Vicksburg and
Chattanooga

ALSO BY JACK H. LEPA AND FROM McFARLAND

*Grant's River Campaign:
Fort Henry to Shiloh* (2014)

*The Civil War in Tennessee,
1862–1863* (2007; paperback 2011)

*Breaking the Confederacy: The Georgia and Tennessee
Campaigns of 1864* (2005; paperback 2011)

*The Shenandoah Valley Campaign
of 1864* (2003; paperback 2010)

Vicksburg and Chattanooga

The Battles That Doomed the Confederacy

Jack H. Lepa

McFarland & Company, Inc., Publishers
Jefferson, North Carolina

LIBRARY OF CONGRESS CATALOGUING-IN-PUBLICATION DATA

Lepa, Jack H., 1949–
Vicksburg and Chattanooga : the battles that doomed the Confederacy / Jack H. Lepa.
p. cm.
Includes bibliographical references and index.

ISBN 978-0-7864-9412-5 (softcover : acid free paper) ∞
ISBN 978-1-4766-1728-2 (ebook)

1. Vicksburg (Miss.)—History—Siege, 1863. 2. Chattanooga, Battle of, Chattanooga, Tenn., 1863. 3. Grant, Ulysses S. (Ulysses Simpson), 1822–1885—Military leadership. I. Title.
E475.27.L47 2014   973.7'34—dc23   2014033722

BRITISH LIBRARY CATALOGUING DATA ARE AVAILABLE

© 2014 Jack H. Lepa. All rights reserved

No part of this book may be reproduced or transmitted in any form or by any means, electronic or mechanical, including photocopying or recording, or by any information storage and retrieval system, without permission in writing from the publisher.

Front cover: *Siege of Vicksburg*, 13, 15 and 17 Corps commanded by General U.S. Grant, July 4, 1863 (Kurz & Allison, Art Publishers); portrait of General Grant on the battlefield of Chattanooga 1863-4 (Library of Congress)

Printed in the United States of America

McFarland & Company, Inc., Publishers
Box 611, Jefferson, North Carolina 28640
www.mcfarlandpub.com

Table of Contents

Preface 1

1. Early Action on the Mississippi 3
2. First Fighting at Vicksburg 9
3. Vicksburg Is the Key 16
4. Chickasaw Bayou 25
5. Victory and Conflict 31
6. One Failure After Another 37
7. Meeting Challenges 47
8. South of Vicksburg at Last 55
9. The Campaign Takes Shape 63
10. Grant Moves Quickly 73
11. Champion's Hill 81
12. Closing In on Vicksburg 87
13. Slaughter Outside the City 93
14. Vicksburg's Fate Is Sealed 100
15. Life and Death Under Siege 111
16. A Great Victory 117
17. Occupation and Politics 126
18. Triumph Turns to Disaster 134
19. A Difficult Time in Chattanooga 145
20. Grant Makes Things Happen 155
21. An Army Unable to Move 164
22. The Battle Begins 173
23. A Change of Plans 181
24. A Legend Is Created 187
25. The Aftermath of Victory 194

Chapter Notes 199
Bibliography 211
Index 217

Preface

Two of the most important military campaigns in American history were for control of Vicksburg, Mississippi, and Chattanooga, Tennessee, in 1863. Taken individually both of these campaigns were significant Federal victories but together they were instrumental in turning the tide of the war in the Union's favor. The opening of the entire length of the Mississippi River was crucial to the North not only for the war effort but for economic and political reasons as well. Control of the relatively small town of Chattanooga was important for the Union to be able to take and hold control of central Tennessee and as a gateway to the Deep South and the industrial center of Atlanta.

The most important common factor and the person most responsible for both these victories was a short, relatively modest looking man named Ulysses S. Grant. This book will detail the events that brought about the Union triumphs at Vicksburg and Chattanooga and how Ulysses S. Grant was possibly the only man who could have overcome the many challenges that had to be faced on the difficult road to victory.

I would like to thank the staff of the University of Nevada, Las Vegas, for their help with research and locating material used in this book. The staff of the Interlibrary Loan Department of the Las Vegas–Clark County Library District provided significant assistance in finding many older and rare books used as references. In addition, the Honnold/Mudd Library at the Claremont Colleges in Claremont, California, has an excellent selection of nineteenth-century material that I was allowed to use.

Chapter 1

Early Action on the Mississippi

At the time of the Civil War the Mississippi River was America's most important thoroughfare. From its modest headwaters a little northwest of central Minnesota to the Gulf of Mexico, no waterway on the continent was more important to the nation as a whole. In the time of dirt roads, many of which became impassable mud holes when it rained, and undependable and frequently dangerous rail service, the nation's rivers were the main highways of commerce. Goods of every kind traveled down the Mississippi: ore from the mines of the upper Midwest, grain from the vast plains and cotton from the south made its way to New Orleans for shipment around the world.

When war broke out between the states the general-in-chief of the United States was Winfield Scott, the hero of the Mexican War. Recognizing how important it would be to cut the rebellious states off from the rest of the world, Scott developed what was known as the "Anaconda Plan." Of the two main parts of this proposal, one was to strangle the South's economy by a naval blockade of coastal ports to restrict the export of cotton that could finance the importation of food and military equipment. The other objective of the plan was to seize control of the Mississippi River by land and naval forces advancing north from New Orleans and south from the Union base at Cairo, Illinois. Newly elected President Abraham Lincoln had intimate knowledge of the Mississippi, having worked down from the Ohio River to New Orleans as a young man, and fully supported this approach.[1]

For multiple reasons control of the Mississippi River was of vital importance to both the North and the South. If the Confederates could disrupt the flow of grain and livestock from the Northwest, this would have a serious economic effect on those states and the Union as a whole. It was also obvious to both sides that the Mississippi, and its many tributaries, could serve as an interstate transportation system for Union forces to invade the heart of the Confederacy. William Tecumseh Sherman, soon to become one of the Union's most important commanders, clearly stated this fact when he wrote to Secretary of the Treasury Salmon P. Chase in October of 1861, "The Power which controls the Ohio and Mississippi will ultimately control this Continent." For the Confederacy, control of the lower part of the Mississippi was imperative, not only to protect against Federal invasion, but to stay connected with the states west of the river. That area, known as the Trans-Mississippi, was comprised of the states of Texas, Arkansas, and Louisiana, and they supplied much needed manpower and provisions that the entire Confederacy depended on.[2]

Having few available warships, the only way the South could hope to prevent the Union from using its overwhelming naval strength to control the Mississippi was by establishing fortifications at key points along the river. Located at the southern tip of Illinois, where the Ohio River runs into the Mississippi, the small town of Cairo became the main Union naval base for operations on the upper Mississippi. Early in the hostilities the Confederates established their most powerful fortification on the Mississippi just over twenty miles downriver from Cairo at Columbus, Kentucky. The other major locations for Confederate fortifications were at Island No. 10 near the Kentucky and Tennessee border; New Madrid, Missouri; Memphis, Tennessee; Vicksburg, Mississippi; Port Hudson, Louisiana; and the forts outside New Orleans. Equipped with heavy guns and manned by determined troops, these citadels effectively closed the Mississippi to Federal shipping.[3]

During the spring and summer of 1861 the Union river force began to take shape when Commander John Rodgers began building a fleet by purchasing three civilian steamboats and converting them to gunboats: the *Tyler, Lexington* and *Conestoga*. About the same time, James B. Eads, a wealthy inventor from St. Louis, was contracted to build seven ironclad gunboats that could operate in shallow water. Completed by the end of the year, they were well armed but underpowered. These ships: the *De Kalb, Cincinnati, Carondelet, Louisville, Mound City, Cairo,* and *Pittsburg*, along with the much larger *Benton*, another ship converted from civilian use, were the backbone of the Union fleet that would contest for control of the Mississippi.[4]

In September 1861 Commander Rodgers was replaced by Flag Officer Andrew Hull Foote. With almost thirty-five years in the Navy, Foote was an experienced sailor and devout Christian. Commander Henry Walke, who was captain of the *Carondelet,* knew Foote for most of his career and described him as "slow and cautious in arriving at conclusions, but firm and tenacious of purpose." During this early period the fleet was actually under the command of the army and did mainly reconnaissance work to keep the Upper Mississippi, Ohio and Cumberland Rivers free of enemy shipping.[5]

Cutting the western Confederate states off from the east would not only curtail the transport of enemy supplies and manpower east, but the capture of territory along the river in Mississippi and Louisiana would give the Federal government access to some of the richest cotton producing areas in the country, cotton that was desperately needed by Northern textile mills. Early in 1862 the war strategy in the west began to take shape; advancing down the Mississippi Valley and opening the river to the Gulf of Mexico was of paramount importance, no matter what it cost. And that the cost would be high, in treasure and lives.

The Union commander in the West was Major General Henry W. Halleck, a graduate of the United States Military Academy in 1839. After serving in the army for fifteen years, Halleck resigned to become a successful attorney in San Francisco. When war broke out, Halleck was quickly offered a commission as major general and was a very skillful administrator adept at bringing order out of the chaos that plagued the Union forces in the West. General Halleck was also a difficult man to get along with. His nickname was "Old Brains" and it was not a term of affection, as he was rude to subordinates and had a bad temper. One of those subordinates that Halleck did not care for and did not trust in command of large bodies of troops was Ulysses Grant.[6]

Ulysses Grant began life on what was then considered the frontier in Ohio in 1822. After a relatively normal childhood, his father, Jesse, with the help of family friends, obtained an appointment for young Ulysses to the United States Military Academy, from which he graduated in 1843. During the Mexican War Lieutenant Grant was twice noted for bravery. In 1848 he married his wife, Julia, and was shortly shipped out to the Pacific Northwest where now Captain Grant grew bored and lonely and developed a fondness for drink. Close to being dismissed from the service, Grant resigned and went back to civilian life where he had little to no success at several endeavors, including working in his father's leather shop. The beginning of the war provided many opportunities to former army officers and Grant soon found himself a colonel in command of the 21st Illinois Volunteers. It was not long before Grant's steady leadership and willingness to push forward in the face of enemy resistance brought victory and promotion to major general. One of Grant's most notable personality traits was that he simply refused to accept defeat. Call it tenacity or just plain stubbornness, but he believed that at some point in any contest, both sides will be near exhaustion and ready to quit and that the side that summons up enough courage and energy to continue past that point will be the victor. Several times during the war Grant put this belief to the test and by doing the unexpected succeeded where others might have failed.[7]

During the next few months one by one the Confederate fortresses on the Upper Mississippi fell as the Union forces relentlessly moved south. Oddly enough, the opening moves to clear the Mississippi River were begun by General Grant about eighty miles to the east along the banks of the Tennessee River. Just below the Kentucky border with Tennessee the Confederates had constructed works to impede river traffic at Fort Henry. On February 6, 1862, after a heavy but brief bombardment by Union gunboats under the command of Flag Officer Foote, the poorly built fort surrendered before the army even arrived on the scene. Most of the troops manning the position had escaped to Fort Donelson about twelve miles away on the banks of the Cumberland River. A week later the Union fleet approached Fort Donelson expecting the same results as at Fort Henry, but was repulsed with serious damage to most of the ships after hours of exchanging heavy fire with the fort. Over several days Grant built up a force of nearly twenty thousand men and was able to cut off Fort Donelson on the land side while Foote's ships controlled the river. After a few days of desperate fighting by both sides in snow and bitter cold, the Confederate garrison was forced to surrender. Over twelve thousand enemy soldiers became prisoners when Grant issued his famous demand for the "unconditional surrender" of the fort on February 16. With the capture of Forts Henry and Donelson, the Confederate riverfront stronghold at Columbus, Kentucky, could not be defended, as thousands of Union troops were now able to approach it from the rear. On March 2, 1862, Columbus was evacuated and the first of the major Confederate fortresses on the Mississippi was eliminated.[8]

Union General Ulysses S. Grant—a few months after Chattanooga he was promoted to lieutenant general and named general-in-chief (Library of Congress).

Near where the northwest corner of Tennessee meets Missouri, the Confederates had built strongholds at New Madrid and Island No. 10. Both positions were heavily fortified and at least partially protected by water and swamps. At the end of February, Union Brigadier General John Pope advanced on New Madrid, and by the first week of March the town was surrounded with siege works manned by about 20,000 Union troops. Pope was able to establish artillery positions below New Madrid, closing the river and cutting off any reinforcements and supplies bound for the stronghold. With no relief in sight and vastly outnumbered, the Confederates evacuated New Madrid on March 13, leaving behind everything they could not carry.[9]

General Pope quickly moved on Island No. 10, but reducing this fortress proved to be a much more difficult task. The defenses around Island No. 10 were well built with over twenty guns on the island itself and thirty guns along the Tennessee side of the river. On March 17, Flag Officer Foote led six iron-clad gunboats and ten mortar boats against the Confederate positions, but the forts proved too strong and neither side suffered serious damage. With his flotilla the only protection for the upper Mississippi against raids by enemy gunboats, Foote had to be careful not to cripple his fleet by acting rashly, so the fighting was limited to long range shelling until April 4. During this time Pope's troops cut a canal through the swamps on the Missouri side of the river allowing small transports to safely pass below Island No. 10. During the night of April 4, the *Carondelet* successfully ran past the enemy batteries during a thunderstorm; three nights later it was joined by the *Pittsburg*. With two powerful gunboats for cover General Pope sent his troops down below Island No. 10 and across to the east side of the river, effectively cutting the Confederate supply line and their line of retreat. On April 7, the Confederate forces abandoned what was now an indefensible trap, and despite doing their best to escape by April 8, over six thousand men had been captured by Pope's troops. General Pope and Flag Officer Foote had taken two more giant steps toward opening the Mississippi.[10]

Right after the relatively bloodless victory at Island No. 10, General Pope began moving south toward Memphis, Tennessee. On April 14 the gunboats and transports carrying the army arrived near Fort Pillow, the last major obstacle before Memphis. It was at this time that General Halleck decided that the main army in Tennessee needed reinforcements after the bloodbath at Shiloh. Except for two regiments that were to stay with the fleet, Pope's entire force was ordered to join the main army near the Shiloh battlefield. For several weeks after the army left the scene two or three of the mortar-boats kept up a light shelling from long range of Fort Pillow but no action was taken to seize the position by force.[11]

On May 9, Flag Officer Foote was relieved of command of the flotilla at his own request. A relatively minor wound suffered at Fort Donelson that never healed and the stress of command had ruined his health. Commodore Charles H. Davis took command of the fleet. The very next day eight Confederate rams came up the river and engaged the Union ships. In the early morning fog only three of the Union gunboats were ready for action, the *Cincinnati*, *Carondelet* and *Mound City*. The *Cincinnati* was struck several times by Confederate rams and sunk near the shoreline; the *Mound City* was also struck and had to withdraw upriver. For a brief period the *Carondelet* engaged several enemy ships on its own but soon the *Benton* and *Pittsburg* were able to add their fire to drive off the Confederate vessels. Three enemy rams were disabled but were able to float downriver with the rest of their ships to the safety of Fort Pillow's batteries. Following this engagement there was about a month of little activity except for occasional shelling by the Union gunboats looking for weak points in the fort's defenses; none were found. General Halleck's campaign resulting in the occupation of Corinth, Mississippi, made further occupation of Fort Pillow pointless, and on June 4 the Confederates abandoned the works and destroyed everything they could not carry.[12]

With no more enemy fortress to deal with, Commodore Davis sailed south with five gunboats and seven newly arrived ships designed for ramming enemy vessels and commanded by Lieutenant Colonel Charles R. Ellet, son of the designer of the ram fleet. The Union fleet arrived within two miles of Memphis, Tennessee, by the night of June 5. The next morning eight Confederate ships were observed just off the city. The battle was joined by five of the Union gunboats: the *Benton, Louisville, Carondelet, St. Louis* and *Cairo* and two of Ellet's rams with thousands of spectators watching from the hills around Memphis. In less than two hours seven of the Confederate ships were sunk or disabled with the loss of only two Union ships temporarily disabled. The same afternoon the city of Memphis surrendered and the Mississippi River was now cleared of enemy ships and fortifications from Cairo to Memphis.[13]

Months before Federal forces began moving down the Mississippi from Cairo, plans were being developed to gain control of the river where it empties into the Gulf of Mexico. New Orleans was the largest city and most important port in the South. Capturing this city would not only give the Federal government access to hundreds of miles of the river but close down one of the main ports used by the Confederacy to ship cotton to Europe and receive contraband goods in return. Getting to New Orleans, however, would not be an easy task for wooden ships. As befitted the city's importance, about thirty-five miles from the Gulf and about seventy miles below the city two strong forts had been built on either side of the river. Long before the current conflict these massive stone forts, heavily armed and well manned, had provided an impenetrable barrier that no wooden ships would dare try to breach. Fort Jackson, on the left bank, mounted over sixty guns of various sizes, and about eight hundred yards upstream on the opposite bank, Fort St. Philip and batteries on either side of the fort itself presented over forty guns of various sizes.[14]

In mid–November of 1861 the Lincoln Administration decided to mount an expedition to capture New Orleans. The command of this expedition was given to Flag Officer David Glasgow Farragut. Although Farragut was well down the seniority list of officers, Secretary of the Navy Gideon Welles decided that he possessed the necessary combination of experience and audacity to command the expedition. In January 1862 Flag Officer Farragut took command of the newly created Western Gulf Squadron with orders to "collect such vessels as can be spared from the blockade and proceed up the Mississippi River and reduce the defenses which guard the approaches to New Orleans." After the city was taken the naval forces would be relieved by army troops command by Major General Benjamin Butler. Farragut's squadron was then to move up the river to capture or destroy all enemy positions encountered until meeting the Western Flotilla heading south from Cairo.[15]

The naval force assigned to the New Orleans expedition consisted of the 40-gun ship *Colorado;* four *Hartford* class steam sloops with over twenty guns each; the side-wheeler *Mississippi;* three steam corvettes with seven to ten guns each; eleven gunboats with two guns each; and a flotilla of twenty mortar boats each with a 13.5 inch gun under the direction of Commander David D. Porter. In March Farragut began the strenuous effort of bringing his ships through the shallow water that covered sand bars guarding the entrance to the Mississippi. After weeks of work removing everything possible from the larger ships, the fleet was into the river and prepared to attack the forts.[16]

On April 18 the mortar boats opened fire from about two miles below the forts. After two days of almost constant bombardment, expending most of the mortar ammunition, there was little apparent damage done to the forts, and more importantly, Farragut's patience had worn thin. On April 20 he held a meeting of his captains on board the flagship *Hartford,* and, despite a protesting letter from Porter, decided that "whatever is to be done will have to be done quickly, or we will be again reduced to a blockading squadron without the means of carrying on the bombardment." As to the next step, Farragut's opinion was clear: "The forts should be run." After the fleet passed the forts General Butler's troops could be landed on the Gulf side and move through the bayou, then the fleet and the army could move up the river, covering each other as they advanced.[17]

In the early morning hours of April 24 the *Hartford* signaled for the fleet to get under way. The mortar boats provided covering fire and the ships opened fire as they approached Fort Jackson. The smoke and the darkness combined to make visibility very poor and gunners on both sides could only fire at the flashes of the enemy guns. All the Union ships were hit by Confederate fire, several had significant damage, a few were too damaged to continue, and a couple others had to turn back after being stuck in a chain and log barrier, but by dawn Farragut had most of his fleet safely past the forts. Several small Confederate gunboats came out to engage the Union ships as they passed the forts, but these were destroyed or damaged and Farragut was soon able to assemble his ships to repair damage and take care of casualties before pushing on to New Orleans.[18]

The Union fleet arrived off New Orleans about noon on April 25. The city had no real fortifications and was virtually defenseless, so Farragut sent only a small naval detachment ashore to raise the U.S. flag and wait for General Butler's occupying troops to arrive. With New Orleans in Union hands and their supply lines now cut off by Federal troops, Forts St. Philip and Jackson surrendered on April 28. The mouth of the Mississippi and the Confederacy's most important port were now under Federal control.[19]

After General Butler's troops took control of the city, Farragut's ships were free to move against other targets. Farragut would have preferred to next attack Mobile, Alabama, one of the South's largest ports, but was instead ordered to send his ships up the Mississippi in an effort to join with the ships of the Western Flotilla working their way downriver and take control of the entire waterway. Seven ships under the command of Captain Thomas Craven headed north, and on May 7 placed Baton Rouge under Federal control and then Natchez, Mississippi, on May 12 with no opposition to speak of. The fleet then sailed past Port Hudson, Louisiana, where crews saw no signs of fortifications or artillery batteries, apparently deciding the place was not worth occupying and continued on to their next assigned target of Vicksburg, Mississippi.[20]

Chapter 2

First Fighting at Vicksburg

In the spring of 1862 Vicksburg, Mississippi, was one of the most defensible locations on the Mississippi River. High bluffs that ran along the eastern side of the river above and below the city coupled with swamps and marshy terrain to the north made it basically impossible to approach Vicksburg from any direction other than from the east or south. Earlier in the war the Confederate government had been confident that Federal warships would not be able to breach the fortifications at places such as Columbus, Island No. 10, and Fort Pillow in the north and New Orleans in the south. When these positions were taken one by one with only moderate difficulty, work was begun to improve the defenses at other positions along the river; chief among these was Vicksburg.

Much of the heavy artillery that was saved from capture at New Orleans was sent to Vicksburg in early May. Working feverishly, in just a couple of weeks Confederate authorities improved the few existing fortifications and increased the defensive works facing both the river and the land side. Especially important was the placing of artillery in commanding positions overlooking the river above and below the city. It was close, but the Confederates won the race to fortify Vicksburg before Federal ships arrived from New Orleans. On May 18 a small advance squadron of four gunboats under Commander S. Phillips Lee approached the city. That day Commander Lee sent a demand for the surrender of the city to "the authorities at Vicksburg." The response from the city was immediate and clear. From Colonel J. L. Autry, military governor of the city: "I have to state that Mississippians don't know, and refuse to learn, how to surrender to an enemy. If Commodore Farragut or Brigadier-General Butler can teach them, let them come and try."[1]

The other senior military and civilian authorities made similar replies. From Brigadier General Martin L. Smith, commander of the military forces defending the city: "Regarding the surrender of the defenses, I have to reply that having been ordered here to hold these defenses, it is my intention to do so as long as in my power." And from the civilian mayor of Vicksburg, L. Lindsay, came a note stating that no defenses had been built "within the corporative limits of the city; but, sir, in further reply, I will state that neither the municipal authorities nor the citizens will ever consent to a surrender of the city." It was quite clear that if the Union wanted Vicksburg it would have to take it by force.[2]

Showing that the war had not yet reached the point where all sense of chivalry was dead, Commander Lee wrote to Mayor Lindsay on May 21, "It becomes my duty to give you notice to remove the women and children beyond the range of our guns within twenty-four hours, as it will be impossible to attack the defenses without injuring or destroying the town, a proceeding which all the authorities of Vicksburg seem determined to require." Mayor Lindsay wrote back to Lee that he did not receive his letter until it was too late to do anything about it and he would consider the time to start the next morning. Commander Lee then replied to the mayor that it would be at the option of his forces as to when or if they would commence a bombardment. At a later date such niceties would be ignored.[3]

Commander Lee's few small ships were not powerful enough to make much of an impression on the city's works, so he decided to wait until the rest of the fleet arrived before opening fire on the fortifications. Within a few days Flag Officer Farragut arrived with more ships and two regiments of infantry commanded by Brigadier General Thomas Williams that had been sent from New Orleans to occupy any important positions taken by the fleet. During the night of May 26 the fleet opened fire on Vicksburg's fortifications, and after a relatively brief bombardment it was clear that the shelling was using up a great quantity of ammunition while doing little damage to the defenses. Relatively safe behind their fortifications, the Confederate gunners just kept their heads down and conserved their ammunition.[4]

The defenders knew full well that they had little to fear from the riverfront. Although at this time there were only twenty-six artillery pieces in place on the bluffs, they were spread out over nearly three miles on the heights that were well over two hundred feet above the river in some places; at these heights the Union ships were unable to elevate their guns enough to hit anything. Farragut and Williams soon decided that the only way to take Vicksburg was from the land side and Williams' force of about 1,500 men was totally inadequate to even make an attempt.[5]

Unable to assault the city from the land side and equally unable to pound it into submission with naval gunfire alone, Farragut saw no good reason for his ships to just sit off Vicksburg and decided to return to New Orleans. The fleet arrived back at New Orleans by June 1, where Farragut immediately received orders from Washington to return to Vicksburg and cooperate with the Western Flotilla coming down the river from the north to take the city and open the full length of the Mississippi River.[6]

Flag Officer Farragut quickly re-supplied his ships and headed north again on June 8, but this time he brought a significantly stronger force. The ships began arriving in the vicinity of Vicksburg on June 18, and within a week Farragut had eleven large gunboats, including the *Brooklyn, Richmond,* the flagship *Hartford,* and seventeen of Porter's small mortar boats. Accompanying the warships were transports loaded with over three thousand troops commanded by General Williams. Farragut also received news that the city of Memphis had fallen to Federal forces and that the Western Flotilla was heading south to rendezvous above Vicksburg. The admiral quickly devised a plan of action. On June 26 the operation was begun.[7]

After the mortar boats established the range, they began an almost continuous bombardment over the next two days. To pass the city Farragut arranged his ships in two lines with the *Richmond, Hartford* and *Brooklyn* on the right, closer to Vicksburg. The line was staggered and enough space was left between the ships on the right so that the gunboats in the left line could fire between them. The column on the left consisted of the *Iroquois* and the *Oneida* sailing ahead of the *Richmond*, with the *Wissahickon* and *Sciota* in the gap between the *Richmond* and *Hartford*. Next on the left was the *Winona* and *Pinola* between the *Hartford* and the *Brooklyn*, with the *Kennebec* and the *Katahdin* at the rear of the formation. This configuration would present a shorter line to the Confederate gunners and allow all the ships to concentrate their fire against Vicksburg's batteries more effectively than having the ships strung out in a long single line.[8]

About two o'clock on the morning of June 28 Farragut ordered the signal to set sail and the fleet began slowly moving up river. Around four o'clock the mortar boats began a heavy bombardment as the leading ships of the fleet began to exchange fire with the city's batteries. The air was filled with shot and shell as the mortars pounded the Confederate fortifications and the ships and shore batteries sent hundreds of shells flying back and forth. Visibility quickly deteriorated as smoke settled down over the river, and most of the firing was done at muzzle flashes rather than actual targets. Frequently the defenders would briefly abandon their guns when the ships were directly in their front, only to quickly return and pour fire into them after the heaviest shelling was over. Trying to navigate the river in the smoke and darkness caused some of the ships to fall out of line and Farragut had the *Hartford* moving forward slowly to wait for the vessels in the rear.[9]

A little over four hours after it weighed anchor, the fleet came to a halt a few miles above Vicksburg. The *Brooklyn* along with the two gunboats behind it, the *Kennebec* and the *Katahdin,* stopped to engage the batteries, and after nearly two hours of exchanging fire these ships pulled back and stayed below the city. Most of the ships that made it past the city received some damage, none seriously, and overall the fleet lost fifteen men killed and thirty wounded. The Confederates suffered only a few casualties with light damage to their works and no loss of any guns. Farragut sent a message to Secretary of the Navy Gideon Welles: "I passed up the river this morning, but to no purpose; the enemy leave their guns for the moment, but return to them as soon as we have passed and rake us.... I am satisfied it is not possible for us to take Vicksburg without an army force of 12,000 or 15,000 men." Farragut also advised Welles that the water in the Mississippi was too low for his large ships to travel more than fifteen miles above Vicksburg.[10]

Although most of the Federal fleet was now above Vicksburg, the mortar boats and General Williams' troops were still below the city. While there were not enough troops to make an assault on the land side of the city, an idea was proposed to put them to work cutting a canal through a piece of land where the river made a sharp turn opposite the city. Vicksburg's most valuable attribute as a military position was that the bluffs on the eastern side of the river were high enough to provide a nearly unassailable position for artillery that could command the river below. By cutting a new channel for the river to run across, this projecting piece of land Vicksburg would become nothing more than a landlocked small town several miles from the river. On June 29 the digging began with the help of about twelve hundred former slaves gathered from nearby plantations. What appeared to be a relatively easy solution came to nothing when the canal was finished on July 22 because the river was too low to flow into the new canal.[11]

On July 1 the gunboats of the Western Flotilla joined Farragut's fleet near the mouth of the Yazoo River, about ten miles above Vicksburg, to begin combined operations. By that time, however, Farragut had become convinced that although he could get his ships past Vicksburg's batteries whenever necessary, even the combined strength of both fleets would not be able to force the city's surrender without a strong land based force. General Halleck, who had previously promised to send troops to assist in taking Vicksburg, had already responded to a request for reinforcements by Secretary of War Edwin M. Stanton, writing, "It is impossible to send forces to Vicksburg at present, but I will give the matter very full attention as soon as circumstances will permit."[12]

In reply to an appeal from Farragut to send troops to assist in attacking Vicksburg's land fortifications, Halleck wrote on July 3, "The scattered and weakened condition of my force renders it impossible for me at the present time to detach any troops to co-operate with you."

After the battle of Shiloh, Halleck had put together an army over 100,000 strong and commenced a slow march to capture the rail center of Corinth, Mississippi. The summer heat had exhausted his army and Halleck was sending reinforcements to various locations, including Arkansas and East Tennessee, but could spare none for the most important operation in the West, opening the Mississippi River.[13]

Flag Officer Farragut received more unwelcome news when he learned that the Confederates were building a strong ironclad gunboat called the *Arkansas* several miles up the Yazoo River. Another situation Farragut had to deal with was the deteriorating condition of his ships and their crews. All his ships had received damage either from the batteries at Vicksburg or from collisions with debris below the city. The engines in the gunboats were woefully underpowered and the recent months spent sailing up and down the river meant that all the ships were in need of extensive maintenance. The crews had been suffering from inadequate food and water and the summer climate was causing much sickness on board the cramped ships. But most worrisome was the fact that the water level in the Mississippi was falling rapidly. It would not be long before his heavy sea-going ships were in danger of not being able to navigate back down the river.[14]

On their own, the ships of the Western Flotilla were certainly strong enough to deal with the *Arkansas* if it were ever finished and also strong enough to bombard Vicksburg if enough land forces were brought in to attack. So, considering the dangers facing his fleet by just sitting in the middle of the Mississippi, on July 10 Farragut wrote to Secretary Welles requesting permission to withdraw the fleet and return to New Orleans. Welles had the same idea, because on July 14 he sent a message to Farragut, "The evacuation of Corinth had much lessened the importance of your continuing your operations on the Mississippi." It was clear that no troops would be coming to aid in capturing Vicksburg, and Farragut should take all proper measures "to get the part of your fleet now above Vicksburg below that place, with as little injury and loss of life as possible. Nothing is to be gained by a contest with the batteries of the enemy." Porter had already received orders to withdraw from the Vicksburg area and bring his mortar fleet back to Hampton Roads, Virginia, so Farragut began making plans to run his ships past Vicksburg once again.[15]

As it turned out, however, while the combined Federal fleets were anchored above Vicksburg, the Confederates were not sitting idle just waiting to be attacked. On the same day Farragut took his ships past the Vicksburg batteries to join with the Western Flotilla, a new military commander was appointed to oversee the city's defenses, Major General Earl Van Dorn. Van Dorn was born about twenty five miles south of Vicksburg near Port Gibson and was a distant relative of Andrew Jackson. At West Point he showed little interest in academics but in fighting Indians and during the Mexican War earned a reputation as a courageous young officer who was willing to take risks. Van Dorn won promotion and, more importantly, the attention of another Mississippi native, Jefferson Davis. Vicksburg's new military commander immediately set to work strengthening the city's defenses and increasing the number of heavy guns covering the river, especially on the heights known as Haynes' Bluff covering the entrance to the Yazoo River.[16]

While Farragut had known for some time that the Confederates were building the ironclad *Arkansas*, it was not expected to be finished anytime soon. Southern shipbuilders along the Mississippi were hampered by a lack of materials required for constructing ships, especially ironclad warships. Despite many obstacles, however, through an extraordinary effort the

Arkansas was completed sooner than any of the Union commanders anticipated and was one of the most powerful ships on the river. It was protected by 4½ inches of railroad iron and armed with ten heavy guns and an underwater ram. Unfortunately for the Confederates, its engines were inadequate to power such a heavy vessel and were poorly constructed and subject to frequent breakdowns. The ship was commanded by Commander Isaac Brown and had a crew of about two hundred mostly untrained men. Once the *Arkansas* was completed, General Van Dorn wanted the ship brought down to Vicksburg as soon as possible. It left Yazoo City on July 14 sailing toward the Mississippi and the Union fleet.[17]

As luck would have it, Farragut had recently received information that the *Arkansas* was nearing completion and had decided to send a reconnaissance squadron to investigate. Early on the morning of July 15 the ironclad *Carondelet* under Commander Henry Walke, accompanied by the *Tyler* and the *Queen of the West*, set sail up the Yazoo. That morning the *Arkansas* was moving down the Yazoo toward the Federal squadron on the Mississippi. As the Union ships moved up the river the *Tyler* was in the lead with the *Carondelet* in the rear.[18]

About 7 a.m. the Union ships saw the *Arkansas* bearing down on them, and both the *Tyler* and *Queen of the West* immediately tried to turn and run. The *Tyler* was able to fire one broadside as the Confederate ship approached and one shell damaged the pilothouse, killing the pilot and wounding Commander Brown. The *Carondelet* attempted to put up a fight but was outgunned and soon was also heading back toward the Mississippi with the *Arkansas* in close pursuit. The ships traded fire as the *Arkansas* pursued the fleeing Federal vessels. Just before they reached the mouth of the Yazoo a broadside from the *Arkansas* damaged the *Carondelet*, forcing that ship to be run up on the riverbank. Believing the *Carondelet* to be sinking, Commander Brown continued the pursuit of the *Tyler* into the Mississippi and right into the midst of the anchored Federal fleet.[19]

Aboard their respective flagships both Farragut and Davis heard the gunfire from the Yazoo and both decided that the reconnaissance squadron was exchanging fire with enemy field artillery known to be posted along the river banks. There was no reason to prepare for battle and none of the ships had steam up in their boilers, nor did they load their guns just in case. About 8:30 a.m. lookouts in the fleet spotted the *Tyler* and *Queen of the West* as they came around the point running for their lives with the *Arkansas* close behind. The Confederate ironclad had been damaged during the running fight down the Yazoo and was moving at only a couple of knots when it encountered the Union fleet. Slowly passing right through the fleet, the *Arkansas* fired broadside after broadside into the unprepared Union ships. But the firing was not all one sided; the *Arkansas* was hit multiple times by Federal shells that riddled its smokestack and destroyed the pilot house, and a couple shells penetrated its side causing casualties among the gun crews. This damage slowed the *Arkansas* even more, but it made it through the gauntlet of Union ships and soon found safety under the guns of Vicksburg's batteries. Aboard the Union ships at least 42 men were killed and 69 wounded, while the *Arkansas* suffered 14 killed and 15 wounded.[20]

Flag Officer Farragut was personally and professionally embarrassed by his fleet's state of unreadiness when the *Arkansas* sailed past his ships and made it safely to Vicksburg. Farragut wanted to immediately follow the Confederate ship and destroy it, but Davis persuaded him to wait until proper preparations could be made. With the water level falling and sickness in his crews increasing, Farragut had already been thinking that it was time to leave the area and return down the river. He now had the perfect opportunity to pass the Vicksburg batteries and destroy the *Arkansas* at the same time. Later that evening Farragut's entire fleet weighed anchor, and in the same formation as they had previously passed Vicksburg heading north, they moved down the river toward the city. Flag Officer Davis brought his gunboats into position to bombard the Confederate batteries while Farragut's ships were moving past. The Confederates had been expecting some sort of attack and the *Arkansas* changed its position after dark, making it impossible for the Union ships to find it between the flashes of the guns. The fleet passed by Vicksburg with little damage, but the *Arkansas* was still there and still a serious threat to the many wooden ships downriver.[21]

On the afternoon of July 22 another attempt was made to destroy the Confederate ironclad sheltered under the guns of Vicksburg's batteries. The gunboat *Essex*, commanded by Commander William D. Porter, and the ram *Queen of the West*, commanded by Lieutenant Colonel Ellet, attacked the *Arkansas* in an effort to either destroy it or force it to run down river into the waiting guns of Farragut's fleet. Ships from both the Western Flotilla above the city and Farragut's fleet below the city joined in a heavy bombardment to provide cover for this daring venture. Both Union ships made it to their target, with the *Essex* hitting the *Arkansas* with several shots before trying to ram it. As the *Essex* approached the Confederate ironclad the *Arkansas* was able to get one of its engines started and swing around so that the *Essex* only grazed its side, after which the Union vessel then ran aground and came under heavy fire for about ten minutes before getting free. The *Queen of the West* had much better luck and was able to squarely ram the Confederate ship, but the damage was not serious enough to cripple the ironclad. Unable to turn about and sail back against the current, the *Essex* continued downriver and joined Farragut's ships while the *Queen of the West* was able to make its way back to the Western Flotilla. This would be the last aggressive Federal naval move for quite a while.[22]

The Union naval presence at and near Vicksburg now wound down to the occasional reconnaissance. With Farragut gone and the mortar boats on their way to the East Coast, the Western Flotilla remained the only Union naval force in the area. Sickness had decimated the army troops under General Williams and they too were withdrawn and sailed down river to Baton Rouge. Along the banks of the Mississippi the Confederates became bolder in attacking transports and setting up small batteries of artillery that, while not strong enough to establish any control over their area, did harass shipping and force Davis to accompany supply and transport ships with armed escorts, thus depleting his strength even further. Sickness also struck the Western Flotilla, and Flag Officer Davis decided to withdraw his fleet to Helena, Arkansas. The only Union ships near Vicksburg were now the *Essex* and *Sumter*, which were stationed below the city basically just to show the flag.[23]

After the Union withdrawal from around Vicksburg, the always aggressive General Van Dorn decided it was time to go on the attack with his eyes set on retaking Baton Rouge and possibly New Orleans. About six thousand Confederate soldiers were dispatched toward Baton Rouge, and on August 3 the *Arkansas* left Vicksburg to provide support for the land forces. Suffering from frequent engine breakdowns, the ship was barely able to crawl down the river, and two days later was still about fifteen miles above Baton Rouge. The infantry attack had gone on without support from the heavy guns of the *Arkansas* and failed, although General Williams and nearly three hundred of his men were casualties. The *Essex* had steamed down to Baton Rouge to assist in the city's defense, and by firing its heavy guns as quickly as they could be loaded and run out, it made a major contribution to the Confederate defeat.[24]

After the danger to Baton Rouge had passed, Commander Porter turned the *Essex* upriver to find the *Arkansas*. The Confederate ship was still having engine problems and could not put up any sort of fight when the *Essex* appeared. Unable to fight or run away, the crew of the *Arkansas* moored to the bank and set fires to destroy the ship. With the *Essex* closing in, the fire reached its magazine and the *Arkansas* blew up around noon. The last Confederate warship of any significance was finally removed from the Mississippi River.[25]

After the failure to take Baton Rouge and the loss of the *Arkansas*, it was clear to General Van Dorn that something had to be done to keep at least a portion of the Mississippi under Confederate control. He decided to fortify Port Hudson, Louisiana, turning it into a mini–Vicksburg. This would give the Confederacy control of about two hundred miles of the river between the two sites through which men and material could flow east on the Red River and then all through the South over railroads that ran from both towns.[26]

The brief delay that General Halleck had predicted when Farragut requested assistance in July turned into six months before there was another serious threat against Vicksburg. During that time both sides worked feverishly to improve their chances for victory when the next campaign began. There was an expansion of the Federal ship building program along the Mississippi with a new type of gunboat capable of drawing less than three feet of water, making them very useful in travelling the shallow water of the many smaller rivers and bayous around Vicksburg. These ships were lightly armored and carried six or eight guns and quickly earned the nickname "tinclads." Several other much larger and more powerful ships were put into service during the summer and fall of 1862, including double turreted monitors with huge 11-inch guns built to trade fire with any fortifications they might come up against. In October the Western Flotilla was officially transferred to the Navy Department and renamed the Mississippi Squadron. Flag Officer Davis was transferred to Washington as chief of the Bureau of Navigation, and David Porter was named the squadron commander with the rank of acting rear admiral.[27]

While Union shipyards were turning out these new gunboats, the Confederates were improving and extending the defenses around Vicksburg. Fortifications were extended nearly twenty miles from Haynes' Bluff on the Yazoo to Warrenton below the city. Confederate work parties repaired damage and made improvements to Vicksburg's fortifications on the river side, and defensive works were also built around the city on the land side. The countryside around the city was a maze of hills, ravines, and ridges, excellent terrain to defend against an approaching army. Colonel S. H. Lockett, the chief engineer for Vicksburg, later wrote about the works he designed, "The most prominent points I purposed to occupy with a system of redoubts, redans, lunettes, and small field-works, connecting them by rifle-pits so as to give a continuous line of defense." As will be seen, Colonel Lockett did his job very well.[28]

Chapter 3

Vicksburg Is the Key

Vicksburg, Mississippi—a place that was soon to be the subject of massive Federal troop movements, the ultimate loss of thousands of casualties and an incalculable amount of wealth—was actually a river-front town much smaller than other river-front cities such as Cincinnati and Memphis. It was also very probably the most important point in the Confederacy at the time.

President Lincoln certainly knew how important Vicksburg was to eventual Union victory. Admiral Porter related that while planning the campaign for New Orleans the president had pointed out on the map, "See what a lot of land these fellows hold, of which Vicksburg is the key." From the Trans-Mississippi states of Louisiana, Texas, and Arkansas, large numbers of cattle and hogs along with tons of grain were sent down the Red, the White, and Arkansas Rivers into the Mississippi and then to Vicksburg, where these essential supplies could be transported to all parts of the Confederacy. As Lincoln said, "Let us get Vicksburg and all that country is ours. The war can never be brought to a close until that key is in our pocket. I am acquainted with that region and know what I am talking about, and, valuable as New Orleans will be to us, Vicksburg will be more so."[1]

Confederate President Jefferson Davis, who owned a plantation just twenty miles south of Vicksburg, compared the city with the British fortress of Gibraltar. Built on steep hills and bluffs, many of which were two hundred feet above the river, Vicksburg was more of a citadel than a city. The town was well protected along the riverfront, and even if ships could survive the heavy fire from Confederate artillery positioned along the shore and on the bluffs and get close enough to the docks to land troops, sending heavily laden soldiers up that steep terrain under fire was unthinkable. The only realistic way to approach the city was from the land side, and this too had its difficulties. To the north Vicksburg was protected by large areas of swamps with rivers and bayous, making it difficult if not impossible for an army to approach from that direction.[2]

The importance of Vicksburg was not just that its artillery virtually closed the Mississippi River to commercial shipping, the town was also a major transportation center. In addition to the vast amount of food that was transported through Vicksburg, the Trans-Mississippi states provided many thousands of men now serving in the Confederate armies. The railroads that ran east from Vicksburg carried large amounts of weapons, munitions, and other military supplies, much of which came from European supporters and was smuggled through Mexico and into Texas to help sustain the Southern war effort. Some of these goods and materials came down the Red River to Shreveport and Alexandria, Louisiana, then up the Mississippi to Vicksburg. Large amounts of supplies were also brought by rail to De Soto Point across the river from Vicksburg where constantly running ferries brought the goods over to the city. Once the supplies reached Vicksburg, they were forwarded on the Southern Railroad of Mississippi, the city's lifeline to the rest of the South. Running east to Jackson, the Southern connected with other railroads that ran in all directions throughout the South bringing the supplies that came through Vicksburg to the Confederate armies in Tennessee and even as far as Virginia. Vicksburg was as vital to the Confederacy's war effort, and its very survival, as any other place in the South.[3]

The man given the responsibility of protecting this vital position was Lieutenant General John C. Pemberton. Born in Philadelphia in 1814, his family was wealthy and socially well-connected. Pemberton graduated from West Point in 1837 with an unremarkable record but excelled in math and horsemanship. He distinguished himself during the Mexican War, being wounded twice and earning promotion. Even as a young man at West Point, Pemberton identified with the South and firmly believed in states' rights. His wife was a Southerner and when the war began Pemberton resigned his commission and offered his services to the South. Pemberton first served under Robert E. Lee in Charleston, South Carolina, later being put in charge of Charleston's defenses. Growing up among the elite in society, Pemberton had always been stiff and aloof with most people, and this demeanor did nothing to endear him to the local residents. Lacking the qualities of a Southern gentleman combined with his Northern roots, John Pemberton soon became unpopular with most of the important people in Charleston, more than a few of whom complained to Confederate President Jefferson Davis.[4]

In October of 1862 Pemberton was transferred west to be commander of the Army of Mississippi, where his most important task was to hold Vicksburg for the Confederacy. By the beginning of 1863, the only portion of the Mississippi still under Confederate control was between Vicksburg and Port Hudson, Louisiana. Knowing how important it was to maintain the connection with the Trans-Mississippi states, President Davis was willing to risk a great deal to retain control of even a small section of the river, and that included Pemberton's army.[5]

On September 26, 1862, Major General John A. McClernand met with Illinois Governor Richard Yates and Secretary of the Treasury Salmon P. Chase in Washington to make a proposal that would open the Mississippi River and carry the war into the heart of the Confederacy. At that meeting the influential politician turned general from Illinois made enough of an impression that Secretary Chase arranged for McClernand to present his ideas to another important person from Illinois, President Lincoln.[6]

McClernand gave President Lincoln on September 28 a detailed proposal for opening the Mississippi River. Seizing the riverfront fortress of Vicksburg was the first step. This could be accomplished, according to McClernand, by landing a large force at Drumgould's Bluff to the north of Vicksburg on the Yazoo River. This would enable Union troops to cut the railroad between Vicksburg and Jackson and then approach Vicksburg from the east, which was the only way to get at the city over solid ground. This expedition would, of course, be commanded by General McClernand.[7]

The merit of McClernand's proposal was obvious to President Lincoln, but he had reservations about the man. John McClernand had been born in Kentucky and raised in Illinois. He was a little below average in height with a heavy beard, unruly hair, and dark, piercing eyes. McClernand could be generous and personable when he wanted to but was also calculating and underhanded when it suited his purpose. In addition he was egotistical, ambitious to a fault, and easily irritated most people he came in contact with. Early in his career he practiced law but politics was where he made his mark. McClernand served in the U.S. House of Representatives on two different occasions, rising to a position of power in the Democratic Party. He was defeated for the speakership in 1860 and in 1861 resigned from Congress to form a brigade of volunteers under his command as brigadier general.[8]

McClernand had little military training or experience before the war, but it was his political connections that made him valuable to the Union. He turned out, however, to be a reasonably capable officer. Personally courageous, McClernand commanded troops under General Grant at the battles of Belmont, Fort Henry, Fort Donelson and Shiloh. He was steady under fire and displayed generally sound judgment on the battlefield. Up to this point in the war the only real successes for Union arms had been in the West, and McClernand had been involved in many of those victories. This successful record coupled with his still impressive political influence made McClernand an asset that Lincoln knew he had to use to the fullest advantage.[9]

Whether McClernand's plan was used, or another plan was decided upon, the president knew that some action to open the Mississippi had to be taken, and soon. The closure of the river had brought severe stress to commerce in the northwest. Farmers in the region were faced with increasing rates when shipping their bulk goods by railroad. In addition to the economic hardships, many citizens in the West were dissatisfied with the government's handling of the war so far, and with congressional elections coming in November, the Republican administration had to do something to improve the chances for their candidates in the region. Using the popular McClernand to raise troops from the states most affected by the closure of the Mississippi for the specific purpose of launching a campaign to open the river could very well result in a political as well as a military triumph.[10]

On October 21, General McClernand received confidential orders from Secretary of War Stanton authorizing him to raise troops in Indiana, Illinois, and Iowa for the campaign to capture Vicksburg. These troops were to be forwarded to Memphis or other points south, and "when a sufficient force not required by the operations of General Grant's command shall be raised, an expedition may be organized under General McClernand's command against Vicksburg and to clear the Mississippi River and open navigation to New Orleans." This certainly sounded to McClernand like he was to have independent command of the expedition. The next paragraph, however, was the real key to the order: "The forces so organized will remain subject to the designation of the general-in-chief, and be employed according to such exigencies as the service in his judgment may require."[11]

In addition to the formal orders from the secretary of war, McClernand also received a handwritten letter from President Lincoln giving the general permission to show his orders to others when it might be necessary to receive assistance in completing his mission. The president added, "I feel deep interest in the success of the expedition, and desire it to be pushed forward with all possible dispatch, consistently with the other parts of the military service." With orders from the secretary of war and a personal endorsement of the president of the United States, McClernand must have been confident that nothing could stand in the way of his raising and then commanding the army that would open the Mississippi River and, just possibly, bring him glory enough to eventually achieve his ultimate goal, the White House.[12]

McClernand's interpretation of his orders would seem reasonable on the surface but he apparently did not read the fine print, a serious mistake for a lawyer. While General Grant was not immediately notified of McClernand's orders, all the troops that would be raised for the Vicksburg expedition were being sent into his department. In essence Halleck's order says that the expedition could proceed only after sufficient forces not needed for the operations of General Grant's command were raised. For all practical purposes, Grant could do what he wanted to do with these newly raised troops once they came under his command. Another fine point McClernand seems to have missed is that the order only gave him command of an expedition against Vicksburg, not the command of an independent army subject only to orders from Washington. Finally, General-in-Chief Halleck reserved for himself the final say as to what use would be made of the troops raised by McClernand's efforts.

General McClernand went right to work recruiting troops for his army. By November 10 he was able to report to Secretary Stanton that he organized, mustered and forwarded from different camps in Illinois "six regiments of infantry and one six-gun battery to Columbus, Ky., and six regiments of infantry and one six-gun battery to Memphis, Tenn. From Indiana I have forwarded five regiments of infantry, and from Iowa three, also to Columbus, Ky." In addition to these twenty regiments thousands more troops would soon be streaming south to join the expedition to Vicksburg, or so everyone believed.[13]

While McClernand was pleading his case for a campaign down the Mississippi to Washington, General Grant was presenting a plan of his own. On October 26 he wrote to Halleck that although he had received no orders and knew nothing of the plans of the commanders on either side of his department, he was prepared to move south into Mississippi: "With small re-enforcements at Memphis I think I would be able to move down the Mississippi Central road and cause the evacuation of Vicksburg and to be able to capture or destroy all the boats in the Yazoo River." Grant felt that he had to stick to the route of the railroad because as he later wrote, "Up to this time it had been regarded as an axiom in war that large bodies of troops must operate from a base of supplies which they always covered and guarded in all forward movements."[14]

Troops that McClernand had been recruiting were pouring into Memphis, and on November 9 Brigadier General James M. Tuttle, commander of the District of Cairo, notified Grant of their arrival. Since Grant had not been informed of McClernand's secret orders he, wrote to Halleck on the tenth seeking clarification, "Am I to understand that I lie here while an expedition is fitted out from Memphis, or do you want me to push as far south as possible?" The next day Halleck replied, "You have command of all troops sent to your department, and have permission to fight the enemy where you please." Halleck's answer confirmed Grant's total control over military operations in his department, putting McClernand and any troops he sent forward under Grant's command. Apparently John McClernand would not be commanding an independent army to clear the enemy from the Mississippi River.[15]

General Grant began his campaign against Vicksburg during the first week of November. Pulling in troops from around the department, Grant concentrated his forces near Grand Junction, Tennessee, just north of the Mississippi border. The original plan was relatively straightforward. Grant would advance down the line of the Mississippi Central Railroad to Jackson, Mississippi, the state capital and more importantly the junction with the Southern Railroad of Mississippi which ran west to Vicksburg and was that city's main transportation link to the rest of the Confederacy. If the Federals could cut that railroad and approach Vicksburg from the east, the city would eventually have to surrender. Just in case more strength was needed, Grant arranged for Brigadier General Frederick Steele to bring another column of troops across the Mississippi and threaten Pemberton's flank. On November 2, Grant's forces left south-central Tennessee and headed toward the first important objective: Holly Springs, Mississippi, about twenty-five miles away.[16]

Moving south along the line of the railroad, the Federal troops soon ran into Confederate defenders. Confederate General Pemberton was not only responsible for defending Vicksburg but the entire state. Trying to do too much with too little, Pemberton's forces were scattered around Northern Mississippi and were unable to seriously affect the movements of the advancing Union army. General Van Dorn, who was now commanding the troops opposing Grant's advance, could do no more than fight a delaying action by harassing the advancing Federals and destroying the railroad and any supplies that might fall into enemy hands.[17]

The progress of the Union army toward Holly Springs could probably be best described as methodical. Recent rains had made the normally poor roads in Northern Mississippi even worse. In addition, the many forests and streams that cut up the landscape made it very difficult to move an army with its artillery and numerous wagons. Grant being tied to the railroad line repairing tracks and bridges destroyed by retreating Confederates and establishing supply depots along the way only added more delays. Several miles out in front of the main column, Grant's cavalry advance pushed the Confederates out of Holly Springs on November 13, and on the 29th the town became the army's headquarters. This was one of the first objectives of the movement, but soon the entire character of the campaign was about to change.[18]

When Grant started moving south he had instructed his friend and most trusted subordinate, Major General William T. Sherman, to remain in Memphis and build up his forces until he could put two full divisions in the field. On November 15, Grant notified Sherman to leave Memphis and bring his divisions south to join the main force. As the Federal army continued south from Holly Springs, they expected the Confederates to make a stand at the natural defensive positions along the Tallahatchie River near Oxford. Pemberton, however, had already pulled his troops farther south to consolidate his scattered forces in the vicinity of Grenada using the Yalobusha River as his main defensive position. During the first week of December, Grant was able to advance about thirty miles south of Holly Springs to Oxford with little enemy interference.[19]

By the time Grant occupied Oxford, Sherman had marched his troops down to College Hill, about ten miles west. On December 8 Grant sent word to Sherman to come over to Oxford to discuss the campaign. Grant had decided to add another facet to the campaign by continuing his advance toward Jackson and at the same time sending Sherman with a large force down the Mississippi. Grant issued these orders to Sherman:

> You will proceed with as little delay as practicable to Memphis, Tennessee, taking with you one division of your present command. On your arrival at Memphis you will assume command of all the troops there, and that portion of General Curtis's forces at present east of the Mississippi River, and organize them into brigades and divisions in your own way.
> As soon as possible move with them down the river to the vicinity of Vicksburg, and, with the cooperation of the gunboat fleet under command of Flag-Officer Porter, proceed to the reduction of that place in such manner as circumstances and your own judgment may dictate.
> Inform me at the earliest practicable day of the time when you will embark, and such plans as may be matured. I will hold the forces here in readiness to cooperate with you in such manner as the movements of the enemy may make necessary.[20]

This sudden and significant departure from the original campaign came about because Grant came to realize that time had become more of a factor than he had originally believed, and he had to move more quickly to capture Vicksburg and open the Mississippi. By continuing his original advance, Grant might draw troops away from Vicksburg, making it easier for Sherman to land his men from the river and take the city. If the Confederates pulled troops from in front of Grant to reinforce Vicksburg, he would continue south and complete the original plan to take Vicksburg from the east. Grant later wrote about what he expected from this new plan: "I hoped to hold Pemberton in my front while Sherman should get in his rear and into Vicksburg. The further north the enemy could be held the better.... It was my intention, and so understood by Sherman and his command, that if the enemy should fall back I would follow him even to the gates of Vicksburg."[21]

This appeared to be a sound strategic decision providing two different ways to approach Vicksburg, and Grant elaborated on the new plan in a telegram to Halleck: "General Sherman will command the expedition down the Mississippi. He will have a force of about 40,000 men. Will land above Vicksburg, up the Yazoo, if practicable, and cut the Mississippi Central Railroad and the road running east from Vicksburg where they cross Black River." Grant would continue moving south, keeping in contact with the Confederates. There was plenty of cavalry with Grant's force and he would use them to raid at different points along the Tallahatchie and Yalabusha to confuse the enemy as to his actual plans. Once Sherman was able to cut the railroad Grant felt that "movements to secure the end desired will necessarily be left to his judgment."[22]

In addition to the sound military reasons for adding a second front to capture Vicksburg, there was another reason that Grant wanted Sherman to move quickly to gather his forces and start off down river—John McClernand. That Grant did not trust McClernand and had little confidence in his ability to lead a large independent command was certainly no secret. Grant later admitted that part of the reason for sending Sherman back to Memphis to command the river expedition was to prevent McClernand from having "a separate and independent command within mine, to operate against Vicksburg by way of the Mississippi River." Grant believed that "two commanders on the same field are always one too many, and in this case I did not think the general selected had either the experience or the qualifications to fit him for so important a position." Grant later wrote that he "feared for the safety of the troops intrusted to him, especially as he was to raise new levies, raw troops, to execute so important a trust." In a wire to Halleck he was even more plain-spoken in saying that McClernand was "unmanageable and incompetent." Grant clearly did not think McClernand was capable of leading the campaign down the Mississippi. In addition to his own doubts, the way the situation had been handled in Washington and Halleck's message that Grant had command of all the troops in his department led Grant to say regarding McClernand's independent command, "I had good reason to believe that in forestalling him I was by no means giving offence to those whose authority to command was above both him and me."[23]

The day after putting Sherman in command of the river expedition, General Grant received a message from General Halleck confirming the need for quick movement. Halleck warned Grant, "Do not make the Mississippi expedition so large as to endanger West Tennessee." Then in response to a previous question as to whether Grant should take command of the river campaign himself, Halleck wrote, "The president may insist upon designating a separate commander; if not, assign such officers as you deem best. Sherman would be my choice as the chief under you." The general-in-chief was apparently warning Grant that he might not have much say in who would command the river expedition, and at the same time Halleck voiced his preference in a commander.[24]

Sherman did indeed make haste, arriving back in Memphis by noon on December 12. He formed four divisions under the command of Brigadier Generals A. J. Smith, George W. Morgan, Morgan L. Smith and Frederick Steele. Sherman had written to Admiral Porter on December 8 emphasizing the need to work quickly: "Time now is the great object. We must not give time for new combinations. I know you will promptly co-operate." To his brother, U.S. Senator John Sherman, the general wrote, "The move is one of vast importance and if successful will remove the chief obstacles to the navigation of the Mississippi.... I take it that now Vicksburg is fortified by land & water and that it is a difficult task, but it must be undertaken."[25]

In his *Memoirs*, General Sherman explained why it was so important to move as soon as practical. "The preparations were necessarily hasty in the extreme, but this was the essence of the whole plan, viz., to reach Vicksburg as it were by surprise, while General Grant held in check Pemberton's army about Grenada." This would leave Sherman free "to deal with the smaller garrison of Vicksburg and its well-known strong batteries and defenses." The troops at Memphis left on December 19 and steamed down to Helena, where General Steele's division was also embarked on the 21st. The troops then rendezvoused at Friar's Point on December 22.[26]

While General Grant's force was slowly moving south, General McClernand had been busy recruiting and sending forward thousands of new soldiers that he was expecting to lead down the Mississippi. Like General Grant, he had been hearing some unpleasant rumors regarding the campaign and decided it was time to head south and put his plan into action. On December 1, McClernand wrote to Secretary Stanton detailing the number of troops he had sent forward and asking for orders to move his headquarters to Memphis to begin "organizing, drilling, and disciplining my command, preparatory to an early and successful movement, having for its object the important end of liberating the navigation of the Mississippi River." McClernand also reminded Stanton that he had "worked early, assiduously, and zealously in this great enterprise," and that the people and politicians of the Northwest supported a campaign down the Mississippi and approved of him as the commander of that campaign.[27]

Receiving no satisfactory reply from Stanton, on December 12 McClernand wrote directly to President Lincoln to let him know that about forty thousand men had been recruited for the Mississippi expedition and that it was time for him to join these troops and prepare them for the coming campaign. He inquired of the president,

Union General Henry W. Halleck was an excellent administrator who would become Grant's chief of staff (Library of Congress).

"May I not ask therefore to be sent forward immediately?" McClernand was now beginning to believe something had gone very wrong and messages started flying between the general and Washington.[28]

On December 16, McClernand wrote to General Halleck informing him of the number of troops sent forward and saying, "I beg to be sent forward, in accordance with the order of the Secretary of War of the 21st of October giving me command of the Mississippi expedition." On December 17, McClernand wired President Lincoln, "I believe I am superseded. Please advise me." He also sent basically the same message to Secretary Stanton, who quickly reassured, "There has been, as I am informed by General Halleck, no order superseding you." However, the rest of Stanton's reply was less soothing. Pointing out that the proposed operation and all the troops sent forward were within General Grant's department, Halleck was to issue orders to "organize all the troops of that department in three army corps, the First Army Corps to be commanded by you, and assigned to the operations on the Mississippi under the general supervision of the general commanding the department." This was hardly the independent command that McClernand had been expecting to lead down the Mississippi.[29]

As frequently happens, orders were changed, and on December 18 instructions were issued by Secretary Stanton for Grant to divide the forces under his command into four corps. McClernand was to have command of the Thirteenth Corps, Sherman the Fifteenth, Major General Stephen A. Hurlbut the Sixteenth and Major General James B. McPherson the Seventeenth. That day Grant wrote to McClernand informing him of the re-organization and that in addition to McClernand's corps, Sherman's would be added to the expedition down the Mississippi. Although he would still technically be under Grant's command, McClernand, who was senior to Sherman by achieving the same rank at an earlier date, would have overall command of the expedition.[30]

McClernand did not receive Grant's order until December 29. In the meantime he became increasingly upset and wired Stanton on the 23rd complaining that he had still not been relieved to join his troops. The secretary of war replied that evening: "It has not been my understanding that you should remain at Springfield a single hour beyond your own pleasure and judgment of the necessity of collecting and forwarding the troops." Stanton added that McClernand was free to "report to General Grant for the purpose specified in the order of the General-in-chief."[31]

John McClernand was finally on his way to join the thousands of troops he had recruited for the campaign down the Mississippi. Leaving Cairo, Illinois, with his new bride, the sister of his late wife, he arrived in Memphis on December 28. Unfortunately his army had already left without him and was at this moment preparing to launch an attack which, if successful, would allow General Sherman to get behind Vicksburg and possibly capture the city without McClernand. Beside himself with anger, McClernand could only follow his missing army downriver as quickly as he could. Clearly the politician turned general had been tricked, first in Washington by the original orders that left much open to interpretation, then by Grant and Halleck, both of whom worked to get the new troops into Grant's department and under his command to use as Grant saw fit. As it turned out, however, at the same time that Sherman was forming the army in Memphis and McClernand was cooling his heels in Illinois, events were taking place elsewhere that would cause a dramatic change in the Federal campaign.[32]

In mid–December famed Confederate cavalry leader Brigadier General Nathan Bedford Forrest led over two thousand troopers into Western Tennessee. For two weeks Forrest ran wild destroying railroads, capturing tons of supplies and weapons, burning what they could not carry off, inflicting over 2000 casualties on local Union troops and generally destroying Federal communication and supply lines throughout the area. Although constantly pursued by Union forces, by the first of January the now well equipped and well fed Confederate raiders crossed the Tennessee River to safety.[33]

In addition to Forrest's disastrous raid, Grant's forces suffered an even more crippling blow in Mississippi. About the same time that Forrest was entering West Tennessee, General Van Dorn was leading about 3,500 cavalrymen north to strike at Grant's supply lines. The Confederate cavalry was able to avoid contact with Federal patrols, and on December 20 it made a surprise attack on the massive Federal supply base at Holly Springs. The commander of the base, Colonel R. C. Murphy, had apparently ignored warnings about a possible raid and the town was totally unprepared for the attack. At dawn Van Dorn led his troopers forward and they struck the Union camp like a bolt of lightning. Most of the Federal soldiers in town were still sleeping and offered little resistance. The 2nd Illinois Cavalry, however, was camped out at the fairground and was preparing to go out on patrol when the Confederates appeared. The Federal cavalry put up a spirited fight but were soon overwhelmed by numbers. By 8 a.m. Van Dorn was in possession of Holly Springs, mountains of supplies, and about 1,500 prisoners.[34]

After the fighting ended, Van Dorn's men went about the work of destruction. Railroad equipment, including two complete trains, were destroyed, machine shops, buildings loaded with quartermaster supplies and ordnance, the courthouse which was serving as an ammunition depot, even a new two thousand bed hospital were consumed by flames. The town contained thousands of bushels of wheat, tons of beef, pork, flour, and coffee, and all that was not taken by the raiders was destroyed. Grant estimated the loss at about $400,000, a tremendous amount at that time. One of Van Dorn's officers, Colonel A. F. Brown, later wrote, "In a few short hours, with a comparatively insignificant force, General Van Dorn had destroyed an accumulation of military supplies which it had taken months to collect from the factories and storehouses of the North."[35]

General Van Dorn's raid on Holly Springs combined with Nathan Bedford Forrest's raid into Western Tennessee crippled Grant's ability to continue his advance and increased the danger to the Mississippi expedition. With his communications disrupted and no reliable supply line, Grant was forced to end his advance and head back to Tennessee. Grant had received no news from Sherman or Memphis concerning the river expedition, so on December 23 he sent a message to "commanding officer expedition down Mississippi" to advise that officer of his withdrawal. In this message Grant admitted that the dual enemy raids "have cut me off from supplies, so that farther advance by this route is perfectly impracticable. The country does not afford supplies for troops, and but a limited supply of forage. I have fallen back to the Tallahatchie."[36]

On the march back to Tennessee the Federal foragers made a wide sweep of about fifteen miles on either side of the main column. At first Grant was unsure that he would be able to find enough provisions for the army, but he would later write, "I was amazed at the quantity of supplies the country afforded. It showed that we could have subsisted off the country for two months instead of two weeks." This ability to live off the land came too late to save this campaign, but it was a lesson that Grant would remember for the future.[37]

Chapter 4

Chickasaw Bayou

On Christmas Day 1862, a fleet of Union gunboats and transports carrying General Sherman and over thirty-five thousand troops arrived at Milliken's Bend, about twenty miles up the Mississippi River from Vicksburg. Sherman was faithfully continuing his part in the campaign as originally planned, unaware of how much the situation had recently changed. The destruction of telegraph lines by Confederate raiders that added to the normal difficulties in communicating over long distances during the Civil War had also prevented Sherman from receiving any information about the raid at Holly Springs and Grant's return to Tennessee. Grant's withdrawal allowed General Pemberton to weaken his force in central Mississippi and send reinforcements to Vicksburg. Ignorant of these events, Sherman wasted little time at Milliken's Bend, and on December 26 the fleet started up the Yazoo River toward Chickasaw Bayou.[1]

Conscious of the need to isolate Vicksburg from receiving assistance, Sherman sent Brigadier General Stephen G. Burbridge's brigade, of A. J. Smith's division, to break the railroad that connected the city with Shreveport. While the remainder of Smith's division waited for Burbridge to return, the other three divisions of the army continued on to the mouth of the Yazoo River. Sherman's force then sailed about thirteen miles up the Yazoo to Johnson's plantation, the only substantial amount of solid ground in the area, where the troops disembarked. J. T. Woods of the 96th Ohio wrote about their march through the foreboding landscape toward the waiting enemy: "The darkness threw around us a sable mantle, as sick and sad, we moved along the narrow roads, heavy with mud, interspersed here and there with still worse old corduroy. The lands were low and marshy, over which the water every year overflowed, leaving its marks on the dense forest of cypress trees, whose branches, laden with trailing moss, seemed to beckon us gloomily on to our burial."[2]

Sherman spread his army out with Steele's division near the mouth of Chickasaw Bayou, Morgan's division near the Johnson house, and Morgan L. Smith below Morgan. When A. J. Smith's division arrived it went into line below Morgan Smith. Sherman would later describe the terrible terrain he found himself in as "an island separated from the high bluff known as Walnut Hills, on which the town of Vicksburg stands, by a broad and shallow bayou.... On our right was another wide bayou, known as Old River; and on the left still another, much narrower, but too deep to be forded, known as Chickasaw Bayou." The vast majority of the island was heavily wooded except for the cultivated land on Johnson's plantation.[3]

To get to the high ground from where he could assault the city, Sherman's men would have to pass through some of the worst ground imaginable. J. T. Woods later remembered that when he and his comrades came up to the front they found themselves facing heavily defended high ground "with only a narrow sheet of water intervening, and our position rendered precarious by the fact that the ground we occupied was often submerged, the marks on the trees showing that frequently the waters were at least ten feet deep." The area the Union forces had to traverse was essentially a large swamp filled with intersecting creeks and bayous that made it impossible for the army to advance in strength. There were only a few narrow corridors of land that were solid enough to support large numbers of troops, and these approaches were heavily defended. Brigadier General Stephen D. Lee was in charge of the Confederate defenses, and he cleverly used every advantage offered by the miserable terrain. There were numerous rifle pits dug in along the base and slopes of the hills with artillery on the high ground commanding every approach that the Union troops might take. Despite the obvious difficulties, it was at Chickasaw Bayou that Sherman decided to launch his attack. There was a decent road through the bayou and behind that was solid higher ground from which it would be possible to advance against Vicksburg.[4]

After Sherman and his senior officers reconnoitered the front on December 27 and 28, the enemy positions were found "to be strong by nature and by art, and seemingly well defended." On the right of the Union line in front of A. J. Smith's troops, the natural and man-made obstacles in their front made it pointless to send his men forward under what was sure to be heavy enemy fire. Sherman also saw that the main bayou was virtually impassable except at two locations. The only points where the Union troops might gain a foothold on the enemy side were in front of Morgan's division near the head of Chickasaw Bayou and about one mile below across from Morgan Smith's division. It was quickly seen that General Steele could not physically reach the bluffs from his current position, so Sherman ordered him to bring his troops closer in to the left of General Morgan's position. Also on the 28th, Morgan Smith was severely wounded during the reconnaissance and the command of his division fell to Brigadier General David Stuart.[5]

It was decided to begin the assault on the morning of December 29. Sherman's plan was "to make a lodgment on the foot-hills and bluffs abreast of our position, while diversions were made by the navy toward Haynes' Bluff, and by the first division directly toward Vicksburg." Not wanting to allow the defenders time to reinforce the most crucial positions, Sherman proposed to "make a show of attack along the whole front." General Morgan's division would lead the assault. Their job was to take the Confederate trenches and occupy the crest of the Walnut Hills, from which they could move against Vicksburg on good ground. General Steele's division would support Morgan's assault and A. J. Smith's division would attack to Morgan's right. Sherman noted that "the front was very narrow, and immediately opposite, at the base of the hills about three hundred yards from the bayou, was a rebel battery, supported by an infantry force posted on the spurs of the hill behind." To try to draw attention from the point of attack, orders were given to begin the assault on both flanks before moving against the center.[6]

As General Morgan's troops marched along the road leading from the Yazoo toward the heights, the bayou was on their left, and on the right was a water filled forest with several creeks running parallel to the bluffs in their front. In addition to these natural obstacles Morgan could clearly see that "opposite the point where the bayou turns abruptly to the left, and on the right side of the road, the forest was felled and formed a tangled abatis." Past this dismal looking terrain the bayou was divided into two branches with a narrow corduroy bridge spanning one of them. When Brigadier General Francis P. Blair studied the ground in front of his troops, he also did not like what he saw; "The works of the enemy on their right were more formidable than from any other approach. Almost every gun and rifle-pit bore upon us and many enfiladed our line of battle. The natural obstructions were certainly as great as from any other direction." There was also concern that there had not yet been as thorough a reconnaissance of the ground as should have been done before launching an assault over such poor terrain. General Blair's conclusion was that "the enemy had improved their naturally strong position with consummate skill." In addition to the bayou itself, there was a "steep bank on the side of the enemy at least 10 feet high, covered with a strong abatis and crowned with rifle pits from end to end." Above this first line was another set of rifle pits and artillery which covered their entire line. "These formidable works, defended by a strong force of desperate men such as held them on the 29th, would seem to require almost superhuman efforts to effect their capture."[7]

General Morgan had discovered that a body of water off Chickasaw Bayou known as McNutt Lake had no defenses between the lake and the bluffs. Here was an opportunity to get Union troops on the same high ground as Vicksburg without having to break through the tough Confederate defenses. During the late night of December 28 and early the next morning, a small group of engineers and troops made two attempts to bridge this undefended body of water. The first failed when the bridge was put up at the wrong location due to the darkness and the men not being familiar with the terrain. The second attempt was at the proper location but the soldiers ran out of bridging material and it was light before they were able to finish. It was too late in any event, because by now the Confederates had brought up troops and artillery that forced Morgan's men to abandon their work. There would be no easy way past the Confederate works.[8]

After studying the terrain over which his men were to advance, Morgan considered that attacking over the narrow road across the bayou was a mistake and made his feelings known to General Sherman. Morgan later wrote that when he and Sherman made their final examination of the ground, "I called his attention to our very narrow and difficult front; to the bayou in its tortuous course on our left; to the mucky marsh beyond the bayou and bridge, all within easy range of the enemy's guns." Morgan's protests had no effect, however, and Sherman ordered the attack to take place as planned. Shortly after sending out his orders for the assault, Colonel John DeCourcy approached Morgan to confirm his orders. Knowing the difficulties facing his troops an obviously distressed, DeCourcy exclaimed to Morgan, "My poor brigade! Your order will be obeyed, General."[9]

A little after noon on December 29, the attack began with an artillery barrage from the Federal lines, quickly followed by return fire from the defenders. Winchester Hall of the 26th Louisiana later wrote that as he waited in

Union General William T. Sherman believed in waging total war against the South. He followed Grant as general-in-chief (Library of Congress).

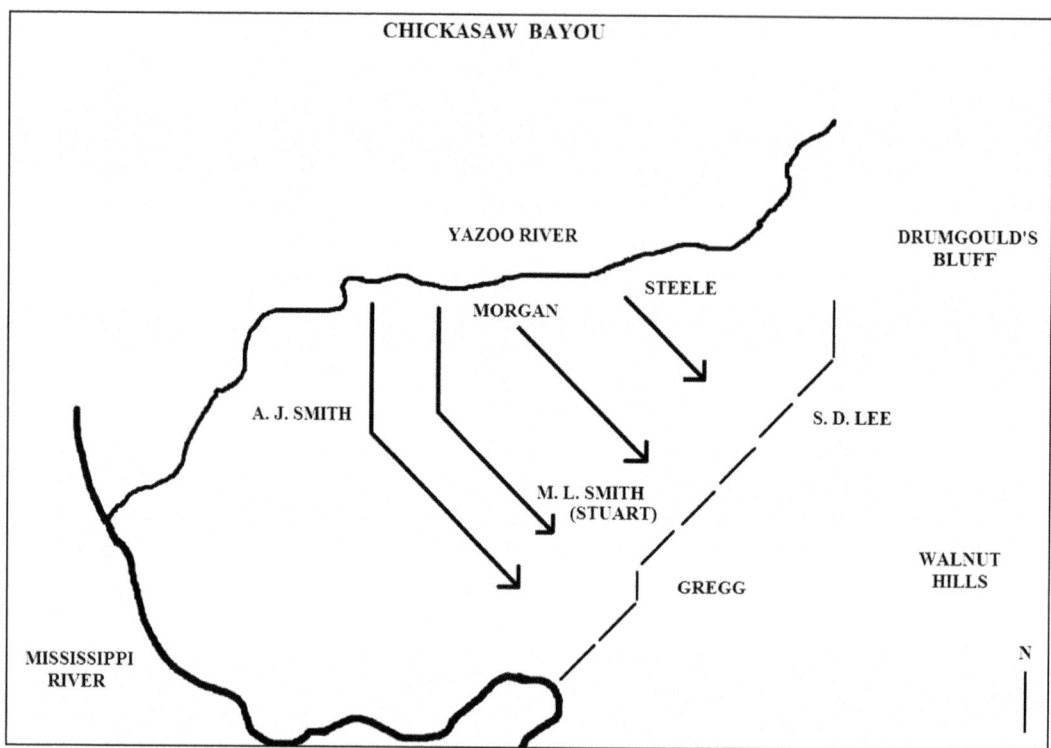

the Confederate works for the coming attack, "A terrific storm of shot and shell now burst upon us, and in its fury it seemed as if no living thing about us could escape." General Blair's brigade was stationed between the bayou and Thompson's Lake. Colonel DeCourcy's brigade occupied the ground from the abatis to across the road with Brigadier General John M. Thayer's brigade in support. With a shout the troops moved forward and the attack began. By the time DeCourcy and Thayer reached the bridge and Blair entered the bayou, they came under heavy fire. Forcing their way through the muddy bayou and over and around the fallen trees, the men reached dry ground, but the cost had been heavy. General Morgan wrote, "All formations were broken; the assaulting forces were jammed together, and, with a yell of desperate determination, they rushed to the assault and were mowed down by a storm of shells, grape and canister, and minie-balls which swept our front like a hurricane of fire." As the Confederates poured their fire into the oncoming Union troops, Winchester Hall noted that the enemy line continued to advance through the storm of lead, "although every weapon on our side was warm, and every man was doing his best. Some approached within fifty yards of our line, but it was their last assault."[10]

As soon as Colonel DeCourcy's men began to move forward, the 42nd Ohio and the 22nd Kentucky came under heavy fire as they worked their way through the abates. They had to stop at the bayou, which was too deep to ford. Lieutenant Owen J. Hopkins of the 42nd Ohio later wrote that "the hill belched forth flame and smoke, with trembling of the earth under the cannons' roar, as though a hundred volcanoes were in violent eruption." DeCourcy reported that the 16th Ohio, 54th Indiana, and a detachment of the 22nd Kentucky had more solid ground to traverse and were able to move relatively quickly through the bayou and advance on a road up to the Confederate works, where they moved forward "in splendid style, and nearly accomplished their object, notwithstanding the immense and fearfully-destructive fire which poured in from front, left, right, and even rear." Moving the 42nd Ohio and 22nd Kentucky to the left, DeCourcy was able to reach the clear ground in front of the enemy works but too late to support the regiments that had made the charge. DeCourcy reported that his assaulting troops "had nearly crossed the large open space of more than half a mile which lay stretched out before them glacis fashion, when the enemy increased his fire of small-arms and grape to such a degree as to render farther advance impossible." Lieutenant Hopkins remembered that during the assault as he and his comrades were "climbing, crawling, fighting our way up the slope" they came under "an awful fire from outnumbering foes nearly surrounding us," and found it impossible to hold their hard-won positions. Seeing no point in sending any more men forward "to useless destruction," DeCourcy held them back to cover the retreat of the survivors of the assault.[11]

On the left of the assaulting Union line, General Blair's four regiments began their attack with the 13th Illinois and the 31st Missouri in the lead, followed by the 58th Ohio and the 29th Missouri. Blair watched as his men "rushed with impetuosity to the attack and pressed over every obstacle and through a storm of shell and rifle-bullets, and carried the first and second ranges of rifle-pits with an irresistible charge." Blair's troops suffered terrible casualties, and by the time his men worked their way to level ground near the hills they ran into a crossfire of artillery and muskets that decimated their ranks before they even reached the main Confederate fortifications. At this point General Morgan's troops were seen moving forward and Blair's men "pushed still farther and to within a short distance of the enemy's last intrenchments. Some reached the foot of these formidable works only to pour out their lives at their base." Blair lost nearly a third of his command before the attack bogged down and the survivors began to slowly pull back across the bayou.[12]

Over on the Federal right General A. J. Smith's men ran into the same problems with the same results. J. T. Woods remembered that when the attackers approached the Confederate works, they ran into "a tornado of musketry, grape and canister. The very air seemed rent into splinters by the fierce, sharp volley they delivered, and in an instant after rose, the strange, wild, half-maniac yell, that drowned the rattle of our musketry." One of Smith's regiments, the 6th Missouri, pressed forward and wound up under a steep embankment where, as Sherman noted, they "actually scooped out with their hands caves in the bank, which sheltered them against the fire of the enemy, who, right over their heads, held their muskets outside the parapet vertically, and fired down." Unable to fall back during the day, the men of the 6th Missouri had to stay under the embankment until dark when they were able to make their way back to the Union lines. All across the battlefield Sherman's army had run into the worst possible situation for attacking troops, terrible ground defended by well fortified and determined veterans.[13]

General Sherman's assault was a complete failure and in his *Memoirs* he candidly wrote, "Our loss had been pretty heavy, and we had accomplished nothing and had inflicted little loss on our enemy." Sherman blamed General Morgan for the defeat but considering the terrible ground they had to cross and the well posted and strong defenses, the attack never really had much chance of success. The effort put forth by the courageous Union troops is evident in the casualty figures. Sherman lost about eighteen hundred men overall with over two hundred killed; the total Confederate casualties were just over two hundred.[14]

Never one to give up after just one try, Sherman considered attacking again, but "soon became satisfied that the enemy's attention having been drawn to the only two practicable points, it would prove too costly." Looking for another location from which he might be able to gain the high ground behind the bayous, Sherman decided to load General Steele's division and one brigade of Stuart's onto transports and land them just below Haynes' Bluff, making a quick move to gain the hills. This attempt was foiled by the weather when on December 30, the night the troops were to sail to the selected landing point, heavy fog descended on the river and the ships could go nowhere. From the Union camps at Chickasaw Bayou reinforcements could be seen arriving in the Confederate works and also heading toward Haynes' Bluff. Sherman noted, "The rain, too, began to fall, and the trees bore water-marks ten feet above our heads, so that I became convinced that the part of wisdom was to withdraw."[15]

General Sherman was able to retrieve most of his supplies and equipment, and the troops were back on their ships by January 2, when Admiral Porter brought the news that General McClernand had arrived at the mouth of the Yazoo River aboard the steamer *Tigress*. Still clinging to the idea that he was to lead an independent army, McClernand named his new command the Army of the Mississippi with General Sherman commanding one of the corps and General Morgan the other. McClernand also brought the news that Grant's army had turned back toward LaGrange and any advance through central Mississippi was out of the question for the near future. This meant that Vicksburg and the defenses in the area would be reinforced by troops that had been facing Grant, and another attempt to break through the Confederate lines from the Yazoo would be pointless.[16]

The most immediate question facing General McClernand was what to do next. Assaulting Vicksburg itself was out of the question and Sherman's defeat showed how difficult it would be to reach the city from the Yazoo area. Shortly after McClernand arrived, however, a relatively minor event occurred that would provide the answer the generals were looking for. A small supply ship, the *Blue Wing*, had been captured on the Mississippi by a Confederate ship based at Fort Hindman, about forty miles to the northwest up the Arkansas River. Commonly called the Post of Arkansas, this fort was manned by about five thousand enemy soldiers. Confederate ships based there would pose a threat to the Union supply lines by attacking shipping coming down the Mississippi during any operation against Vicksburg. It did not take Sherman long to decide this serious threat must be eliminated.[17]

General Sherman enlisted the support of Admiral Porter in moving against Fort Hindman, and they brought the matter to McClernand. Porter, who had been acquainted with McClernand in Washington, did not like or trust the new commanding general and made his feelings clear during the meeting, so much so in fact that at one point Sherman asked Porter to go with him to another cabin before the situation got too heated. When the meeting resumed it was decided that a combined attack by gunboats and infantry would be launched against the Post of Arkansas. Admiral Porter personally took commanded of the naval force that transported both infantry corps while General McClernand was in overall command of the expedition.[18]

Chapter 5

Victory and Conflict

With the Federal troops already on board their transports, the fleet was able to set sail up the Mississippi River on January 4. In addition to Porter's flagship *Black Hawk*, the transports were accompanied by the gunboats *Louisville, Lexington, Cincinnati*, and the *Baron de Kalb* (formerly the *St. Louis*), and several of the smaller and lighter fighting ships known as tinclads. To save coal and to move faster the gunboats were towed by transports. The fleet first sailed past the Arkansas River to the White River in an attempt to conceal their real target, then went through a cutoff that joined both rivers to enter the Arkansas. After an uneventful trip it landed about four miles below the fort on January 9.[1]

Square in shape, Fort Hindman was about three hundred feet long on each side and located on high ground on the left bank of the river. The fort was protected by three casemates for heavy artillery, mounting 8-inch and 9-inch guns situated so they could cover the river approach and at least a dozen smaller pieces located around the work. On January 10, General Sherman sent Stuart's division along the embankment up-river, where they ran into a line of trenches extending from the river to a swamp on the left. General Sherman led Steele's division along a road through the swamp and around to the rear of the fort. As they were advancing, General McClernand rode up and informed Sherman that the Confederates had abandoned their outer lines and fallen back to the fort. Sherman re-crossed the swamp and approached the fort following Stuart's route. While the troops were moving forward during the evening, the *Louisville, Baron de Kalb,* and *Cincinnati* approached the fort to get the range and exchanged some heavy fire with the shore batteries. Admiral Porter also brought up several of the lighter gunboats to bombard the fort with shrapnel and light shells.[2]

On the morning of January 11, the Federal forces were in position about five to six hundred yards from the outer works of the fort with Sherman's corps on the right and Morgan's corps to his left. The gunboats had already begun firing on the fort, and about 1:30 p.m. the infantry began its advance. The ground in front was mostly flat with little cover for the advancing troops, and Sherman reported that his men "advanced well under a heavy fire, once or twice falling to the ground for a sort of rest or pause." Fortunately for Sherman's men, most of the artillery in the fort was focusing on the gunboats and Morgan's troops. However, crossing open ground against well-manned trenches was still dangerous work. Charles Miller, of the 76th Ohio, recorded that as his regiment went forward the first volley from the defenders was too high, but "the second volley however fell plump into our lines and made considerable havoc." They could get no closer than about 100 yards from the Confederate lines, where "the men all dropped on their faces in the grass and underbrush and commenced skimming the enemy's parapets with musket balls."[3]

Over on the left General Morgan's troops faced even tougher going. With General Burbridge's brigade in the lead, A. J. Smith's division advanced slowly but steadily, driving enemy skirmishers ahead of them until they came to within about 200 yards of the fort. As on the right, Smith's advance stalled and General Morgan reported that "a galling fire was kept up between General Smith's division and the enemy." The fighting here continued with both sides stubbornly holding their ground amid heavy firing. General Morgan noted that more than a third of the Union casualties during the battle were suffered by Burbridge's brigade. General Smith now brought Colonel DeCourcy's brigade up from his position below the fort, and soon Smith's entire force was engaged.[4]

While the infantry was advancing, the gunboats had been keeping up a steady fire during the afternoon, and by 4 p.m. all but a couple of the fort's artillery pieces had been put out of commission. By late afternoon, confident of the outcome, two gunboats moved past the fort and headed upriver to cut off the Confederates' route of retreat. Virtually surrounded by land and water, their artillery out of action, heavily outnumbered, the Confederates had little choice other than to surrender or be destroyed. Around 4:30 p.m. white flags appeared on the parapets. The Confederate commander, Brigadier General Thomas J. Churchill, surrendered about 5,000 troops. Not only did General McClernand achieve an important victory at the relatively modest cost of about one thousand total casualties, he eliminated a major threat to future Federal operations against Vicksburg.[5]

The next morning the *Baron de Kalb* and the *Cincinnati,* escorting several transports full of troops, headed farther up the Arkansas River to look for other enemy outposts. They sailed about fifty miles, passing St. George, which had been evacuated, and reached a railroad depot at Duvall's Bluff where they destroyed as much railroad equipment as they could. The little fleet then retraced its route and joined the rest of the army as they made their way back toward the Mississippi.[6]

Meanwhile, General Grant, unable to communicate directly with the Mississippi expedition since the disaster at Holly Springs, returned to Memphis unaware of what was taking place along the Mississippi. The first solid news he received was from General Halleck on January 7. Informing Grant of Sherman's defeat at Chickasaw Bayou, the general-in-chief wrote, "Every possible effort must be made to re-enforce him. Take everything you can dispense with in Tennessee and Mississippi. We must not fail in this if within human power to accomplish it." Included in Halleck's message was a reference to Major General Nathaniel Banks, who was headquartered in New Orleans and had orders to advance up the Mississippi to join with the troops coming down the river and converge on Vicksburg. Unaware that Banks had made little progress and was nowhere near Vicksburg at this time, Grant felt it was most important that the army now led by McClernand be available to join with Banks when he appeared.[7]

Grant barely had time to digest the information from Halleck when he received the first news from McClernand in a message sent on January 8. He was most definitely not pleased with what he read. McClernand informed Grant that the army had left Milliken's Bend and was heading for the Post of Arkansas. McClernand gave several reasons for this movement, including the failure of Sherman's attack and the "present impracticability of reducing that place with the force under my command by a front attack unsupported by a co-operative movement in the rear of the place." He noted the "importance of reducing the Post as a means of freeing the navigation of the Mississippi River" and preventing enemy raiders from coming out of the White and Arkansas Rivers. There was also concern about the morale of the army, and McClernand decided that "the counteraction of the moral effect of the failure of the attack near Vicksburg and the reinspiration of the forces repulsed by making them the champions of new, important, and successful enterprises" was another important objective. After completing the expedition to Arkansas, McClernand pledged to return to the Mississippi near Vicksburg and continue with the main objective of the campaign.[8]

McClernand's message sent Grant over the edge. As far as anyone knew Banks was approaching Vicksburg at the very time that McClernand decided to leave the area to pursue his own agenda. Grant expressed his anger in a wire to Halleck on January 11: "General McClernand has fallen back to White River and gone on a wild-goose chase to the Post of Arkansas. I am ready to re-enforce but must await further information before knowing what to do."[9]

Also on the 11th, Grant composed a terse message to McClernand reminding that officer that the goal of the expedition was Vicksburg. "Unless absolutely necessary for the object of your expedition you will abstain from all moves not connected with it. I do not approve of your move on the Post of Arkansas." Grant could see no great advantage to taking the army up the Arkansas River and made it clear that "unless you are acting under authority not derived from me keep your command where it can soonest be assembled for the renewal of the attack on Vicksburg." It was of the utmost importance that McClernand's force be available to join Banks when he arrived, and Grant reiterated that he wanted McClernand to wait at Milliken's Bend. He wrote, "Unless there is some great reason of which I am not advised you will immediately proceed to that point and await the arrival of re-enforcements and General Banks' expedition, keeping me fully advised of your movements."[10]

As it turned out, this message never reached McClernand due to a lack of transportation downriver. On January 13 Grant wrote another, less strident message to McClernand, saying in part, "I cannot tell positively what is best for you to do; but unless there is some object not visible at this distance your forces should return to Milliken's Bend, or some point convenient for operating on Vicksburg, and where they can co-operate with Banks should he come up the river." Grant admitted that he did not know Banks' current position or whether he was even moving north, but stated to McClernand that "it is our duty to be prepared to co-operate."[11]

By now it had become obvious to Grant that in order for the Vicksburg campaign to proceed as he wanted, he would have to take over the command in the field. Halleck had wired to Grant on January 12, "You are hereby authorized to relieve General McClernand from command of the expedition against Vicksburg, giving it to the next in rank or taking it yourself." Halleck had no more faith in McClernand than did Grant, and this order would put either Sherman or Grant in charge of the Vicksburg expedition, which is probably what Washington had in mind all along. The same day Grant sent his second message to McClernand, he wrote to General McPherson settling the question of who was in charge: "It is my present intention to command the expedition down the river in person."[12]

By the time Grant had decided to take over command of the Vicksburg expedition, General McClernand had already captured the Post of Arkansas and was heading back to the Mississippi. On January 17 Sherman wrote to Grant concerning his disapproval of the move up the Arkansas River. Sherman admitted that if Banks was approaching Vicksburg it would have been a mistake to leave the area, but felt "so assured that we will again be at Vicksburg before Banks is there that I cannot think any bad result of this kind can occur." Sherman also justified the move, stating that "as long as the Post of Arkansas existed on our flank, with boats to ship cannon and men to the mouth of the Arkansas, we would be annoyed beyond measure whilst operating below. The capture of the Blue Wing was a mere sample. We were compelled to reduce it." After receiving Sherman's message, Grant modified his objections, later writing, "I was at first disposed to disapprove of this move as an unnecessary side movement having no especial bearing upon the work before us; but when the result was understood I regarded it as very important."[13]

Sherman also suggested possible ways to assault Vicksburg, and once again made it clear that he had no confidence in McClernand as overall commander of the expedition, saying to Grant, "I wish you would come down and see. I only fear McClernand may attempt impossibilities." Sherman did not have long to worry about who commanded the expedition, because General Grant arrived at McClernand's headquarters on January 17. Grant later wrote that he had received letters from both Sherman and Admiral Porter asking him to take command in person, and when he arrived, "It was here made evident to me that both the army and navy were so distrustful of McClernand's fitness to command that, while they would do all they could to insure success, this distrust was an element of weakness. It would have been criminal to send troops under these circumstances into such danger."[14]

General Grant immediately went to work to straighten out the situation on the Mississippi. McClernand was ordered to take his troops back to Vicksburg and concentrate at Young's Point, about nine miles above the city. Grant returned to Memphis, where he issued orders that sent General McPherson's corps downriver to join the expanding army near Vicksburg. On January 29, Grant arrived in person at Young's Point and assumed overall command the next day.[15]

Even before Grant took over the command of the Mississippi expedition, McClernand had been complaining about his treatment by Grant and Halleck. After writing to Secretary of War Stanton and others, McClernand received a letter from President Lincoln stating that he was already dealing with enough problems and did not need McClernand to cause any more; he also noted that McClernand had done very well for a politician with no military training and should avoid making enemies in the high command, especially General Halleck. The president also stated in plain words that everyone involved, including McClernand, would be better off if he would just concentrate on performing his duties to the best of his ability and stop complaining. This letter from President Lincoln should have been the final word on who was in command of what, but apparently McClernand's ego and belief that he had been used by Grant and Halleck overrode any common sense that he might have possessed.[16]

A series of messages now passed between Grant and McClernand concerning who was

Union General John McClernand—after being relieved from command at Vicksburg, he became active in Illinois politics (Library of Congress).

in command of the Mississippi expedition. Grant later wrote that "General McClernand took exception in a most characteristic way—for him. His correspondence with me on the subject was more in the nature of a reprimand than a protest. It was highly insubordinate, but I overlooked it, as I believed, for the good of the service." The issuance of General Orders No. 13 by Grant began the exchange. In this order, Grant assumed command of the expedition against Vicksburg and ordered McClernand, as commander of the Thirteenth Corps, to take control of Helena, Arkansas, and other points on the west bank of the Mississippi.[17]

On January 30 McClernand wrote to Grant registering dissatisfaction with his assignment: "I hasten to inquire whether its purpose is to relieve me from the command of all or any portion of the forces composing the Mississippi River expedition." McClernand then cited his orders from Secretary Stanton the previous October which stated in part that "an expedition may be organized under General McClernand's command against Vicksburg and to clear the Mississippi to New Orleans." However, the key to the orders and the portion that McClernand chose to ignore stated that the "forces so organized will remain subject to the designation of the general-in-chief and be employed according to such exigencies as the service in his judgment may require." In other words, General Halleck could assign whomever he wanted to the command, and he wanted Grant.[18]

Also on the thirtieth, McClernand sent a second message that basically challenged Grant to prove he had the authority to take command of the expedition. Complaining about Grant's headquarters issuing orders directly to corps commanders without first going through his own headquarters, McClernand stated, "As I am invested, by order of the Secretary of War, indorsed by the President, and by order of the President communicated to you by the General-in-Chief, with the command of all the forces operating on the Mississippi River, I claim that all orders affecting the condition or operations of those forces should pass through these headquarters." If this was not confrontational enough, McClernand continued, "If different views are entertained by you, then the question should be immediately referred to Washington, and one or the other, or both of us, relieved. One thing is certain, two generals cannot command this army."[19]

Grant replied to McClernand's messages on January 31 in relatively measured terms stating that, indeed, the intention of General Orders No. 13 was "that I will take direct command of the Mississippi River expedition, which necessarily limits your command to the Thirteenth Army Corps." Grant referred to both McClernand's original orders and Halleck's wire of January 12, saying that while he acknowledged President Lincoln as commander-in chief and would certainly obey his orders, "I have seen no order to prevent my taking immediate command in the field, and since the dispatch referred to in your note, I have received another from the General-in-Chief of the Army, authorizing me directly to take command of this army."[20]

General McClernand refused to give in. His in final message on the subject of command wanted the question decided by the highest authorities. "I acquiesce in the order for the purpose of avoiding a conflict of authority in the presence of the enemy." Citing his orders from Secretary Stanton once again, McClernand protested losing command of what he considered to be his expedition and requested that the matter be submitted to General Halleck and through him to Secretary Stanton and President Lincoln for resolution. McClernand closed his message saying, "I request this, not only in respect for the President and Secretary, under whose express authority I claim the right to command the expedition, but in justice to myself as its author and actual promoter."[21]

To be fair, McClernand had a legitimate complaint. The Illinois general did put together the troops making up the expedition and certainly Stanton and Halleck knew full well that McClernand believed he was to command an independent army. The careful wording of the orders left a loophole that was now being used to deprive McClernand of overall command. It was not particularly fair, but the fact is that no one in the Federal leadership believed McClernand was capable of commanding one of the most important campaigns of the war.

On February 1, Grant sent the correspondence between himself and McClernand back to Washington to get a definitive ruling concerning the command situation on the Mississippi. Grant stated that per instructions from Washington, he assigned McClernand "command of an army corps operating on the Mississippi River, and to give him the chief command, under my direction." After receiving Halleck's order to give the command to the most competent officer or take command himself, Grant decided to do just that. The heart of the problem was that Grant felt "if General Sherman had been left in command here, such is my confidence in him that I would not have thought my presence necessary. But whether I do General McClernand injustice or not, I have not confidence in his ability as a soldier to conduct an expedition of the magnitude of this one successfully." Grant was confident that most of the senior officers in the Mississippi Expedition felt the same doubts about McClernand as he did. Finally, Grant stated that in submitting this question to higher authorities, he would "cheerfully submit to and give a hearty support" to whatever they decide. The authorities in Washington quickly made it clear that there was no interest in having anyone but Grant in command of the campaign to take Vicksburg.[22]

Chapter 6

One Failure After Another

The situation facing General Grant at Vicksburg was stated quite accurately by Admiral Porter in a dispatch to Secretary Welles in January: "The front of Vicksburg is heavily fortified, and unless we can get troops in the rear of the city I see no chance of taking it at present, though we cut off all their supplies from Texas and Louisiana." No matter how strong Vicksburg's defenses were, however, the city had to be taken to open the Mississippi. In another letter to Welles, the admiral wrote to emphasize the stronghold's importance: "My opinion is that Vicksburg is the main point. When that falls all subordinate posts will fall with it."[1]

With Vicksburg on the east side of the Mississippi, it was obvious that Grant would have to somehow get his army on the same side of the river in order to launch any type of assault or siege. The advance through central Mississippi the previous fall did not produce the desired results, and Sherman's defeat at Chickasaw Bluff illustrated how difficult it would be to approach the city from the north. Getting past Vicksburg and then approaching the city from the south or east held the most promise for success. Clearly Porter's armored gunboats could get past the city's batteries without too much difficulty, but trying to run flimsy transports crammed with thousands of troops past those batteries was just asking for disaster. Marching the army down the western side of the river and then crossing to the eastern side below Vicksburg was clearly the most logical solution, but the heavy winter rains had turned the ground in every direction into swamp-like quagmires and the few roads into impassable ribbons of mud. This approach would have to wait months for the ground to dry out. In the meantime Grant could not just sit off Vicksburg and wait.

At this time the Federal army confronting Vicksburg contained well over forty thousand men. One of the biggest problems facing Grant, and most Civil War commanders, was that in the unsanitary camps where these men lived, disease was common. Thousands of Union soldiers would get sick and many would die from just sitting around in camp. Something had to be done to get the men out into the countryside and working at anything to keep them busy. Another situation that Grant had to keep in mind was the generally poor state of the Union war effort. In December, Major General Ambrose Burnside had led the Army of the Potomac into a disastrous defeat at the hands of General Robert E. Lee at Fredericksburg, Virginia. At the turn of the year, as Sherman was pulling back from his defeat at Chickasaw Bayou, the armies of Union Major General William Rosecrans and Confederate General Braxton Bragg fought a fearful battle near Murfreesboro, Tennessee, at Stone's River. Casualties on both sides were horrendous, and although the battle was considered a Union victory because Bragg fell back, Rosecrans' army was so shattered that it would be months before it could begin another campaign. Politically and militarily the Lincoln administration was in trouble and right now the main hope of any type of Northern victory lay with Grant's army on the Mississippi.[2]

Grant knew full well that the people in the North were becoming weary of supporting a war they appeared to be losing. He would not consider pulling back to Memphis and starting over when the weather improved; this would surely be seen as another setback. It was at this time that the best qualities of Grant's character came out. Failure did not cause immobilizing discouragement in Grant, but instead he displayed a natural tenacity and the resolve to use all the resources at his disposal. He simply would not acknowledge defeat. This characteristic was displayed at Fort Donelson and again at Shiloh when all looked lost. On the outside Grant always appeared to be a very ordinary man who went about his work in a very ordinary manner. But on the inside he was tough and determined and was loath to give up on a project. He could be patient when necessary and audacious when it was called for, and was always ready to take advantage of any small opportunity that might present itself to accomplish the task at hand. Grant was determined to stay at Vicksburg and get the job done no matter what it took.[3]

When Grant took over command of the river-based campaign he began to look for other possible routes to get around the Vicksburg fortifications, since he had little faith in the canal at Young's Point that had been started the previous summer and was supposed to leave Vicksburg high and dry. He noted in a message to Assistant Adjutant-General Colonel J. C. Kelton in Washington on February 4, "The canal is at right angles with the thread of the current at both ends, and both ends are in an eddy, the lower coming out under bluffs completely commanding it."[4]

Looking over the entire scene, Grant mentioned three other potential routes to Kelton:

> One of these is by the way of Yazoo Pass into Coldwater, the Tallahatchee, and Yazoo Rivers. This is conducted by Lieutenant-Colonel Wilson, from whom no report is yet received. This route, if practicable, would enable us to get high ground above Haynes' Bluff, and would turn all the enemy's river batteries.
>
> Another is by Lake Providence and the network of bayous connecting it with Red River. The accompanying reports show the feasibility of this route.
>
> A third is by the way of Willow and Roundaway Bayous, leaving the Mississippi at Milliken's Bend, and coming in at New Carthage. There is no question but that this route is much more practicable than the present undertaking, and would have been accomplished with much less labor if commenced before the water had got all over the country. The work on the present canal is being pushed. New inlet and outlet are being made, so that the water will be received where the current strikes the shore, and will be carried through in a current.[5]

Even though Grant had little faith in the canal across Young's Point as a viable solution to getting past Vicksburg he had to try it because Washington wanted it tried. On January 19 Secretary of the Navy Welles wrote to Admiral Porter, "The President is exceedingly anxious that a canal from which practical and useful results would follow should be cut through the peninsula opposite Vicksburg." And, if the president's wishes were not enough, Welles continued, "The Department desires that this plan may be tried whenever you may deem it expedient and can have the cooperation of the army."[6]

Young's Point was a peninsula about a mile wide that jutted out into the river to the northeast across from the city forming a hairpin curve in the river. If a canal could be cut near the base of the peninsula and if the river could be induced to enter the canal instead of flowing around the end of this finger of land, Vicksburg would left well away from the new course of the Mississippi. The advantages of cutting across Young's Point had always been apparent to Union commanders, and this was where General Thomas Williams had begun digging a canal when his small army accompanied Admiral Farragut to Vicksburg the previous summer. The work had been abandoned when Farragut returned to New Orleans, but now Grant was going to try to finish it.[7]

Although it may have seemed like a good idea from afar, the flaws in the canal plan were readily apparent to the men working on it. First was the simple fact that even if the canal could be completed and provided a passage below Vicksburg, the point in the river where it came out was above Warrenton, and when the Confederates learned of the project they simply erected several batteries of heavy artillery at that point. These batteries commanded the end of the canal and a large portion of its length, leaving the Confederates in control of the river no matter what path it followed. The other problem with the canal project was that it was designed wrong from the beginning. The current at the point where the river was supposed to enter the canal flowed toward the opposite side of the river, away from the canal entrance. It was unlikely that any water entering the canal would have enough force to create a new river channel.[8]

Despite his misgivings, Grant had to try to make the canal work; at the worst it would get some of his troops doing something. The job was assigned to General Sherman's Fifteenth Corps and soon several thousand Union soldiers were at work widening the present narrow ditch to over fifty feet. Dredges were brought in to speed the work and engineer officers tried to redesign the canal so that the river would actually flow into it and create the new channel across Young's Point. Digging in the wet clay was backbreaking work and the weather did not help, as Grant noted in his report, "The task was much more Herculean than it at first appeared, and was made much more so by the almost continuous rains that fell during the whole of the time this work was prosecuted." To protect the army camps from flooding, the dirt from excavation was piled high on the west side of the canal to form a levee.[9]

The men doing the work were also not convinced the canal would ever be a success. In the 55th Illinois there were hundreds of men well acquainted with the river, and during many a discussion around the campfires, they "talked wisely about the eddy before the proposed entrance and the clayey nature of the subsoil, prophesied that the wayward current could not be coaxed to enter the channel being laboriously prepared for it." Charles Miller of the 76th Ohio remembered that his regiment sent men to work on the canal daily and that "the almost continuous rain rendered slow progress in this work and the occupation of camp on the low ground was anything but pleasant. With the rains and hard work came much sickness and the hospitals were filled with diseased and dying soldiers."[10]

General Sherman wrote to his brother on January 25 that although the river had risen and filled the narrow original canal, as had been feared the current was not powerful enough to cut the channel larger, "but on the contrary threatens to overflow the low ground embraced in the Levee. All my soldiers are busy day and night in throwing up a levee on the inside of this Canal to prevent the water overflowing us." William Wiley of the 77th Illinois wrote in his diary on January 24, "We spent the day draining our camp we had to dig a deep ditch on each side of our rows of tents and between each tent to drain the water away from the tents and throw the dirt inside of the tents to raise us above the water line."[11]

Across the river the Confederates were well aware of the canal project. General Joseph E. Johnston, Pemberton's immediate superior in the West, wrote to Jefferson Davis on February 12, "In Mississippi every thing depends upon the result of the labour opposite to Vicksburg. If Grant should succeed in making a navigable canal, & thro' it pass Vicksburg & invest Port Hudson with the combined armies, it would be difficult for us to succor the place." Johnston candidly admitted to Davis, "Indeed we have not the means of forming a relieving army." He also noted, however, that General Pemberton seemed less concerned about the viability of the canal, probably because he knew they could simply move some artillery a short distance south and still retain control of the river.[12]

General Johnston need not have worried, because on March 8 the quickly rising river broke through the dam at the head of the canal. A wall of water came roaring through and over the canal, flooding everything in sight. The men had to run for their lives and try to save anything they could from the camps before they were flooded. Virtually all the equipment being used on the canal was lost. The men were forced to take to the tops of the levees to save themselves. It was clear that this project would never amount to anything, and a few weeks later Grant abandoned the project to concentrate on other possibilities to pass Vicksburg that looked more promising.[13]

During the same period that Sherman's troops were toiling on the canal, there was another project being explored using mostly existing waterways. On January 30, Grant wrote to General McClernand, "I find that Lake Providence, some 60 miles above here, which connects with Red River, through Tensas Bayou, Washita and Black Rivers, is a wide and navigable way; the distance to be cut to enter it from the Mississippi not great." Putting General McPherson in command of the project, Grant told him, "This bids fair to be the most practicable route for turning Vicksburg." Using troops from both McPherson's and McClernand's command to work on this new route, Grant also wrote to Admiral Porter requesting one of the light tinclads to accompany this expedition.[14]

Much of the Louisiana side of the Mississippi was flooded, and it looked as if it might be feasible to put together a water route by connecting several small rivers and bayous. Only about a mile inland from the Mississippi, the six mile long Lake Providence eventually flowed into a muddy stream called Bayou Baxter, which flowed through about six miles of swamp before joining a wider and deeper stream. This next waterway, known as Bayou Macon, flowed into the Tensas River, which flowed into the Washita River, which ran into the Red River, a major waterway that joined the Mississippi just above Port Hudson. This nearly four hundred mile route appeared promising since the vast majority of the distance was on navigable waters.[15]

For weeks the Union troops worked in the swamps trying to clear a passage wide enough for ships to traverse. They struggled with dredging out tons of mud and cutting off trees and stumps several feet under water. Eventually it became obvious that this route was going to take much more time to open than had been originally expected. In addition, it turned out that there were not nearly enough light transports available to carry sufficient troops down to the Red River to make the work worth the effort. The Lake Providence project turned out to be as impractical as the Young's Point canal and was abandoned about the same time as the canal.[16]

While the canal and Lake Providence projects were still active, General Grant was looking into a third possible route to get behind Vicksburg, one that involved the swamp filled Yazoo Delta region above Vicksburg. Grant had suggested to Admiral Porter that a route might be opened "through the Pass into Coldwater River, thence down that stream into the Tallahatchee, which, with its junction with the Yalabusha, forms the Yazoo, which it is the great object of the expedition to enter." Far up the Mississippi just below Helena, Arkansas, was a levee that closed off the river entrance to Yazoo Pass. Behind this levee was Moon Lake at the northern end of the Yazoo Valley, an oval area about two hundred miles long that extended from just below Memphis to Vicksburg filled with rivers and bayous. If this levee were opened up, water from the Mississippi would flood the area and hopefully open a channel large enough for ships to advance through the chain of waterways Grant had noted and then into the Yazoo River.

Once the ships were in the Yazoo, they would be able to travel far enough inland to reach the high ground past the Confederate defenses along the bluffs and get behind Vicksburg's fortifications. This was the same area that had been Sherman's target during the Chickasaw Bayou fighting.[17]

An officer on Grant's staff, Lieutenant Colonel James H. Wilson, was sent up river to look into the possibility of such a project succeeding. Wilson was a young and energetic recent engineering graduate of West Point who had already impressed both Grant and McPherson, who had known him during duty in California. Colonel Wilson reached the levee on February 2; digging began immediately and what was left of the levee was blown up the next day. As expected, water from the Mississippi rushed through the opening, carrying along trees, logs and anything else that got in the way. Because of the vast area of the Yazoo Valley that had to be flooded, it took several days before the water was deep enough for any of the ships to enter.[18]

The expedition that finally sailed through the opening of the levee and into Moon Lake was certainly powerful enough. To provide protection for the fleet, Porter had assigned the ironclads *Chillicothe* and *Baron de Kalb,* the tinclads *Rattler, Marmora, Signal, Romeo, Petrel* and *Fort Rose* and two rams the *Lioness* and *Fulton.* Accompanying the warships were coal barges and transports carrying a division of McClernand's troops commanded by Brigadier General Leonard Ross. The ships, under the command of Lieutenant Commander Watson Smith, slowly made their way through the lake and into Yazoo Pass, where they began to encounter some of the many natural and man-made obstructions that would torment the expedition as it crept toward the Yazoo River.[19]

During the days it took for ships to sail down Moon Lake, the Confederates were not idle. News of the expedition had reached Confederate commanders in the area, and they immediately sent men to cut down trees to block the narrow channels in Yazoo Pass and the rivers beyond. The floodwaters covered many trees and stumps that also had to be removed for the ships to proceed. For three days the Union soldiers and sailors were laboring constantly to open a passageway. Huge trees had to be cleared out of the way. Underwater obstructions had to be removed so they did not tear the bottoms out of the light ships. Limbs from trees on the shore hung over the channel and crashed down, tearing into the light upper works of the unarmored ships.[20]

One of the soldiers on the expedition, Aaron Dunbar of the 93rd Illinois, later wrote about the damage caused by the overhanging trees that were so thick they practically blotted out the sun. "The railings and cornices and fancy woodwork of the upper decks were broken into splinters and carried away. The outside walls of the cabins were penetrated in many places by great limbs of trees and considerable portions of the same practically destroyed." Although many ships suffered damage to their upper works, this was mostly cosmetic; the real problems came from damage to vital parts of the ships. "Smokestacks were thrown down, and pilothouses riddled. Paddle wheels were half destroyed, and rudders many times broken.... The crashing and smashing through the timber was full of danger and accident to those on board, as well as fearfully disastrous and destructive to the boats." Alonzo Brown of the 4th Minnesota remembered that the current was so fast that his ship was frequently out of control, "first striking the trees on one side, which fortunately, would spring, so the blow was broken; then the trees bending like whips, she would rebound to the other side. The pilot turned pale, the troops were almost breathless."[21]

The flotilla finally worked its way through Yazoo Pass and entered the Coldwater River on February 28. The waterway here was wider and the current less forceful, but the channel was almost as winding and difficult to negotiate as the pass had been, and progress was slow. Most of the vessels had suffered some kind of damage, and Lieutenant Commander Smith was careful not to push his battered ships too fast, lest some accident cause severe damage or even the loss of any of the vessels. Due to the zigzag course of the river there were still more incidents of hitting submerged snags and trees along the shore, but after six days of moving along at a crawl, the ships emerged into the Tallahatchie River.[22]

Entering the Tallahatchie on March 6, the flotilla had a relatively easy four day journey down the river until the vessels arrived at the junction with the Yalobusha River that formed the Yazoo River. The Tallahatchie makes a sharp horseshoe turn to the east at this point near the town of Greenwood. While the Federal ships were slowly making their way through the winding waterways, the Confederates had put the time to good use and built a modest fort of earthworks and cotton bales on the narrow strip of land in between the two rivers, named Fort Pemberton. The fort, commanded by Major General William W. Loring, was armed with one heavy and three light rifled artillery pieces and several smaller smoothbore field cannon and was cleverly positioned so that it could not be attacked by land. The fort's armament was not very physically imposing, but because of the way the fort faced the river, the Confederate gunners had a clear, straight shot at any ships approaching from the Tallahatchie. Although the Union flotilla vastly outgunned the fort, due to the narrowness of the channel at this point there was only enough room for two ships to approach the fort at the same time, and that would have to be head-on.[23]

At ten o'clock on the morning of March 11, the *Chillicothe* and the *Baron de Kalb* steamed downstream to confront the fort, which was the flotilla's last major obstacle to gaining access to the Yazoo River. Soon after the engagement began the *Chillicothe* was hit four times. One Confederate shell struck a gun being loaded, killing two men and wounding eleven. Both ships soon withdrew for the men to place some cotton bales in front of their casemates for added protection from the rifled Confederate guns. Later that afternoon the ships renewed the engagement, but both ships were hit a number of times and withdrew after causing little damage to Fort Pemberton.[24]

On March 13 the gunboats again attacked the fort with the firing lasting all day. The *Chillicothe* was again sufficiently damaged that it had to withdraw while the *Baron de Kalb* continued to exchange fire with the fort until dark. This time the fort was heavily damaged with the earth and cotton bale walls being carried away at several points and the cotton set on fire. On the 16th, both ships renewed the attack, but the *Chillicothe* was once again severely damaged and both ships withdrew. With both the *Chillicothe* and *Baron de Kalb* damaged and the total loss of seven men killed and at least two dozen wounded, Lieutenant Commander Smith could see that his ships would not be able to get past Fort Pemberton. On March 17, the flotilla began heading back to the Mississippi.[25]

As the ships were retracing their route, on March 22 they met Brigadier General Isaac F. Quinby, who was bringing a force of infantry to assist the ships. Lieutenant Commander Smith, who had been in poor health since the expedition began, was taken back to a hospital where he died soon after. General Quinby decided to try taking Fort Pemberton with his infantry and convinced the new naval commander, Lieutenant Commander John G. Foster, to return with the gunboats. With most of the area under water and the little dry land available firmly in Confederate hands, Quinby had no better luck than the gunboats in silencing the fort. After about twelve days the Federal expedition abandoned the attempt to take or destroy Fort Pemberton and headed back to the Mississippi, where they arrived at their starting point on April 10.[26]

Even as the Yazoo Pass expedition was still trying to complete its mission, Grant and Porter were busy devising yet another scheme to bypass Vicksburg's batteries. Grant wrote to General Sherman on March 16, "I have just returned from a reconnaissance up Steele's Bayou, with the admiral [Porter], and five of his gunboats. With some labor in cutting tree-tops out of the way, it will be navigable for any class of steamers."[27]

Admiral Porter was a tough old sea dog who had the ambition and energy of a much younger man. Basically he would try almost anything at least once. In March he developed a roundabout but feasible route that just might solve Grant's problem of getting on solid ground behind Vicksburg. A few miles up the Yazoo River from the Mississippi, but well short of the Confederate positions at Snyder's Bluff, was Steele's Bayou. This modest stream flowed into another waterway known as Black Bayou, which was little more than a narrow ditch filled with floodwaters. Black Bayou connected with another narrow and winding waterway called Deer Creek, which flowed into another bayou known as Rolling Fork. Getting to this point was the objective because Rolling Fork connected Deer Creek with the Sunflower River, a decent size waterway that flowed south for about fifty miles where it joined the Yazoo, well above Snyder's Bluff. The entire route covered about two hundred miles of mostly narrow, crooked and shallow channels filled with overhanging trees and submerged stumps that frequently blocked the passageway.[28]

Union Admiral David D. Porter, after the war, became superintendent of the U.S. Naval Academy (Library of Congress).

Admiral Porter quickly made his preparations, and on March 14 five gunboats, the *Carondelet, Cincinnati, Louisville, Mound City* and the *Pittsburg* accompanied by four mortar boats and four tugs, set out for the Yazoo River. Admiral Porter commanded this flotilla in person with General Sherman commanding a division of his infantry following along through the swamps in support.[29]

Moving up the Yazoo and through Steele's Bayou, the expedition made good time. They encountered overhanging tree limbs that crashed on the decks of the ships but few serious obstacles. All that changed, however, when they entered the four mile long Black Bayou. Porter reported, "Here the crews of the vessels had to go to work to clear the way, pulling up trees by the roots or pushing them over with the ironclads, and cutting away the branches above. It was terrible work." The ironclads were able to force their way through the bayou, but the channel was too difficult for the wooden ships to follow. After twenty-four hours of backbreaking work, the gunboats arrived at Hill's plantation, where Black Bayou joined Deer Creek. Sherman's troops, who had been following the ships through the bayou, remained there to clear a channel for the transports.[30]

Pushing on, Porter was under the impression given by locals that his ships would encounter few difficulties moving through Deer Creek, but it was soon apparent that was untrue. Porter reported the "channel much narrower than I expected, filled with small willows, through which we could scarce make our way, and the branches much overhanging." The water was deep enough for the gunboats, but in addition to the trees, the channel contained numerous sharp bends that made it extremely difficult to maneuver the ships through the creek. Progress was necessarily slow with the ships advancing less than a mile an hour on average. It took three days of cutting down trees and chopping at branches and underwater roots before the ships got close to Rolling Fork.[31]

So far the expedition had only natural obstacles to contend with. Porter wrote, "We had succeeded in getting well into the heart of the country before we were discovered. No one would believe that anything in the shape of a vessel could get through Black Bayou, or anywhere on the route." Local inhabitants and many slaves had been congregating along the banks of the creek to watch the progress of the ships and it was only a matter of time before Confederate authorities were informed. Soon cotton as well as other supplies that might be taken by the invaders were being destroyed, and as Porter noted, "All along, as far as the eye could see, there was nothing but cotton fires burning up, and many dwellings consuming with it."[32]

Once Confederate military leaders learned of Porter's expedition they acted quickly. On March 17 Colonel Samuel Ferguson sent a battalion of sharpshooters and several field artillery pieces from Fort Pemberton to Rolling Fork. Shortly after Ferguson's movement, word of the Federal incursion reached Vicksburg, and Major General Carter L. Stevenson sent Brigadier General Winfield Featherston's brigade to the junction of Deer Creek and Rolling Fork. Artillery batteries were set up and infantry stationed along the banks to fire on any sailors who showed themselves outside the armored ships. Trees were cut down to block the channel. The situation was rapidly going from bad to worse for the Federal flotilla.[33]

Admiral Porter sent Lieutenant J. M. Murphy ahead of the gunboats with three hundred men and a few howitzers to take control of Rolling Fork until the ships could arrive and control the area with their guns. Murphy accomplished his task by occupying an Indian mound that overlooked the nearby country. With men working all night and the next day to clear the obstructions, the ships advanced to about 800 yards of Rolling Fork, where Porter halted the work for the night. The next morning, March 20, the work began again, but cutting through the willow trees slowed progress to a crawl. Porter noted, "The lithe trees defied our utmost efforts to get by them, and we had to go to work and pull them up separately, or cut them off under water, which was a most tedious job."[34]

While the gunboats were inching forward, Confederate infantry under Colonel Ferguson launched an assault with 800 men on Murphy's position, which he was forced to abandon. Later that afternoon General Featherstone's brigade and artillery arrived from Vicksburg and a heavy fire was opened on the stalled ships. With his sailors unable to go outside the safety of the armored ships to clear the channel of obstructions and the enemy positions being strengthened almost hourly, it was apparent that Porter could not go forward. At this point the admiral received word that a detachment of Confederates was busily cutting down trees to block the channel behind the gunboats. This presented the very real possibility of Porter and five of his best ships being trapped in the narrow channel with no way out, a disaster of the first magnitude. Porter could not wait for Sherman's help since there was no way to know when, or if, the infantry could make its way through the swamps to where the ships were located. Porter wrote that he knew he could not afford "to risk the least thing; at all events, never to let my communication be closed behind me.... I saw at once the difficulties we had to encounter, with a constant fire on our working parties and no prospect at present of the troops getting along.... I hesitated no longer what to do."[35]

It was impossible to turn the ships around in the narrow channel, so the rudders were unshipped and the gunboats began the long, tortuous trip back the way they had come, bouncing from tree to tree. Porter sent out a party of about 300 men to stop the enemy from creating more obstructions in the waterway, and on March 21 they met up with a force of 800 men commanded by Colonel Giles A. Smith that Sherman had sent ahead of his main body. With Smith's troops controlling the shoreline the sailors were able to begin clearing the many trees blocking the waterway, although progress was still desperately slow. There were a few skirmishes with Confederate troops but Smith's men, and occasional fire from the ships, were able to keep them from interfering with the progress of the flotilla.[36]

The next day General Sherman arrived with his main force and Porter's men were finally able to work undisturbed to clear the channel. Porter later admitted, "I do not know when I felt more pleased to see that gallant officer, for without the assistance of the troops we could not, without great loss, have performed the arduous work of clearing out the obstructions.... I never knew how helpless a thing an ironclad could be when unsupported by troops." General Sherman later wrote that Porter told him, "At one time things looked so critical that he had made up his mind to blow up the gunboats, and to escape with his men through the swamp to the Mississippi River." The battered gunboats arrived back at Hill's plantation on March 24. It was another failed attempt to use the Yazoo River to bypass Vicksburg, and the last.[37]

It was now clear that passage through the thick forests and impenetrable swamps could not be forced by any amount of human effort. While no substantial military benefit had been realized, there had been some advantages for Grant's army. Thousands of men had been put to work doing something instead of just sitting around the dirty camps where sickness was rampant. The Confederates were forced to move many of their troops around Western Mississippi, preventing Pemberton from concentrating his forces. One more point that was of vital importance in the campaign was that Grant was finally convinced that there was only one way to accomplish the goal of taking the Confederate citadel.[38]

These few positives were only minor factors, however, when compared to the biggest problem facing Grant at this point in the campaign, the health of his army. There was little enough dry land in the area under normal conditions and the almost constant rain had turned even that into muddy bogs. Most of the Union camps were on low ground that made them even more susceptible to disease than was usual for the period. Stuck in unhealthy camps or confined on transports in the river, thousands of Union soldiers got sick and many hundreds died from everything from measles to smallpox. Isacc Jackson wrote that for the men in his Ohio regiment, sickness and death were constantly present: "Go any day down the levee and you could see a squad or two of soldiers burying a companion, until the levee was nearly full of graves and the hospitals still full of sick."[39]

The morale of the army dropped noticeably as the miserable conditions and constant danger of illness brought many of the men to new levels of pessimism. J. Grecian of the 83rd Indiana wrote, "Our stay in this dismal, swampy valley ... was one of unparalleled discouragement. Scarcely a man had any thing like good health; about one-half were prostrated with various diseases, many dying almost daily.... In fact, these were the worst times the 15th Army Corps ever saw." For now the greatest enemy facing Grant's army was not the Confederates across the river. Something had to be done before his army disintegrated.[40]

Chapter 7

Meeting Challenges

While the capture of Vicksburg was clearly Grant's highest priority, he had other important issues to deal with during the early months of 1863. In addition to the health of the army, one of the most challenging problems he faced that spring was what to do with the thousands of former slaves who were crossing into Union held territory looking to escape from their bondage. Grant had already set up an organization to put able-bodied former slaves to work for the army and care for those who could not work under the supervision of Chaplain John Eaton of the 27th Ohio, but the problem had grown so large that it was affecting the war effort. It had always been the policy of the government to welcome fugitive slaves and do what was possible to care for them and provide labor at fair wages, a policy Grant supported. But the flood of former slaves that inundated Grant's department was starting to affect the army's ability to wage war.[1]

Grant had to do something, and in February he issued Special Field Orders No. 2 stating that the needs of the current campaign had made it impractical for the army to transport and house fugitive slaves, so he ordered that "the enticing of negroes to leave their homes to come within the lines of the army is positively forbidden." Former slaves that were already within Union lines would not be forced out, but "in future no persons, white or black, who are not duly authorized to pass the lines of sentinels will be permitted to enter or leave camp." In a letter to General McPherson, Grant explained that the question of what to do with the former slaves "is a troublesome one. I am not permitted to send them out of the department, and such numbers as we have it is hard to keep them in."[2]

When General Halleck learned of Grant's order he wasted little time in refuting it. At the end of March the general-in-chief wrote to Grant, "It is the policy of the Government to withdraw from the enemy as much productive labor as possible." Halleck went on to point out the obvious fact that the more slaves the South could put in the fields, the more white men would be free to serve in the Confederate Army: "Every slave withdrawn from the enemy is equivalent to a white man put *hors de combat*." As far as any effort to turn escaped slaves away from Union controlled territory, Halleck wrote, "This is not only bad policy in itself but is directly opposed to the policy adopted by the government." Halleck made it clear that Grant was expected to use his authority and influence to enforce the policy of the government regardless of personal opinions, and "that policy is to withdraw from the use of the enemy all the slaves you can, and to employ those so withdrawn to the best possible advantage against the enemy."[3]

In the same letter, Halleck went on to give his views on the overall war effort, declaring that the conflict was entering a new phase and explaining how the situation had changed in the last year: "There is now no possible hope of reconciliation with the rebels. The Union party in the South is virtually destroyed. There can be no peace but that which is forced by the sword.

We must conquer the rebels or be conquered by them." The rivers of blood that had flowed since Shiloh had hardened the resolve of both sides, and it was now obvious to the Union leadership that a military victory was the only solution. Halleck could see that it was going to take an all-out effort on the part of the Federal government to bring the fighting to a satisfactory end, and commanders like Ulysses Grant would be needed to bring total war to the enemy.[4]

Orders were orders and Grant promptly reversed his position on fugitive slaves. In a letter to Major General Frederick Steele on April 11, he wrote that since the war must be fought out to the bitter end, "It is our duty, therefore, to use every means to weaken the enemy, by destroying their means of subsistence, withdrawing their means of cultivating their fields, and in every other way possible." Steele was informed that he must provide rations for all former slaves under his jurisdiction, and furthermore, "You will also encourage all Negroes, particularly middle-aged males, to come within our lines. General L. Thomas is now here, with authority to make ample provision for the negro."[5]

The man Grant was referring to was Major General Lorenzo Thomas, adjutant general of the army, who was currently visiting Grant's army on a two-part mission. The first was to simply see how the campaign was proceeding and report on Grant himself. Thomas's second task was to promote a new program to enlist able-bodied former slaves into the army. There were many thousands of these men living in and around army camps. The government had decided to make soldiers out of those who would volunteer, and not just to fill out labor battalions but to create new combat regiments. To help raise support for this controversial plan, these new regiments would be led by white officers, many chosen from the ranks of veteran enlisted men who would suddenly become commissioned officers, something that few could ever achieve in their current units. General Thomas was also making it clear that this plan had the full support of the government and that while he was authorized to promote enlisted volunteers to officers, he was also authorized to dismiss any man who openly opposed the new policy, no matter what his rank.[6]

There was quite a bit of opposition to the raising of regiments filled with former slaves, and there were threats by some officers and men to put down their weapons and fight no more. This type of resistance to the government's policy did not last long, however, as the threat of court-martial for refusing to obey orders was enough for most of these protestors to settle down and accept the inevitable. Also, as John K. Duke of the 53rd Ohio noted another, more practical realization quickly spread through the army, as it was obvious that "a negro could stop a bullet as well as a white man, and that for every one so sacrificed there would be just that many more white soldiers to return north to their friends and families."[7]

General Grant did his best to support the government policy and issued orders on April 22 that all corps, division and post commanders were to "afford all facilities for the completion of the negro regiments now organizing in this department." Supplies were to be issued to these new regiments on the same basis as existing units, and "it is expected that all commanders will especially exert themselves in carrying out the policy of the Administration, not only in organizing colored regiments and rendering them efficient, but also in removing prejudice against them." No matter what Grant believed personally, he was a soldier. Shortly before the bloodbath at Shiloh, Grant had written to his friend and sponsor Congressman Elihu B. Washburne stating as a soldier it was his duty to obey orders: "No man can be efficient as a commander who sets his own notions above the law and those whom he has sworn to obey. When Congress enacts anything too odious for me to execute, I will resign."[8]

The war was entering a new phase and Grant was one of the men most fit to conduct the type of warfare that was coming. Whatever slim possibility of a political solution that might have existed was now gone for good. Only a complete military victory would end this tragic conflict. The real change was not just that the government would authorize the arming of ex-slaves and send them to fight against their former masters or that destroying civilian property was now approved policy. The real change was that the conflict had gone from soldiers trying to win battles to nation trying to destroy nation. The capture of Vicksburg was a vital step in the dismemberment of the Confederacy.

In addition to enforcing the government policy toward former slaves, there was another situation facing Grant that he had little control over—the persistent rumors about his drinking and fitness to command such an important campaign. The stain of his early years in the army had always followed Grant, and every once in a while a newspaper or disgruntled former subordinate would bring up the subject of his drinking. With setback following setback over the past several months, doubt about Grant's abilities were beginning to form in the minds of some in the government. Secretary of War Stanton decided to send what amounted to a spy to Grant's army to keep himself and the president informed of the true conditions in the army and whether Grant was the best man to command it.[9]

Secretary Stanton's eyes and ears in Grant's headquarters was Assistant Secretary of War Charles A. Dana. He had been the managing editor of Horace Greeley's *New York Tribune*, and Stanton decided he was the right man to send objective reports back to Washington. Dana later wrote that his assignment was "to give such information as would enable Mr. Lincoln and himself to settle their minds as to Grant, about whom at that time there were many doubts, and against whom there was some complaint."[10]

When Dana arrived at Grant's headquarters on April 6 he was given a warm welcome. Dana was supposedly there to look into problems with the army's payroll, but Grant and his staff were well aware of his real mission and decided to work with him. Dana came to believe that Grant was actually pleased with his presence since Dana's frequent reports back to Stanton meant that Grant would have to make fewer reports himself and could get on with the business of running the army rather than spending valuable time on paperwork.[11]

The decision to cooperate with Dana proved to be wise. Stanton's man soon developed a favorable impression of the general, and his reports to Washington contained little negative information about Grant or the way he was running the campaign. The assistant secretary later would write that Grant was "the most honest man I ever knew, with a temper that nothing could disturb and a judgment that was judicial in its comprehensiveness and wisdom ... not an original or brilliant man, but sincere, thoughtful, deep and gifted with courage that never faltered." Grant was already known for his calmness in the face of pressure and adversity, and Dana noted that "when the time came to risk all, he went in like a simple-hearted, unaffected, unpretending hero, whom no ill omens could deject and no triumph unduly exalt."[12]

Another assessment of Grant's character and abilities came from James H. Wilson, one of Grant's aides who would later in the war become the commander of all the Federal cavalry in the West: "He gave his best attention to learning the position, strength, and probable plans of his adversary, and then made his own plans as best he might to foil or overthrow him, modifying or changing them only after it became clearly necessary to do so." Wilson noted that Grant didn't stay up nights worrying about what the enemy might be planning: "He never worried over what he could not help, but was always cool, level-headed, and reasonable, never in the least excitable or imaginative. He always had the nerve to play his game through calmly and without any external exhibition of uneasiness or anxiety." Now that he was playing for one of the greatest prizes of the war, Grant would need to use all of his talents.[13]

In addition to Dana's reports, several independent observers helped to dispel the rumors of Grant having a drinking problem during these dark months. One of these civilians was Mary Livermore, who brought a delegation of the Sanitary Commission to see for themselves the conditions facing the army along the Mississippi. Expecting the worst based on the stories they had heard, the women of the delegation were pleasantly surprised when they actually met and talked with Grant. Livermore related, "In the first five minutes of our interview, we learned, by some sort of spiritual telegraphy, that reticence, patience, and persistence were the dominant traits of General Grant." The women quickly saw that "the clear eye, clean skin, firm flesh, and steady nerves of General Grant gave the lie to the universal calumnies, then current, concerning his intemperate habits and those of the officers of his staff."[14]

The final word on Grant's character came from President Lincoln himself. While visiting Washington to discuss possible solutions to the problem of dealing with the flood of refugees coming into Union lines, Chaplain Eaton said that Lincoln told him about a delegation of congressmen who were complaining that Grant's drinking made him unfit for command. The president told Eaton that he seriously asked them if anyone knew what brand of whiskey Grant drank, which no one knew. Lincoln then related, "I urged them to ascertain and let me know, for if it made fighting generals like Grant, I should like to get some of it for distribution." Throughout all the doubt about his ability, General Grant ignored his critics and remained focused on the objective, confident that he was the right man in the right place and all he had to do was take care of business.[15]

All of the men involved in making the decision knew there were basically three ways to attack Vicksburg. The first was a direct assault from the river against the fortifications protecting the city, a virtual suicide mission that no one believed could succeed. Another option was to abandon the river approach altogether and return to Memphis for another try down the route Grant had taken the previous fall. Most of the army's high ranking officers, including General Sherman, recommended this course of action. Sherman contended that the best way to take Vicksburg was "to resume the movement which had been so well begun the previous November, viz., for the main army to march by land down the country inland of the Mississippi River; while the gun-boat fleet and a minor land-force should threaten Vicksburg on its riverfront." Admiral Porter also supported abandoning the river approach. In a report on March 26 detailing the failures to get through the swamps and bayous north of the city, he wrote, "There is but one thing now to be done, and that is to start an army of 150,000 men from Memphis, via Grenada, and let them go supplied with everything required to take Vicksburg. Let all minor considerations give way to this and Vicksburg will be ours."[16]

Considering the obstacles the army currently faced, starting the campaign over appeared to be the most sensible approach, but to the people back home it would look like another defeat. There had been little good news for the North since Grant's capture of Fort Donelson over a year ago. Even the few victories won by Union armies had come at such a high cost that there had been little to celebrate. A decisive victory was needed to raise morale in the North and ensure the continued support of the war effort. Grant later wrote that while discussing the situation with General Sherman, he stated, "The country is already disheartened over the lack of success on the part of our armies.... The problem for us was to move forward to a decisive victory, or our cause was lost. No progress was being made in any other field, and we had to go on." There would be no turning back now. Grant had to find a way to take Vicksburg.[17]

There was a third option that also contained great risk along with the potential for great rewards. Grant had already considered marching the army down the western side of the Mississippi and then transferring the troops over to the eastern side below Vicksburg. The problem with this approach was getting sufficient ships below the enemy fortress to transport thousands of men across the river and provide security from enemy attack during the crossing. Something else that had to be considered was supplying the army from above Vicksburg. The armored warships would have little trouble running past the city's guns, but light, unarmored supply ships were another matter. In addition, the weather this time of the year made moving large numbers of men through flooded terrain on roads that were little more than muddy ruts a very difficult proposition. There were, however, several options that made this plan interesting.

A couple hundred miles below Vicksburg was the town of Port Hudson, a smaller version of Vicksburg, that closed the river to Union ships heading north from New Orleans. The Confederacy controlled the river between these two strongholds. Major General Nathaniel Banks was in the process of moving his Army of the Gulf against Port Hudson. Grant wrote to Banks on March 22 suggesting that if Banks were able to capture Port Hudson, Grant could send troops south to meet him, crossing the river where Admiral Farragut's ships were in control of the waterway. Together the combined army could then turn on Vicksburg, or head toward any other target, from the south and east on solid, dry ground. With Federal forces controlling the lower Mississippi, there would be no problem obtaining supplies through New Orleans. If Banks could not actually capture Port Hudson it was hoped that his presence in the vicinity would at least prevent reinforcements from being sent to Pemberton.[18]

How long Grant had been thinking about making this move down the western side of the river is known only to him, but to come up with what turned out to be a relatively complicated movement, he must have at least considered it during the months of trying to work through the bayous and swamps above Vicksburg. The first objective of the march would be New Carthage, a village about thirty-five miles below Vicksburg. New Carthage seemed to be an excellent place to position the army. It was well below the enemy batteries at Warrenton and at least fifteen miles above the next Confederate stronghold at Grand Gulf. With his troops at this point Grant could attack either of those places to expand his hold on the eastern bank or advance east between them and leave them to be cut off by troops in their rear. Another factor that was taken into consideration was that below Milliken's Bend the countryside was filled with small lakes and bayous, including Bayou Vidal and Lake St. Joseph, that might be turned into a narrow waterway. By breaking some levees and clearing paths through the swamps, it might be possible to float shallow draft transports down to New Carthage. This would be an important time saver because the terrain on the western side of the river was almost as bad as on the Vicksburg side.[19]

On March 29, Grant instructed General McClernand to begin moving his Thirteenth Corps to New Carthage. After weeks of enduring sickness and backbreaking work in the muddy swamps, the army was finally on the move. At first McClernand's advance troops made slow but steady progress over the poor roads until they arrived at Smith's plantation on Bayou Vidal about two miles from New Carthage. Owen J. Hopkins, a young soldier from Ohio, described some of the difficulties facing the men during that march: "The heavy artillery wheels cut through the slime and the mud, making the path a perfect mortar bed through which we waded knee deep, and where the hubs of the wheels often disappeared out of sight." The only way the troops could advance was by building corduroy roads over the muck.[20]

South of Smith's plantation, the levees in the area had already broken and the countryside was badly flooded. New Carthage was practically an island. At first boats were brought up to continue the move south, but there were nowhere near enough boats to transport all the troops and equipment in a timely manner. Another route was found around Bayou Vidal that added another twelve miles or so to the march, but McClernand's advance troops were soon in New Carthage waiting for their comrades to come up.[21]

While the infantry was slowly moving south on the west side of the river, Grant had been in contact with Admiral Porter to prepare for the next phase of the plan—getting the men across the river. On March 29 Grant wrote to Porter apprising him of the infantry movement and stating that it was "a matter of vast importance that one or two vessels should be put below Vicksburg, both to cut off the enemy's intercourse with the west bank of the river entirely and to insure a landing on the east bank for our forces." Grant stated the obvious by closing, "Without the aid of gunboats it will hardly be worth while to send troops to New Carthage, or to open the passage from here there."[22]

Responding to Grant's request the same day, Admiral Porter wrote that he was ready to co-operate with Grant's plan, but warned him, "You must recollect that, when these gunboats once go below, we give up all hopes of ever getting them up again." Porter also approved of taking Grand Gulf but noted, "If I do send vessels below, it will be the best vessels I have, and there will be nothing left to attack Hayne's Bluff." Porter's comment about not being able to bring his ships back above Vicksburg was not merely his being overly cautious. The current in the river was about four knots going downstream. The ironclads had a top speed of about six knots, which meant that moving with the current they would be under fire for about twenty minutes. Any ship could certainly be damaged or even sunk by a lucky shot, but considering their speed going downriver and assuming the attempt would be made at night, there was a good chance of all the ships getting through. Going upstream against the current, however, the ships would have an actual speed of only about two knots, leaving them under fire for close to ninety minutes, too long to avoid major damage or sinking.[23]

Well aware of the risks inherent in his plan, Grant made his decision and was determined to see it through. Grant wrote to Porter to explain that he had given up on the idea of a direct assault on Vicksburg, as the cost would be too great. The admiral was informed of the troop movements down to New Carthage. Additional barges and transports had been requested, and if all went well Grant felt he would be able to move up to 20,000 men at one time. Planning to operate from New Carthage and cross the river near Grand Gulf or Warrenton, Grant was confident that "one army corps, with the aid of two gunboats, can take and hold Grand Gulf until such time as I might be able to get my whole army there and make provision for supplying them."[24]

On April 4, Grant wrote to General Halleck informing him of the plan to get down to New Carthage, "Once there, I will move either to Warrenton or Grand Gulf; most probably the latter. From either of these points there are good roads to Vicksburg, and from Grand Gulf there is a good road to Jackson and the Black River Bridge without crossing the Black River."

Grant also noted that the "discipline and health of this army is now good, and I am satisfied the greatest confidence of success prevails." The comment about Jackson shows Grant's ability to think several moves ahead and keep his options open. Instead of heading directly for Vicksburg or Port Hudson, he might move east toward the capital of Mississippi and the railroad that was Vicksburg's lifeline to the rest of the Confederacy.[25]

Admiral Porter decided to use seven of his gunboats to make the run past Vicksburg's batteries: the *Benton, Lafayette, Louisville, Mound City, Pittsburg, Carondelet, Tuscumbia* the ram *General Sterling Price*, and three transports carrying 300,000 rations. The admiral went to great lengths to ensure his ships' survival. Each ship had a barge loaded with coal for later use lashed to its starboard side, leaving the port side open for the gunboats to fire on the batteries as they passed. Porter made it clear, however, that these barges were expendable if the ships needed more speed to save themselves. Wet bales of cotton were placed around the boilers and other unprotected areas of the ships, especially the unarmored sterns of the gunboats. All ships were to keep their gun ports closed and lights out until the firing began. The ships were to proceed down the river close to the opposite shore at least fifty yards apart and in staggered formation so that any damaged ships could be easily passed. Damaged ships that could still travel but might be unable to keep up with the rest of the flotilla were to be grounded below the batteries. Sinking ships or ships grounded under fire were to be abandoned and destroyed. There was to be no stopping under the city's guns for any reason.[26]

When Grant selected McClernand to lead the advance to New Carthage, protests came from Sherman, Porter and other high ranking officers, but Grant's decision was final. There were several practical reasons for McClernand's corps to lead the march, the most obvious being that they were in the best position to take the advance. In addition, McClernand was the senior corps commander. His own ambition along with the support he received from President Lincoln, and the fact that he was one of the few senior commanders who enthusiastically supported the overall plan, made Grant believe that McClernand would put forth a maximum effort to succeed. As it turned out, Grant was correct, because despite the difficulties in advancing through the waterlogged terrain, McClernand kept his men moving steadily forward.[27]

As the Union troops made their way south they collected whatever food and forage they could find to supplement their basic rations and feed the animals that struggled to pull the wagons and guns through the muddy landscape. At the

Confederate General Joseph E. Johnston was so highly respected by his adversaries that he served as a pallbearer at General Sherman's funeral (Library of Congress).

few farms and plantations on the Louisiana side of the river where the Union soldiers passed, little was spared for the civilians. A soldier from Iowa, Taylor Peirce, wrote to his wife on April 18, "The country is being laid waste so that there will be nothing raised here this year and what the people is to do for something to eat is more than I can tell." The taking of food and destroying of buildings and crops during this march through the eastern edge of Louisiana was but a small taste of what was to soon befall Mississippi.[28]

Once the ships caught up with McClernand's troops, Grant told him to "get possession of Grand Gulf at the earliest practicable moment. Concentrate your entire corps there with all rapidity, and, as soon as transportation can be got through for them, move down the river to Bayou Sara. From there you can operate on the rear of Port Hudson." At this stage of the campaign Grant was still expecting to cooperate with General Banks in capturing Port Hudson, then move with the combined armies to take Vicksburg and complete the opening of the entire Mississippi River.[29]

While Porter was preparing his gunboats to run past the city's batteries and Grant's infantry was already moving south, the citizens of Vicksburg came to believe that the danger had passed. The various failures of the Federal boats in the swamps and bayous were well known in the city and it appeared to Confederate observers that most of the gunboats had pulled back upriver. The intelligence reports received by General Pemberton in early April convinced him that Grant was giving up, and on April 11 he wrote to General Johnston that he believed the Union forces were being withdrawn back to Memphis. Thinking that perhaps Grant was going to again try to approach Vicksburg through the center of Mississippi, Pemberton asked for and received permission to begin assembling troops at Jackson to oppose such a Federal movement. The majority of the Confederate cavalry had already been dispatched to Tennessee to assist Braxton Bragg in holding the strategic southern part of the state, and one of Pemberton's infantry divisions was preparing to join Bragg's army where there appeared to be more imminent danger than at Vicksburg. Unaware that Grant was on the move, Pemberton was unknowingly making it easier for Grant's plan to succeed by weakening his forces in the very area that Grant was targeting.[30]

Chapter 8

South of Vicksburg at Last

Months of hard marching and fighting lay ahead, but the fate of Vicksburg, and in some large part the outcome of the war itself, was determined on the water in front of the city during the night of April 15, 1863.

With coal barges lashed to the sides of the warships, Admiral Porter's flotilla was lined up and ready to begin its run past Vicksburg's formidable batteries by 9 o'clock that night. The guns on the warships were loaded with canister and grape and the gunners had orders not to fire until the Confederates spotted the fleet and opened fire. Stacks of wet hay and cotton bales had been strategically placed to protect machinery, giving the powerful warships the look of old tramp steamers. Porter tried to anticipate all possible problems and even stationed the *Tuscumbia* at the rear of the fleet to make sure the captains of the three transports did not have a change of heart and turn back when the firing began.[1]

As the Federal fleet waited for the order to weigh anchor and head down the river, the inhabitants of Vicksburg had no idea what was about to happen. General Pemberton, like most of the men in his command, believed that the lack of enemy activity after all the failed attempts to get troops or ships through the bayous meant that Grant had finally decided to give up and was withdrawing his troops. On April 11, Pemberton wrote to General Stevenson, "My information indicates that the enemy is moving up to Memphis." It was not that intelligence was lacking; the Confederate commanders simply believed what they wanted to believe. Pemberton also received a report from Stevenson on the thirteenth advising him that "a spy from the enemy reports that they are preparing two or three boats to pass our batteries, as re-enforcements for Farragut." But this report was not taken seriously and the city's defenders had the utmost confidence that their massive array of artillery would keep the enemy at bay.[2]

At 9:15 p.m. Admiral Porter gave the order to get underway. His flagship *Benton,* commanded by Lieutenant Commander James A. Greer, slowly moved out into the river's current. Behind the *Benton* came the rest of the rest of the fleet: the *Lafayette, Louisville, Mound City, Pittsburg, Carondelet,* and the *Tuscumbia.* In addition to these warships, lashed to the other side of the *Lafayette*'s coal barge was the captured Confederate vessel *General Price*, and between the *Carondelet* and the *Tuscumbia* were three army transports—the *Silver Wave, Henry Clay,* and *Forest Queen*—loaded down with supplies the army would need later.[3]

Through the darkness the ships slowly headed downriver, barely making a sound as they let the current quietly carry them along. General Grant and his family, who were visiting at this time, were on the headquarters ship along with other staff officers and dignitaries, including Assistant Secretary of War Dana. There were other smaller boats in the river containing Union officers and their wives who had assembled to watch the fireworks. Along the shore and the levees many others had gathered, all hoping to see something of the coming excitement. For several hours after night fell there was nothing to see but the blackness of the water and the faint line of the opposite shore. Then, when the fleet began to move, it appeared as if massive shadows were drifting out into the water and slowly floating through the darkness. As the ships made their way toward whatever fate held for them, there was a tense silence among the spectators. For now all was quiet along the Mississippi.[4]

All went well until the ships came around De Soto Point a little after 11 p.m. Porter was keeping a close watch on the dark ships as they silently glided over the black water and even remarked to Greer, "We will, no doubt, slip by unnoticed, the Rebels seem to keep a very poor watch." The Confederate lookouts were there, however, and as the fleet rounded the point an abandoned house was set on fire as a signal to their comrades farther down river. Within minutes fires were blazing all along the western shore and the ships were silhouetted against the light, making excellent targets for Vicksburg's experienced gunners.[5]

In Vicksburg, Major J. T. Hogane later wrote about what he witnessed that night: "About the middle watch of the night the belching of a cannon in one of the water batteries awoke the city from its easy slumbers. Officers and men rushed to the river front to gaze upon the Yankee gun boats slowly steaming down the river; nearer they came with almost a death-like motion, slow, and in harmony with the black, lith, sinuous gliding of the river."[6]

As the *Benton* advanced, small-arms fire from shore pinged off the side of the ironclad. First a single cannon fired at the lead vessel was followed in minutes by the thunder of the Confederate batteries and the reply from Porter's ships. As the fleet came around the point, it was caught in the swift current and swung back and forth, falling out of formation under the increasing fire from the guns on the bluffs. The light from the blazing houses, the smoke from the fires, and the flashes from the belching cannon combined with the roaring thunder of the guns to form a vision that General Grant called "magnificent, but terrible."[7]

Admiral Porter spent much of the passage standing out on the exposed deck of the *Benton* and would later write that as the fleet approached Vicksburg. "Every fort and hill-top vomited forth shot and shell, many of the latter bursting in the air and doing no damage, but adding to the grandeur of the scene." From his position on deck, Porter had a good view of the action and remembered that "the sight was a grand one, and I stood on deck admiring it, while the captain fought his vessel and the pilot steered her through fire and smoke as coolly as if he was performing an everyday duty." From inside the Confederate works, Major Hogane noted that the guns were worked and aimed "with the precision of parade practice, but it seemed with no effect, for boat after boat kept on with steady thud passing gun after gun that opened singly one after the other upon them." Enough of the Confederate fire did, however, find its mark, and most of the Federal ships suffered multiple hits by the heavy shells.[8]

The flagship *Benton* was hit four times and had four men wounded, one losing a leg. The *Lafayette* was struck nine times and had to cut loose its sinking coal barge but luckily suffered no serious damage. The *General Sterling Price* was struck thirteen times and collided with the *Louisville* but surprisingly suffered no casualties. The *Louisville* briefly lost the coal barge it was towing, but was able to retrieve it a little farther down river. The *Mound City* was hit by six shells that caused only six casualties. The *Pittsburg* was also fortunate that the seven hits it received caused little damage and no casualties. The *Carondelet* had to circle around to avoid a collision and still escaped with only two hits and four men slightly wounded. The only ship actually sunk was the transport *Henry Clay,* but the crew was saved. Another transport, the *Forest Queen,* became disabled but was assisted to safety by the last ship in the line, the *Tus-*

cumbia, which shortly afterward ran aground on the Louisiana side of the river. After a brief but harrowing experience the crew freed it and got through with no serious casualties, although the vessel was taking on water from a shot in the bow.[9]

Just below the city several small boats were waiting to help any of the Federal warships that might need assistance. On board one of them was General Sherman, who later gave this account:

> I was out in the stream when the fleet passed Vicksburg, and the scene was truly sublime. As soon as the rebel gunners detected the Benton, which was in the lead, they opened on her, and on the others in succession, with shot and shell; houses on the Vicksburg side and on the opposite shore were set on fire, which lighted up the whole river; and the roar of cannon, the bursting of shells, and finally the burning of the Henry Clay, drifting with the current, made up a picture of the terrible not often seen.[10]

Despite the ferocious fire from Vicksburg's batteries, only one ship was actually lost and the rest of the fleet suffered only minor damage with no fatalities. In his report Admiral Porter admitted, "Altogether we were very fortunate; the vessels had some narrow escapes, but were saved in most instances by the precautions taken to protect them." The ships assembled near Diamond Island, about twelve miles above New Carthage, where Porter decided to rest his men until daylight before continuing downriver. He later wrote, "The danger to the vessels was more apparent than real." Passing Vicksburg, he felt, was not as risky as running the forts that had protected New Orleans.[11]

Now that the Union fleet had successfully passed Vicksburg, the availability of supplies for the city and its garrison would be substantially restricted. The Mississippi between Vicksburg and Port Hudson had remained mostly open to Confederate shipping, especially provisions that were shipped down the Red River to the Mississippi and then to Vicksburg. Now that Federal gunboats were below Vicksburg that important source of supply was cut off, and the only way to bring large amounts of food and military supplies to the city was railroad lines that came from Jackson, Mississippi. On April 18, General Pemberton wrote, "I regard the navigation of Mississippi River as shut out from us now. No more supplies can be gotten from trans–Mississippi department."[12]

Before running past Vicksburg's batteries, Admiral Porter had been very explicit in warning Grant that once his ships had gone downriver, they could not return north of Vicksburg. Now that the Federal fleet was safely past the fortress and could begin to implement Grant's plan to move the army to the eastern shore, the river itself began to cause problems. All winter the river had been swollen by frequent rain but now the water level was falling. This meant that Grant could not use the numerous small lakes and streams on the western side of the river to create a waterway that could transport troops and supplies down from Milliken's Bend to New Carthage. Trying to run past the Vicksburg batteries with wooden transports filled with soldiers was a disaster waiting to happen. If necessary the men could move down the western side of the river; it would be a difficult march but possible. However, it was unrealistic to expect that enough provisions and ammunition for the entire army could be transported by wagon trains down those narrow muddy roads.[13]

General Grant had ridden down to New Carthage to view the situation for himself. Unfortunately there was no good place on the eastern side of the river to put the troops ashore, so Grant had to order the army to move farther south to Hard Times. Realizing that sufficient supplies could not be moved overland, he decided to tempt fate again. The gunboats had gotten past Vicksburg's batteries—perhaps transports carrying supplies could also. After returning to Milliken's Bend on April 20, Grant ordered six transports loaded with supplies and protected by coal-carrying barges on each side to be prepared to run past Vicksburg at the earliest opportunity. The civilian crews were not too happy about risking their lives, so the ships were manned mostly by army volunteers. Protected by cotton bales and barrels of beef, the transports made their try on the night of April 22. All but one ship made it past Vicksburg; the one loss was the ship carrying medical supplies and equipment. Now Grant had over half a million rations and the ships to ferry the army across the river below Vicksburg. All he needed was the army itself.[14]

Even before the transports passed Vicksburg, General Grant was issuing orders for the movement of the army south. General McClernand had already been instructed to cross the river and get possession of Grand Gulf as quickly as possible. On the 20th, Special Orders No. 110 was issued stating that the reason for the movement was "to obtain a foothold on the east bank of the Mississippi River, from which Vicksburg can be approached by practicable roads." McClernand would take the lead with his Thirteenth Corps, followed by McPherson with the Seventeenth Corps and the Fifteenth Corps commanded by Sherman. The army was to travel light with no tents or shelters for the troops and only the very barest of equipment for unit headquarters. Officers were authorized to requisition needed supplies from the civilian population only so long as they filled a military need and according to the orders, which stated in part, "insulting citizens, going into and searching houses without proper orders from division commanders, are positively prohibited. All such irregularities must be summarily punished."[15]

John McClernand was no favorite of Grant's, or most of the other high ranking commanders for that matter, but he had performed well in previous battles and his corps was made up of mostly veteran regiments, so he was in the lead. Admiral Porter was one of those who complained that McClernand was moving too slowly and told Grant plainly, "I wish 20 times a day that Sherman was here, or yourself, but I suppose we cannot have all we wish." General Sherman was also not convinced Grant's plan was the best way to take Vicksburg and wrote to Major General Frederick Steele, "I confess I don't like this roundabout project, but we must support Grant in whatever he undertakes."[16]

Despite the misgivings of others, McClernand himself had few doubts about the coming campaign, at least his part of it. On April 19 he wrote to Grant: "My present movement, if properly sustained, ought, and I believe will, eventuate in the extinguishments of the rebellion in the Gulf States, and limit it in the East." Following a request for a dozen transports to speed the movement of his troops so as to attack the Confederates before they had a chance to fortify new positions, he stated, "They will be worth untold millions to our cause, not only in money, but in momentous military results." Unlike many other commanders, McClernand approved of Grant's plan for the campaign: "Earnestly sympathizing in your plans and purposes, no effort or personal sacrifice on my part will be spared to give them complete success."[17]

While the army was moving south on the western side of the Mississippi, Admiral Porter had sent ships downriver to reconnoiter Grand Gulf and the surrounding shoreline. He reported to Grant that the Confederates were very busy improving their existing fortifications: "My opinion is that they will move heaven and earth to stop us if we don't go ahead. I could go down and settle the batteries, but if disabled would not be in condition to cover the landing when it takes place, and I think it should be done together." Porter was thinking along the same lines as Grant when he suggested that the troops leave their equipment behind and head south as quickly as possible. Looking to overwhelm the defenders, the admiral wrote, "I don't want to make a failure, and am sure that a combined attack will succeed beautifully."[18]

With the transports below Vicksburg, the provisions for the troops and the ships to ferry them across the river were now available. All that needed to be done was to capture Grand Gulf and begin the campaign on the east side of the river. It turned out, however, that Grand Gulf would not be an easy nut to crack. On April 22, Porter, who had stationed his ships just off Grand Gulf, wrote to McClernand: "They have built extensive works and have guns in them. If left to themselves, they will make this place impregnable." He ended the message with a plea for quick action: "This is a case where a dash will save everything.... Dispatch is all-important at this moment."[19]

On April 24 Grant took a look at Grand Gulf for himself and updated Sherman on the situation: "My impressions are, that if an attack can be made within the next two days, the place will easily fall. But the difficulties of getting from here [Smith's plantation] to the river are great." Even though it was only a matter of time before the army was in position to cross the river, he was well aware that the overall success of the campaign was still very much in doubt: "I foresee great difficulties in our present position, but it will not do to let these retard any movements." Grant added, "The line from here to Milliken's Bend is a long one for the transportation of supplies and to defend, and an impossible one for the transportation of wounded men." With the water level in the streams and bayous adjacent to the river falling, Grant noted that "it is exceedingly doubtful whether they can be made use of for the purposes of navigation." Despite having Porter's ships below Vicksburg, there were still many challenges for Grant and his army to overcome.[20]

While the navy was doing its part in moving ships and supplies below Vicksburg, the army itself was still moving south along the west side of the Mississippi. The roads were poor to begin with and frequent rain made them even worse. Albert O. Marshall of the 33rd Illinois later wrote that the men had to march along the tops of the levees, as "this is the only ground we can find to walk on here now. Everything except the high levees is under water." Marshall also added that concern about sickness was on the minds of most of the men. "To add to all else, our supply of quinine gave out. Chills and fever in such a damp and unhealthy place and climate without any quinine to check them, are fearful. Then the dread of being left when the advance was made." Another soldier writing about the tough march south was S. C. Jones of the 22nd Iowa, who commented that they moved along on "the levee with the roaring Mississippi on one side and the submerged swamp on the other. The whole country is a water waste."[21]

Day after day the troops pressed on through the mud and rain toward Hard Times. On April 28, Alonzo Brown of the 4th Minnesota wrote that his division started at six in the morning and only advanced four miles that day: "It rained and the mud is very deep. We have only one team along with the regiment. Empty wagons get stuck and fourteen span of horses were pulling a caisson through the mud. We had to step in the tracks of the men ahead of us." Colonel John B. Sanborn of the 4th Minnesota summed up the situation: "A worse march no army ever made."[22]

No matter the obstacles, however, the army kept moving south. Finally, many of the men thought, we are getting somewhere. After months of sitting around soaked to the skin in their tents or working in the mud and rain, and accomplishing nothing worthwhile, the men could at last see a campaign taking shape. The troops tore down local houses and barns, using the lumber to build roads and bridges over the swamps and bayous they had to march through. Many of the men in Grant's army were from pioneer families and were accustomed to using whatever materials they could find to get the job done. In his report on the campaign, General Grant paid tribute to the ability of his men to improvise in any situation when he wrote, "It is a striking feature, so far as my observation goes, of the present volunteer army of the United States, that there is nothing which men are called upon to do, mechanical or professional, that accomplished adepts cannot be found for the duty required in almost every regiment."[23]

General Grant worked himself as hard as his men. He was constantly riding up and down the columns of men straightening out traffic jams and urging them to keep moving. Captain S.H.M. Byers observed Grant during this time and later wrote that he was not posturing for effect like many generals did, but rather, "There was no nonsense, no sentiment. Only a plain business man of the republic there for the one single purpose of getting that army across the river in the shortest time possible."[24]

The next obstacle to be overcome was the Confederate works at Grand Gulf. Admiral Porter had already seen how strong the fortifications were, and he decided to bombard the enemy forts with his most powerful ships: *Benton, Tuscumbia, Carondelet, Louisville, Mound City, Pittsburg,* and the *Lafayette.* About 8 a.m. on April 29 the gunboats sailed to Grand Gulf and a fierce battle began. Part of the fleet steamed past the fortifications and turned around so the vessels could present their most heavily armored front to the enemy. For over five hours the big guns thundered as the ships hammered the works and the Confederates replied shot for shot. By early afternoon it was obvious that the ships could not silence the enemy guns. Grant reported that even though the ships frequently closed to "within pistol-shot of the enemy's batteries. It soon became evident that the guns of the enemy were too elevated and their fortifications too strong to be taken from the water side." Porter finally had to pull his battered fleet back out of range. All the ships in the Union fleet suffered serious damage and Porter would report casualties of 18 killed and 57 wounded. Grant's army would not be crossing the Mississippi River at Grand Gulf.[25]

While the troops were slogging their way south, another possible problem had weighed heavily on Grant's mind. If General Pemberton was to figure out what Grant was attempting to do, he could easily move thousands of his men down the eastern side of the river to oppose any Federal landing. The only way to prevent this potential disaster was to keep Pemberton guessing as to Grant's real strategy by diverting his attention away from the potential landing sites. As early as April 17, Grant had sent a cavalry expedition out of La Grange, Tennessee, commanded by Colonel Benjamin H. Grierson, who had been a small-town music teacher before the war. Leading three cavalry regiments, the 6th and 7th Illinois and the 2nd Iowa, totaling about seventeen hundred troopers, Grierson's raid was one of the most important and successful in the entire war.[26]

Colonel Grierson left La Grange the day after Porter's ships ran past Vicksburg. One objective of the raid was to wreck railroad equipment and telegraph lines, and generally destroy any military equipment he could find. With much of his cavalry up in Tennessee, Pemberton's command was short of mounted troops, so there was no way he could learn if Grierson's raid was just an annoyance or the precursor of a major Federal move. During the next two weeks Grierson's force rode nearly four hundred miles through the heart of Mississippi burning supplies and destroying railroad equipment until they arrived safely at Baton Rouge by May 2.

Grant wrote to Halleck that Grierson had "spread excitement throughout the State, destroying railroads, trestle-works, bridges, burning locomotives and railway stock, taking prisoners, and destroying stores of all kinds. To use the expression of my informant, 'Grierson knocked the heart out of the State.'"[27]

While the few cavalrymen Pemberton had were running themselves ragged chasing Federal troopers through Mississippi, Grant wanted to make sure that Pemberton did not send any large reinforcements south to oppose his landing on the eastern shore of the river. To keep the Confederates guessing, Sherman's corps remained north of Vicksburg when the rest of the army began to head south. On April 27, Grant had written to Sherman concerning his making a diversionary attack, saying that he liked the idea of making a "heavy demonstration" against Haynes' Bluff but didn't want to order it because "it would be so hard to make our own troops understand that only a demonstration was intended, and our people at home would characterize it as a repulse." Grant decided in the end to leave the decision to attack or not to his trusted friend.[28]

The next day Sherman replied that he had already made arrangements with the navy to provide escorts and transports, and he would take ten regiments up the Yazoo River to Haynes' Bluff: "We will make as strong a demonstration as possible. The troops will all understand the purpose, and will not be hurt by the repulse." As for the northern civilian population, Sherman dismissed any concerns: "The people of the country must find out the truth as they best can; it is none of their business. You are engaged in a hazardous enterprise, and, for good reasons, wish to divert attention; that is sufficient to me, and it shall be done."[29]

In a second message on April 28, Sherman confirmed that the naval support had arrived and he would be setting out the next day to demonstrate at Chickasaw Bayou, where he was previously repulsed, and then Haynes' Bluff. Never shy about his feelings toward newspapermen, Sherman also wrote: "As to the reports in newspapers, we must scorn them, else they will ruin us and our country. They are as much enemies to good government as the secesh, and between the two I like the secesh best, because they are a brave, open enemy, and not a set of sneaking, croaking scoundrels." Sherman fully supported the idea of making a diversion at Haynes' Bluff, believing that it "is proper and right, and will make it, let whatever reports of repulse be made." Sherman and his men did a good enough job of pretending to launch an attack that the Confederate commander at Haynes' Bluff urgently called for reinforcements. Troops that might have been used against Grant were instead used to defend against a nonexistent attack.[30]

Back at Grand Gulf, the repulse suffered by the navy convinced Grant to find another place farther downriver to land his troops. That same night, under cover of darkness and heavy covering fire from the fleet, the transports ran past Grand Gulf followed by the warships. The troops marched down to Hard Times, about two miles past Grand Gulf, where they were loaded onto the transports and headed south once again. About ten miles below Grand Gulf was a good landing point called Bruinsburg that offered access inland. On April 30, the first of McClernand's troops went ashore and quickly moved inland to occupy the high ground past Bruinsburg and secure the landing site. During the rest of the day and night transports and gunboats sailed back and forth across the river loaded with troops. With the success of the landing there was no need for Sherman to keep up the pretext of attacking Haynes' Bluff. Grant ordered him to bring his corps south with as much supplies as he could transport.[31]

Finally, after months of work and sacrifice, Grant had achieved his goal of getting on the same side of the Mississippi as Vicksburg. He later wrote:

> When this was effected I felt a degree of relief scarcely ever equaled since. Vicksburg was not yet taken, it is true, nor were its defenders demoralized by any of our previous moves. I was now in the enemy's country, with a vast river and the stronghold of Vicksburg between me and my base of supplies. But I was on dry ground on the same side of the river with the enemy. All the campaigns, labors, hardships and exposures from the month of December previous to this time that had been made and endured, were for the accomplishment of this one object.[32]

Now the campaign for Vicksburg would really begin.

Chapter 9

The Campaign Takes Shape

Once the landing site was secure and troops were moving inland, Grant had to make one of the most important decisions of the campaign, and make it quickly. The most obvious move was to drive north toward Vicksburg, maintaining contact with the river to receive supplies. It was well known, however, that Joseph E. Johnston was raising an army at Jackson, the capital of Mississippi, about forty miles east of Vicksburg. If Grant marched straight for Vicksburg, that would expose the right flank of the Federal army to an attack by the very capable Johnston. Grant had to decide if he was going to head south to join with General Banks to operate against Port Hudson or continue north toward Vicksburg, or perhaps head east toward Jackson to destroy Johnston's force and cut the railroad to isolate Vicksburg from the rest of the Confederacy.

But, before the army could begin to drive too far inland, a secure supply depot had to be set up on the east side of the river. Bruinsburg could not handle the amount of traffic that would be needed to keep the army supplied, so Grant looked north to Grand Gulf. The Confederate fortress was closer to the Union supply lines, had good roads inland and was easily defended. The best route to Grand Gulf lay through Port Gibson, about ten miles inland from Bruinsburg and about the same distance southeast of Grand Gulf, using the bridge located there to cross over Bayou Pierre. During the night of April 30, while troops were still crossing the river, Grant put the operation into motion. "As soon as the Thirteenth Army Corps was landed, and could draw three days' rations to put in haversacks (no wagons were allowed to cross until the troops were all over), they were started on the road to Port Gibson." Grant wanted troops on the move toward high ground as quickly as possible.[1]

Before the rest of the army moved forward, however, Grant needed to make sure that a sufficient supply of ammunition was available. The local countryside could supply food, but ammunition was another matter since each man could carry only enough in his cartridge case for a relatively brief engagement. Grant ordered "immediately on landing that all the vehicles and draft animals, whether horses, mules, or oxen, in the vicinity should be collected and loaded to their capacity with ammunition." A very un-military looking wagon train was quickly put together using whatever animals could be rounded up to pull anything on wheels. Thomas Durham remembered that in addition to fine carriages, "there were cotton wagons, ox carts and even dog carts—everything that could be found in the country that had wheels, and every kind of an animal and harness with which to pull them, were pressed into service," all loaded with ammunition and other military equipment.[2]

The lead troops moving toward Port Gibson were from Brigadier General Eugene Carr's division of McClernand's corps. Isacc Elliott, of the 33rd Illinois, remembered that they marched all night: "It was a most tedious tramp, although the roads were good and it was bright moonlight. During the frequent halts the men would drop upon the ground and go instantly to sleep, and it was no little trouble to rouse them to move on again." Around two o'clock in the morning of May 1, advance Union troops ran into the enemy's pickets a couple miles outside Port Gibson and scattered firing broke out on several fronts. As more and more Federal soldiers moved up, the firing became heavier until it was light enough to see. Then the real fighting began.[3]

There were six thousand to seven thousand Confederates from Grand Gulf defending Port Gibson, commanded by Brigadier General John Bowen. One of the few Confederate commanders who seemed to grasp what Grant was planning, Bowen knew he had to delay the Federals long enough for Pemberton to pull his spread out command together and hopefully contain the invaders before they were able to move inland. Bowen dispatched troops under Brigadier General Martin Green to defend the western approaches to Port Gibson while Brigadier General Edward Tracy's brigade was defending the route from Bruinsburg. Another brigade, commanded by Brigadier General William Baldwin, was on its way from Vicksburg to reinforce Bowen's small force.[4]

Although the Confederates would be outnumbered by the approaching Federal troops, the difficult terrain in the area provided strong natural defensive positions. Grant described the ground over which his men had to advance: "The country in this part of Mississippi stands on edge, as it were, the roads running along the ridges except when they occasionally pass from one ridge to another. Where there are no clearings the sides of the hills are covered with a very heavy growth of timber and with undergrowth." The surrounding terrain was broken by ravines filled with vines and heavy undergrowth, making many of them almost impenetrable.[5]

During the early morning hours McClernand's men continued to move up from the landing site, and by first light most of them were up to the front and ready to advance. The rugged terrain caused serious problems for the Union commanders. It was clear that it would be nearly impossible to make coordinated attacks against the well protected enemy lines. Just before reaching the Confederate lines, the road to Port Gibson divides and runs along the top of two separate ridges about a mile apart until they come together again just outside the town. Between these two ridges is a deep ravine that makes moving between them virtually impossible. McClernand was forced to divide his command between these two roads, advancing the divisions of Carr, A. J. Smith and Brigadier General Charles E. Hovey on the right, and Brigadier General Peter J. Osterhaus on the left side road.[6]

Thomas Durham, of the 11th Indiana, remembered that his unit came upon the enemy at Magnolia Church, where "there was a little skirmishing before day, but soon after daylight we got down to business." Around the church was a forest of magnolia trees in full bloom and Durham decided "the beauty of the large blooms and their fragrance made me feel more like admiring the beauties of nature than fighting." But the battle continued just the same. The Confederates put up a stubborn defense with Bowen moving troops around to shore up weakening positions. Tracy was killed trying to hold the Bruinsburg Road where Osterhaus was advancing, and Carr and Hovey's troops slowly drove Green back from the Magnolia Church. General Baldwin's brigade arrived to reinforce the Confederate left, and the fighting went on for hours with the terrain limiting the use of the overwhelming Federal manpower and turning the battle into a series of fights in the woods between small units. Fresh Union troops were frequently sent down into the jungle-like ravines in fruitless attempts to outflank the Confederate lines.[7]

Grant was in the field checking on the progress of his men and was not happy with what he was seeing: "On the right the enemy, if not being pressed back, was at least not repulsing our advance. On the left, however, Osterhaus was not faring so well. He had been repulsed with some loss." Fortunately, around noon Major General John A. Logan's division of McPherson's corps had come up, and Brigadier General John E. Smith's brigade was sent forward to reinforce Osterhaus and move to the left to flank the Confederate lines. Another brigade went to the right to reinforce that side of the Union lines. These fresh troops tipped the scale, and by mid-afternoon the Federals were pushing back the exhausted defenders and the outcome of the battle was certain.[8]

Late in the afternoon General Bowen's struggling command was barely holding together, and shortly before dark he finally ordered his men to withdraw across Bayou Pierre, burn the bridges behind them and evacuate Port Gibson. By nine o'clock Bowen's men had taken up a new position between Port Gibson and Grand Gulf. Considering they were vastly outnumbered, Bowen's men put up a remarkable fight, delaying the Federal troops for most of the day, time that was critical for Pemberton to bring together his scattered forces. Just before he fell back, Bowen sent a quick wire to Pemberton informing him of the battle and acknowledging that "the men did nobly, holding out the whole day against overwhelming odds. The town will be in possession of the enemy in a few hours."[9]

That evening Grant told McClernand to "push the enemy, with skirmishers well thrown out, until it gets too dark to see him ... and renew the attack at early dawn." Pemberton was also sending messages. After rushing back to Vicksburg from Jackson, he realized that the Union landing was not a feint as was originally believed but an invasion. To Jefferson Davis he wrote "enemy can cross all his army from Hard Times to Bruinsburg, below Bayou Pierre. Large re-enforcements should be sent me from other departments. Enemy's movement threatens Jackson, and, if successful, cuts off Vicksburg and Port Hudson from the east." Pemberton also noted that the, "Enemy's success in passing our batteries has completely changed character of defense."[10]

Early on May 2 the Federals renewed their advance and found Port Gibson abandoned and the nearby bridges across Bayou Pierre destroyed. Union engineers and work details feverishly labored throughout the day, and by nightfall most of McPherson's corps was again on the move. It encountered scattered resistance from small Confederate units but easily brushed them aside, repaired another bridge over the North Fork of Bayou Pierre, and on the morning of the 3rd moved into the village of Willow Springs. A few miles north the road to Vicksburg crossed the Big Black River, and the road to Jackson headed off to the northeast. McPherson ran into a sizeable number of Confederates at this point and heavy skirmishing broke out, but Logan's division was sent around the left toward Grand Gulf and flanked the defenders out of their positions. McClernand brought his corps up for support and soon this important road junction was firmly under Federal control.[11]

On the morning of May 3, Admiral Porter brought his fleet up to attack Grand Gulf but found the defenders gone. With Grant's army now below Grand Gulf, that position lost its value and Bowen abandoned the fortress and pulled most of his troops back behind the Big Black on the 3rd. When Grant arrived in Grand Gulf he immediately began making arrangements to make that location the main supply base.[12]

Also on May 3, Grant sent a message to General Halleck from Grand Gulf in which he stated that Bowen's "defense was a very bold one and well carried out. My force, however, was too heavy for his, and composed of well-disciplined and hardy men, who know no defeat, and are not willing to learn what it is." Grant was clearly pleased with how they had performed so far: "This army is in the finest health and spirits. Since leaving Milliken's Bend they have marched as much by night as by day, through mud and rain, without tents or much other baggage, and on irregular rations, without a complaint, and with less straggling than I have ever before witnessed."[13]

In his *Memoirs*, Grant described the situation he faced and how he came to make the audacious decision that sealed the fate of Vicksburg. Before leaving Grand Gulf, Grant received a message from General Banks, who had taken his army on a campaign up the Red River and who informed Grant that "he could not be at Port Hudson before the 10th of May and then with only 15,000 men." Grant later wrote, "Up to this time my intention had been to secure Grand Gulf, as a base of supplies, detach McClernand's corps to Banks and co-operate with him in the reduction of Port Hudson." After Port Hudson was secured the main Federal supply base could be shifted to New Orleans. With a secure supply route, Banks could bring his army north to join Grant, and the combined army would then be in a position to attack Pemberton with overwhelming force.[14]

All too often during the war when the original plan for a campaign fell apart, many Union commanders would have pulled back to a safer position and sent to Washington for instructions. Fortunately Ulysses Grant was not like most Federal commanders; he would wait for no one. As he explained:

> The news from Banks forced upon me a different plan of campaign from the one intended. To wait for his co-operation would have detained me at least a month. The reinforcements would not have reached ten thousand men after deducting casualties and necessary river guards at all high points close to the river for over three hundred miles. The enemy would have strengthened his position and been reinforced by more men than Banks could have brought. I therefore determined to move independently of Banks, cut loose from my base, destroy the rebel force in rear of Vicksburg and invest or capture the city.[15]

Establishing a supply base at Grand Gulf shortened the army's supply line, but material still had to come down from above Vicksburg, be ferried across the river and then reach the army, wherever it was. The countryside could provide plenty of food, and if not, the men could make do on short rations if necessary, but the army needed powder, shells and bullets to fight, and these had to come through the supply line. Now was the turning point in the campaign and Grant could not afford to delay. The Confederates had been taken by surprise but Pemberton was pulling his forces together to defend Vicksburg against the expected advance from the south. On May 3, Grant wrote to Sherman, who was already moving his corps south to join the rest of the army, that Grand Gulf was captured and that "it is unnecessary for me to remind you of the overwhelming importance of celerity in your movements.... The enemy is badly beaten, greatly demoralized, and exhausted of ammunition. The road to Vicksburg is open. All we want now are men, ammunition and hard bread." But Grant knew full well that he had only a small window of opportunity to take advantage of the enemy's confusion.[16]

To break from your supply line was a dangerous and unprecedented move and in conventional military thinking this simply was not done. The accepted strategy would have been to advance north close to the river where supplies would be easily obtained. If the army should be defeated in battle, it would be a simple matter to escape across the river. Moving inland, however, presented significant problems and dangers. The supply line would stretch over many miles of poor roads subject to raids by enemy guerrillas. The army would have to live off the land, which meant that they had to keep moving since an army that size would quickly clean out the provisions in the surrounding area. But most dangerous was the possibility of defeat in battle. Deep in enemy territory there would be no safe place to retreat to; the army could be virtually destroyed.

Once Grant made up his mind, there was no time to lose. When Sherman's corps arrived the army would contain over forty thousand men, a lot of mouths to feed. It would not take long for Pemberton and Johnston to recognize what Grant was attempting to do, so it was imperative to act quickly. Even before crossing the Mississippi, orders had gone back to Milliken's Bend to send four more barges past Vicksburg loaded with supplies. Grant told Chief Quartermaster Colonel J. D. Bingham to "do this with all expedition, in forty-eight hours from receipt of orders if possible. Time is of immense importance." Colonel Bingham was also given the authority to replace the civilian crews with army volunteers if the crews refused to make the run past Vicksburg. Also on May 3, Grant sent orders to Brigadier General J. C. Sullivan, who commanded the area on the west side of the Mississippi, to construct a road from Young's Point to below Warrenton in order to speed supplies south, ending with "everything depends upon the promptitude with which our supplies are forwarded." Orders also went out to General Sherman to bring 120 wagons down to Grand Gulf to be filled with supplies for the march east. Sherman was to take five days' rations for his own men but was cautioned to "see that they last five days." With the plan set in motion, Assistant Secretary Dana wrote to Secretary Stanton on May 4, "As soon as Sherman comes up and the rations on the way arrive, he will disregard his base and depend on the country for meat and even for bread. Beef cattle and corn are both abundant everywhere."[17]

Once Grant's troops began moving inland it would be obvious to Pemberton that Vicksburg was not the immediate target, but it was still important that the Confederates be kept guessing as to exactly where Grant was heading. There were several routes the Union army could take, depending on what target Grant was going to go after first. Grant was focusing his attention on the Southern Railroad of Mississippi which ran from Vicksburg east through Jackson. At Jackson the railroad crossed the tracks of the New Orleans, Jackson & Great Northern line that went down to New Orleans from western Tennessee. This line connected Vicksburg with the rest of the Confederacy, and on these rails would come supplies and reinforcements

Union General James McPherson—a favorite of both Grant and Sherman, he was killed outside Atlanta in July 1864 (Library of Congress).

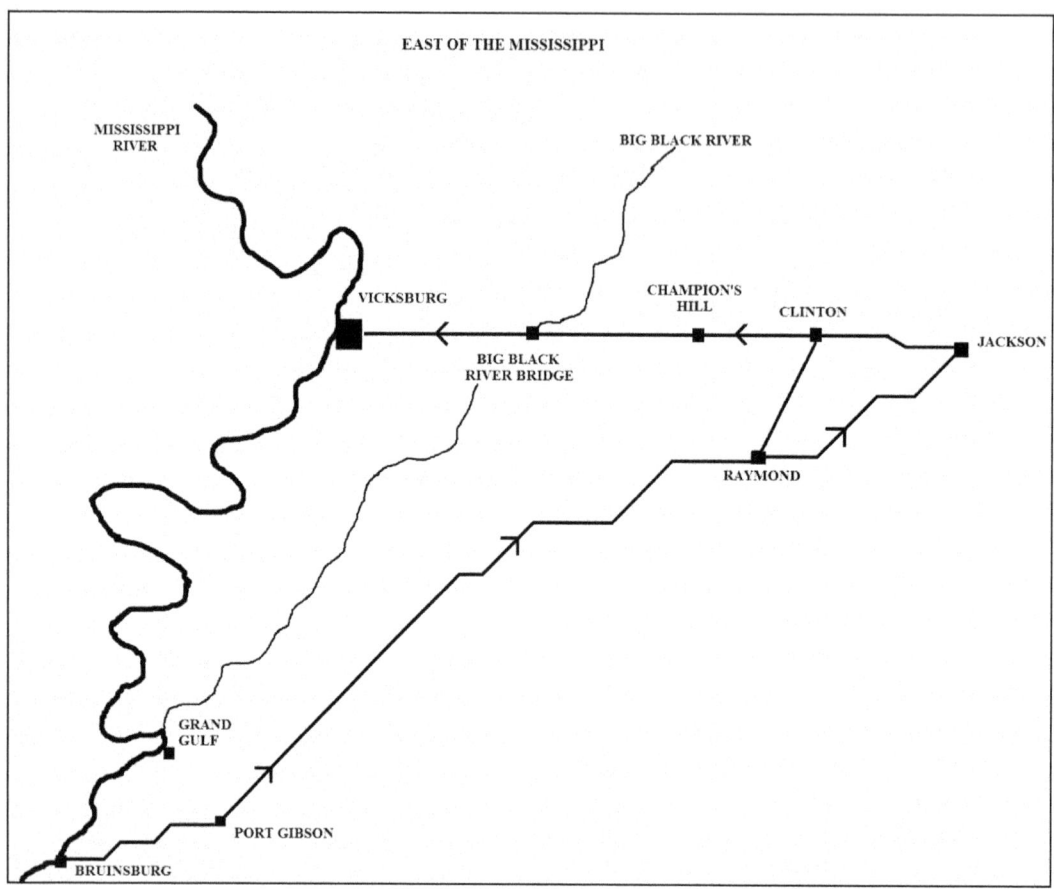

for Pemberton's army. In addition, it was at Jackson that Joe Johnston would be building his new army. Breaking the railroad would cut Vicksburg's communications and deprive the city of any further supplies and reinforcements. If Grant could take Jackson, the large stores of military supplies there could be destroyed and Johnston's growing army might be destroyed or at least damaged enough so they would be unable to interfere with the rest of the campaign.

General Sherman reached Grand Gulf on May 6 with two of his divisions. General Blair's division was still moving down the west side of the Mississippi. By the end of the first week in May the Federal army had grown to about thirty-three thousand men with eight thousand more on the way, it was time to move. On May 7 the army headed northeast with "McPherson's corps keeping the road nearest Big Black River, to Rocky Springs, McClernand's corps keeping the ridge road from Willow Springs, and Sherman following with his corps divided on the two roads." The crossings of the Big Black were closely guarded to prevent Pemberton from attacking the army from behind. Grant had decided on a two-pronged advance in order to keep Pemberton guessing his intentions and create two opportunities to destroy Vicksburg's communications with Jackson. Grant reported: "It was my intention here to hug the Big Black River as closely as possible with McClernand's and Sherman's corps, and get them to the railroad at some place between Edwards Station and Bolton." McPherson's task was to march to Raymond, "and from there into Jackson, destroying the railroad, telegraph, public stores, &c., and push west to rejoin the main force."[18]

Grant had to move quickly, not only so the enemy could not have time to build up a large force large enough to oppose him, but also so that his superiors in Washington would be unable to order him not to attempt such a risky move. Grant later wrote, "I knew well that Halleck's caution would lead him to disapprove of this course; but it was the only one that gave any chance of success." The difficulty in sending messages back and forth to Washington worked in Grant's favor since he knew that "the time it would take to communicate with Washington and get a reply would be so great that I could not be interfered with until it was demonstrated whether my plan was practicable."[19]

Grant was correct in assuming that his plan was too risky for the high command back in Washington, but to be fair there were reasons to be cautious. The Army of the Potomac had just suffered a terrible defeat at Chancellorsville and was trying to pull itself together just outside Washington. The masterful Robert E Lee was preparing to invade Pennsylvania with the nation's capital as his final objective. If Grant's army were destroyed, as it very well could be so deep in enemy territory, the Union cause might be irreparably damaged.

The authorities in Washington were not the only opposition to Grant's plans; even his old friend Sherman had urged caution saying that it would be impossible to supply the army over the one road from Grand Gulf and that the troops should stay where they were until sufficient supplies could be brought up and stockpiled. Grant replied on May 9, "I do not calculate upon the possibility of supplying the army with full rations from Grand Gulf. What I do expect, however, is to get up what rations of hard bread, coffee, and salt we can, and make the country furnish the balance.... A delay would give the enemy time to re-enforce and fortify."[20]

The march toward Jackson and the railroad was hard on the Federal troops, but even harder on the Mississippi countryside. Thomas Durham later wrote that everyone knew that speed was essential for their survival, "therefore, rain or no rain, roads or no roads, hungry or thirsty, we had to move rapidly. Very little time was taken for sleep and we were on the move almost constantly both day and most of the night." S.H.M. Byers of the 5th Iowa would remember, "For days we scarcely slept at all; it was hurry here and quickstep there, day or night. None of us soldiers or subordinates could tell the direction we were marching. We had few rations, little water, and almost no rest." Ira Blanchard, of the 20th Illinois, echoed these comments: "We found little time to eat, much less to sleep, but were pushed forward before we had time to make a little coffee in the morning."[21]

Moving quickly through the enemy territory was only one of the priorities on this march; finding food was the other, but this turned out to be less difficult than expected. Wilber Crummer, of the 45th Illinois, wrote, "Our rations are getting short, but the country affords us a fair supply of some things, such as fresh pigs, chickens and vegetables, which we take as a matter of crippling the enemy as well as to satisfy the hungry boys in blue." John A. Bering, an officer in the 48th Ohio, described how the foraging parties, also known as "bummers," obtained provisions from the countryside: "They left camp every morning, in advance of the infantry ... mounted on such 'critters' as they could gather up in their expeditions." These foragers began their collections as soon as they got beyond the Federal lines: "They slaughtered the pigs in the pens; the cattle and horses were driven from the fields; smokehouses and cellars were ransacked for flour, meal, and bacon; the chickens and turkeys were captured in the yard; the mules were hitched to the family carriage, and the provisions stowed away in it." Then, with their plunder in tow, they went on to the next plantation and repeated the process. The foragers would return to the army by evening and distribute their booty to the men of their unit.[22]

Grant's troops continued the march northeast using the Big Black to shield their movements. Sherman and McClernand met little enemy resistance until they arrived at Fourteen-Mile Creek, where there was considerable skirmishing before they were able to gain control of the crossings. McPherson's troops also met only light skirmishers as they moved toward the town of Raymond. As Grant's army moved closer and closer to Vicksburg's lifeline, John Pemberton was grappling with a series of conflicting problems and orders.[23]

On May 7, Jefferson Davis sent a message to Pemberton that had a major effect on the remainder of the campaign. Along with announcing that upwards of five thousand reinforcements were on the way from the East Coast, Davis told Pemberton, "To hold both Vicksburg and Port Hudson is necessary to a connection with Trans-Mississippi. You may expect whatever is in my power to do." Although not an outright order, it is very clear what the president expected of Pemberton. Pemberton had already received orders from Johnston, his immediate superior, to the effect that due to Grant's landing on the east side of the Mississippi the safety of the entire state would depend on beating him before he grew too strong and "for that object you should unite your whole force." In another dispatch, Johnston again wrote for Pemberton to "unite all your troops to beat him. Success will give back what was abandoned to win it."[24]

Before receiving Davis' message to hold both Vicksburg and Port Hudson, orders had gone out to General Franklin Gardner, commander of Port Hudson, to send one of his brigades to Jackson. On May 4, Pemberton sent another dispatch to Gardner: "You must come and bring with you 5,000 infantry." Since General Banks was off in Louisiana there was no immediate threat to Port Hudson, so it seemed safe to bring most of those troops up to protect Vicksburg. The fact was that if Vicksburg fell, Port Hudson could not be held for long no matter how many troops were there. Once Pemberton received the dispatch from his commander-in-chief to defend both Vicksburg and Port Hudson, the conscientious general felt it was his duty to obey and immediately contacted Gardner telling him to "return with 2,000 troops to Port Hudson, and hold it to the last. President says both places must be held."[25]

General Pemberton had too many places to guard and too few troops do the job properly. He was not bold by nature, and taking the risk of concentrating all his forces for one major decisive battle was out of character. Pemberton was much more comfortable defending a few important points and letting the enemy come to him. He was, however, intelligent enough to look for help anywhere he could get it. On May 9, Pemberton wrote to Lieutenant General Edward Kirby Smith in Shreveport, Louisiana, informing him of Grant's landing and asking Kirby Smith to make "a movement upon the line of communications of the enemy on the western side of the river.... To break this would render a most important service." Little came of this very good idea. On May 12 Pemberton sent a message to President Davis detailing the situation: "The enemy is apparently moving in heavy force toward Edwards Depot, Southern Railroad. With my limited force, I will do all I can to meet him.... The enemy largely outnumbers me, and I am obliged to hold back large forces at the ferries on Big Black, lest he cross and take this place." Pemberton also noted that he felt "compelled to keep a considerable force on either flank of Vicksburg, out of supporting distance of Edwards, to prevent his approach in those directions."[26]

As Grant's troops approached the railroad the question of cooperating with Banks came up again. On May 10, Grant wrote to Banks to let him know that his original intention had been to send forces to capture Port Hudson to ensure the capture of that place. But, as Grant wrote, "Meeting the enemy, however, as I did, south of Port Gibson, I followed him to the Big

Black, and could not afford to retrace my steps." The original campaign was also still on the minds of the high command in Washington, which was unaware of Grant's movements. On the 11th Halleck wrote to Grant, "If possible, the forces of yourself and of General Banks should be united between Vicksburg and Port Hudson, so as to attack these places separately with the combined forces. The same thing had been urged upon General Banks." Considering how close he was to the first major target, there was little chance that Grant would now turn his army around.[27]

The first real fight since Port Gibson began during the morning of May 12, when McPherson's advance division, commanded by General John Logan, ran into over five thousand Confederates commanded by Brigadier General John Gregg, a few miles outside of Raymond. Gregg originally thought he was facing just one Federal brigade out on a scouting mission. Gregg positioned two regiments to attack the Federal troops as they approached Fourteen Mile Creek and positioned three more regiments to hit the flank and rear of the advancing Federals. Unknown to Gregg, however was that the rest of Logan's division was moving up to attack Gregg's much smaller force.[28]

At first the Confederates had the advantage when General Gregg launched his attack against the 23rd Indiana as they approached the creek out in front of the main force. Soon the 45th Illinois, 20th Illinois and the 20th Ohio were also under heavy attack. Outnumbered and with bullets raining down on them, the Federals took cover in the creek bed. Osborn H. Oldroyd of the 20th Ohio later wrote, "Every man of us knew it would be sure death to all to retreat, for we had behind us a bank seven feet high. Made slippery by the wading and climbing back of the wounded, and where the foe could be at our heels in a moment."[29]

The initial violence of the Confederate attack had caught Logan's men by surprise, but in pushing past the advanced Federal regiments, the Confederates ran right into the rest of the Union line. Ira Blanchard of the 20th Illinois described the scene: "Both lines stood equally firm; both equally determined as a couple of bull dogs engaged in a death struggle. The air was full of hissing bullets; they cut up the ground and made the dust fly in our rear as though a heavy shower of hail was falling."[30]

General Logan pulled his men back to a fenceline for more protection as both sides continued to exchange heavy fire. On the Union right, two Confederate regiments were moving to attack that flank defended by Federal cavalry and just one infantry regiment. General Logan, never one to panic during battle, suddenly realized that his entire line was in grave danger. Riding back and forth yelling at his troops to stand fast, he was able to move two Illinois regiments from the main line to establish a position on the right. When the Confederates came out of the woods they ran into a solid line of Federal troops. Even worse was that Logan had sent troops to flank them on their left and the Confederates were forced to fall back. By now Gregg knew he was facing a much larger force than just one brigade and was in danger of falling into the same type of trap he had planned to spring on the Federal troops.[31]

The Confederate left flank was in danger of collapsing when Colonel Hiram Granbury of the 7th Texas decided it was time to pull back before his regiment and the 3rd Tennessee were totally destroyed. As they were pulling back, Colonel Randal McGavock led his 10th Tennessee and the 30th Tennessee forward straight into the strength of the Union line. Lieutenant Colonel James J. Turner of the 30th Tennessee reported that both regiments "charged forward gallantly, cheering and firing as they went. The enemy, being on our right flank and strongly posted in the woods in our front, poured into our ranks a most destructive fire."

McGavock was killed and both regiments suffered heavy casualties, but the advancing Federal troops were forced to stop and take cover.³²

The battle now became a fight for position with Logan bringing up more of his division on the right and the Confederates working hard to avoid being flanked. By mid-afternoon the weight of the Federal forces were becoming too much for Gregg's beleaguered men. He decided to pull his forces back through Raymond and head for Jackson, where they would live to fight another day. The engagement at Raymond was not large in terms of number of men involved or casualties, with Gregg's brigade losing just over five hundred men and Logan's division 442 total. The real importance of Raymond was that it caused General Grant to once again change the focus of the campaign.³³

Chapter 10

Grant Moves Quickly

The determined stand made by the Confederates at Raymond led Grant to consider that maybe they had more strength at Jackson and the surrounding area than had been initially assumed. Also, there were rumors of enemy reinforcements arriving soon, and Joseph Johnston was expected to assume command in person at any time. Grant was faced with the very real possibility that there could be more than ten thousand Confederate soldiers in Jackson under the command of one of the South's most able generals. Grant was with Sherman when he received news of the battle at Raymond and "decided at once to turn the whole column towards Jackson and capture that place without delay."[1]

There was danger no matter which way the Federal army moved. By turning east toward Jackson there was the possibility that Pemberton would strike at the Federal rear with the forces at Edwards Station. If Grant moved to attack the enemy gathering at Edwards Station, he could be attacked by Johnston's force on the flank. The truth was, however, that Grant knew Pemberton was too cautious to leave his defenses and come too far out into the open. Turning the entire army toward Jackson would give Grant enough strength to defeat any number of troops that Johnston could reasonably have gathered. Another very good reason to go after Mississippi's capital was that the city was a valuable supply depot and railroad center with tracks connecting to all areas of the Confederacy. If Vicksburg were to be eventually put under a siege it would be necessary to cut the city's communications, so why not destroy the only link to the rest of the South. As Grant later wrote, "As I hoped in the end to besiege Vicksburg I must first destroy all possibility of aid. I therefore determined to move swiftly towards Jackson, destroy or drive any force in that direction and then turn upon Pemberton." In addition, Jackson was also a good sized industrial center with an arsenal, foundries, and mills, the destruction of which would damage the war effort for the entire Confederacy.[2]

During the advance Grant had been careful to guard the crossings over the Big Black to prevent Pemberton from breaking his communication with Grand Gulf. But as he had already decided to bring all the army forward, there would be no communication line for the enemy to cut. As Grant later wrote, "By moving against Jackson, I uncovered my own communication. So I finally decided to have none—to cut loose altogether from my base and move my whole force eastward." There was every reason to believe that Grant's force could move quickly enough to take Jackson and still have time to turn west before the cautious Pemberton was able to bring troops forward to attack the army from the rear.[3]

The decision was made. Grant wrote to General Halleck on May 11, "As I shall communicate with Grand Gulf no more, except it becomes necessary to send a train with heavy escort, you may not hear from me again for several days." New orders were sent out to all the corps commanders. McPherson was to leave Raymond first thing in the morning and move north to Clinton. Sherman was to move toward Jackson through Raymond and Mississippi Springs, approaching the city from the southwest. McClernand, who had been fighting sharp skirmishes outside of Edwards Station, had the difficult task of disengaging with Bowen and marching three divisions toward Raymond north of Fourteen Mile Creek, leaving one to guard the crossing at the Big Black. Since Grant had no way of knowing for sure the Confederate response to an attack, he decided to make a two-pronged advance—from the west along the road from Clinton and from the southwest on the road from Raymond. It would be difficult to coordinate the attacks of two separated columns but even more difficult to defend against them.[4]

With Grant's army moving rapidly and brushing aside any attempt to halt or even slow them down, the Confederate high command was growing desperate. The crisis demanded that the most able commander available should be in charge. Secretary of War James Seddon ordered General Johnston to "proceed at once to Mississippi and take chief command of the forces, giving to those in the field, as far as practicable, the encouragement and benefit of your personal direction." Johnston, who was still recovering from a serious illness in Tullahoma, Tennessee, acknowledged the orders: "I shall go immediately, although unfit for field service."[5]

When Johnston arrived in Jackson on May 13, General Gregg informed him that there were several Federal divisions moving toward Jackson from Edwards Station. This was McPherson who was mistakenly believed to be Sherman, but Sherman's forces coming from the southwest were not yet detected. Johnston also learned that there were currently about six thousand Confederate troops in the Jackson area and several thousand more on the way. If Johnston could gather as many as twelve thousand men he could put up a good fight from inside the city's fortifications. Johnston sent a dispatch to Pemberton letting him know of his arrival and informing Pemberton of the Federal occupation of Clinton. Johnston wanted Pemberton to move his command forward and come up from behind the enemy troops at Clinton: "To beat such a detachment would be of immense value; the troops here could cooperate; all the strength you can quickly assemble should be brought; time is all-important." General Johnston also sent an ominous telegram to Secretary Seddon, "I arrived this evening, finding the enemy's force between this place and General Pemberton, cutting off the communication. I am too late."[6]

Pemberton informed Johnston that he would immediately begin marching toward Clinton, but after a council of war with his generals decided against the movement. Instead he proposed to move with seventeen thousand men to Dillon's on the main road between Raymond and Port Gibson. Pemberton informed Johnston of this move: "The object is to cut enemy's communications and force him to attack me, as I do not consider my force sufficient to justify an attack on enemy in position or to attempt to cut my way to Jackson." Pemberton was apparently unaware that Grant had no communications with Port Gibson to cut and that he would be more than happy to let Pemberton have control of that road if it meant seventeen thousand fewer enemy troops between the Federal army and Vicksburg.[7]

The Federal army was converging on Jackson from two directions on May 13. With Brigadier General Marcellus Crocker's division in the lead, McPherson had occupied Clinton during the afternoon and set his men to work destroying railroad equipment. Sherman's Fifteenth Corps left their camps before dawn, and the advance elements of General James Tuttle's division reached Raymond just as McPherson's last troops were still moving out of the town. Tuttle had a brief skirmish just east of Raymond, but his troops pushed forward to Mississippi Springs that evening.[8]

General McClernand had the most difficult task to accomplish—disengage from the skirmishing in front of Edwards Station and turn his division toward Raymond. McClernand left Hovey's division behind to keep in contact with the enemy while Osterhaus and Carr moved their divisions north of Fourteen Mile Creek, moving to the Raymond road. Hovey's division was able to safely pull back from Edwards Station and McClernand's three divisions made the long march to Raymond, which they reached near midnight. Another of McClernand's divisions, that commanded by A. J. Smith, had already been sent south to meet Frank Blair's division of Sherman's corps as they moved up from Grand Gulf with a supply train. Even Grant was complimentary of the way McClernand handled his corps, writing that he executed his orders "with much skill and without loss."[9]

During the night of May 13, Grant's orders to all his corps commanders for the morning were basically the same, advance on Jackson: "McPherson was ordered to march at early dawn upon Jackson, only fifteen miles away. Sherman was given the same order; but he was to move by the direct road from Raymond to Jackson, which is south of the road McPherson was on." Grant did not really need McClernand's troops for the assault on Jackson, so "McClernand was ordered to move one division of his command to Clinton, one division a few miles beyond Mississippi Springs following Sherman's line, and a third to Raymond."[10]

Grant felt that dividing McClernand's troops in this way provided several advantages at the same time. The division at Clinton was in good position to reinforce McPherson and the division beyond Mississippi Springs could reinforce Sherman if they were needed. The troops at Raymond were close enough to support either of the two advancing columns. In addition, A. J. Smith's and Blair's divisions that were escorting the supply wagons from Grand Gulf were now only about a day's march from Jackson, which also meant they were one day closer to Vicksburg. As Grant later put it, "the most important consideration in my mind was to have a force confronting Pemberton if he should come out to attack my rear."[11]

The weather was miserable for marching with heavy rain falling most of the night of the 13th that turned the roads into muddy trails. But McPherson kept his men moving through the night. In his diary, Owen Johnston Hopkins of the 42nd Ohio wrote, "Last night's rest not very comfortable. It rained until Midnight, when we were ordered to roll up our Blankets for marching immediately. Of course this was no welcome order, But we might as well be marching as Sleeping in the rain (for we had seen no tents since leaving Carthage)." The troops made good time despite the weather, and during the morning of May 14 two columns of Federal troops were converging on Jackson from different directions.[12]

Back in Jackson the defenders had made a very basic and a very bad mistake. General Gregg had sent out patrols that discovered Sherman's skirmishers as they were moving northeast. Since the idea of making an attack with two forces converging from different directions was exceptionally difficult to coordinate, Gregg dismissed that possibility and assumed the skirmishers were merely a screen to protect troops moving to join McPherson's force that was known to be at Clinton. When Johnston arrived he was only informed of the Union troops advancing from Clinton, which is where the Confederates placed most of their forces to defend the Clinton-Jackson road. Sherman's troops approaching from Mississippi Springs were able to close in on Jackson with little opposition.[13]

Convinced that at least four Federal divisions were approaching Jackson, and well aware that Grant had several more divisions behind them, Joe Johnston decided that the city could not be successfully defended and decided to save as much of his little army as possible. By 3 a.m. on May 14, orders went out to begin evacuating the city. Gregg was put in charge of fighting a delaying action, and Brigadier General John Adams was to use the time bought by Gregg to remove any useful military material east to Canton. About nine hundred men commanded by Colonel P. H. Colquitt took up position about three miles out of town to block the road from Clinton with Brigadier General William H. T. Walker's command stationed behind them for support. Another brigade commanded by Colonel Robert Farquharson was ordered to march out a little over two miles on the Clinton road, then move to the right to defend against an attack from that direction. Adding to the problems facing the defenders, Sherman's force was finally detected and a small force of mounted infantry, sharpshooters and a battery of artillery was sent out about two miles on the road from Mississippi Springs to delay him as best they could.[14]

McPherson and Sherman contacted each other during the night and tried to time their advance to arrive outside Jackson as near simultaneously as possible. As McPherson's corps approached the city, General Crocker's division was in the lead with Colonel Samuel A. Holmes' brigade out in front. About 9 a.m. Federal skirmishers engaged the Confederate picket line and quickly forced them back to the main body of defenders. Colonel Colquitt had taken up a good position on some high ground outside the main defenses, and as Holmes' men approached and moved into line, the Confederate artillery began firing. Federal guns were quickly brought up and a heavy artillery duel developed while General Crocker formed the rest of his division into line of battle.[15]

Now that they had found the enemy, General McPherson ordered General Logan to bring his division up as quickly as possible to join the attack on the enemy lines. It took McPherson some time to form his troops for the assault, and just before the men were to advance, a violent rainstorm hit the area. Unable to see any distance in the downpour and concerned that the rain could make the fragile musket cartridges useless, McPherson decided to wait until the weather moderated before launching his assault.[16]

A few miles south of McPherson's position, Sherman's Fifteenth Corps was moving steadily up from Mississippi Springs accompanied by General Grant. The 5th Minnesota, from Tuttle's division, was in the lead, and it had the occasional brief fight with Confederate patrols as they moved through the difficult terrain and heavily wooded areas. As they drew nearer to Jackson they could hear the booming of the big guns firing to the north. About two miles outside Jackson the lead troops ran into an enemy force commanded by Colonel Alfred P. Thompson in position behind a creek that ran across the road. Due to the heavy rains the creek was unfordable, and the Confederates had control of the only bridge in the vicinity.[17]

As the Federal vanguard approached the bridge, Thompson's artillery began firing on it. Tuttle quickly brought up his own artillery and began forming his division for an assault with Brigadier General Joseph A. Mower's brigade on the left and Colonel C. L. Matthies' brigade on the right. There was no need for an infantry attack, however, because after being pounded by the superior Federal artillery the defenders were soon forced back from the creek to a patch of woods in front of the prepared trenches protecting the approaches to Jackson.[18]

With just one bridge being the only way over the swollen creek, it took some time for Tuttle's division to cross over and form up to continue the advance. Seeing how outnumbered they were, the defenders wisely fell back through the woods into Jackson's main fortifications. When the pursuing Federals emerged from the other side of the woods they ran into heavy artillery fire from the Confederate fortifications. Tuttle's advance ground to a halt. With his attack stalled, Sherman sent the 95th Ohio, commanded by Colonel William L. McMillen, to the right to see if there was any way around the defenses.[19]

The Ohio regiment moved through the woods on the left of the defenses until they came to the tracks of the New Orleans, Jackson & Great Northern Railroad and found the nearby fortifications empty. Here they learned that most of the Confederates had left the fortifications and were pulling back through the city, leaving only a small rear guard to keep up the artillery fire and hold the Federals back as long as possible. When General Steele's division arrived at the front, Sherman had sent them over to the right to take advantage of any opening found by the 95th Ohio. With Steele's troops in support, McMillen led his regiment through some of Jackson's suburbs and around behind the still firing Confederate artillery that was holding up Sherman's main body on the Raymond road. In a surprise attack from the undefended rear of the works, McMillen's troops captured ten guns and over fifty prisoners. When McMillen began his assault Tuttle sent his men forward and the nearly empty fortifications were easily occupied. It was now after 5 p.m. and with the enemy works in his hands, Sherman decided to halt his men for a well-deserved rest.[20]

Back on the road from Clinton, McPherson's men were having a much more difficult time. With the rain subsiding and the newly arrived men from Logan's division in support, McPherson ordered Crocker to advance against the Confederate lines about 11 a.m. Crocker's men advanced with little difficulty until coming to a ravine about five hundred yards from the enemy position, where they briefly halted to regroup. Realizing that he was facing a much smaller force than his own, General Crocker gave the order to attack. Colonel John Sanborn, commanding the First Brigade, reported that he received the order to "fix bayonets and charge through the ravine and all the way to the batteries, if possible" from General Crocker. The men in blue rose up and cheered as they ran toward the enemy sweeping them from their advance position. After another brief pause Cocker's men continued their gallant assault despite heavy artillery and musket fire. At the main defensive lines there was savage fighting for control of the position. Major Francis C. Deimling of the 10th Missouri reported that the fighting with the 24th South Carolina was especially violent, with both sides resorting to the bayonet, and his regiment "suffering severely from the streams of fire which issued from behind every object which could furnish a protection to the enemy." The weight of the Federal attack was too much for the shorthanded Confederates, however, and they were slowly forced back until Colquitt's men retired to Jackson's main fortifications. Realizing that it was futile to continue to resist against the overwhelming Federal numbers, General Walker also fell back inside the city's main works. Colonel Farquharson, who was far out on the right, decided he could not reach the city and took his men north on the road to Canton.[21]

After taking possession of the Confederate position along the road, McPherson had his troops halt to rest and regroup before taking on the final defenses of Jackson. After a short rest Crocker's men again moved forward in the face of artillery fire from the fortifications. Patrols were sent out to see how strong the defenses were, and it was soon discovered that the works were empty. General Gregg had received word from General John Adams, who was in charge of the evacuation, that the last of the army's supply trains had left Jackson. With this accomplished, Gregg's responsibility was to save as many of his men as possible and fall back on the road to Canton, protecting the rear of the wagon trains. Around 3 p.m. McPherson learned the Confederates had abandoned their defenses and ordered Crocker to enter and occupy the city, sending Brigadier General John D. Stevenson's brigade of Logan's division to pursue the fleeing enemy. The cost to Grant's army to capture the capital of Mississippi was relatively light, about three hundred total casualties, while Gregg lost a little over two hundred men.[22]

When General Grant entered the city that afternoon he took a room at what appeared to be the best hotel in town, supposedly the same room that General Johnston had the day before. During a meeting between Grant, Sherman and McPherson, it was learned that one of McPherson's men had found a copy of a dispatch sent by Johnston to Pemberton telling him that both forces were to unite their commands along the railroad west of Clinton. It was imperative to keep Johnston and Pemberton apart so Grant immediately ordered McPherson to turn his corps around and head back toward Clinton. Grant wrote orders to McClernand explaining that, "It is evidently the design of the enemy to get north of us and cross the Black river and beat us into Vicksburg. We must not allow them to do this. Turn all your forces toward Bolton station and make all dispatch in getting there." With most of two corps concentrated west of Clinton, there were enough Federal troops in position to confront Pemberton, if he moved east.[23]

On the May 15, Grant updated Halleck on the situation, "This place fell into our hands yesterday, after a fight of about three hours.... The enemy retreated north, evidently with the design of joining the Vicksburg forces. I am concentrating my forces at Bolton, to cut them off, if possible." Also on May 15, Sherman's troops, who had been assigned the duty of destroying any military property in Jackson, began their work. Generals Tuttle and Steele basically divided the city between themselves, and their men enthusiastically went to work. Miles of track were pulled up and the rails heated over roaring fires made from the wooden ties until the center glowed red. The heat would warp the rails to such an extent that they could not be used again without being rolled out in a mill. The railroad bridge over the Pearl River and another bridge were burned.[24]

Inside the city, a textile factory, arsenal, and iron foundry were destroyed along with a multitude of workshops. The textile factory provided an interesting situation that Grant wrote about in his *Memoirs*. He and Sherman visited this factory, which had not shut down even during the battle outside the city. The workers, mostly young women, were turning out material for tents with "C.S.A." woven into the material, continuing to work even while the generals were watching. Grant remembered, "Finally I told Sherman 'I thought they had done work enough.' The operatives were told they could leave and take with them what cloth they could carry." The factory and an immense stock of cotton were soon blazing. Years later, when Grant was president, the owner of the factory visited him in Washington claiming that the factory had been private property. He asked Grant for "a statement of the fact that his property had been destroyed by National troops, so that he might use it with Congress where he was pressing, or proposed to press, his claim." Grant declined.[25]

General Mower's brigade had been assigned to keep order in the city but was quickly overwhelmed by their comrades and hundreds of civilians who decided to take what they could get wherever they found it. Looting and destruction of private property became a serious problem, and quite a few civilian buildings, including a church and a hotel, were burned, some accidently, some not. Despite his reputation as an advocate of total war, General Sherman tried to halt the looting and destruction of private property. He wrote to Mower, "This, if true, is wrong. Only such articles should be taken as are necessary to the subsistence of troops, and the private rights of citizens should be respected. The feeling of pillage and booty will injure the morals of the troops, and bring disgrace on our cause."[26]

Despite being deep in enemy territory with no supply line, this was a good time for Ulysses Grant. The gamble he took by breaking contact with Grand Gulf and taking the army east had worked out just fine so far. The troops were in good spirits and eager to move forward toward the next target, Vicksburg itself, and important news had arrived from Washington. The conflict with McClernand had never really been settled, it had just been pushed aside temporarily. Now Grant received word from Secretary Stanton through Dana: "General Grant has full and absolute authority to enforce his own commands, and to remove any person who, by ignorance, inaction, or any cause, interferes with or delays his operations. He has the full confidence of the Government, is expected to enforce his authority, and will be firmly and heartily supported; but he will be responsible for any failure to exert his powers."[27]

Unfortunately for the Confederacy, General Pemberton enjoyed no such support from his superiors; in fact he was trying to deal with totally opposite instructions from President Davis and General Johnston. Davis was insisting that Vicksburg was too important to the Confederacy and must be held at all costs, and he did not want the city put at risk by Pemberton accepting battle too far away from the city. General Johnston, on the other hand, believed the only way to really protect the city was to combine Pemberton's forces with his and defeat Grant in the field, thus eliminating the threat to Vicksburg. Pemberton wanted to compromise by taking a strong defensive position along the Big Black and let Grant smash his army in futile attacks. If Pemberton was able to implement this strategy, with no base of supplies and deep in enemy territory, the Federal survivors would be lucky to escape back to the Mississippi River for evacuation and the threat to Vicksburg would be eliminated.[28]

Pemberton received a dispatch from Johnston back on May 14 requesting that he bring his force east to attack the Federal army from the rear. A little over twenty thousand Confederate soldiers marched through rain and mud and crossed over the Big Black during the night of the fifteenth. Early on May 16, Pemberton received word from Johnston that Jackson had been abandoned and that Pemberton should bring his army north of the railroad to unite with Johnston's forces. Orders had already gone out to change the direction of the march when sporadic firing broke out at the front of the column. The firing quickly increased and Pemberton's troops began to form their lines for battle.[29]

On May 15, Grant had two Federal corps converging between Clinton and Edwards Station. General McClernand's corps was still somewhat scattered and were marching on three separate roads with Hovey moving west on the northernmost direct road to Vicksburg, Osterhaus in the center and A. J. Smith to the south. General McPherson's troops were march-

Confederate General John C. Pemberton—although he was following orders, many in the South never forgave him for losing Vicksburg (Library of Congress).

ing west from Clinton coming up to support Hovey as quickly as possible but ran into delays because of supply trains occupying the roads. Early on the morning of the 16th, Grant learned of Pemberton's position and the approximate size of the Confederate force and immediately sent out orders to concentrate the entire army. At 5:30 a.m. Grant sent a dispatch to Sherman, who was still in Jackson, "to move with all possible speed until he came up with the main force near Bolton.... A dispatch was sent to Blair at the same time to push forward his division in the direction of Edwards Station with all possible dispatch." General Smith's skirmishers ran into the Confederate pickets first with Hovey and Osterhaus encountering the enemy shortly afterward near a modest rise in the ground called Champion's Hill. By the time Grant arrived at the front, the skirmishing had grown heavy, with Hovey's troops becoming engaged to the extent that the fighting "amounted almost to a battle."[30]

Chapter 11

Champion's Hill

When it was discovered that Federal troops were rapidly approaching from multiple routes, General Pemberton canceled the movement north and as quickly as possible set up defensive positions. As it happened Pemberton's forces were already at one of the best defensive positions in the area, a series of hills with the highest being Champion's Hill. About sixty to eighty feet above the countryside, the hill commanded the surrounding terrain. The top of the hill was relatively cleared, which provided an excellent view in all directions. The east side was covered with dense forests and cut up with ravines while the western slope was smoother with fewer natural obstructions. The Confederate position ran from the north end of the hill, where it blocked the road from Clinton, southward across the middle road from Raymond. Baker's Creek ran across the northern end of the position around behind the hills, then mostly south, where it flowed into Fourteen Mile Creek.[1]

The Confederate forces were spread out in a line over three miles long. General Carter Stevenson's division defended the left end of the line on Champion's Hill covering the road from Clinton. In the center was General Bowen, who was stationed on the eastern slopes of the hills, and on the right was General Loring where terrain was more gentle and open and the middle road from Raymond came in on his left.[2]

As the Federal army approached they were spread out on several roads. General Hovey came up to the Confederate position on the northern end where it faced east. Behind Hovey on the same road, General Logan's division was hurrying forward with Crocker behind him. When Logan came up he moved to the right, coming in on the northern facing end of the enemy lines with Crocker supporting Hovey. Advancing west on the middle road from Raymond, the divisions of Osterhaus and Carr moved forward and centered their lines along the road and south of the Champion's Hill defenses. The divisions of A. J. Smith and Blair came forward on the Raymond road and formed up facing the far right of the Confederate lines opposite Loring.[3]

General Hovey's troops were the first to make serious contact with the Confederates. Hovey had been a lawyer in Indiana before the war who took his military duties very seriously and had developed into a good battlefield leader. Pushing his men forward, Hovey sent skirmishers ahead as he formed his division in line. The firing between the advanced parties gradually increased as more and more Federal troops came up. By about 10:30 a.m. Logan's men had reached a position on the right of Hovey, who ordered his men to advance, and as he reported, "In a few minutes the fire opened briskly along the whole line, from my extreme left to the right of the forces engaged under Major-General McPherson, and at 11 o'clock the battle opened hotly all along the line." Hovey's men continued to press forward against heavy enemy fire for about an hour.[4]

Up on the hillside Confederate General Carter Stevenson realized he was in trouble even before the battle began. Stevenson's division was defending the far left or northern end of the Confederate line and was charged with protecting the road from Clinton and preventing the Federal forces from coming around the left flank. General Stephen D. Lee's brigade was on the far left facing mostly north, with Brigadier General Alfred Cumming's brigade to Lee's right and Brigadier General Seth M. Barton's Georgia brigade on the right of Lee's brigade. The Confederate line was in the shape of the number seven with Stevenson across the top and Bowen and Loring down the vertical part. As John Logan's division arrived on the scene and the Union line stretched westward, it was clear that the Confederate position was in danger of being flanked and cut off from Vicksburg. Stevenson had to order Barton to leave his position on the right and move over to extend the line to the left. With Barton's men gone, Cumming was now the right end of Stevenson's line and his position was at the turn of the line where it headed south. It was against this angle defended by Cumming that Hovey's troops were advancing facing Stevenson's right and center. As Logan came up, his men were facing mostly south against Barton and Lee.[5]

Colonel James R. Slack, one of General Hovey's brigade commanders, occupied the right of Hovey's line and reported that as the men moved forward, "the thick growth of underbrush and vines, ravines and hills made it very difficult to advance, but it was accomplished with little disorder, until we reached the crest of the hill." Here Slack's men ran into the Confederate defenders under the cover of woods. Hovey's other brigade commander, Brigadier General George F. McGinnis, reported that after advancing about five hundred yards his men ran into heavy artillery fire and were forced to briefly take cover before the advance continued. About seventy-five yards from the Confederate battery another hail of grape and canister came at the attacking men, forcing them to lie down. This time, however, as soon as the storm of lead passed over them, the order was given to charge. General McGinnis reported that his "whole line moved forward as one man, and so suddenly and apparently so unexpected to the rebels was the movement, that, after a desperate conflict of five minutes, in which bayonets and butts of muskets were freely used, the battery of four guns was in our possession."[6]

One of the soldiers who made this charge, Thomas Durham of the 11th Indiana, remembered that although he had heard stories about hand-to-hand fighting, "this was the only real hand-to-hand battle I saw during the war. We were stabbing with bayonets, clubbing with guns, officers shooting with revolvers and slashing and thrusting with swords." On Colonel Slack's front the 24th Iowa valiantly charged a battery of five guns "driving the enemy away, killing gunners and horses, and capturing several prisoners." All told Hovey's division advanced about six hundred yards as they "gallantly drove the enemy before them, capturing 11 guns and over 300 prisoners."[7]

While Hovey's men were pushing the Confederates on his front, over on the right of the Federal lines, General Logan ran into a more obstinate defense. On the far right of the Federal line Brigadier General John D. Stevenson's brigade hit the Confederate defenders; the fighting went back and forth with each side giving as good as they got. The terrain here was broken and covered with woods, and General Barton reported that by the time his men arrived on the left of the Confederate line the fighting had already begun, "the enemy having turned Lee's left flank, were already in the timber, pressing vigorously forward." Barton launched his men against the advancing enemy and pushed them back until Federal reinforcements came up and stopped the Confederate advance.[8]

Now the weight of numbers was beginning to tell and John Stevenson's attack in combination with Hovey's advance broke the Confederate line. General Barton reported that "the troops on the right now gave way, and my right flank was soon turned and overwhelmed. The left was in like manner enveloped and a heavy fire poured in from the rear.... I was compelled to fall back." Barton's brigade was close to being surrounded and he had to act quickly. As he began to pull back, Barton admitted in his report that "this movement was necessarily accompanied with some confusion." One of the attacking soldiers, E. Z. Hays of the 32nd Ohio, recalled that as his regiment was moving forward they targeted a battery of artillery that turned out to be the 1st Mississippi Artillery located between Barton and Lee. The infantry supporting these guns "seemed dazed by the boldness and intrepidity of the assault, and before they had time to recover their wits we were upon them, the battery they should have defended was in our hands ready to be turned upon them, and they realized that the time for resistance had passed." Hays paid compliment to the artillerymen, however, acknowledging that they "fought their guns to the last moment, most of them falling on the ground where their battery stood."[9]

By early afternoon it looked as if General Grant was on the verge of another victory. The left of the Confederate line had been smashed by Logan and Hovey. Several thousand Federal troops were approaching a position from which they could move south behind the Confederate lines and hit Bowen and Loring from the rear at the same time they were being attacked from the front by three divisions of McClernand's corps and Blair's division of Sherman's corps. The Confederates would soon be cut off from their avenue of retreat, and attacked in front and rear by overwhelming force, there could be only one result—the destruction of Pemberton's army.

General Pemberton had to act quickly if he were to save his army. Obviously the crucial area was the left and something had to be done to stem the Federal advance. Around 1 p.m. Pemberton sent orders for General Bowen to reinforce the left. Bowen sent Colonel Francis Cockrell's brigade over to the left and shortly after sent his other brigade commanded by General Martin Green. As soon as Cockrell's troops arrived at their assigned position, they immediately ran into heavy fighting. Cockrell found that the defenders he was supposed to link with on his right "had almost wholly disappeared." Federal troops were already occupying the ground that Cockrell was supposed to defend and "were firing a most destructive enfilading fire into the brigade," pushing back the right of his force. In an extraordinary effort, Cockrell was able to form his brigade and moved forward against the still advancing enemy.[10]

Colonel Cockrell launched his men against Hovey's advancing troops and "in the most gallant, dashing, fearless manner, officers and men with loud cheers threw themselves forward at a run against the enemy's hitherto victorious lines." On Bowen's left, General Lee was able to pull together stragglers and troops from his second line and advanced against Logan's left. Brigadier General McGinnis reported, "At this point occurred one of the most obstinate and murderous conflicts of the war." Each side took turns in pushing the other back and forth over the same ground, but eventually Bowen's tough veterans forced Hovey's troops back over most of the ground they had taken earlier.[11]

General McGinnis informed General Hovey of the situation and requested help, but the entire division, including reserves, had already been committed and there were no men left to send. Hovey had to ask General Grant to send reinforcements from other divisions. Fortunately, another of McPherson's divisions commanded by General Crocker was just now arriving on the scene between Logan and Hovey. Grant ordered Crocker to send help to Hovey's hard pressed men who, as Hovey recorded, "in the mean time had been compelled to yield ground before overwhelming numbers. Slowly and stubbornly they fell back, contesting with death every inch of the field they had won."[12]

General McGinnis reported that his exhausted men were finally forced back "after having been engaged in continual conflict for nearly three hours." Even after emptying the ammunition boxes of the dead and wounded, many Union soldiers were out or nearly out of ammunition and could not stand against the ferocious Confederate attack. McGinnis' men fell back "not in disorder and confusion, but in good order, step by step, contesting every inch of ground." As they were approaching the area where the enemy artillery had been captured during the morning assault, reinforcements from General Crocker's division began joining the fight. Colonel George Boomer's 3rd Brigade arrived just in time to prevent Hovey's line from breaking. Aaron Dunbar of the 93rd Illinois remembered that "in line of battle, still at double-quick time, down the slope of the hill, the brigade rushed into the thickest of the fight."[13]

One of Boomer's men, John Quincy Adams Campbell of the 5th Iowa, later wrote that as they reached the top of a ridge, "Hovey's troops were breaking back through our ranks and the rebel bullets were whizzing by us." The Iowans "charged with a yell ... and chased the rebels from their position on one of the side ridges." Another member of the 5th Iowa, S.H.M. Byers, would recall that "we were met in a minute by a storm of bullets from the wood, but the lines in blue kept steadily on." Pushing forward through heavy fire, the 5th Iowa came up against a solid line of Confederates. Both lines held their ground "and for over an hour we loaded our guns and killed each other as fast as we could. The firing and the noise were simply appalling."[14]

Coming up close behind Boomer's brigade were troops from Crocker's Second Brigade commanded by Colonel Samuel Holmes, who joined the fighting with as much zeal as their comrades. But even these reinforcements did not immediately turn the tide. Aaron Dunbar later wrote that the "battle was a continuous flame of fire from thousands of muskets" as both sides were locked in a death grip of charges and counter-charges. General Hovey admitted that he "never saw fighting like this," and later wrote in his report, "I cannot think of this bloody hill without sadness and pride. Sadness for the great loss of my true and gallant men; pride for the heroic bravery they displayed." Fighting just as hard as their opponents, Bowen's Confederates stubbornly held their ground against these multiple assaults until the weight of numbers and the relatively fresh troops from Crocker's division began to be felt.[15]

By late afternoon Union officers had been able to concentrate several batteries of artillery along the right and center of the Federal lines, and Hovey reported that "through the rebel ranks these batteries hurled an incessant shower of shot and shell, entirely enfilading the rebel columns." G. B. McDonald of the 30th Illinois later wrote that the "artillery opened on the Johny's and for about thirty minutes, the earth trembled and the smoke rolled up as from a prairie fire." Finally, around 3 p.m. the combination of this heavy artillery fire and the fierce attacks from the Union infantry began to take its toll. The Confederates were slowly forced back over the bloody ground once again, this time for good.[16]

While Hovey and Crocker were engaged in desperate fighting in what could be called the center, Union forces were also advancing on the right and left. On the far right of the Federal line, John Stevenson's brigade of Logan's division had swung well around the left of the Confederate defenses, caving in that portion of their line, and had taken control of the road from Jackson west of Champion's Hill. This effectively gave them control of the northern crossing of Bakers Creek and cut off the direct line of retreat to Vicksburg. Unfortunately, neither Logan nor General Grant realized this and failed to take advantage of this splendid opportunity.[17]

Over on the Union left, McClernand's troops finally began to arrive on the battle line. Grant had sent several messages to McClernand to hurry his forces forward, but it was not until late afternoon that General Osterhaus' division was close enough to threaten the right side of Bowen's line. McClernand had run into a small but well placed force that blocked his path, but instead of moving to the right to close up with the rest of the army, he sent orders to Hovey, who was heavily engaged, to close up with McClernand's right. Grant learned of this and quickly canceled McClernand's order. Isacc Elliott, of the 33rd Illinois, did not understand why his division, commanded by General Carr, and the rest of the corps did not advance to the sound of the raging battle: "For four hours we stood there listening, waiting and wondering why we were not put into the fight. Fifteen minutes would have put us into the battle any time that day." This delay, coupled with the missed opportunity to cut off Pemberton's line of retreat, caused Grant to later admit his frustration in achieving anything less than the total destruction of the enemy: "Had McClernand come up with reasonable promptness, or had I known the ground as I did afterwards, I cannot see how Pemberton could have escaped with any organized force."[18]

Just as Osterhaus was moving forward toward Bowen's right, General Loring's Confederates were moving north to confront this new threat. Pemberton had issued orders for Loring to slide to his left hours earlier, but he delayed the move because of McClernand's approaching troops, who didn't show up until it was too late to have much influence on the battle. Loring left one brigade under Brigadier General Lloyd Tilghman behind to cover the road from Raymond and moved the rest of his division up to the middle road, where he was able to block Osterhaus from attacking Bowen's right flank.[19]

Union General Peter J. Osterhaus became a corps commander during Sherman's March to the Sea in the fall of 1864 (Library of Congress).

General Loring's move north made little difference in the outcome of the battle since the Confederate line was already collapsing on all fronts. On the far left Logan's forces were now advancing behind Lee and Bowen's lines, in the center Hovey and Crocker were steadily pushing the defenders back, and with two of McClernand's divisions moving up to engage the Confederate right, the outcome of the battle was obvious. Pemberton finally ordered what was left of his army to fall back on Vicksburg, reporting, "Finding that the enemy's vastly superior numbers were pressing all my forces engaged steadily back into old fields, where all advantages of position would be in his favor, I felt it to be too late to save the day."[20]

With the route along the Jackson road cut off by Union troops commanded by General John Stevenson, Confederate Generals

Bowen and Carter Stevenson had to move their men to the southwest to get over Bakers Creek using the Raymond Road crossing. General Loring's division was ordered to stay east of the creek and cover the withdrawal until the rest of the army was able to get away. General Tilghman's brigade formed the rear guard to prevent any Federal forces from marching down the Raymond Road and cutting off the Confederates' only escape route. It was during this final action of the day that Tilghman was killed by a Federal artillery shell.[21]

Most of Pemberton's men made good their escape during the evening, but when Loring tried to cross the creek to follow the main body of the Confederate army, he learned that Federal troops, commanded by General Eugene Carr, had already moved over to the west side of Bakers Creek and were heading south to cut off the escape route. Loring believed it was already too late to head west, so he decided to march his troops south along the east side of the creek to escape capture. As it turned out, Loring never did rejoin the main army. He marched south and east for a few days, then headed back north, where he eventually joined up with Joseph Johnston's forces.[22]

The battle at Champion's Hill, or Bakers Creek as the Confederates called it, was the decisive battle of the campaign so far. Pemberton's army was shattered by the heavy losses and the string of defeats they had suffered. The victory gave Grant a clear path to Vicksburg with only the Big Black River between him and the prize. But the victory had been costly. Hovey lost nearly a third of his division and the total Federal casualties were a little over 2,400 men. In his report, Hovey wrote, "It was, after the conflict, literally the hill of death; men, horses, cannon, and the debris of an army lay scattered in wild confusion." Confederate losses are more difficult to arrive at, but between reported casualties and conservative estimates, Pemberton's total loss could be put at close to 3,800 men. That evening as the beaten Confederates streamed toward Vicksburg, Grant ordered Generals Carr and Osterhaus to continue the pursuit to the Big Black and sent orders for Sherman to bring his corps west as quickly as possible. The race to Vicksburg was on.[23]

Chapter 12

Closing In on Vicksburg

John Pemberton had a decision to make. In the aftermath of the defeat at Champion's Hill, his Confederate troops fell back to the Big Black River, about ten miles east of Vicksburg. Pemberton could retire back to Vicksburg and occupy the extensive fortifications around the city where his men would be relatively safe and avoid the possibility that his army might be destroyed in a battle in the open field. The reality was, however, that this choice provided a false sense of security, with the most likely result of a siege being the loss of both the city and the army. The other option for Pemberton was to move his army north behind the Big Black and try to join forces with Joseph Johnston. This would obviously give Vicksburg to Grant, but at least the majority of the Confederate army would be saved to fight another day. Even Grant thought Pemberton should abandon Vicksburg to save his army, writing later, "It would have been his proper move, however, and the one Johnston would have made had he been in Pemberton's place." Whatever Pemberton decided, one thing was clear, Grant would eventually get Vicksburg, because as he noted, "We were now assured of our position between Johnston and Pemberton, without a possibility of a junction of their forces."[1]

Although he had just won the biggest battle of the campaign to date, General Grant had his own problems to deal with. In addition to the actual fighting still to take place, there was a growing concern about supplies. The route through Grand Gulf had been working well up to now, but such a long supply line could not be made secure for any extended period of time. Grant must get his troops across the Big Black and make contact with the Yazoo River north of Vicksburg so that the army could be supplied from the Mississippi. The last thing Grant wanted was to be forced to halt his army before reaching a place where he could make a connection with the river. Despite all the success the Union forces had enjoyed up to this point, with Pemberton's army in front and the very real possibility that Joe Johnston's force might be advancing on their rear, this campaign could still end in disaster.

As soon as it was physically possible after the fighting at Champion's Hill ended, Grant had his army on the move pursuing the defeated Confederates. After resting and reorganizing briefly during the middle of the night, the men began the chase again about 3:30 a.m. on May 17. Leading the pursuit was Carr's division followed by Osterhaus, both from McClernand's corps, with McPherson's corps in support. The Confederate rear guard, comprised of three brigades commanded by General John Bowen, was waiting along the Big Black River, and they had chosen their position well. On the eastern side of the Big Black there were relatively clear fields several hundred yards wide with a water and mud filled bayou between the solid land and the river. The Confederates had constructed rifle-pits and fortifications using cotton bales from a nearby plantation. Due to the winding course of the river the defenses could not be flanked, and trees had been cut down to further inhibit passage through the bayou. Isacc Elliott, of the 33rd Illinois, wrote that while waiting to move forward, he could see in front of his regiment "an open cornfield a few hundred yards across, and just beyond that were the enemy in their trenches, which were protected by cotton bales; they were also protected by a deep bayou, which served as a moat." Any Federal assault would have to come right at the enemy works across open ground exposed to rifle and artillery fire, and as Albert Marshall another member of the 33rd Illinois later wrote, "The rebels doubtless thought that they could easily destroy all who attempted to approach, before their works could be reached."[2]

Despite the formidable appearance of the Confederate position, they were vastly outnumbered, morale was low, and they were exhausted after their recent defeat and an all-night retreat. Pemberton was taking a huge risk in trying to hold the east side of the river, but he was hoping to keep the bridges open long enough for General Loring's errant division to rejoin the rest of the army. The Confederate commander was unaware that Loring was not coming back. Grant's troops, on the other hand, triumphant in every engagement in the campaign, were anxious to come to grips with the enemy. Confident they were about to win another victory, the soldiers in blue needed no urging to move up quickly and form their lines for the assault. If they could capture the bridges over the Big Black intact, Grant's army could follow the Confederates right into Vicksburg before they could get set in their fortifications. Carr's division formed to the right with Brigadier General Michael K. Lawler's brigade on the end of the line, where there was some cover provided by a wooded area. Osterhaus' division formed to Carr's left and directly in front of the main portion of the Confederate works.[3]

During the afternoon both sides exchanged light artillery and rifle fire, which gradually increased as the Federal troops came up into position and during which time General Osterhaus was wounded. Late in the day General Lawler took his brigade around the far left of the Confederate line looking for a location that he might successfully attack. Mike Lawler was one of the more conspicuous officers in the army. He was a large man, so large in fact that he had to wear his swordbelt over the shoulder because it would not fit around his waist. Usually dressed in a checkered shirt, loose grey pants, and a worn and battered hat, Lawler was easily found on any battlefield. More important than his appearance was that Lawler was a fighter who could be counted on to do his duty and then some. As they moved up and came out from the protection of the woods to form their lines, Lawler's men became the prime target for much of the Confederate fire.[4]

As Lawler's men waited for orders, the Confederate fire was taking its toll and they had to do something other than just stand there. Lawler could wait no longer, so coatless, with his sword flashing in the air, Lawler led his brigade forward, the men cheering as they ran toward the enemy. General Lawler reported that during that incredible charge his men advanced "over the open field, 500 yards, under a wasting fire, and up to the edge of the bayou." Stopping just long enough to "pour into the enemy a deadly volley, they dashed forward through the bayou, filled with water, fallen timber, and brush, on to the rebel works with the shout of victors, driving the enemy in with confusion from their breastworks and rifle-pits." As Lawler's men went forward, Isacc Elliott saw that "officers and men went down; flags went down, but were snatched up and borne grandly forward; there was not a halt or a waver in the splendid brigade."[5]

Shortly after Lawler's men went forward, other units joined in the assault. Colonel W. K. Bailey of the 99th Illinois had enough of the enemy fire while his men were waiting for orders and yelled out, "Boys, it is getting too damned hot here. Let us go for the cussed rebels!" With a cheer the Federal line surged forward across the open ground, through the bayou and up to the Confederate works.[6]

The fight was over in a matter of minutes. With the memory of the rout at Champion's Hill still fresh, the tired and demoralized Confederates could not stand up to the frenzied Union charge. A few were able to swim to the safety of the west bank of the river or run across the railroad bridge, but most of the defenders were captured. Leading a column of troops toward the battlefield, Brigadier General Mortimer Leggett of McPherson's corps came upon Lawler riding down the road and asked, "Did you get any of them?" Lawler yelled back, "Whole acres of them, whole acres of them."[7]

Federal casualties totaled fewer than three hundred, exceptionally low considering the ground and the defenses they were up against. The Confederates lost over 1,700 men captured and 18 pieces of artillery, with Lawler's brigade taking the majority of the prisoners. He reported, "By our brigade were captured 1,460 small-arms ... 1,120 prisoners, and 4 stand of colors. It is, perhaps, worthy of remark that more men were captured by my brigade than I had men in the charge." That evening Grant made a point of riding over to Lawler's camp to personally commend him for the work he did that day. When the army's commanding general arrived, Lawler was casually sitting with a few of his men around a campfire waiting for their coffee to boil.[8]

An interesting side event occurred during the day. An officer from the staff of General Nathaniel Banks appeared and presented Grant with the letter Halleck had written on May 11 instructing him to suspend his campaign and return to Grand Gulf to join Banks in reducing Port Hudson, after which the combined armies would move north to attack Vicksburg. Washington had never approved Grant's plan to attack Jackson before moving on Vicksburg, but Grant was certainly not going to abandon his campaign at this point. He later recalled, "I told the officer that the order came too late, and that Halleck would not give it now if he knew our position." Banks' officer was trying to convince Grant to obey the order when Lawler began his attack on the right. Grant simply mounted his horse and rode off in the direction of the fighting and never saw the officer again.[9]

The Confederates on the west side of the river had burned the bridge before they pulled out, so there was no way for the Federals to cross that day. Grant later wrote about how important that one bridge was: "But for the successful and complete destruction of the bridge, I have but little doubt that we should have followed the enemy so closely as to prevent his occupying his defences around Vicksburg." Despite being routed from their position, the Confederate rear guard had done its job. Union troops immediately went to work building bridges and the next morning were crossing over the Big Black. Sherman's corps was moving north of the rest of the army toward Bridgeport, and during the night of May 17 and the next morning, his three divisions also crossed over the Big Black. Grant joined his old friend Sherman that night as the troops crossed the pontoon bridge. Many years later Sherman remembered, "After dark, the whole scene was lit up with fires of pitch-pine. General Grant joined me there, and we sat on a log, looking at the passage of the troops by the light of those fires; the bridge swayed to and fro under the passing feet, and made a fine war-picture." Grant's army now had clear roads to Vicksburg. On the seventeenth he wrote to Sherman, "If the information you gain after crossing warrants you in believing you can go immediately into the city, do so." With his army moving west in three columns and the enemy falling back as quickly as they could, Grant was confident that he would "either have Vicksburg or Haynes' Bluff to-morrow night." This confidence was based on Grant's belief that "the enemy have been so terribly beaten yesterday and to-day that I cannot believe that a stand will be made unless the troops are relying on Johnston's arriving with large re-enforcements."[10]

While Grant's army was pressing forward, the remnants of Pemberton's shattered force made their way into Vicksburg. The men that poured into the city that night looked more like a crowd of fugitives than an army. The appearance of the troops and the rumors of Yankees killing and destroying everything in sight sent many of the city's civilians into a panic. Confederate soldier John Guilford Earnest of the 60th Tennessee wrote in his diary for May 17 that after being forced back from the Big Black, "then commenced a pel mel retreat. We had a foot race to Vicksburg. I at length arrived at our old camp—completely broken down and nearly strangling for water."[11]

A civilian witness to the confusion and terror that filled Vicksburg was Dora Miller Richards, who recorded, "About three o'clock the rush began. I shall never forget that woful sight of a beaten, demoralized army that came rushing back,—humanity in the last throes of endurance." Unaccustomed to the horrors of war, Dora was among many of Vicksburg's civilians who were shocked by what they saw as the defeated troops dragged themselves into the city. "Wan, hollow-eyed, ragged, footsore, bloody, the men limped along unarmed, but followed by siege-guns, ambulances, gun-carriages, and wagons in aimless confusion."[12]

Another resident of Vicksburg, Mary Loughborough, also left a record of what she witnessed as the retreating troops came into the city: "Wagons came rattling down the street—going rapidly one way, and then returning, seemingly, without aim or purpose: now and then a worn and dusty soldier would be seen passing with his blanket and canteen; soon, straggler after straggler came by, then groups of soldiers worn and dusty with the long march." Soon the streets were full of dirty and exhausted men slowly shuffling along as if in a daze. Confused and afraid, Mary asked what had happened and the reply was, "We are whipped; and the Federals are after us."[13]

As usually happens after a defeat, the first soldiers to seek shelter were the worst of the army, deserters, cowards, and those who abandoned their comrades and ran for safety before the battle was decided. Of course, the impression they gave was one of defeat and ruin. As the survivors of fighting units arrived, they seemed stunned by what they had gone through and afraid of what might be coming, but the panic had abated. Units were reorganized, and as fear subsided most of the men regained their dignity and the mob became soldiers again. The massive fortifications to the east were manned and fresh units from north and south of the city began arriving to bolster the defenses. By nightfall some semblance of order had been restored and the fears that the Yankees would be marching into Vicksburg the next day diminished.

Still east of Vicksburg, the Federal army approached the city on a wide front with Sherman to the north heading for Haynes' Bluff, General McPherson in the center along the road from Jackson, and McClernand in the south. By the night of May 18, Sherman had taken possession of Walnut Hills, giving the army access to the Yazoo River, the same objective of his disastrous fight at Chickasaw Bayou five months earlier. Grant had accompanied Sherman as they came to the Walnut Hills and both men were able to look down on the Yazoo River and realize what they had finally achieved: high, dry ground north of Vicksburg. With access to the Mississippi there was no longer any doubt about obtaining sufficient supplies for the army. Sherman turned to his friend and candidly admitted, "Until this moment, I never thought your expedition a success. I never could see the end clearly, until now. But this is a campaign; this is a success, if we never take the town."[14]

Joseph Johnston knew just as well as Grant what the result would be once the Federal army gained access to the Yazoo River. On May 17 he wrote to Pemberton: "If Haynes' Bluff is untenable, Vicksburg is of no value, and cannot be held. If, therefore, you are invested in Vicksburg, you must ultimately surrender. Under such circumstances, instead of losing both troops and place, we must, if possible, save the troops. If it is not too late, evacuate Vicksburg and its dependencies, and march to the northeast." When Johnston wrote this, there was still a chance for Pemberton to escape and save the army, but when Sherman arrived on the bluff overlooking the Yazoo, the fate of Vicksburg and Pemberton's army was sealed.[15]

The only way for the Confederates to get out of Vicksburg now was to fight their way out, and considering the low morale and physical condition of the troops this seemed like the road to disaster. With two fresh divisions added to the men already in the strong fortifications, Pemberton began to feel more confident that he could save the city that was so important to the survival of the Confederacy. During a council of war his generals pointed out that even if the army were able to break out past Grant's troops, the cost would probably be so heavy that the army would become useless as a fighting force. Facing little real choice, Pemberton notified Johnston, "I have decided to hold Vicksburg as long as is possible, with the firm hope that the Government may yet be able to assist me in keeping this obstruction to the enemy's free navigation of the Mississippi River. I still conceive it to be the most important point in the Confederacy."[16]

Before the Federals were able to spread out around the outside of Vicksburg's fortifications, the Confederates tried to bring as much food and equipment as possible into the city in preparation for a siege. Brigadier General J. H. Forney reported that as his troops moved back into the city, he "directed them to drive inside of the fortification all the beef-cattle, hogs, and sheep that had been collected from the surrounding country, and squads of mounted men had previously been sent out for this purpose." All during the day and night soldiers filled whatever transportation they could find with chickens, hams, corn, rice, bacon, and anything else that might be of use. Long processions of wagons headed into the city, and to some residents it probably looked like there would be enough to eat for months. There was little worry about suffering through an extended siege because nearly everyone was sure the Yankees would soon be caught between Vicksburg's impregnable fortifications and Joe Johnston's army, and destroyed.[17]

Outside the city's fortifications, Grant's army was gradually filling in their lines around the city. The weather had been hot and many of the men were still far behind the front lines, overcome with fatigue and just trying to get a little rest wherever and whenever they could. Some tried to grab a brief nap in the shade of a tree but others were too exhausted to do more than just lie down by the side of the road. The Confederates had faced the same problems, but now they were within the safety of their fortifications and could rest and regroup.[18]

As the Federal army closed up to the fortifications around Vicksburg, the men saw for themselves the rough terrain and the massive works they would have to contend with. Even Grant had to admit that "the ground about Vicksburg is admirable for defence." The fortifications designed by Major Lockett were mostly situated on the crest of a ridge that began at the river north of the city and formed a semicircle about three miles out from the city and ended at the river to the south of Vicksburg. All along this line the ground was broken up by steep ravines, streams, and wooded areas. Two Federal engineers, Captains Frederick E. Prime and Cyrus B. Comstock, would later write a report detailing some of the obstacles the Union troops faced: "The sides of the smaller and newer ravines were often so steep that their ascent was difficult to a footman unless he aided himself with his hands." Most of the ground in and around the ravines were covered with woods, but "near the enemy's line the trees had been felled, forming in many places entanglements which under fire were absolutely impassable."[19]

The Confederate works were a mixture of large and small forts and rifle pits cleverly located to take advantage of the local terrain. All the main roads and the railroad line were protected by large earthen forts with smaller forts located at strategic sites all along the lines. Confederate artillery batteries were spread out at important points along the entire line to support the troops in the trenches. In front of the forts, deep ditches had been dug so that attacking troops would have a difficult climb just to reach the parapet. In addition, as much as practical the ground in front of the lines had been cleared of most anything that might provide shelter for advancing troops, giving the defenders clear fields of fire. To sum up what the Federals were facing, Captains Prime and Comstock concluded: "Vicksburg was, then, rather an intrenched camp than a fortified place, owing much of its strength to the difficult ground, obstructed by fallen trees in its front, which rendered rapidity of movement and *ensemble* in an assault impossible."[20]

General Pemberton had about 30,000 troops in his command, more than enough to effectively man the fortifications. General Carter Stevenson's division occupied the right of the Confederate lines north to the railroad. General Forney's division was stationed in the center and General Martin Smith's division manned the works on the left up to the river. A reserve force was made up of General Bowen's troops and Colonel Thomas Waul's Texas Legion. Although the Confederate troops were tired and discouraged when they reached Vicksburg, once they were safely behind the fortifications these veteran soldiers quickly recovered their fighting spirit.[21]

Outside the works, Grant and most of his commanders were confident that Vicksburg would soon be theirs. Grant believed that right now he had the upper hand, and if an attack were pressed the dispirited Confederates could be driven out of their trenches, but he had to act quickly. If the assault were postponed until all the Federal troops were up to the front the delay would give the enemy time to recover their morale. Grant knew full well how difficult it would be to assault fortifications manned by tough, veteran soldiers. He had to attack quickly and with as many men as were available. Besides, the men were ready. In just seventeen days Grant had brought his army nearly 200 miles through enemy territory had fought and won five battles, causing nearly twice as many enemy casualties as his army lost. These Federal soldiers had just completed one of the greatest campaigns of the war and now the prize was right in front of them. They had suffered through all the marching and fighting for this one objective, to possess Vicksburg. As he came up to Vicksburg's fortifications, Owen Hopkins wrote in his diary on May 18, "The sun was extremely hot and water scarce, But highly elated at our repeated Victories we marched on in good Spirits." The commander was ready, the army was ready, all that was needed was the order to attack.[22]

Chapter 13

Slaughter Outside the City

Throughout the early morning hours of May 19, Grant's troops continued to file into position around Vicksburg. Union doctor Charles B. Johnson later wrote, "As the Confederates had, so far, been defeated and had in the last engagement yielded what seemed a strong position with so little resistance, the opinion came to prevail throughout the Federal Army that Vicksburg would yield without further resistance." As Doctor Johnson noted, the men were anxious to put an end to the campaign, and, "Filled with this idea the Union forces confidently approached the out-works of Vicksburg on the morning of May 19."[1]

While the Union army was growing in strength and consolidating positions outside the fortifications, inside the city the situation brought about a much different attitude. General Pemberton wrote to President Jefferson Davis summarizing events since Champion's Hill, commenting that "the army was much demoralized; many regiments behaved badly." Pemberton's message ended with a dire prediction, "Our men have considerably recovered their morale, but unless a large force is sent at once to relieve it, Vicksburg must before long fall. I have used every effort to prevent this, but in vain."[2]

As the Federal troops approached Vicksburg they spread out in a semi-circle around the fortifications with Sherman's corps, consisting of the divisions of Steele, Blair and Tuttle, on the far right starting at Haynes' Bluff. McPherson's corps moved into the center, spreading out on both sides of the road from Jackson. He had divisions commanded by Logan, Crocker and Quinby under his command. On the left extending to the river below Vicksburg were the four divisions of McClernand's corps commanded by Carr, A. J. Smith, Osterhaus and Hovey.[3]

These Union troops were all veterans and confident in their abilities and in their commanders. And who could blame them? Since landing on the east side of the Mississippi less than three weeks earlier, they had seen nothing but success. In fight after fight the enemy had fled before them, and after the rout at Champion's Hill and the debacle at the Big Black the men in blue were confident they could beat the rebels anytime and anywhere. Of course the fortifications in their front were intimidating, but they were manned by men the Federals had beaten every time they met. There was no reason to suppose the next time would be any different.

The commander of the Federal army was just as confident as his men. Grant later wrote, "The enemy had been much demoralized by his defeats at Champion's Hill and the Big Black, and I believed he would not make much effort to hold Vicksburg." Grant also had to consider that the longer it took to capture the city, the greater was the chance that General Johnston could pull together enough men to mount a serious attack on the rear of his lines. And if Pemberton and Johnston were able to coordinate attacks on the same part of the Union line from opposite sides, there was the potential for a real disaster. Grant was not the kind of man to wait: "On the 19th there was constant skirmishing with the enemy while we were getting into better position.... Accordingly, at two o'clock I ordered an assault."[4]

While the commanders were making preparations for the assault, the men who were shortly going to be fighting for their lives had time to prepare themselves for the coming ordeal. No matter how much confidence they had in themselves and their officers, the works they were about to assault were the strongest they had ever seen, and these men were veterans who knew they were in for a tough time. John Bering of the 48th Ohio later wrote, "The news was received by the Regiment in a quiet and serious manner, and the suspense until 2 o'clock was somewhat like that of the culprit awaiting the hour of his execution." J. J. Kellogg, of the 113th Illinois, carefully crept over the hill in his front to take a look at the defenses his regiment was facing, and he did not like what he saw, "Three strong bastioned forts on the right, center and left on high grounds within a line of entrenchments and stockades confronted us. It required but a brief inspection to satisfy me that more than likely we wouldn't go into town that day."[5]

The attack began on schedule as the Federal troops went forward confident they would once again be victorious. This time, however, the Confederates didn't run but let loose a storm of bullets and shells as the Yankees approached. In some locations sheets of fire met the attackers and their lines melted away. William Wiley of the 77th Illinois wrote in his diary, "The ground over which we had to advance was very rough being a sucession of hills and hollows and when we would reach top of the hills or ridges we were exposed to a murderous fire from the rebel forts. When one part of our line was exposed the rebels would consentrate their fire on them from all directions." J. J. Kellogg remembered, "The leaden hail from the enemy was absolutely blinding. The very sticks and chips scattered over the ground were jumping under the hot shower of rebel bullets.... I can but wonder that any of us survived that charge."[6]

One of McClernand's brigade commanders, Brigadier General Albert L. Lee, reported that "as our line appeared on the brow of the hill and in full view of the enemy, he opened upon us a most murderous and raking fire from his many batteries on our front and flanks." It was the same all along the line, Grant's men advanced bravely and they were cut down by the defenders before most could even get close to the fortifications. The experience of William Wiley's regiment was typical: "Our men would charge forward on the run until we would reach the next hollow where we would reform our lines and advance again over the next ridge and at each advance the rebels fire became more deadly."[7]

The assault failed miserably, with many Union soldiers being trapped in the ravines or just lying flat trying to find some cover in the undergrowth. Unable to move forward or fall back because of the heavy fire from the defenders, they had to wait until dark before they could return to their lines. J. J. Kellogg was one of these soldiers, and he later wrote, "Such a long dreadful day it was without food or water, under the excessive heat of the sun, lying flat in that old gully, but hardly daring to move a limb or change our position for fear of attracting a rebel volley."[8]

The only area where the attack came even close to success was Sherman's command, and even there too few men were able to close with the enemy works. Sherman reported, "My troops reached the top of the parapet, but could not cross over. The rebel parapets were strongly manned, and the enemy fought hard and well. My loss was pretty heavy." Grant summed up the results of the attack in his report: "The Fifteenth Army Corps, from having arrived in front of the enemy's works in time on the 18th to get a good position, were enabled to make a vigorous assault. The Thirteenth and Seventeenth Army Corps succeeded no further than to gain advanced position covered from the fire of the enemy." The assault was not properly coordinated and too many units were not yet at full strength. Grant's impatience cost his army over nine hundred casualties.[9]

The total repulse of the attack on May 19 proved that the Confederates within Vicksburg's fortifications were not the beaten and discouraged mob that most of the Federal army believed them to be. The obvious next step was to settle down to a formal siege, which almost surely would be successful in time. May 20 and 21 were spent bringing up the remainder of the army and consolidating the Federal positions. After constantly marching and fighting for twenty days the troops received some much needed rest and provisions. Before committing to a siege, however, Grant had to consider many factors, among which were the urgings of many top officers to launch another attack. The attack on the nineteenth was not properly coordinated, only Sherman's corps was at full strength, and the artillery support had been inadequate. Grant also had to consider how a siege at Vicksburg would affect other Federal operations.

It was well known that Joseph Johnston was building an army to attack the Federal lines from the rear. A quick victory at Vicksburg would allow Grant to turn on Johnston, destroy his much smaller force and gain control of most of Northern Mississippi. Another reason to move quickly was a question of manpower. Putting Vicksburg under siege would require that Grant be reinforced by thousands of fresh troops, not only to man the siege lines but to have enough men to face Johnston if he advanced. Once Vicksburg was secured large numbers of men could be transferred to Tennessee to join the campaign against Braxton Bragg's Army of Tennessee and seize the strategically important town of Chattanooga. The fall of Vicksburg would almost certainly result in the capture of the only other major fortress on the Mississippi still in Confederate hands—Port Hudson, Louisiana. Opening the Mississippi was one of the primary objectives of the Union forces in the West and the military and political benefits would be enormous. Finally, although certainly not least in importance, were the soldiers themselves. Grant felt that "the first consideration of all was—the troops believed they could carry the works in their front, and would not have worked so patiently in the trenches if they had not been allowed to try." All things considered, the possibility of taking Vicksburg sooner rather than later was worth the risk. The decision was made and "on the 21st, orders were issued for a general assault on the whole line, to commence at 10 a.m. in the 22d."[10]

Even after the bloody repulse of the first assault, many of the Federal troops were still confident they could take the works in a coordinated all-out attack. R. L. Howard, of the 124th Illinois, was one man who believed there was still a chance of taking Vicksburg: "It could not be that the men whom we had just whipped so terribly, and who had strewn their retreat with the proofs of their demoralization, would make any stand." Still believing the Confederates were exhausted and demoralized, Howard and many of his comrades "doubted if they would fully man their lines, and every hour of the 20th and 21st we expected some new development, a conflict it might be for a little time, or some discovery of their weakness which we could take advantage of, that would end the campaign."[11]

There was, however, another side to the belief that one good attack could end the campaign. All through the Union army men spent at least some of the night before the attack to write what might be their last letters home to loved ones. Usually these letters were given to one of their comrades who would not take part in the assault. This man would keep the letters safe to make sure they were mailed if the author failed to return after the attack. Personal mementos, watches, rings and photos were also gathered up and held in safekeeping to be returned after the attack, or sent home if the owner failed to survive the day. The men knew they had a tough fight ahead and tried to prepare for any eventuality.

Early on the morning of May 22 preparations for the assault were in full swing. Ammunition was brought up and the men filled their cartridge boxes; canteens were filled and the surgeons got their tents set up and equipment ready to receive the wounded. The artillery began firing well before the attack began, but despite the heavy bombardment all that really occurred was to rearrange a lot of dirt; little real damage was done to the fortifications. One of McClernand's men, Isacc H. Elliott of the 33rd Illinois, remembered that as he stood in line waiting to advance, he looked down the line of his comrades and "saw that the faces of the men were pale, but determined; everyone knew what was coming, but there were no cases of sudden illness or important engagements to meet elsewhere." As the men waited, quietly talking among themselves, "some were exchanging last messages for home and giving directions for the disposal of their simple effects. Other attempted jokes that were received with a good deal of solemnity."[12]

Promptly at 10 a.m. all three Federal corps began the assault. Wilber F. Crummer, of the 45th Illinois remembered that when the attack began, "every piece of artillery was brought to bear on the works; sharpshooters at the same time began their part; nothing could be heard but the continual shrieking of shells, the booming of cannon and the sharp whiz of the minieball." With a line of skirmishers ahead of the main body, thousands of Union troops stepped out hoping that this would be the last battle of the campaign. For many a brave man it was.[13]

General Sherman was watching his men advance from an observation point less than two hundred yards from the enemy works and later wrote, "I could see every thing. The rebel line, concealed by the parapet, showed no sign of unusual activity, but as our troops came in fair view, the enemy rose behind their parapet and poured furious fire upon our lines." One of Sherman's men, Cloyd Bryner of the 47th Illinois, remembered that at first his regiment was at least partially sheltered by hills, but "then it came to the top of a ridge exposed to the full fire from the enemy's works. From every part of the line rose the Confederates in double rank and poured in a terrible fire; grape and canister from the enemy's guns swept the ridge so clean that no living thing could pass it."[14]

The men in the center of the Federal lines, where McPherson's corps was stationed, faced the same terrible fire as Sherman's men. John Quincy Adams Campbell, of the 5th Iowa, wrote in his diary, "No rebels were to be seen until our force had approached close up to the rebel works, when their breastworks and forts swarmed with butternuts who poured volley after volley into our advancing columns." Another of McPherson's men, R. L. Howard of the 124th Illinois, remembered that no matter how valiantly the men who made it to the parapets tried to gain the Confederate works, "it was of no use, they were too few, and the enemy's fire was too galling, concentrated as so much of it was on single points, reached by our enfeebled columns." All up and down the line about all the surviving Union troops could do was stay low in the ditches and wait.[15]

General McClernand's men ran into the same hailstorm of bullets as did the rest of the army. In his diary William Wiley wrote that they were "determined to enter Vicksburg or die in the attempt. When we reached the top of the ridge we encountered a terrible fire of shell and shot from the rebel forts which made sad morale in our ranks but we pressed steadily forward leaving a path strewn with our dead and wounded." Albert O. Marshall, of the 33rd Illinois, was in the ranks that day: "As the head of the column raised upon the brow of the hill and came in sight of the rebel line, the fearful storm, with all of its unbounded fury, burst upon our ranks. The first of the column was virtually swept away. Of all of Company E only one was left unharmed." All around Albert men were falling but they kept on going. "How a single man ever went through that leaden storm and lived I do not know.... On we went, unheeding those who fell. I do not suppose that there was a single one in the advance of that fierce charge who expected to pass through it in safety. I did not."[16]

Here and there the Union troops had some minor success but the price was too high for the results. As usual Mike Lawler's men were in the thick of it, as he reported, "Officers and men fell on every side; but, with a courage that could not be daunted, the Twenty-second and Twenty-first Iowa on the right, and the Eleventh Wisconsin and a portion of the Ninety-seventh Illinois on the left, moved upon the enemy's works." Braving the deadly fire, men from the Iowa regiments were able to capture and hold the outer ring of one of the forts after a brief but savage hand-to-hand fight. Captain Charles N. Lee, of the 22nd Iowa, reported that his men "went through the most galling fire of musketry, grape, and canister, until retarded by an almost impassable abatis. This obstacle overcome, they gained the top of the hill, gathered around, driving the enemy from the rifle-pits in front, and planting the Stars and Stripes on the ramparts." About fifty men from Lee's regiment were able to enter the fort and take fifteen prisoners until fire from rifle pits behind the fort drove them back, losing nearly half of the men who made the charge.[17]

By mid-day it was pretty obvious that the Federals were not going to be entering Vicksburg this day. Grant rode over to meet with Sherman, who later wrote, "I pointed out to him the rebel works, admitted that my assault had failed, and he said the result with McPherson and McClernand was about the same." While they were discussing the situation Grant received a message from McClernand saying "positively and unequivocally that he was in possession of and still held two of the enemy's forts; that the American flag then waved over them, and asking me to have Sherman and McPherson make a diversion in his favor."[18]

To say the least Grant was skeptical of McClernand's claim to have control of part of the Confederate works. Grant later wrote that during most of the morning he "occupied a position from which I believed I could see as well as he what took place in his front, and I did not see the success he reported." Sherman said that Grant simply stated to him, "I don't believe a word of it." But, as Sherman pointed out, this was an official message and could not be ignored. Also, there was always the chance that even if McClernand was exaggerating, just a small break in the enemy's lines might be exploited into something important. Grant decided to consult with McPherson and told Sherman to renew the attack if he did not receive different orders by 3 p.m.[19]

While on his way to McPherson's position Grant received another message from McClernand saying, "We have gained the enemy's intrenchments at several points, but are brought to a stand." Grant could not ignore multiple dispatches from a major general in command of an entire army corps. After consulting with McPherson, Grant sent Isaac Quinby's division to reinforce McClernand and decided that diversionary attacks by McPherson and Sherman on both ends of the line had to be made, and orders went out to renew the assault at three o'clock. Around 3:50 p.m. Grant received yet another message from McClernand stating that when the fresh troops arrived, "I will press the enemy with all possible speed, and doubt not I will force my way through. I have lost no ground. My men are in two of the enemy's forts, but they are commanded by rifle-pits in the rear."[20]

Once again the men bravely went forward, but the only results from the afternoon assault on Vicksburg's fortifications were hundreds more killed and wounded Union soldiers. After looking over the fortifications they were about to attack, one of General Quinby's men who just arrived in McClernand's lines, Aaron Dunbar of the 93rd Illinois, decided, "If a soldier might at any time, or at all, weigh his life, in the scales, against his honor, that was a time to determine which he would lose." But Dunbar and the rest of his regiment went forward with their comrades and ran into the same hail of lead that other troops had already faced. "The storm of bullets and shot and shell that was hurled against those lines was simply appalling. Increasing the speed every second, the command rushed across the ravine to the protection afforded by the ridge on the other side, and there halted." The brigade commander, Colonel George Boomer, was killed and when Colonel Holden Putnam, the new commander, called for the men to renew the advance Dunbar recalled, "The brigade rose up, but only to take one quick glance into the jaws of certain death. The sheet of flame, from thousands of muskets, that burst from those rifle pits in front, the thousands of bullets that came whistling over, and screaming shells and grape and canister from both forts, foretold nothing less than the complete annihilation of the entire command if it should pass beyond the protection of that ridge." Colonel Putnam reported back to division headquarters that his men would advance no farther without positive orders to do so. Putnam soon received orders to stay where he was until it was safe to withdraw.[21]

R. L. Howard witnessed a portion of the second attack from McPherson's lines and later wrote, "Clear up to the works our boys surged only to be mowed down by scores. They fired up the works, and tried to fire over, but it was in vain." Once again the assault was stopped at the base of the ridge and it was pretty much suicide for anyone to try to advance or fall back. A young private in the 83rd Ohio, Isaac Jackson, remembered, "It was the hottest place for men to be in that I ever seen." There was nothing for the Union soldiers to do but remain under what shelter they could find until darkness gave them enough cover to return to their own lines. Isaac Elliott later wrote that the men on both sides of the parapet would fire their guns by "holding them over their heads, depressing the muzzle and pulling the trigger with the thumb." Besides bullets flying through the air, Elliott described another danger facing the men along the parapets. "The enemy lighted shells and threw them over the parapet into the ditch, where they were snatched up and thrown back. It was a mere matter of chance on which side they would explode."[22]

General Carter Stevenson, who commanded the Confederate division opposite McClernand, gave an account that could probably be used to describe the fighting all along the line: "They were allowed to approach unmolested to within good musket range, when every available gun was opened upon them with grape and canister, and the men, rising in the trenches, poured into their ranks volley after volley with so deadly an effect that, leaving the ground literally covered in some places with their dead and wounded, they precipitately retreated."[23]

General Sherman candidly said that this second assault "was a repetition of the first, equally unsuccessful and bloody." To his wife Sherman wrote that on that bloody day "the heads of Columns are swept away as Chaff thrown from the hand on a windy day." Many of the common soldiers were angry that so many of their comrades' lives were seemingly thrown away on fruitless attacks. Owen Hopkins, of the 42nd Ohio, wrote in his diary, "It was not a charge; it was not a Battle, nor an assault; But a Slaughter of Human beings in cold blood. We done our best; we struggled manfully; we fought desperately; all would not do, we were repulsed and with fearful loss." The Union army's loss for the day was too high considering there were virtually no gains to speak of, with over three thousand Federal soldiers dead, wounded or missing. The defenders lost fewer than five hundred men.[24]

The results of this terrible day left a bad taste in the mouths of the Union commanders, especially the afternoon assaults that were launched only because of McClernand's insistence that he had broken the enemy line. One civilian witness was reporter Sylvanus Cadwallader, who was in a good position to view the battle on McClernand's front and clearly saw that only a few of McClernand's men ever reached or went into the main works, and those did not return. Cadwallader later reported, "I was questioned closely concerning it; and shall never forget the fearful burst of indignation and disgust which settled down on Grant's usually placid countenance, when he was convinced of McClernand's duplicity, and realized its cost in dead and wounded."[25]

In addition to the normal disdain that McClernand brought on himself by his attitude and frequent use of political influence, the circumstances of the second assault brought outright condemnation of his abilities by fellow high ranking officers, including both Sherman and McPherson. Grant, who never trusted McClernand, bitterly denounced him in a dispatch to Halleck on May 24, saying that McClernand's repeated requests for assistance "misled me as to the real state of the facts, and caused much of this loss. He is entirely unfit for the position of corps commander, both on the march and on the battlefield. Looking after his corps gives me more labor and infinitely more uneasiness than all the remainder of my department."[26]

It would be unfair, however, to lay all the blame for the failed attacks only on McClernand. Grant's attempt to take Vicksburg with one massive assault and quickly end the campaign could reasonably be considered a calculated risk that did not work. A major portion of the blame should be placed on the overconfidence of both the Union commanders and the troops themselves. They believed they were facing an already beaten foe that would not stand against a determined assault. In their final report, Engineer Captains Frederick Prime and Cyrus Comstock stated that the strength of the Confederates was underestimated and, echoing Grant's reasoning, believed that "our own troops, buoyant with success, were eager for an assault, and would not work well if the slow process of a siege was undertaken." One of the soldiers who participated in the assault that day also seemed to agree with the army's commander. W. H. Bentley of the 77th Illinois would later write:

> We failed to carry the formidable works of the enemy, not for any lack of courage, or want of discipline in the army. On the contrary this check—for it was not a defeat—only inspired the men to endure any hardships and suffer any losses for the accomplishment of their darling object—*the reduction of Vicksburg*. Our losses were great, but not irreparable. Our failure was not so disheartening as might have been supposed. At all events, there seemed to be a stronger determination than ever to succeed.[27]

There would be no more assaults on Vicksburg's fortifications. The Union troops withdrew a few hundred yards and began to build their own extensive lines of fortifications, completely cutting off the city from the rest of the Confederacy. Grant "now determined upon a regular siege—to 'out-camp the enemy,' as it were, and to incur no more major losses. The experience of the 22d convinced officers and men that this was best, and they went to work on the defences and approaches with a will." In the same dispatch containing Grant's complaints about McClernand, he informed General Halleck, "The enemy are now undoubtedly in our grasp. The fall of Vicksburg and the capture of most of the garrison can only be a question of time."[28]

Chapter 14

Vicksburg's Fate Is Sealed

Shortly after the fighting died down on May 22, Grant sent a dispatch to General Halleck informing him of the situation as it now stood: "Vicksburg is now completely invested. I have possession of Haynes' Bluff and the Yazoo; consequently have supplies. To-day an attempt was made to carry the city by assault, but was not entirely successful." At the time he wrote this Grant obviously did not know the severity of his casualties, but he did realize that further attacks would be useless, admitting that "the nature of the ground about Vicksburg is such that it can only be taken by a siege."[1]

In the message of May 24 Grant gave Halleck more details of the assault, describing the positions of his troops, and his assessment of the enemy's works around Vicksburg: "The position is as strong by nature as can possibly be conceived of, and is well fortified. The garrison the enemy have to defend it I have no means of knowing, but their force is variously estimated from 10,000 to 20,000." He also noted that he was aware that Johnston was building up his forces "to effect a raising of the siege. They may attempt something of the kind, but I do not see how they can do it." With the railroad destroyed, any Confederate relief force would have to march fifty miles carrying enough food and ammunition for a prolonged battle. Grant stated, "My position is so strong that I could hold out for several days against a vastly superior force. I do not see how the enemy could possibly maintain a long attack under these circumstances." Although confident of ultimate success, Grant promised to keep a close watch on any approaching enemy force.[2]

The Federal siege lines would eventually stretch from Haynes' Bluff south to near Warrenton, a distance of about fifteen miles. Grant felt confident that with this ring of troops and "with the navy holding the river, the investment of Vicksburg was complete. As long as we could hold our position the enemy was limited in supplies of food, men and munitions of war to what they had on hand. These could not last always."[3]

Grant's appraisal of the situation was pretty accurate. The Confederates within Vicksburg's fortifications were not going anywhere. They could not replenish their supplies, and even without another Union assault it was clearly only a matter of time before hunger and illness forced Pemberton to capitulate. The only hope of breaking Grant's lines lay with Joe Johnston, who was working with limited success to build up a force large enough to launch an attack against the rear of the Federal lines. With Haynes' Bluff securely under Union control, Grant could be supplied from the river almost as well as if the army were still in Memphis. Thousands of reinforcements were on the way and soon the Federal lines would be virtually impregnable.

Siege warfare was slow and laborious; success was measured in how many feet the besieger's lines drew closer to the enemy's lines. But siege warfare was also as close to a sure thing as there was in war. Slowly, but inexorably, the Federal lines would approach the Confederate lines.

Mines would be dug under certain important Confederate positions that would reduce them to piles of indefensible rubble. If the Confederates could not be starved out, then eventually, when the lines were close enough, another assault would take place where the defenders would not have enough time to put up much of a fight before overwhelming numbers of Union soldiers were inside their works. Starvation or a surprise attack, one way or another, barring complete mismanagement by the Federal commanders, Vicksburg would eventually be in Union hands.

Work on the Federal siege lines began on May 23 with several batteries of artillery located in the best positions to fire on the Confederate strong points. These batteries were then quickly connected by lines of parapet and rifle pits manned by sharpshooters whose job it was to keep the heads of the defenders down while work was being done on the lines. Under normal conditions the design and construction of siege lines would be done by military engineers familiar with this type of construction. Unfortunately, Grant had only a few experienced officers assigned to engineering duty in his army when the siege began, which made it impossible to spend much time supervising the work in any one location. In the early part of the siege these officers spent most of their time working on the overall planning and location of the lines and issuing instructions for specific locations to officers detailed from headquarters or the fighting units.[4]

The actual labor of building the Union siege lines was done by pioneer companies, small details taken out of the lines, and by former slaves who were paid ten dollars a month. Engineer Captains Prime and Comstock issued a report after the siege was over giving much of the credit for constructing the siege lines to the troops and laborers who were able to learn how to do almost anything if given the chance:

> The want of officers of engineers has already been referred to, there being at no time more than three on engineer duty. Over a line so extended and ground so rough as that which surrounds Vicksburg, only a general supervision was possible, and this gave to the siege one of its peculiar characteristics, namely, that many times, at different places, the work that should be done, and the way it should be done, depended on officers, or even on men, without either theoretical or practical knowledge of siege operations, and who had to rely upon their native good sense and ingenuity. Whether a battery was to be constructed by men who had never built one before, a sap-roller made by those who had never heard the name, or a ship's gun-carriage to be built, it was done, and, after a few trials, was well done.... Officers and men had to learn to be engineers while the siege was going on.[5]

Between the digging and the shooting the men were kept pretty busy. Lucius Barber of the 15th Illinois wrote in his diary, "One day we were on the skirmish and picket line and the next in the trenches. There was no rest for us, but labor, fight and dig was the order." William Wiley wrote in his diary that the men working on the trenches would stay under cover during the day and only come out to work at night: "Working parties would be sent out after dark which would follow up some hollow to some point as near to the rebel works as they thought best where we would start our rifle pits below the brow of the hill and run them up towards the rebel works...." These trenches would be covered with boards and then dirt so that the men inside could not been seen by the Confederate pickets. After moving forward a certain distance, side trenches would be dug parallel to the enemy works in a zigzag pattern. The earth that was dug up would be piled up in front of the trench to increase the height of the protection against enemy bullets. Artillery would be brought up behind the new trenches and once the position was established the routine would be repeated moving still closer to the enemy's fortifications.

As Wiley noted, "Our aim would be to keep up such a rain of balls and grape and schapnell from the batteries over the top of their works that they did not dare to raise their heads above their works."[6]

Ira Blanchard of the 20th Illinois remembered that the Union works pretty much mirrored the shape of the enemy fortifications. One of the ways the troops tried to provide as much protection for themselves as possible was to "put logs on top of our defenses to protect our heads, under which we had a line of port-holes where we could sit and pop away all day with perfect safety." The work proceeded quickly, and on May 28 Owen Hopkins of the 42nd Ohio wrote in his diary, "We have entrenchments within a few yards of those of the enemy, and death is dealt out to the Rebel who is Brave enough to show his head above the parapets of the enemies Breastworks." J. T. Woods of the 96th Ohio recalled that another device used by the troops to provide some protection while building the works was called a "sap." A sap was made from baskets or barrels held together with tree saplings and filled with cotton and dirt. "Men lying down pushed these 'saps' before them as a protection until reaching the desired spot, then they instantly began securing themselves by throwing over them earth enough to make a bullet and cannon shot proof embankment."[7]

On May 28, Assistant Secretary Dana was able to report to Secretary of War Stanton that "Sherman has his parallels completed to within 80 yards of the rebel fortifications. He is able to carry artillery and wagons with horses under cover to that point." The works in McPherson's front had advanced to about the same distance from the enemy's lines, and as Dana noted, "On both these lines our sharpshooters keep the rebels under cover and never allow them to load a cannon." While the Union line was not yet completed, on the far left Dana was convinced that "the enemy cannot either escape by that route or receive supplies."[8]

Not the type of commander to just sit in headquarters reading reports, General Grant made frequent trips up to the firing line to measure the progress of the siege, often exposing himself and those around him to enemy fire. One day Grant rode up on a mule and stopped out in the open behind troops of the 96th Ohio to survey the Confederate works in their front. With enemy fire coming in above the heads of the soldiers in the trenches one, of the men apparently had enough of being in the line of fire and yelled at the unknown figure on a mule "See here, you damned old fool, if you don't get off that mule you'll get shot." One of the man's comrades who recognized Grant informed him that he was yelling at the commanding general, which apparently made little difference, as the man replied, "I don't care who it is; what's he foolin' round here for, any way? We're shot at enough without taking any chances with him." In another instance Grant was studying the enemy fortifications from a wooden observation tower that was the target of frequent fire when a soldier from the 4th Minnesota, not recognizing Grant, yelled at him "You old ***, you'd better keep down off of there or you'll be shot. When one of his friends told him who he had been yelling at the soldier quickly found a way to disappear. Whether Grant heard admonishments like these or not is unknown, but he did not stop visiting the front lines in person.[9]

Immediately after it was decided to begin a formal siege of Vicksburg, Grant began requesting reinforcements to make sure he had enough manpower to seal Pemberton's army inside their works and man his own defensive lines to keep Johnston from breaking through from the outside. In Memphis, General Hurlbut forwarded all the available men he could find from Western Tennessee. On June 3, a brigade from Memphis, commanded by Brigadier General Nathan Kimball, arrived and was sent to man positions between the Yazoo and Big Black.

On June 8, a full division from Memphis commanded by Brigadier General Sooy Smith joined the army and was also sent to the Haynes' Bluff area. On the eleventh a division from Missouri, commanded by Major General Francis J. Herron, arrived and took up a position on the left of the Federal lines. On June 14 two more divisions from the Ninth Army Corps in Kentucky arrived commanded by Major General John G. Parke and were sent to join the troops at Haynes' Bluff. It was not long before Grant had about seventy thousand men under his command in the vicinity of Vicksburg.[10]

With Admiral Porter's gunboats in control of the river above and below Vicksburg and reinforcements flooding in, Grant felt confident enough to send General Frank Blair with a full division on an expedition up the Yazoo River. Grant later wrote, "The country was rich and full of supplies of both food and forage. Blair was instructed to take all of it." Whatever supplies the expedition could not bring back were to be destroyed along with bridges and roads so that nothing was left for the enemy to use. General Sherman and about thirty thousand troops were sent to occupy the area between the Yazoo and Big Black rivers. They built a formidable line of works from Haynes' Bluff running east and then south to the railroad bridge over the Big Black right across the route that Joseph Johnston would have to use if he were to march to the relief of Vicksburg.[11]

By the middle of June there were about fifteen miles of Federal trenches and artillery emplacements from the Yazoo River to the Mississippi south of the city. With nearly half of his men too sick or too weak to actively participate in heavy fighting, Pemberton could do nothing but watch while the Union lines got closer and closer as the days passed. Winchester Hall of the 26th Louisiana later wrote, "When the real investment began, a cat could not have crept out of Vicksburg without being discovered. Every yard of river and foot of land was watched and guarded, and the horrors of a siege were felt alike in the streets of the city, and trenches at the front."[12]

With the Confederates in Vicksburg unable to do anything but wait for the inevitable end and Sherman's force protecting the rear of the Federal lines, Grant had good reason to be confident of eventual victory. In response to a comment that Johnston might fight his way in, Grant suggested that might not be so bad since it would only increase the number of Confederate soldiers who would be prisoners once the city surrendered. Grant's confidence spread to the soldiers in the trenches that ringed Vicksburg; they could see what a commanding position they held just as well as the senior officers. A soldier from Wisconsin, James K. Newton, wrote to his parents on May 24, "There is not much news only that we have the rebels in a pretty tight place. They are completely surrounded and if we cant make them surrender any other way we can starve them out." During the rest of May and into June the Union siege lines were gradually extended and strengthened until the city of Vicksburg was totally cut off from the rest of the Confederacy. No meaningful amount of supplies could get into the city and no one was going to get out. The only thing the citizens and soldiers of Vicksburg had to look forward to was to try and survive one more day.[13]

Grant's attitude toward the enemy was one of hit them as hard as you can during the fighting with the full weight of Federal power until they broke, but be magnanimous when the battle was over. One incident illustrating this occurred when General Sherman removed the wives and daughters of several Confederate soldiers from a fine plantation house that he was concerned was being used to supply the enemy with information about Federal troop movements. Proving that chivalry was not quite dead, Sherman wrote to headquarters to make sure Grant would approve treating these women in such a harsh manner, admitting that "I moved them all by force, leaving a fine house filled with elegant furniture and costly painting to the chances of war," suggesting that his actions "may not appeal to the tender heart of our commanding general, but he will not reverse my decision when he knows a family accessible to the enemy—keen scouts—can collect and impart more information than the most expert spies."[14]

When Grant learned of his friend's concern, his reply illustrated a fundamental part of Grant's nature: "You need not fear, general, my tender heart getting the better of me, so as to send the secession ladies to your front; on the contrary, I rather think it advisable to send out every living being from your lines, and arrest all persons found within who are not connected with the army." Grant did not enjoy the idea of driving helpless civilians out of their homes, but if it aided the war effort he had no problem with it. He was willing to use all the power the government had put in his hands to destroy the enemy, whether they were found on the battlefield or in stately plantation manors.[15]

For the Union soldiers manning the trenches outside Vicksburg there was constant danger, and despite every effort to shield the men from enemy fire there were really no safe places near the front lines. J. J. Kellogg of the 113th Illinois noted that the firing was almost continuous, "Every minute, almost, a tick-a-ka-tick of minie bullets was registered by the twigs and leaves above and around us. Many of our boys were killed or wounded in their bowers and beds by the stray bullets." R.L. Howard of the 124th Illinois wrote in his diary for May 31, "Opened at three o'clock in the morning, with the most terrific cannonade on our part I ever heard. Up and in line. The night was perfectly hideous. A hundred guns at once, and half as many exploding shells answering back, with streams of fire and dense smoke. Like pandemonium...."[16]

Wilber Crummer of the 45th Illinois remembered, "The work of slaughter and destruction went on day and night. The roar of cannon, the rattle of musketry, the sharp crack of the rifle in the hands of the sharpshooters, reached the ear from all sides. There was no cessation, no let up." Isacc Jackson wrote home after four weeks in front of Vicksburg telling his family that "during that time there has been a constant firing of cannon. There has not been an hour hardly but we can hear the report of a gun along the line somewhere. We have become very much used to it." The Union soldiers in the trenches were confident that even if they had to wait for the Vicksburg garrison to be starved out of their fortifications, the city would eventually be taken. They were also aware of how dangerous the defenders were, no matter how hungry they might be. Thomas M. Stevenson of the 78th Ohio later wrote, "We have got the animal caged, but dare not enter the cage."[17]

One of the more spectacular visual sights during the siege were the mortar shells fired from ships in the river. J. J. Kellogg wrote that the men would hear the boom of the mortar, then soon after saw "the ponderous bomb mounting up into the sky, spinning out its fiery web along its wild track from its first appearance until it stood still for a second, then gracefully curved downward and dropped swiftly down, down into the doomed city." Shortly after the tail of the shell disappeared would come the terrible crash of its detonation.[18]

An old saying that familiarity breeds contempt seemed to hold true in the trenches around Vicksburg. The constant danger facing the troops on both sides gradually seemed to lessen simply because they got used to it. The sharp crack of musket fire and the roar of artillery that made men dive for cover in the early days of the siege seemed like nothing more than annoying

Union troops approaching trenches at Vicksburg (Library of Congress).

noises after a few weeks. Wilber Crummer noted that "danger had long since ceased to cause any fear." Violence had become so familiar that even the death of a comrade seldom produced more than an expression of sadness at his passing, but mostly the men wondered who might be next. Crummer wrote, "Men are not naturally unmindful of danger, nor do their hearts usually exhibit such indifference to human agony and suffering; yet the occurrence of daily scenes of horror and bloodshed through which they passed, the shadow of the angel of death constantly hovering over them, made them undisturbed spectators of every occurrence, making the most of today, heedless of the morrow."[19]

On June 15 Grant wrote a letter to his father that expressed the confidence that ran throughout the army: "I have the enemy closely hemmed in all round. My position is naturally strong and fortified against an attack from outside. I have been so strongly reinforced that Johnston will have to come with a mighty host to drive me away. I do not look upon the fall of Vicksburg as in the least doubtful." Grant noted that if he had been able to take Vicksburg by assault, he could have turned east and campaigned throughout Mississippi, admitting, "The fall of Vicksburg now will only result in the opening of the Mississippi River and demoralization of the enemy. I intended more from it. I did my best, however, and looking back can see no blunder committed."[20]

Some of the most serious difficulties facing Grant was not from the Confederates but from within his own ranks. From the beginning of the campaign John McClernand had felt that the wishes of the president had been cleverly nullified by Grant and Halleck. The Missis-

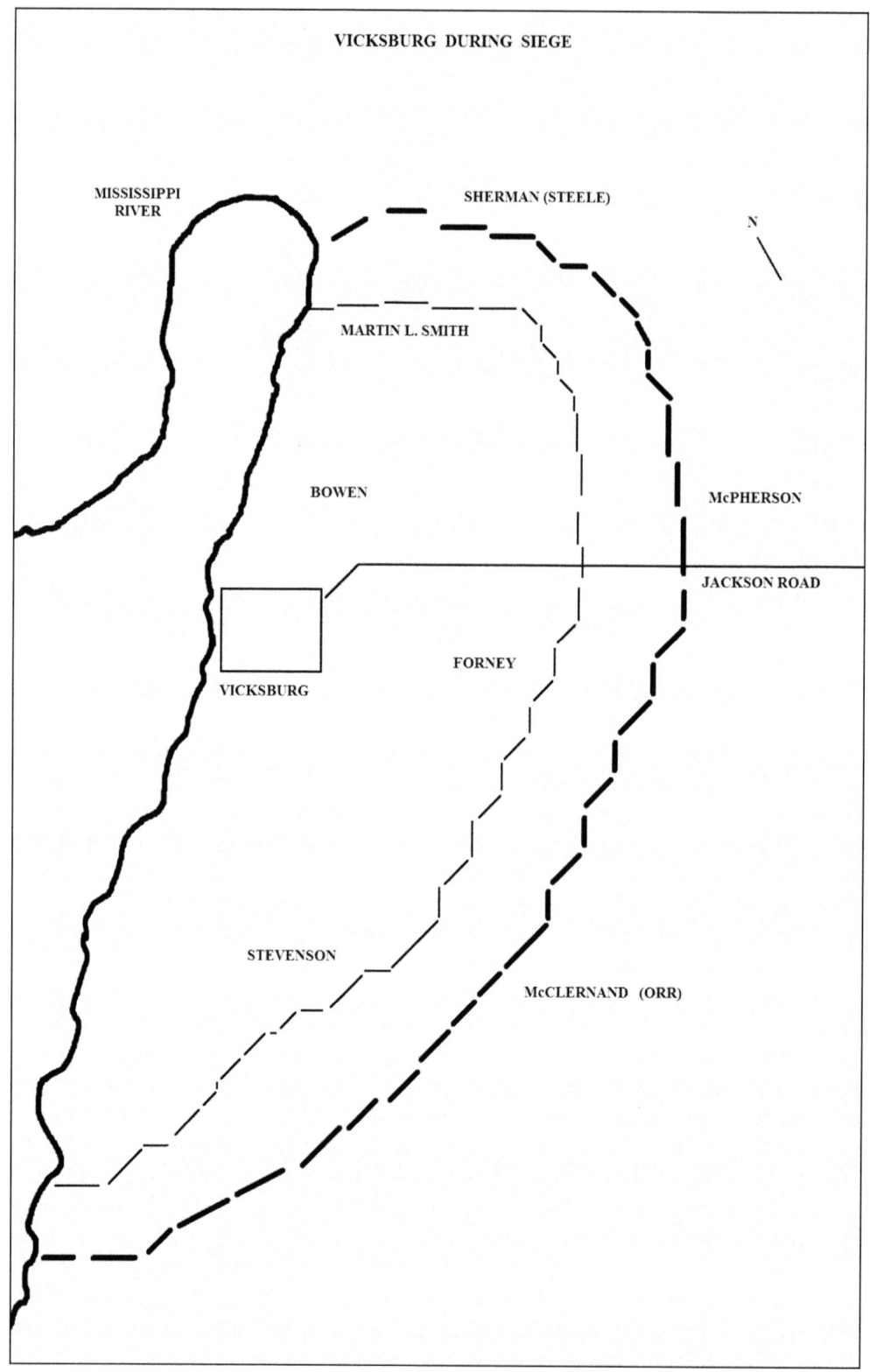

sippi campaign had been his idea from the start; he had raised thousands of troops specifically for this campaign and had been promised, he thought, an independent command to open the Mississippi River. Brooding in his tent, a mere corps commander, he saw the glory he was expecting to win being usurped by Grant and it made him angry. This anger exploded when one of Grant's aides, Colonel Wilson, brought a relatively routine order to McClernand to reinforce a detachment from his corps currently guarding a ferry crossing on the Big Black. Colonel Wilson later wrote that when he delivered the orders, McClernand burst out with, "I'll be god-damned if I'll do it. I am tired of being dictated to—I won't stand it any longer, and you can go back and tell General Grant."[21]

This kind of language was generally not used between officers and gentlemen, and after McClernand made a few more similar remarks Wilson also lost all semblance of formality. He told McClernand in plain English that not only was he insulting the commanding general but Wilson himself, and that if that were the case he would ignore the difference in their rank and "pull you off that horse and beat the boots off you!" McClernand quickly said that his remarks were not directed at the young colonel, whose father had been a close friend of his, but rather he was "expressing my intense vehemence on the subject matter, sir, and I beg your pardon." When Wilson reported the outburst to Grant he took no action, but this obviously was added to the long list of reasons Grant was anxious to rid himself of McClernand.[22]

By the middle of June it was apparent that Grant had a stranglehold on Vicksburg and that he had the backing of the authorities in Washington. He was now finally able to take care of one of the most vexing problems he faced, what to do with John McClernand. That Grant disliked the arrogant, politically well-connected general was no secret, but Grant had decided to keep McClernand in his present position as commander of the Thirteenth Corps until after Vicksburg was taken and then move him out with as little fanfare as possible. As it turned out, however, McClernand himself provided the grounds for his own dismissal when he wrote a supposed order to his troops congratulating them on their effort in the failed assaults on Vicksburg's lines and suggesting that lack of action on the part of other commanders had cost his men a victory. This unfortunate paper quickly made its way back to Illinois newspapers, violating War Department regulations that any such communications be submitted to headquarters before being printed in any civilian publications.[23]

When the news of McClernand's order reached the army around Vicksburg, both Sherman and McPherson were incensed that they were being blamed for the failure of the assault. On June 17 Sherman wrote to Grant, "It certainly gives me no pleasure or satisfaction to notice such a catalogue of nonsense—such an effusion of vain-glory and hypocrisy." Sherman felt that the order was not published for the troops in McClernand's corps because "I know too well that the brave and intelligent soldiers and officers who compose that corps will not be humbugged by such stuff." Sherman believed that the order was addressed "not to an army, but to a constituency in Illinois, far distant from the scene of the events attempted to be described, who might innocently be induced to think General McClernand the sagacious leader and bold hero he so complacently paints himself."[24]

Sherman complained that although the document in question is called an order:

> It orders nothing, but is in the nature of an address to soldiers, manifestly designed for publication for ulterior political purposes. It perverts the truth to the ends of flattery and self-glorification, and contains many untruths, among which is one monstrous falsehood. It substantially accuses General McPherson and myself with disobeying the orders of General Grant

in not assaulting on May 19 and 22, and allowing on the latter day the enemy to mass his forces against the Thirteenth Corps alone.

Sherman noted that McClernand should have confined his paper to the portion of the action that was under his own observation. The angry general went on to write, "In cases of repulse and failure, congratulatory addresses by subordinate commanders are not common, and are only resorted to by weak and vain men to shift the burden of responsibility from their own to the shoulders of others."[25]

General McPherson's comments on the subject were received at army headquarters on June 18 and also displayed that officer's indignation: "The whole tenor of the order is so ungenerous, and the insinuations and crimination against the other corps of your army are so manifestly at variance with the facts, that a sense of duty to my command, as well as the verbal protest of every one of my division and brigade commanders against allowing such an order to go forth to the public unanswered, require that I should call your attention to it." McPherson noted that after reading McClernand's order he concluded "that it was written more to influence public sentiment at the North and impress the public mind with the magnificent strategy, superior tactics, and brilliant deeds of the major-general commanding the Thirteenth Army Corps than to congratulate his troops upon their well-merited successes." McPherson ended his letter by saying that although McClernand considers himself a warrior, "he has evidently forgotten one of the most essential qualities, viz, that elevated, refined sense of honor, which, while guarding his own rights with zealous care, at all times renders justice to others."[26]

When the complaints of corps commanders that he knew well and respected were added to Grant's own misgivings about McClernand, it was time to act. On June 18 Grant issued Special Orders, No. 164: "Maj. Gen. John A. McClernand is hereby relieved from the command of the Thirteenth Army Corps. He will proceed to any point he may select in the State of Illinois, and report by letter to headquarters of the Army for orders." Grant immediately appointed Major General E.O.C. Ord to replace McClernand.[27]

The order was written up and signed during the evening and was to be delivered next morning. Colonel Wilson and Grant's aide, Colonel John Rawlins decided on their own that the order should be served immediately. There were rumors that the Confederates were going to attempt at breakout at any time and if that happened Grant would not relieve a corps commander during the fighting. Wilson and a small escort set out for McClernand's headquarters, where they arrived at about two o'clock in the morning. Wilson was kept waiting until McClernand, who had retired for the night, was fully dressed in his proper uniform. Wilson handed the letter to McClernand saying that he had been instructed to witness the reading of the order and McClernand's acknowledgement that he understood the order and would obey it. McClernand immediately realized the meaning of the order and burst out, "Well sir! I am relieved!" After a brief pause he added, "By God sir, we are both relieved!" a comment that Wilson took to mean Grant also.[28]

By the middle of June the Confederates had little hope of saving Vicksburg. The Union lines facing the city were just as strong as the Confederate lines keeping them out, and Sherman had constructed and manned strong works covering the route that Joe Johnston would have to take if he tried to break the siege. Johnston, in fact, had pretty much decided that any attack on Grant's lines from outside would be a waste of effort. Writing to Confederate Secretary of War Seddon, the general said that he might be able to put together an army of a little over twenty thousand men. Johnston noted that "Grant's army is estimated at 60,000 or 80,000 men, and his troops are worth double the number of northeastern troops. We cannot relieve General Pemberton except by defeating Grant, who is believed to be fortifying."[29]

In late June General Grant received information that Johnston was advancing toward Vicksburg with the idea of trying to break the Federal lines long enough to allow at least some of Pemberton's troops to escape. Grant decided to take no action against Johnston, believing that "we were strong enough to have taken the offensive against him; but I did not feel disposed to take any risk of losing our hold upon Pemberton's army, while I would have rejoiced at the opportunity of defending ourselves against an attack by Johnston."[30]

As the siege went on the summer weather arrived with a vengeance, especially affecting the Union troops who were unused to the hot temperatures. Clean water was difficult to come by and the hot sun baked the men in exposed trenches. The men in the lines on both sides tried to make the best of a bad situation. By now the lines were so close together in most places that the opposing pickets seldom fired at one another unless some officer came up and gave orders to do so. At some points in the lines the troops were close enough to each other to exchange conversation and trade items such as Federal coffee and hardtack for good Southern tobacco. Elisha Stockwell of the 14th Wisconsin wrote, "It was two rods from the outside of our fort to the outside of the Rebs' fort. Moonlight nights they used to agree to have a talk, and both sides would get up on the breastworks and blackguard each other and laugh and sing songs for an hour at a time." Of course, later that day they would be shooting at each other again.[31]

Life in the trenches did have some amusements, such as putting a cap on the end of a stick and seeing how often the opposing sharpshooters could hit it. Wilber Crummer remembered some of the comments that went back and forth between the lines. "One day a 'johnnie' calls out: 'What are you men doing over there?' and quick comes the answer: 'Guarding 30,000 Johnnies in Vicksburg, and making them board themselves....' The pickets of both armies were good natured and used to brag of their ability to whip each other."[32]

Trading for hard to get items like coffee and tobacco and the occasional friendly discussions across the trenches helped to relieve some of the tension felt by the soldiers on both sides, but they were still at war and in the end they would not hesitate to kill each other. Taylor Peirce of the 22nd Iowa wrote his wife that although conditions in the trenches were improving and "we are doing very well now.... We have to stay in the hollows for as soon as a man sticks his head above the top of the hill hiss comes a bullet at him and admonishes us to keep out of sight." Another soldier from Iowa, William Clayton, wrote to his parents, "The discharge of small arms is almost constant along the line, but they don't do much damage on either side. A fellow has to keep his head pretty low though, for some ball would whistle by, very close." In spite of the hardships and danger, as the siege continued the Union troops grew more confident of the final outcome. William Winters of the 67th Indiana correctly summed up the situation in a letter to his wife, "We will go into the city of Vicksburgh after awhile, that is shure, for we can live outside of their works longer than they can inside of them, that is certain, for we can get everything we want, and they can get nothing at all."[33]

For centuries one of the tactics used during a siege was that of digging mines beneath the enemy's works, and the siege of Vicksburg was no different. The most ambitious Federal mining project occurred near the Jackson Road under the strongest Confederate position in the area known as Fort Hill, which was defended by the 3rd Louisiana. As the main Union lines grew closer to the enemy positions work was begun on June 22 on a mine under the hill on which the fort stood. General Logan's division occupied the area in front of Fort Hill and his men did the digging in cramped, poorly ventilated shafts. The work proceeded relatively quickly and by June 25 they had dug a main gallery forty-five feet in with a smaller tunnel another fifteen feet farther. Where the main gallery ended, two other tunnels were dug at forty-five degree angles for another fifteen feet.[34]

The Confederates had been expecting some mining and were actively digging countermines, but although they came close did not discover the mine under Fort Hill. Preparing for the worst, however, they did build another strong redoubt behind Fort Hill that was connected to the rest of the defensive lines and moved most of the 3rd Louisiana troops to this new position. The gallery and tunnels under Fort Hill were packed with over a ton of gunpowder, and on June 25 around 3 o'clock in the afternoon the fuses were lit. A massive explosion blew off most of the top of the hill, leaving a crater twelve feet deep and about fifty feet across where the Confederate fort had once been.[35]

As soon as the mine exploded, a heavy artillery bombardment began all along the Union line. Moving quickly after the dust settled, volunteers from Logan's division charged forward into the crater formed by the explosion. Entering the crater proved to be no problem for the assaulting force, but as they tried to climb out of the opposite side where the debris had piled up, they ran into heavy fire from the new redoubt in their front. Wilber Crummer recalled that as the Union troops tried to charge over the edge of the crater, they were met with such a devastating fire that "the line wavers, staggers, and then falls back into the crater. The enemy charge on us, but we repel them at the west bank of the crater, and a hand-to-hand conflict rages for hours." For several terrible hours there was close-in fighting as the Federals were forced to take cover behind the crest of the crater. W. S. Morris of the 31st Illinois later wrote that during this desperate fight, "the Confederates threw grenades over the embankment; the Union soldiers threw them back. Shells from the twenty pounders were thrown by hand. Men pitched muskets at each other. Some had rifles snatched out of their hands." Men along the front line had their backs to the enemy and would reach their muskets over the parapet in an attempt to hit an enemy soldier on the other side. General Logan's men could not break through the new Confederate position and the survivors had to wait until after dark before they could return to their original lines.[36]

This assault was the last offensive action by the Union army in June. There was another mine being dug across from Sherman's lines which was going to be used to coincide with what Union headquarters was expecting to be the breakthrough on July 6. Despite whatever plans were being made in headquarters, however, many of the men on both sides were beginning to believe, or at least hope, that the siege would not last much longer. The Union soldiers could see that their opponents were exhausted, physically and emotionally. All they had to do was hold on and starvation would bring the inevitable victory. This was not the time to take excessive risks on the front line. The outcome of the siege was already decided; it would probably only be a matter of days, or a couple weeks at most, and no one wanted to die for a victory already achieved.[37]

Chapter 15

Life and Death Under Siege

From the end of May through June as the Federal forces besieging Vicksburg steadily grew in strength, the situation facing the Confederate soldiers in the trenches and the civilians in the city just as steadily went from bad to worse to desperate. The Confederate troops had regained much of their confidence by repulsing the Union assaults, but it was soon clear to both soldiers and civilians that they were trapped and that the only chance for relief would be to break the Federal stranglehold from outside the city—and that meant Joseph E. Johnston. On May 24 President Davis wrote to General Johnston agreeing with the general's opinion that Pemberton would stubbornly defend Vicksburg, adding, "but the disparity of numbers renders prolonged defence dangerous. I hope you will soon be able to break the investment, make a junction & carry in munitions." On May 29 Johnston sent a courier to Pemberton admitting, "I am too weak to save Vicksburg. Can do no more than attempt to save you and your garrison. It will be impossible to extricate you, unless you co-operate, and we make mutually supporting movements." Pemberton replied that he had only 18,000 men well enough to man the fortifications and no reserves. Johnston would need at least 30,000 men to break Grant's lines and suggested Snyder's Mill as the point of attack. Pemberton added, "The enemy encompass my lines from right to left, occupying all roads…. My men are in good spirits, awaiting your arrival…. You may depend on my holding the place as long as possible."[1]

Back in Richmond, Jefferson Davis, who was ill and very probably distracted by Robert E. Lee's soon to begin invasion of Pennsylvania, apparently did not totally understand the situation in and around Vicksburg. Davis was unhappy that Johnston did not immediately rush to Pemberton's aid earlier in the campaign, and the relationship between Davis and Johnston became more strained. Davis wanted Johnston to cut Grant's nonexistent supply line to force him to abandon the siege while Johnston kept requesting reinforcements before taking any action. Johnston seemed not to grasp the fact that there were no Confederate troops available to reinforce his command; he would have to act with what he had, and the longer he delayed the more difficult it would be to relieve Vicksburg. Jefferson Davis, who owned a plantation near Vicksburg, wrote to his brother Joseph, "Reinforcements to the extent now asked is impossible without ruin to the Confederacy. I have spared no effort and am still striving to give aid to the defenders of my home, but that is not my only duty. I mourn over opportunities lost." Pemberton and the troops in Vicksburg were on their own.[2]

As the soldiers of both sides settled down to a formal siege, the civilians in and around Vicksburg were forced to endure many of the same dangers faced by the fighting men in the trenches. Once fired, Federal shells could be headed toward civilians or soldiers. Dora Richards wrote in her diary on May 28: "We are utterly cut off from the world, surrounded by a circle of fire…. The fiery shower of shells goes on day and night…. People do nothing but eat what they can get, sleep when they can, and dodge the shells." Another resident, Mary Ann Loughborough, later wrote, "The rapid firing from the boats, the roar of the Confederate batteries, and, above all, the screaming, booming sound of the shells, as they exploded in the air and around the city, made at once a new and fearful scene to me." Giving vent to her feelings of outrage, Emilie Riley McKinley wrote, "Can the people in the North know or conceive what we suffer? We are tried beyond endurance, and suffer more than we can tell. We will be obliged to coin words to express our utter detestation of the hated."[3]

As the siege went on conditions in Vicksburg grew more wretched by the day. With thousands of troops added to the civilian population, fresh water was hard to come by after the rainy season and food became scarce and then practically nonexistent. Mary Ann Loughborough related that early in the siege many people were able to live on cornbread and milk "provided their cows were not killed from one milking time to another." The standard meal consisted of cornbread and bacon "served three times a day, the only luxury of the meal consisting in its warmth." But as the siege dragged on the cows disappeared and pretty much anything edible was consumed by the hungry population.[4]

The city itself was soon turned into a desolate place with piles of rubble everywhere. Many buildings were totally destroyed and those that had not suffered some type of damage from the shelling were few and far between. During earlier bombardments when the city was under fire from naval vessels, the people simply evacuated to the side of the hills away from the river. The naval guns fired in a flat trajectory that could not reach the far side of the hills. When the mortar boats were brought up, however, the danger increased dramatically. The mortars fired their huge shells almost straight up into the air, and they came down the same way so that no open place was safe from the deadly shells. The only way the citizens of Vicksburg could find shelter from the storm of steel raining down was to burrow into the hillsides.

The number and size of the caves around the city were directly affected by the scope of the war around Vicksburg. During the earlier attacks the caves were few in number and just basically holes scooped out of the hillsides. When Grant's army arrived, however, all that changed. The fury of the bombardment from both the river and the land side forced everyone who could to take shelter. The hills around Vicksburg soon became honeycombed with caves and tunnels; some provided basic shelter and some were deep and elaborate tunnels where multiple families could live for days at a time in relative safety.

It did not take long for cave building to become a growth industry. Laborers hired themselves out to dig new shelters in the hillsides or extend existing caves deeper into the earth. Some shelters could be made relatively comfortable by their occupants with the addition of furnishings brought from their homes. Wood planks laid over dirt floors could be covered with carpet. Some people brought furniture from their damaged homes; chairs, tables and even beds adorned some of the larger caves. Curtains or rugs hung over the walls of the cave helped to control the dirt and dampness. Sometimes even the smallest touch of home could make a cave a little more livable.[5]

About the best that could be said of life in Vicksburg's caves was that it was difficult. This was summer in Mississippi and the weather was hot and humid in the open air and oppressively worse inside the poorly ventilated caves. There was little enough water for drinking and cooking and almost none for bathing. Sickness affected the civilians nearly as much as the soldiers, with malnutrition a common problem accompanied by malaria and dysentery. In the end, however, no matter how unpleasant it was in the caves, they were the only protection from the shells that rained down upon the city, and sometimes even this was not enough.

Mary Ann Loughborough recalled two incidents that illustrated the terrors faced by the civilians. "A little Negro child, playing in the yard, had found a shell; in rolling and turning it, had innocently pounded the fuse; the terrible explosion followed, showing, as the white cloud of smoke floated away, the mangled remains of a life that to the mother's heart had possessed all of beauty and joy." In another tragedy: "A young girl, becoming weary in the confinement of the cave, hastily ran to the house in the interval that elapsed between the slowly falling shells. On returning, an explosion sounded near her—one wild scream, and she ran into her mother's presence, sinking like a wounded dove, the life blood flowing over the light summer dress in crimson ripples from a death-wound in her side, caused by the shell fragment."[6]

While the civilians in Vicksburg had to cope with the constant danger from shelling and the lack of food, life for the soldiers in the trenches was even worse. The shelling and rifle fire was virtually non-ending, what little food that was available was barely edible, and the heat from the Mississippi summer sun made conditions almost unbearable. Yet day after day the Confederate soldiers manned their earthworks and returned shell for shell and bullet for bullet. Willie Tunnard of the 3rd Louisiana wrote: "There was no shrinking or quailing. Danger had long since ceased to cause any fear, and fighting was a recreation and pastime with the majority of the men. Exploding shells and whistling bullets attracted but little notice. Even death had become so familiar, the fall of a comrade was looked upon with almost stoical indifference; eliciting, perhaps, a monosyllabic expression of pity, and most generally the remark, 'I wonder who will be the next one.'"[7]

The defenders manning the trenches seldom got any relief from duty. Between the poor food, heat exhaustion, the filthy conditions in the trenches, and casualties from enemy fire, there were simply not enough healthy men available to properly man the fortifications, and at the same time allow others to fall back to more comfortable quarters. If it rained the men had to remain in their wet and dirty clothes, which only increased the number of troops that became too sick to man the lines. All these factors combined to force the remaining men to take on more and more duties. The biggest problem facing the defenders was, of course, supplies. It didn't take long for the daily rations to dwindle down to just enough to keep the men functioning. Winchester Hall, of the 26th Louisiana, wrote that "as time passed by, food and forage were at a premium; the law of demand and supply was entirely ignored, and various expedients were resorted to. The privates of the regiment successfully undertook a decrease in the rodent population."[8]

Another Confederate soldier, John Guilford Earnest, wrote in his diary, "We endured as much as mortals ever endured in an army—every day from daylight until late in the night—sometimes all night, we were in the midst of hissing shells and balls of every character that were ever manufactured. Besides this, we lived on less than quarter rations—ate pea bread, mule meat, and rats." While the defenders stubbornly kept on fighting, they were also smart enough to see that without relief from Johnston there was only one possible end to the siege. Willie Tunnard wrote on June 14 that the Union troops knew "the true condition of affairs, knowing full well, and confidently expecting that the gaunt skeleton of famine, then seizing the besieged forces, would ultimately prove the conqueror. They needed but to wait, while they kept up, with unabated fury, their daily and nightly attack on the place."[9]

By the middle of June it was obvious that there was only one hope of saving Vicksburg and the thousands of Confederate soldiers defending the city—the totally inadequate force that General Johnston had been able to pull together. On June 15 Pemberton made another appeal for help to Johnston: "The enemy had placed several very heavy guns in position against our works, and is approaching them very nearly by sap. His fire is almost continuous. Our men have no relief; are becoming much fatigued, but are still in pretty good spirits. I think your movement should be made as soon as possible. The enemy is receiving re-enforcements. We are living on greatly reduced rations, but I think sufficient for twenty days yet."[10]

Since the siege had begun the soldiers and civilians in Vicksburg had been expecting to hear the thunder of Johnston's artillery hitting the Union lines at any moment, all they had to do was hang on a few more days. The only problem was that Johnston was making little effort toward mounting a relief expedition. He was well aware that Grant's army greatly outnumbered his force at Jackson, and the only way Johnston might make a successful assault would be if he could coordinate with Pemberton so that they hit the same area of the Union lines from opposite sides at the same time. Considering the difficulties in getting messages through the Union lines and the weakened condition of Pemberton's troops, this was an unlikely scenario and Johnston knew it.

In a message to Secretary of War Seddon on June 15, Johnston bluntly gave his views on the probability of saving Vicksburg. Speaking about what was more important to the Confederacy, Mississippi or Tennessee, Johnston candidly wrote, "Without some great blunder of the enemy we cannot hold both. The odds against me are much greater than those you express. I consider saving Vicksburg hopeless." The next day Seddon replied, "Your telegram grieves and alarms me. Vicksburg must not be lost without a desperate struggle. The interest and honor of the Confederacy forbid it. I rely on you to avert the loss. If better resources do not offer, you must hazard attack." Seddon was not interested in the specifics, just that the effort must be made: "It may be made in concert with the garrison, if practicable, but otherwise without, by day or night, as you think best."[11]

General Johnston replied to Seddon's message urging he take action with a more complete explanation of the situation. "I think that you do not appreciate the difficulties in the course you direct nor the probabilities or consequences of failure. Grant's position, naturally very strong, is intrenched and protected by powerful artillery, and the roads obstructed." Johnston also pointed out that Grant's army had grown significantly in numbers during the last month, vastly outnumbering Johnston's force, and the Federal forces were well entrenched behind the Big Black River. He also pointed out, "We cannot combine operations with General Pemberton from uncertain and slow communication. The defeat of this little army would at once open Mississippi and Alabama to Grant. I will do all I can, without hope of doing more than aid to extricate the garrison."[12]

On June 21 Seddon again urged Johnston to take some action, no matter how desperate. "Consequences are realized and difficulties are recognized as very great, but I still think, other means failing, the course recommended should be hazarded. The aim, in my judgment, justifies any risk and all probable consequences." That same day Seddon sent a more detailed message to Johnston offering to take responsibility for any failed action:

> Only my conviction of almost imperative necessity for action induces the official dispatch I have just sent you. On every ground I have great deference to your superior knowledge of the position, your judgment and military genius, but I feel it right to share, if need be to take, the responsibility, and leave you free to follow the most desperate course the occasion may demand. Rely upon it, the eyes and hopes of the whole Confederacy are upon you, with the full confidence that you will act, and with the sentiment that it were better to fail nobly daring than through prudence even to be inactive. I look to attack in last resort, but rely on your resources of generalship to suggest less desperate modes of relief.

Seddon then made several suggestions as to how Johnston might break the siege, including attacking General Banks at Port Hudson and uniting the Confederates there to attack Grant or to bombard the Union lines around Vicksburg with long-range artillery from dry swamps north of the Yazoo River. Seddon closed with, "I rely on you for all possible [efforts] to save Vicksburg." The only problem with Seddon's urging Johnston to do something was that Grant probably would have liked nothing more than to have Johnston leave the relative safety of the works at Jackson and smash his modest force against the Union lines.[13]

Desperation began to set in by the end of June as Confederate commanders began to consider a variety of ideas that might at least save the army if not Vicksburg itself. On June 23, Pemberton sent a message with a very unusual suggestion to Johnston: "If I cut my way out, this important position is lost, and many of my men, too. Can we afford that? If I cannot cut my way out, both position and all my men are lost. This we cannot afford." Pemberton then proposed that in return for the surrender of the city, Grant might be open to giving terms that would be much more advantageous to the Confederacy than the loss of both city and army. "Not knowing your force or plans, he may accede to your proposition to pass this army out with all its arms and equipage. This proposal would come with greater prospects of success and better grace from you, while it necessarily could not come at all from me." Pemberton thought that if Grant could be made to believe that the city could hold out for at least several more weeks and if Johnston could give the impression of being stronger than he really was, Grant might be inclined to offer good terms rather than face fighting on two fronts at the same time. "While I make this suggestion, I still renew my hope of your being, by force of arms, enabled to act with me in saving this vital point. I will strain every nerve to hold out, if there is hope of our ultimate relief, for fifteen days longer." Even if Johnston had been willing to try this outlandish proposal, which he was not, it would have been a waste of time because Grant wanted Pemberton's army even more than he wanted Vicksburg.[14]

Another scheme that might have done some good if it had been handled properly was to get General E. Kirby Smith, commander of the Confederacy's Trans-Mississippi Department, to launch a relief campaign from across the Mississippi. Aid from Smith's forces had already been requested but little had been accomplished when Johnston wrote to him on June 26: "Our only hope of saving Vicksburg now depends on the operations of your troops.... If you can contrive either to plant artillery on the Mississippi banks, drive beef into Vicksburg, or join the garrison, should it be practicable or expedient, we may be able to save the city." Realistically, the most that might be accomplished with artillery fire from across the river or getting fresh troops into the city would be to aid in a breakout by the garrison if they could coordinate an attack with Johnston's forces. Smuggling supplies into the city would only prolong the inevitable. In appealing for Smith to personally take command of the relief force, Johnston flatly told him, "Your troops up to this time have done nothing."[15]

The next day Johnston wrote again to Pemberton informing him that Smith's force had been "mismanaged" but that "his expected co-operation, encourage me to hope that something may yet be done to save Vicksburg." In the same message, however, Johnston refuses to consider approaching Grant for surrender terms and opens up the possibility of losing the city: "Negotiations with Grant for the relief of the garrison, should they become necessary, must be made by you. It would be a confession of weakness on my part, which I ought not to make, to propose them. When it becomes necessary to make terms, they may be considered as made under my authority."[16]

On June 28 Pemberton received a letter from "many soldiers" that was respectful but also made it clear that the men had suffered enough:

> We as an army have as much confidence in you as a commanding general as we perhaps ought to have. We believe you have displayed as much generalship as any other man could have done under similar circumstances. We give you great credit for the stern patriotism you have evinced in the defense of Vicksburg during a protracted and unparalleled siege.
>
> I also feel proud of the gallant conduct of the soldiers under your command in repulsing the enemy at every assault, and bearing with patient endurance all the privations and hardships incident to a siege of forty odd days' duration.
>
> Everybody admits that we have all covered ourselves in glory, but alas! alas! general, a crisis has arrived in the midst of our siege.
>
> Our rations have been cut down to one biscuit and a small bit of bacon per day, not enough scarcely to keep soul and body together, much less to stand the hardships we are called upon to stand.
>
> We are actually on sufferance, and the consequence is, as far as I can hear, there is complaining and general dissatisfaction throughout our lines.
>
> We are, and have been kept close in the trenches day and night, not allowed to forage any at all, and even if permitted, there is nothing to be had among the citizens.
>
> Men don't want to starve, and don't intend to, but they call upon you for justice, if the commissary department can give it; if it can't, you must adopt some means to relieve us very soon. The emergency of the case demands prompt and decided action on your part.
>
> If you can't feed us, you had better surrender us, horrible as the idea is, than suffer this noble army to disgrace themselves by desertion. I tell you plainly, men are not going to lie here and perish, if they do love their country dearly. Self-preservation is the first law of nature, and hunger will compel a man to do almost anything.
>
> You had better heed a warning voice, though it is the voice of a private soldier.
>
> This army is now ripe for mutiny, unless it can be fed.
>
> Just think of one small biscuit and one or two mouthfuls of bacon per day. General, please direct your inquiries in the proper channel, and see if I have not stated stubborn facts, which had better be heeded before we are disgraced.

While this letter may just be the complaints of a few disgruntled soldiers, the suffering described was real enough, and it would be unrealistic not to believe that many of Pemberton's men were already of the same mind as the anonymous author.[17]

As the month of June came to an end it was obvious to all but the worst diehards that the end was at hand. The Vicksburg defenders were starving and could not hold out much longer. Any assault to break through the strong Union lines would only result in the useless sacrifice of the few brave men who were still fit enough to make the attempt. Pemberton had only one realistic option available—try to get the best possible terms for surrendering the city and save as many of his men as possible.

Chapter 16

A Great Victory

The month of July began very badly for Vicksburg's defenders. About 1:30 p.m. on July 1 a tremendous explosion literally blew apart one of the Confederate forts in front of Sherman's lines. Federal troops had been hard at work digging under this position for some time and their tunnels beneath the enemy lines were packed with over a ton of gun powder. The explosion created a twenty foot crater where the fort had been, but unlike the mine that was exploded on June 25, there was no assault by Union troops, only a heavy artillery bombardment. Learning from previous mistakes, General Grant noted that this mine resulted in "destroying an entire rebel redan, killing and wounding a considerable number of its occupants and leaving an immense chasm where it stood. No attempt to charge was made this time, the experience of the 25th admonishing us." Brig. General J. H. Forney reported to Pemberton that since there was no attack on the position, perhaps the enemy "only wished to destroy life and weaken the position. In this he has succeeded but too well. The redan itself is entirely gone, and the interior line considerably weakened." Forney also noted that the artillery bombardment after the explosion tended "much to dishearten the men."[1]

It was finally time for General Pemberton to accept the reality of the situation his army was facing. He was surrounded by a vastly superior force, no help was coming, and food was practically non-existent. In a letter to his division commanders, Pemberton asked for an honest appraisal of the condition of their men, "Unless the siege of Vicksburg is raised or supplies are thrown in, it will be necessary very shortly to evacuate the place. I see no prospect of the former, and there are very great, if not insuperable, obstacles in the way of the latter." The commanding general was already well aware that his troops were too weak to fight their way through the Union lines, but he wanted written confirmation by his subordinate commanders before contemplating the next inevitable step.[2]

The replies to Pemberton's inquiry were universally pessimistic. From Stevenson's division came General Barton's comments that "probably half of them are fit to take the field. The command suffers greatly from intermittent fever, and is generally debilitated from the long exposure and inaction of the trenches." Another of Stevenson's officers, Colonel A. W. Reynolds, reported, "It would be utterly impossible for most of them to make a forced march of any distance. Many of my men are in the hospital, and many of those reported for duty in the trenches are extremely weak and unable to undergo the slightest fatigue."[3]

In Major General Forney's division, Brigadier General Louis Hebert answered that he had consulted with most of his senior officers and "without exception all concurred in one single and positive opinion—*that their men could not fight and march 10 miles in one day; that even without being harassed by the enemy or having to fight, they could not expect their men to march 15 miles the first day*." Based on the reply of Hebert and his other regimental commanders, General Forney reported that in his division "although the spirit of the men was good, their physical condition and health was so much impaired by their long confinement in narrow trenches, without exercise and without relief, being constantly under fire and necessarily on the alert, and living upon greatly reduced rations," he felt they could not "make the marches they would have to make and fight the battles they would have to fight" in order to break through the heavily manned Union lines that surrounded the city. Forney was willing to admit that he "favored a capitulation rather than make this attempt, attended, as I thought, with such little hope of success."[4]

The candid replies Pemberton received from his inquiry dashed any hope he might have been clinging to that there was still some way of salvaging the army even if the city was lost. Pemberton called his senior officers together for a council of war on the evening of July 2 to discuss what options might be available in the face of their hopeless situation. And hopeless was certainly a proper description of the circumstances facing Vicksburg's defenders. When the siege began both soldiers and civilians had expected Joseph Johnston to appear at any time to break the Union lines from the rear and relieve the city. It was now obvious that Johnston was not coming, at least not in time. For forty-eight days and nights the troops had manned the trenches suffering through the summer heat and living on such poor rations that by now mule and rat meat were considered a feast. The Federal lines had moved so close in some places that when they launched their next attack, which was expected on July 4, overwhelming numbers of blue uniformed men would be on top of the exhausted Confederates so quickly that a successful defense would be impossible.[5]

During the officers' meeting Major Lockett remembered that Pemberton expressed his opinion that there were only two realistic alternatives, "Either to surrender while we still had ammunition enough left to give us the right to demand terms, or to sell our lives as dearly as possible in what he knew must be a hopeless effort to cut our way through the Federal lines." Each officer was asked to offer their opinion and to vote on whether they wanted to fight or surrender. Only two, Generals S. D. Lee and Baldwin, voted to fight, and they could give no logical reason to do so.[6]

After the vote the final decision was still up to the commanding general. Major Lockett later wrote that Pemberton said that although he agreed with the vote to surrender,

> My own preference would be to put myself at the head of my troops and make a desperate effort to cut our way through the enemy. That is my only hope of saving myself from shame and disgrace. Far better would it be for me to die at the head of my army, even in a vain effort to force the enemy's lines, than to surrender it and live and meet the obloquy which I know will be heaped upon me. But my duty is to sacrifice myself to save the army which has so nobly done its duty to defend Vicksburg. I therefore concur with you and shall offer to surrender this army on the 4th of July.[7]

Several of the officers present objected to surrendering on the birthday of the United States, but Pemberton noted, "I am a Northern man; I know my people; I know their peculiar weaknesses and their national vanity; I know we can get better terms from them on the 4th of July than any other day of the year. We must sacrifice our pride to these considerations." So the fate of Vicksburg and its garrison was finally decided.[8]

Before anything was decided, however, Pemberton had to formally request a cease fire and offer to open negotiations to surrender the city and garrison. Pemberton felt that although his situation was dire, he was still in a position to negotiate with General Grant to receive favorable terms. After all, even if the outcome was certain, the Union forces would still suffer high casualties if Grant tried to take the city by force. On July 3, Pemberton wrote what was probably the most difficult letter of his life:

> I have the honor to propose to you an armistice for—hours, with a view to arranging terms for the capitulation of Vicksburg. To this end, if agreeable to you, I will appoint three commissioners to meet a like number, to be named by yourself, at such place and hour to-day as you may find convenient.
>
> I make this proposition to save the further effusion of blood, which must otherwise be shed to a frightful extent, feeling myself fully able to maintain my position for a yet indefinite period.[9]

General John Bowen, who had fought so well at Port Gibson, was chosen to deliver Pemberton's letter to Grant. Bowen and Grant had been friends in Missouri before the war and it was hoped that this association would make it easier to negotiate favorable terms. As it turned out, however, Grant's attitude toward dealing with former friends who were now fighting for the Confederacy had not changed since Fort Donelson. While the fighting was continuing, Grant had no friends among his country's enemies; he would use every means at his disposal to beat them into submission. As at Fort Donelson, where he accepted the unconditional surrender of old friend, Simon Bolivar Buckner, once the fighting ended Grant would be cordial and friendly as if nothing had happened between them, but only after the surrender.

About ten o'clock on the morning of the 3rd, white flags appeared along a portion of the Confederate works and the firing ceased for the first time since the siege began. General Bowen and Colonel Louis Montgomery, one of Pemberton's aides, emerged from the works carrying a white flag and Pemberton's letter to Grant. Upon reaching the Union lines, Bowen and Montgomery met with Union General A. J. Smith. An audience with Grant was refused, but Smith forwarded Pemberton's letter to him. Grant had little inclination to discuss terms; he was in a position of strength and he knew it.[10]

Grant's reply to Pemberton's offer to discuss terms for surrender left little to negotiate:

> The useless effusion of blood you propose stopping by this course can be ended at any time you may choose, by an unconditional surrender of the city and garrison. Men who have shown so much endurance and courage as those now in Vicksburg will always challenge the respect of an adversary, and I can assure you will be treated with all the respect due to prisoners of war.
>
> I do not favor the proposition of appointing commissioners to arrange terms of capitulation, because I have no terms other than those indicated above.

Despite the apparent harshness of his letter, Grant was not totally opposed to working out a deal that would allow him to quickly and bloodlessly win the prize that had already cost so much, and he agreed to meet personally with Pemberton at three o'clock that afternoon between the lines in front of General McPherson's position.[11]

General Pemberton arrived at the appointed time and place accompanied by Bowen and Montgomery. In addition to several staff officers, General Grant brought Generals A. J. Smith, Edward Ord, James McPherson, and John Logan to the meeting. Grant later wrote that "Pemberton and I had served in the same division during part of the Mexican War. I knew him very well therefore, and greeted him as an old acquaintance." Pemberton was not in a particularly friendly mood that afternoon. He knew that even if he could get good terms for his army, he would be scorned and ridiculed for losing a position that was vital to the survival of the Confederacy. Quickly getting down to the business at hand, Pemberton asked Grant what terms he was willing to offer for the surrender of the Confederate army. When Grant replied that he had none other than he proposed in his earlier letter, meaning unconditional surrender, Pemberton replied, "The conference might as well end," and turned to leave. Grant said that Bowen then proposed that he and one of Grant's officers might be allowed to discuss the situation to find a possible middle ground. Bowen and A. J. Smith met separately for a brief time while Grant and Pemberton walked a short distance away to also discuss matters further.[12]

General Pemberton remembered the meeting a little differently than did Grant. After Grant confirmed that he had no new offer of terms, Pemberton replied, "Then, sir, it is unnecessary that you and I should hold any further conversation; we will go to fighting again at once," adding, "I can assure you, sir, you will bury many more of your men before you will enter Vicksburg." Pemberton says that it was Grant who suggested that they step aside for a private discussion and also that Bowen and Smith try to arrive at a mutually satisfactory agreement.[13]

Generals Bowen and Smith rejoined the rest of the officers after a brief discussion and as Grant remembered it, Bowen proposed that "the Confederate Army was to be permitted to march out with the honors of war, carrying with them their arms, colors, and field artillery." After the city was evacuated Grant's troops could move in and keep any artillery or other equipment left behind. "This was promptly and unceremoniously rejected." The meeting was apparently over and the Confederates assumed that firing would begin again as soon as Pemberton, Bowen and Montgomery were back within their own lines. Before leaving, however, Grant told Pemberton that he would send him a letter containing a final offer of terms by ten o'clock that night and that the cease fire would remain in effect until Pemberton replied.[14]

Back in his headquarters, Grant called a meeting of corps and division commanders in the vicinity. Grant generally did not believe in conducting a council of war when important decisions were to be made. He was in command, the responsibilities were his and the decisions would be his. He was willing, however, to hear the opinions of officers he trusted and respected before making his final decision. The Union officers in that meeting knew full well that sooner or later Vicksburg would be theirs, if not by assault then surely from starvation. The real question to be decided was whether it was better to stick to the demand for unconditional surrender, delaying the victory and perhaps losing hundreds if not thousands of men if they had to take the city by storm, or to offer terms good enough to convince Pemberton to surrender immediately. In the end the question of parole for the Confederate troops would be the determining factor.

Grant knew that if he took all the Confederates prisoner it would create a transportation nightmare for both the army and the navy. Admiral Porter had already informed Grant that shipping nearly thirty thousand prisoners of war up the river to Cairo, Illinois, which was the closest transportation hub to prison camps in the north, would tie up most of his transports for a month. The obvious solution was to make use of the parole system. At this point in the war both sides were still operating under the system of paroling prisoners of war. Paroled troops were men who had been surrendered but were allowed to remain with their own army. They were supposed to remain in camp and simply wait until they could be exchanged for an equal number of opposing troops and then rejoin the fighting units.[15]

The obvious question concerning the parole system was whether the opposing forces could trust each other not to violate the agreement and release troops for active duty before they were formally paroled. Letting thirty thousand Confederate troops stay in the South was a huge gamble, but one that Grant was willing to take. He knew that paroled prisoners were difficult for their own authorities to control. Almost all the soldiers on both sides were just civilians serving briefly in the army, discipline was loose and men on parole frequently decided they since they were technically prisoners they were basically out of the army and free to do what they wanted. Releasing thirty thousand such men into the Deep South might just cause the Confederacy more harm than good. Grant reasoned that most of the released men might simply go home and only a relatively small percentage would ever take up arms again. In addition, Grant had another reason for being willing to let the captured enemy soldiers be released on parole. Once again looking toward the future, Grant believed that "the men had behaved so well that I did not want to humiliate them. I believed that consideration for their feelings would make them less dangerous foes during the continuance of hostilities, and better citizens after the war was over."[16]

Grant made up his mind and later that evening offered his terms to Pemberton:

> I will submit the following proposition for the surrender of the city of Vicksburg, public stores, &c.
> On your accepting the terms proposed, I will march in one division as a guard, and take possession at 8 a.m. to-morrow. As soon as rolls can be made out, and paroles signed by officers and men, you will be allowed to march out of our lines, the officers taking with them their side-arms and clothing, and the field, staff, and cavalry officers one horse each. The rank and file will be allowed all their clothing, but no other property. If these conditions are accepted, any amount of rations you may deem necessary can be taken from the stores you now have, and also the necessary cooking utensils for preparing them. Thirty wagons also, counting two two-horse or mule teams as one, will be allowed to transport such articles as cannot be carried along.
> The same conditions will be allowed to all sick and wounded officers and soldiers as fast as they become able to travel.
> The paroles for these latter must be signed, however, while officers are present authorized to sign the roll of prisoners.

Once Grant's letter had been dispatched, he instructed several of his commanders to make sure that their men standing guard duty informed their Confederate counterparts of Grant's generous offer to parole them and send them home instead of to Northern prison camps.[17]

General Pemberton had believed all along that Grant would offer his men parole, since he had already received intelligence reports about the concerns the Union commanders had about their ability to send so many prisoners north. Trying to get the best terms possible, Pemberton wrote back to Grant:

> In the main, your terms are accepted; but in justice both to the honor and spirit of my troops, manifested in the defense of Vicksburg, I have to submit the following amendments, which, if acceded to by you, with perfect the agreement between us.
> At 10 a.m. to-morrow I propose to evacuate the works in and around Vicksburg, and to surrender the city and garrison under my command, by marching out with my colors and arms, staking them in front of my present lines, after which you will take possession.
> Officers to retain their side-arms and personal property, and the rights and property of citizens to be respected.[18]

Pemberton's letter was received at Grant's headquarters early in the morning on July 4. If Vicksburg was to be his on that celebrated day, an agreement would have to be reached quickly. However, Grant was adamantly against letting the Confederates simply march out of Vicksburg without formally signing paroles. Under these circumstances there would be nothing to stop them from heading east, joining up with Johnston's army, and resume fighting as soon as they were fit again. Grant's reply made it clear that the negotiations were at an end:

The amendment proposed by you cannot be acceded to in full. It will be necessary to furnish every officer and man with a parole signed by himself, which with the completion of the rolls of prisoners, will necessarily take some time.

Again, I can make no stipulations with regard to the treatment of citizens and their private property. While I do not propose to cause them any undue annoyance or loss, I cannot consent to leave myself under any restraint by stipulations. The property which officers will be allowed to take with them will be as stated in my proposition of last evening; that is, officers will be allowed their private baggage and side-arms, and mounted officers one horse each.

If you mean by your proposition for each brigade to march to the front of the lines now occupied by it, and stack arms at 10 a.m., and then return to the inside, and there remain as prisoners until properly paroled, I will make no objection to it.

Should no notification be received of your acceptance of my terms by 9 a.m., I shall regard them as having been rejected, and shall act accordingly. Should these terms be accepted, white flags should be displayed along your lines to prevent such of my troops as may not have been notified from firing upon your men.[19]

Pemberton had no choice but to accept Grant's terms and he knew it. Well before the deadline, Grant received a message from the Confederate commander, "I have the honor to acknowledge the receipt of your communication of this day, and in reply to say that the terms proposed by you are accepted." The siege of Vicksburg was over and Ulysses Grant had just won the biggest prize of the war to date.[20]

While Grant was negotiating with Pemberton, he did not forget about Joseph Johnston's Confederate army in his rear. So confident was Grant that the Confederates were going to surrender that before a deal was finalized he wrote to General Sherman on July 3 advising him of the negotiations and giving him general instructions with the freedom to act as he thought best to accomplish the mission: "I want Johnston broken up as effectually as possible, and the roads destroyed. I cannot say where you will find the most effective place to strike; I would say move so as to strike Canton and Jackson, whichever might seem most desirable." In another dispatch that day, Grant told his old friend that he could have the use of all the troops in the army except McPherson's corps and that Grant especially wanted Sherman to "drive Johnston from the Mississippi Central Railroad; destroy bridges as far as Grenada with your cavalry, and do the enemy all the harm possible."[21]

While the dispatches were going back and forth between the Union and Confederate headquarters during the night, the men out in the trenches could only wait to see what the morning would bring. R. L. Howard of the 124th Illinois later remembered that the silence from the cease fire became "fearfully oppressive. For so many long days and nights it had been a continuous battle. Not a minute but the crack of the rifle or the boom of the cannon had been in our ears. And much of the time it had been deafening. Now it was still, absolutely still." Rumors of the negotiations would have leaked out to the men in the trenches during the night and combined with the cease-fire, many of the soldiers on both sides were wondering what was going on. The tension of waiting to hear something, anything, through that long, dark night surely kept most of them awake waiting to hear if the fighting was really over and there would be no more killing, at least for a little while.[22]

Soldiers from both sides took advantage of the cease fire to get out of their trenches and walk around in the open, action that would have brought instant death a few hours earlier. In a letter home, William Clayton, a Union soldier from Iowa, wrote that when the firing ceased on July 3 he and some of the boys in his unit left their rifle pits to chat with the Confederates, who had done the same thing. "It looked singular to see men, who but a few minutes previously were shooting at each other, mingle together and shake hands, and be as friendly, apparently, as brothers, but such is among the incidents of war."[23]

At last dawn came and word of the surrender became known throughout both armies. Alonzo Brown of the 4th Minnesota saw that "white flags were displayed all along the Confederate lines.... The lines along which the vision extended, for nearly a mile and a half each way, were quiet. The men were seen standing upon both sides and near enough together to converse." R. L. Howard later wrote, "The morning of Saturday, the 4th of July, dawned gloriously. It was our nation's birthday, and we felt it. We sympathized with it as never before. The oppression of the day and night had given place to light feeling. We seemed to tread on air." Taylor Peirce of the 22nd Iowa wrote home, "To us who have been in turmoil and strife of battle day and night for so long a time it seemed as though a weight was lifted from us that well nigh bore us down."[24]

Most of Vicksburg's citizens and defenders did not learn that the siege was over until the morning of July 4. During the previous night many of the city's cave dwellers were able to go outside and walk around the unusually quiet city surveying the desolation or go to their homes to check on damage and retrieve items they might be able to use in the caves. When the soldiers learned of the surrender, many of them were more surprised and angry than relieved that their ordeal was over and the constant threat of a violent death had been averted. Many soldiers cursed their leaders long and loud, some destroyed their weapons, and the worn flags of more than a few regiments were cut up and distributed among the men as keepsakes.[25]

As agreed, the Confederates began leaving their trenches at ten o'clock. Moving out to designated points between the lines, they stacked their arms and marched back to the city to await their paroles. John H. Thurston of the 4th Minnesota remembered, "I have just been up on the hill and saw the rebels marching out and stacking their arms.... This is the most glorious Fourth of July I ever spent." Despite the obvious elation in the Union ranks, there was little cheering as they watched their opponents perform this ritual act of surrender. The Confederates had put up too good a fight and were too weak and dispirited for the victors to gloat.[26]

Soon after the Confederates returned to the city, General John Logan's division with the 45th Illinois at the head of the column marched into town to formally take possession of the city. They had taken great pains to look their best as they entered Vicksburg: boots shined, clean uniforms, even wearing their white parade ground gloves. Logan's men headed for the center of town and raised their flag at the courthouse. Wilber Crummer, a member of the 45th Illinois, remembered that once inside the city the men of both armies freely associated with each other. "Groups of Union and Confederate soldiers could be seen wherever there was a shady place; the Union soldier pumping the rebel and giving him in return for the information hard tack and bacon, which the poor famished fellows accepted with a grateful look."[27]

The Union soldiers who entered Vicksburg that morning were surprised and shocked by what they saw. The city was in ruins, scarcely a building was not damaged in some way, many nothing but rubble. The Confederates, who had fought so well for so long, beating back two assaults in May and trading shot for shot with their besiegers, appeared pathetic in comparison to the well-fed and well-dressed Union troops. The hostility felt by the victors toward these enemy soldiers was soon replaced by sympathy for a beaten and starving foe. Most Union troops quickly emptied their haversacks, passing out hardtack and coffee to men who had been going hungry for weeks. The troops mingled together with so little apparent animosity that few outsiders would have guessed they had been trying to kill each other for the past few months.[28]

Edmund Newsome of the 81st Illinois noted that a few days later, "It seemed strange to see men mix together in pleasant conversation, passing jokes, comparing notes of the siege, or in social argument about the cause of the war, who, a few days ago, were shooting each other on every opportunity." To be sure, not all the Confederates were friendly, some were bitter about the surrender and some simply hated the Yankee invaders. Many were tired of the war and only wanted to get their paroles and head home, but there were others who were ready to fight again the first chance they got.[29]

Shortly after the first Union troops entered the city, General Grant and his staff made their way to Pemberton's headquarters to make a courtesy visit. Unfortunately, the relatively friendly and respectful conduct of the troops did not extend to their commander. The normally aloof Pemberton was simply rude and inhospitable to Grant and his officers. Colonel Wilson later wrote about their reception, "No one even offered Grant a seat, and when he asked for a glass of water a member of the Confederate staff merely told him where he could find it. The situation was a trying one, but Pemberton and his officers met it badly. Their behavior was unhandsome and disagreeable in the extreme." In contrast to most of the senior Confederate officers, three young staff members, including Major Lockett, "were polite and courteous, in recognition of which their haversacks and canteens were well filled with provisions and whiskey when they bade us good-by."[30]

Grant soon left the inhospitable Confederate headquarters and headed down to the docks, where he met Admiral Porter on board his flagship the *Black Hawk*. Here the celebrating really got started when the admiral opened his liquor cabinet, although Grant was content to exchange congratulations and relax with a few cigars. Later in the day Grant and his staff rode through the rubble filled streets past groups of cheering former slaves and quiet, incredulous citizens. The new Union headquarters was established in the home of a wealthy planter, and Grant and his staff got down to the business of implementing the terms of the surrender.[31]

During the day and evening Federal soldiers flooded into Vicksburg to see what they had been fighting for. Most were disappointed. In a letter home, Isaac Jackson of the 83rd Ohio wrote, "It was a desolate looking place, I tell you—I did not notice a house but that was shot through. None was occupied. They had caves in the ground. I was in some of them. The men were a hard looking set. They were nearly starved." William Winters of the 67th Indiana wrote to his wife that he took a walk around the city "looking at the work of destruction which is visable on every hand. The effects of our mortor shell is frightful to look at, for where ever they struck they lef a frightful mark."[32]

The Union troops quickly saw that there was little animosity toward them by the defeated Confederate soldiers. Wisconsin soldier James K. Newton wrote his parents, "It looked strange to see Uncle Sam's troops marching through the city, and the Secesh standing in groups at every street corner." Newton felt that the former enemy "seem to have formed quite a good opinion of our men since we came in here. They did not expect to be treated so kindly and so respectfully, as they have been: and by treating them so we have quite won their esteem."[33]

The Confederate soldiers had much less kind thoughts toward their commanding general, as he had predicted. Dora Richards remembered what one soldier told her when she asked if the rumor of surrender was true. After confirming the news the man said that "the men in Vicksburg will never forgive Pemberton. An old granny! A child would have known better than to shut men up in this cursed trap to starve to death like useless vermin.... Starved to death because we had a fool for a general." Many years later, former Lieutenant Colonel Frank

Montgomery of the 1st Mississippi Cavalry wrote: "It is thirty-seven years since this humiliating and disastrous surrender, but I cannot recall it not without anger and indignation at the incompetent man who had its destiny in his hands. Some thought he was a traitor then." Even though Pemberton was following explicit orders from Jefferson Davis to hold Vicksburg at the risk of losing both the city and the army, the blame that was cast on him for the surrender would never diminish.[34]

Never one to rest on his laurels, General Grant immediately got down to the business of continuing the war. Sherman had already been instructed to head east to confront Joe Johnston's force, and in a dispatch on July 4 Grant displayed his trust in his friend's ability to do whatever was needed: "I have no suggestions or orders to give. I want you to drive Johnston out in your own way, and inflict on the enemy all the punishment you can. I will support you to the last man that can be spared." Grant also wrote to General Banks at Port Hudson informing him of the details of the surrender and that Sherman was moving east to attack Johnston, which would prevent the Confederates from sending any relief force to interfere with Banks' current siege of Port Hudson.[35]

Shortly before he was to head east after Joseph Johnston's army, General Sherman wrote two long letters to the men he deemed most responsible for the victory. To Admiral Porter he wrote:

> No event in my life could have given me more personal pride or pleasure than to have met you to-day on the wharf at Vicksburg....
> I can appreciate the intense satisfaction you must feel at lying before the very monster which has defied us with such deep and malignant hate, and seeing your once disunited fleet again a unit; and better still, the chain that made an inclosed sea of a link in the great river broken forever.... God grant that the harmony and mutual respect that exist between our respective commanders, and shared by all the true men of the joint service, may continue forever, and serve to elevate our national character, threatened with shipwreck.... I assure you I shall never reach the banks of the river or see a gunboat but I will think of Admiral Porter, Captain Breese, and the many elegant and accomplished gentlemen it has been my good fortune to meet on armed or unarmed decks of the Mississippi squadron.[36]

The other letter went to Sherman's good friend Ulysses Grant:

> I can hardly contain myself.... Did I not know the honesty, modesty, and purity of your nature, I would be tempted to follow the examples of my standard enemies of the press in indulging in wanton flattery; but as a man and soldier, and ardent friend of yours, I warn you against the incense of flattery that will fill our land from one extreme to the other. Be natural and yourself, and this glittering flattery will be as the passing breeze of the sea on a warm summer day. To me the delicacy with which you have treated a brave but deluded enemy is more eloquent than the most gorgeous oratory of an Everett.
> This is a day of jubilee, a day of rejoicing to the faithful, and I would like to hear the shout of my old patient troops.... Already are my orders out to give one big huzza and sling the knapsack for new fields.[37]

Chapter 17

Occupation and Politics

It did not take very long for Ulysses Grant and his senior commanders to begin reaping the rewards for their victory. On July 7, General Halleck submitted Grant's name for promotion to major general in the regular army to date from July 4. The promotion was quickly approved by the Senate. Less than four years earlier Grant had been a former infantry captain who had resigned his commission under a cloud of debt and drinking and had been a less than successful civilian. Now he had won the most prized position in the army, a well-paid job until he retired, financial security in his old age, and the respect and admiration of the nation.[1]

A week after the surrender of Vicksburg, Halleck wrote to Grant recommending that he submit both Sherman and McPherson for promotion to brigadier general in the Regular Army. After suggesting that Grant write a letter urging their appointment listing the service record of both generals, Halleck added, "The feeling is very strong here in [favor of] your generals." On a personal note, he said, "Give my kindest regards to my old friends among your officers. I sincerely wish I was with you again in the West. I am utterly sick of this political hell."[2]

On July 22, Grant wrote his recommendations for both Sherman and McPherson in a letter to President Lincoln prefacing the details of their previous service by stating "their great fitness for any command that it may ever become necessary to entrust to them." In a separate letter to General Halleck on July 24, Grant made it plain that he valued more than just their military abilities: "The army does not afford an officer superior to either, in my estimation. With such men commanding corps or armies, there will never be any jealousies or lack of hearty co-operation." This last part was important to Grant, because he had seen firsthand how many problems an uncooperative general can cause, as in the case of John McClernand.[3]

Promotion and praise were all very nice of course, but a letter Grant received from President Lincoln was possibly the most satisfying of all. The two men had never met, but they were moving in the same direction as to how to fight and win the war. Grant had been the most dependable commander Lincoln had. The President wrote to him on July 13:

> I do not remember that you and I ever met personally. I write this now as a grateful acknowledgment for the almost inestimable service you have done the country. I wish to say a word further. When you first reached the vicinity of Vicksburg, I thought you should do, what you finally did—march the troops across the neck, run the batteries with the transports, and thus go below; and I never had any faith, except a general hope that you knew better than I, that the Yazoo Pass expedition, and the like, could succeed. When you got below, and took Port Gibson, Grand Gulf and vicinity, I thought you should go down the river and join Gen. Banks; and when you turned Northward East of the Big Black, I feared it was a mistake. I now wish to make the personal acknowledgment that you were right, and I was wrong.[4]

Despite all the acclaim coming Grant's way, he did not let it get in the way of taking care of business. The terms of surrender had barely been settled when General Sherman was on his way toward Jackson. General Johnston learned of Vicksburg's surrender on July 5 and immediately returned to Jackson and went to work improving the city's defenses. Moving quickly with the Ninth, Thirteenth and Fifteenth Corps, Sherman crossed the Big Black and concentrated his forces at Bolton, about twenty miles west of Jackson. By July 10, Sherman's forces were ready to lay siege to Jackson with the Ninth Corps above the city, the Thirteenth Corps to the south, and Fifteenth Corps on the west. The next day Federal artillery began shelling the town from all three directions, but Sherman refused to launch a costly infantry assault. As Sherman wrote later, "The weather was fearfully hot, but we continued to press the siege day and night, using our artillery pretty freely."[5]

Sherman gradually moved his lines around the city in an effort to surround it and force Johnston to surrender without a major engagement. Joe Johnston, however was not Pemberton; he recognized a trap when he saw it. During the night of July 16 he withdrew his forces across the Pearl River and headed toward Alabama. The next day Sherman learned that Jackson had been evacuated and immediately entered the city, sending General Steele's division to pursue the retreating Confederates. On July 18 Grant told Sherman to "continue the pursuit as long as you have reasonable hopes of favorable results, but do not wear your men out." When Sherman decided to call off the chase and return to Vicksburg, Grant recommended that he take his time and "return by easy marches." The weather was dreadfully hot, the roads bad, and Sherman realized that "pursuit in that hot weather would have been fatal to my command." Steele was instructed to end the pursuit and return to the main force.[6]

The fate of the city of Jackson was sealed when Grant wrote to Sherman, "When you leave, leave nothing of value for the enemy to carry on the war with. I would like the road destroyed east of Jackson as far as possible." Here was a task that Sherman's men were admirably fitted for, and they went at it with a vengeance. A few days later Sherman reported that tracks, bridges, machine shops and railroad cars had been destroyed a distance of forty miles to the north, sixty miles south, and about twenty miles east. In the city of Jackson itself, little was spared. Most public buildings and anything that might possibly help the Confederate war effort, including cotton, was put to the torch. Sherman reported that "Jackson cannot again become a place for the assemblage of men and material with which to threaten the Mississippi River."[7]

After making sure that Jackson and the immediate vicinity would be of no use to the Confederate military for many months, Sherman turned his troops back to Vicksburg, reaching the same area around the Big Black they had occupied before the movement to Jackson on July 27. Behind the army was a devastated countryside that had been stripped of food by both armies during the past several months. The vast majority of the people occupying this area were women, children and old men. There would be no assistance from the Confederate government, so the only way many of these helpless people would be able to survive was to accept assistance from the hated enemy. Large stockpiles of food and forage were established along the east side of the Big Black, and these supplies were freely given out to thousands of desperate citizens who asked for help. Grant, who was possibly thinking of the future and the reuniting of the nation, had written to Sherman that his troops "should try to create as favorable an impression as possible upon the people."[8]

One area where Grant went against convention was in his treatment of the captured enemy troops. At that time the standard military practice was to hold prisoners until exchanged for similar troops by the opposing side. Grant, however, decided to parole the entire Confederate garrison immediately except for some of them who wanted to go to prison camps in the

North to avoid being forced to fight again. The business of paroling enemy troops was heavy with paperwork, as both units and individuals had to have duplicate signed parole forms, one for the Confederates and one for the Federals. Pemberton tried to get Grant to force the several hundred men who refused to sign their paroles to force them to do so, but Grant refused.[9]

There was little doubt that many of the prisoners were planning to desert from the army and simply go home once they were released. Pemberton asked for weapons to arm a battalion to act as guards to keep his army together until they could reach a camp where they could be properly exchanged. Grant also refused this request. Grant later wrote that having Pemberton's army break up "was precisely what I expected and hoped that they would do." Grant did promise that he would keep Pemberton's troops together until they were beyond the Union lines. By July 11 all was ready and the Confederates began marching out of Vicksburg.[10]

General Pemberton sent an accounting of the troops surrendered to Jefferson Davis on the eleventh. In addition to himself, there were thirteen various ranking general officers, and about 29,000 officers and men, with about 10,000 of these ineffective due to illness and wounds. A week later Pemberton wrote to Davis acknowledging the dissipation of his army. "The men, misled by many officers, insist on going home. I have no arms to prevent. It is not to avoid a camp for paroled prisoners, but a determination to see their families. I have done everything in my power to keep them together, but in vain."[11]

General Grant wrote to Halleck on July 18, "The army paroled here have, to a great extent, deserted, and are scattered over the country in every direction." Besides avoiding the expense and effort it would have taken to transport 30,000 prisoners North, Grant was hoping that the release of so many defeated soldiers in the heart of the Confederacy would affect the morale of the citizens as well as cost the Confederacy thousands of veteran soldiers.[12]

Grant's policy toward the release of the prisoners worked as well as it could have. By the time Pemberton's force was east of Jackson probably fewer than 5,000 men were still marching with the army. On July 24 Grant again wrote to Halleck commenting on the fact that Pemberton's army was disintegrating: "The country is full of these paroled prisoners, all of them swearing that they will not take up arms again if they are exchanged. Thousands have crossed the Mississippi river and gone west; many buy passages north." While many of these men did eventually take up arms again, for all practical purposes the Confederate army that defended Vicksburg ceased to exist as a fighting force.[13]

Among the other situations Grant had to deal with that summer was the old subject of the cotton trade. There was no doubt where Grant stood on the question of the cotton trade, as he wrote to Sherman, "I am very much opposed to any trade whatever until the rebellion in this part of the country is entirely crushed out." For economic reasons, Secretary of the Treasury Chase, among many back in Washington, wanted to expand the cotton trade into the newly conquered territory as quickly as possible. Grant, as he had been in Tennessee, was very much against this, writing to Chase that "the people in the Mississippi Valley are now nearly subjugated. Keep trade out but for a few months, and I doubt not but that the work of subjugation will be so complete that trade can be opened freely with the states of Arkansas, Louisiana and Mississippi." Grant also noted that while he would always faithfully execute and orders from his superiors, "My position has given me an opportunity of seeing what could not be known by persons away from the scene of the war, and I suggest, therefore, a great caution in opening trade with rebels."[14]

The cotton trade in the occupied areas of the Confederacy was rife with corruption. All cotton traders had to obtain a permit from the Treasury Department to do business, and these permits were little different from a license to print money. Profits could be enormous and most traders cared little how they obtained their cotton or what side of the lines it came from. Grant reminded Secretary Chase of problems that occurred in Tennessee, saying that his forces were weakened by a third while trying to manage the cotton trade and that "no matter what the restriction thrown around trade, if any whatever is allowed it will be made the means of supplying to the enemy all they want. Restrictions, if lived up to, make trade unprofitable, and hence none but dishonest men go into it." As might be expected, however, Grant's desires meant little when compared to human greed and the economic necessities of a continent. Northern mills needed cotton, the South needed everything and money was to be made fulfilling the needs of both sides.[15]

With all the problems and decisions Grant had to deal with after the capture of Vicksburg, perhaps the most vexing was deciding what his army should do next and then figuring out how to do it. Neither Grant nor Sherman wanted to pursue Johnston's Confederates very far; the weather was terribly hot, the roads were bad, and all that they really wanted at this time was for Johnston to leave Mississippi, which he eventually did. Right now Grant wanted his men to get some rest, but not too much, since it was well known that sickness was more prevalent while an army was in camp than while on the march. Dana wrote to Secretary Stanton just after the fall of Vicksburg saying that Grant was looking for instructions: "He would like to be informed whether the Government wishes him to follow his own judgment or to co-operate in some particular scheme of operations." Grant admitted to Banks that "I have but little idea what is to be done with our western forces. Hope to have instructions from Washington, however."[16]

Several possible actions were being contemplated. First, and most obvious, was Mississippi. The state was wide open and Union troops could move into pretty much any part of the state they wanted to. Moving across the river into the Trans-Mississippi Confederate territory was also considered. However, as long as Union forces controlled the river, the Confederates in the Trans-Mississippi were cut off from the rest of the Confederacy and there was little strategic value in launching a campaign in that vast and arid territory. The biggest threat from Kirby Smith's force was if he decided to launch an attack in Missouri. To counter these possibilities, Grant sent five thousand men to the Union commander in Missouri, Major General John M. Schofield. Other sizeable units were also sent to reinforce Memphis and Natchez, Mississippi.[17]

On July 11, Grant wrote to Banks to congratulate him on the surrender of Port Hudson and advise him of the progress being made in transferring reinforcements. Grant stated that he could spare no troops at this time, but that once Sherman returned from Jackson, "So far as anything I know of being expected from my force, I can spare you an army corps of as good troops as ever trod American soil. No better are found on any other. It will afford me pleasure to send them if I am not required to do some duty requiring them."[18]

In a letter dated July 11, General Halleck wrote to Grant detailing some of the possible options for his troops. In addition to what had already been done to secure the flanks of Mississippi, there was a suggestion of sending more troops to General Rosecrans in Tennessee and the possibility that Banks might need more reinforcements to clear the enemy from Louisiana. Halleck also noted that Johnston might be reinforced enough that Grant would have to confront him with a large force. With all the possible options for action that might present themselves in the near future, Halleck closed with the comment, "Wherever the enemy concentrates we must concentrate to oppose him." The one place that Halleck did not mention, however, was the one that made the most sense to target next, the port of Mobile, Alabama.[19]

Grant was well aware of the importance of Mobile and had started making suggestions about moving against that city. He said in a message to Halleck on July 18: "It seems to me now that Mobile should be captured, the expedition starting from some point on Lake Pontchartrain." Also on the 18th, Banks sent a message to thank Grant for the troops being transferred south and suggested that "the capture of Mobile is of importance second only in the history of the war to the opening of the Mississippi. Mobile is the last stronghold in the West and Southwest. No pains should be spared to effect its reduction." Mobile was the last major Confederate port on the Gulf Coast east of Texas. Capturing the city would be a major blow to the Confederacy and a strategic victory for the North. Not only would closing the port significantly tighten the Federal blockade, but a Federal army in Mobile would be in position to move northeast in the rear of the Confederate armies in Virginia and Tennessee.[20]

Both Grant and Banks continued to suggest that the best use of their troops would be a campaign against Mobile. On August 1, both men wrote to General Halleck concerning Mobile. Grant said, "Mobile can be taken from the Gulf Department, with only one or two gunboats to protect the debarkation. I can send the necessary force." He also asked permission to visit Banks in New Orleans if the movement were authorized. General Banks made a much more detailed plea, noting that most of the city's defenses were concentrated along the Gulf shoreline and Mobile Bay. The landward defenses were incomplete at present but were in the process of being strengthened. The capture of Mobile would give the Federals control of the Alabama River and several railroads that ran east and west connecting Charleston and Savannah to Vicksburg. Most important of all, Banks felt was that "if the rebel Government loses this position, it has no outlet to the Gulf except Galveston."[21]

As it turned out, however, international complications prevented launching a campaign against Mobile at this time. Taking advantage of the war, the French Emperor Napoleon III was in the process of taking control of Mexico and installing Austrian Archduke Maximilian as emperor. Other than lodging protests, the United States was in no position to take any serious action against this violation of the Monroe Doctrine. What Washington could do was to send troops to Texas as a warning against any further incursion by the French. On August 6, Halleck sent a message to Grant for him to forward to Banks, "There are important reasons why our flag should be restored in some part of Texas with the least possible delay. Do this by land, at Galveston, at Indianola, or at any other point you may deem preferable. If by sea, Flag Officer Farragut will co-operate." Halleck noted that this movement should be made quickly.[22]

President Lincoln was well aware of how important Mobile was and that Grant believed that place should be the army's next target. Writing to Grant on August 9, Lincoln explained that an expedition against Mobile "would appear tempting to me also, were it not that, in view of recent events in Mexico, I am greatly impressed with the importance of re-establishing the national authority in Western Texas as soon as possible." The matter of Mobile was settled for the present.[23]

The president also touched on another subject—bringing former slaves into the army. "I believe it is a resource which, if vigorously applied now, will soon close this contest. It works doubly—weakening the enemy and strengthening us." Lincoln wanted to turn 100,000 ex-slaves into soldiers in the Mississippi Valley, "relieving all the white troops to serve elsewhere." Grant had cooperated with this effort from the beginning and was building fortifications around Vicksburg that could be defended by 5,000 troops, using mostly these new soldiers to man the garrison. Grant had already reported to Halleck that "the Negro troops are easier to preserve discipline among than our white troops, and I doubt not will prove equally good for garrison duty. All that have been tried have fought bravely."[24]

The war had finally taken a turn in the Union's favor this summer. General Lee's defeat at Gettysburg and Grant's capture of Vicksburg had been twin disasters for the South. Federal armies were in control of most of Mississippi and Tennessee, the Trans-Mississippi states were now cut off from the rest of the Confederacy, and many in the South were beginning to lose faith in Confederate victory. For men like Grant and Sherman, this was the time to strike even harder, but unlike his friend, Grant was starting to think forward to the time when the enemy might once again become countrymen.

On August 1, Grant issued General Orders No. 50 putting down on paper what conduct was expected from the civilians and soldiers in Mississippi. As long as the citizens went about their business peacefully and obeyed the laws of the government, "all United States forces are prohibited from molesting them in any way." Former slave owners were urged to hire back their former servants for fair wages, as "such a system as this, honestly followed, will result in substantial advantages to all parties." Grant made a point of ordering that all private property was to be respected, and in cases where the army needed to take property for its use, officers were to give receipts to the owners so they could be reimbursed for their loss. The cotton trade was opened to all who brought their cotton to military posts or allowed it to be sent to Memphis, where treasury agents would dispose of it according to regulations. In the war-ravaged areas between Vicksburg and Jackson, both Sherman and McPherson were to set up "a commissary of subsistence, who will issue articles of prime necessity to all destitute families calling for them." To counter disgraceful conduct by soldiers, Grant decided that "if the guilty parties cannot be reached, the commanders of regiments and detachments will be held responsible." And finally, "Summary punishment must be inflicted upon all officers and soldiers apprehended in acts of violence of lawlessness." In essence Grant was offering Federal protection to citizens of the conquered territory if they obeyed the laws of the government they wanted to destroy.[25]

In late August, Halleck wrote to Sherman asking for the views of the senior commanders concerning reconstruction in the states now back under Federal control. Halleck noted, "It is a difficult matter, but I believe it can be successfully solved, if the President will consult opinions of cool and discreet men, who are capable of looking at it in all its bearings and effects." Taking the advice of the commanders who had served in these states was probably the best way to learn the true feelings of the citizens, but it might be debatable whether William T. Sherman could be considered "cool and discreet."[26]

A few weeks later General Sherman replied in a lengthy and less than conciliatory message that included his thoughts on the war in general. Sherman was against reviving civil government in the conquered states for years to come: "They had a government, and so mild and paternal that they gradually forgot they had any at all, save what they themselves controlled.... They chose war.... We accepted the issue, and now they begin to realize that was is a two-edged sword." Winning the war was the only real subject to be considered at this point. Sherman believed that whoever won the war will have the natural right to govern.[27]

Sherman admitted that he "deplored this fratricidal war as much as any man living," but he knew that the only way to end this terrible conflict was to ruthlessly use all the power at the government's disposal to take control of every part of enemy territory. He wrote:

> I would banish all minor questions ... that it makes no difference whether it be in one year or two, or ten or twenty; that we will remove and destroy every obstacle—if need be, take every life, every acre of land, every particle of property, everything that to us seems proper; that we will not cease until the end is attained. That all who do not aid are enemies, and we will not account to them for our acts. If the people of the South oppose, they do so at their peril; and if they stand by mere lookers-on the domestic tragedy, they have no right to immunity, protection, or share in the final result.[28]

As far as negotiating or convincing the people of the conquered states to again become law-abiding citizens of the United States, Sherman's answer was, "I would not coax them or even meet them half way, but make them so sick of war that generations would pass before they would again appeal to it." As to creating new civilian governments in former Confederate states, Sherman suggested that "the only government now needed or deserved by the states of Louisiana, Arkansas, and Mississippi now exists in Grant's army." Like most soldiers, Sherman had seen firsthand the battlefields covered with dead and wounded men; he had seen the rows of bodies waiting for burial in mass graves and the ground outside hospitals that was littered with arms and legs of his troops after every battle. He knew there could be only one outcome of this national horror: "We must conquer them ourselves or be conquered. There is no middle course."[29]

Ulysses Grant was as anxious to get on with the war as anyone that summer, but he also knew how important it was to pay attention to the inevitable political problems that came with civil war. During the campaign for Vicksburg, he had pretty much dismantled one of President Lincoln's most important political deals, namely the one where the president appeared to have promised John McClernand an independent command to take Vicksburg if he could raise the troops to accomplish the task. Grant, with Halleck's assistance, took McClernand's troops for his own use, took over command of the Vicksburg expedition, reducing McClernand to command of a corps, and then while in front of Vicksburg with victory all but assured, dismissed him from the army altogether. McClernand had spent several weeks sitting at home in Illinois seething with anger at what he saw as a betrayal and was complaining to anyone who would listen about Grant's deficiencies. At the end of July, Grant sent his most trusted aide, John Rawlins, to Washington with a copy of the paroles for Pemberton's troops, a letter to the president, and perhaps most importantly to represent Grant's side in what happened with McClernand.[30]

Grant displayed his understanding of the pressures that President Lincoln was under in an introduction letter:

> Colonel Rawlins goes to Washington now by my order as bearer of the reports of the campaign just ended, and rolls and paroles of prisoners captured. Any information desired of any matter connected with this department, from his official position he can give better probably than any other officer in it. I would be pleased if you could give Colonel Rawlins an interview, and I know in asking this you will feel relieved when I tell you he has not a favor to ask for himself or any other living being. Even in my position it is a great luxury to meet a gentleman who has no ax to grind, and I can appreciate that it is infinitely more so in yours.[31]

Colonel Rawlins was well received by everyone he met from Lincoln on down, and he made a good impression on everyone he talked with. Assistant Secretary Dana thought Rawlins was "a very industrious, conscientious man who never loses a moment and never gives himself any indulgence except swearing and scolding." Secretary of the Navy Gideon Welles was "much pleased with him, his frank, intelligent and interesting description of men and account of army operations."[32]

The real reason Rawlins was in Washington, however, was to explain Grant's actions toward McClernand and soothe any possible anger that might be stirred up by the politically powerful and now unemployed general. Considering that Grant was the most successful of all Federal commanders, it is unlikely that McClernand's comments about drinking and Grant being an inept commander who relied on subordinates to get things done would have done Grant much harm, but it could not hurt to have a loyal spokesman available to answer any questions.[33]

Secretary Welles later wrote that the evidence given by Rawlins when questioned about McClernand proved that he was "an impracticable and unfit man—that he has not been subordinate and intelligent but has been an embarrassment. And instead of assisting has really been an obstruction to army movements and operations." Clearly Rawlins was in Washington to give Grant's side of the story and his personal dislike for McClernand was obvious, but Welles felt that "there can be hardly a doubt McClernand is in fault, and Rawlins has been sent here by Grant to enlist the President rather than bring dispatches. In this I think he has succeeded."[34]

By the end of the summer of 1863, Grant was ready to move on with the war. The situation with McClernand had been cleared up, troops that had joined Grant during the campaign had been returned to their original locations, and other troops had been sent to reinforce several key points to protect Mississippi. The army Grant now commanded was smaller but made up of tough veterans and capable officers who were accustomed to winning battles and had every expectation that they would continue.

Before Grant could initiate any campaign of his choosing, however, disturbing news began coming in from Tennessee, and on September 13 Halleck wrote to Grant and Sherman to let them know that it was feared that Braxton Bragg and Joseph Johnston might be combining their forces to attack William Rosecrans' Army of the Cumberland in Tennessee. Halleck ordered that "all of General Grant's available forces should be sent to Memphis, thence to Corinth and Tuscumbia, to co-operate with Rosecrans, should the rebels attempt that movement." Any plans Grant might have been entertaining were suddenly put on hold.[35]

Chapter 18

Triumph Turns to Disaster

During the early morning hours of June 24, 1863, the Federal troops of the Army of the Cumberland tightened their belts and shouldered their muskets as they began leaving their camps around Murfreesboro, Tennessee, heading out on what would be a long and bloody campaign for control of the strategically important town of Chattanooga. Major General William S. Rosecrans, commanding those Union troops, was setting in motion a complicated plan to maneuver General Braxton Bragg's Confederate Army of Tennessee out of their fortifications around Tullahoma, about midway between the Federal base at Murfreesboro and Chattanooga.[1]

During the six months since the battle at Stones River, both armies had been resting and rebuilding from the horrendous casualties they had suffered on those three terrible days between December 31, 1862, and January 2, 1863. Content to just stay where he was, General Bragg spent the majority of his time preparing defensive lines just north of Tullahoma to block the expected Federal advance toward Chattanooga and dealing with a near mutiny by some of his senior commanders. Many of the corps and division commanders were dissatisfied with Bragg as the army's commander and complaints to Jefferson Davis led him to launch an investigation by General Johnston. In the end, however, Johnston decided that the army was in good condition and he found no fault with Bragg's strategy and conduct during the battle. There was no one else of sufficient rank and experience that Davis trusted to command the Army of Tennessee, so Bragg stayed.[2]

General Rosecrans also spent months rebuilding and refitting his shattered army, but unlike his adversary, he was expected to resume offensive movements as soon as the army was ready. In March the authorities in Washington began pressing Rosecrans to take some action. Responding to urgings from General Halleck that he make some effort to engage the enemy, Rosecrans replied, "I do not think it prudent or practicable to advance from this position until I am better or differently informed." Of course, the capture of Chattanooga was a high priority, but it was also hoped that if Rosecrans could occupy Bragg's army, he would be unable to transfer troops to aid in the defense of Vicksburg, the most important Federal objective in the West at that time.[3]

Week after week went by and still Rosecrans did not move. By May 28 even President Lincoln got involved, writing, "I would not push you to any rashness but I am very anxious that you do your utmost, short of rashness, to keep Bragg from getting on to help Johnston against Grant." Even a request for action from the president made little impression on Rosecrans, who pretty much ignored Lincoln's message with this response: "Dispatch received. I will attend to it." General Halleck's patience was close to exhausted on June 3 when he wrote to Rosecrans informing that officer that information had been received that General Johnston was in fact receiving reinforcements from Bragg. Halleck also suggested that if Rosecrans did not act soon he would consider transferring troops from the Army of the Cumberland to reinforce General Grant at Vicksburg. Still Rosecrans did not move.[4]

Telegrams containing orders and warnings and threats poured into Murfreesboro from Washington with seemingly little effect on General Rosecrans. On June 11, Halleck wrote, "I deem it my duty to repeat to you the great dissatisfaction that is felt here at your inactivity." On June 16 Halleck again tried to get Rosecrans to commit to a date to begin an advance: "Is it your intention to make an immediate movement forward? A definite answer, yes or no, is required." Not backing down, Rosecrans answered, "In reply to your inquiry, if immediate means to-night or to-morrow, no. If it means as soon as all things are ready, say five days, yes."[5]

The small town of Chattanooga, home to fewer than three thousand inhabitants, was important to both the Federals and Confederates because of its location. Nestled in a modest valley among the mountains just north of the Georgia border, Chattanooga was the most important rail center the Confederacy still controlled after Richmond and Atlanta. The Virginia & Tennessee Railroad ran from Richmond through Knoxville and all the way to Chattanooga. The Western & Atlantic Railroad ran south from Chattanooga through Dalton, Georgia, and then to Atlanta and other points south. The Nashville & Chattanooga Railroad headed west from Chattanooga through the mountains to Stevenson, Alabama, where it turned north to Nashville. Also from Stevenson, the Memphis & Charleston Railroad connected with Memphis and the Mississippi River. Almost every important point in the Confederacy east of the Mississippi was linked by the railroads that ran through or connected with Chattanooga. The importance of Chattanooga was so obvious to anyone who could read a map that a few months later, during the Federal occupation of the city, George W. Squier of the 44th Indiana wrote to his wife that Chattanooga was "the key to the heart of the southern confederacy, a point of really moore importance than Richmond." He was probably right.[6]

General Rosecrans had a great deal of latitude as to how he would approach Chattanooga just as long as he tried to stay in contact with the army of General Burnside, who was operating in Eastern Tennessee. Burnside was also ordered to try to keep in contact with Rosecrans' left as he moved south so that if the Confederates tried to concentrate their forces on either army, the other could move to its assistance. Both Rosecrans and Burnside pretty much ignored this sound military concept and never got anywhere near close enough to support the other during the entire campaign. After months of preparation, Rosecrans finally began his campaign for Chattanooga early in the morning on June 24 when he sent a message to Halleck simply stating, "The army begins to move at 3 o'clock this morning."[7]

It might have taken General Rosecrans a long time to move, but when the army finally advanced, Rosecrans and his corps commanders conducted a brilliant nine day campaign of deception and maneuver. Lightning quick cavalry attacks and aggressive action by Major General Alexander McCook, who pushed units of his Twentieth Corps through gaps in the mountainous terrain, allowed Rosecrans to bring the full strength of his force to bear on the Confederate positions. In addition, Rosecrans sent units circling around both ends of the Confederate defenses so that General Bragg's scattered forces saw the enemy coming at them from all directions. At the end of the first day of the advance Rosecrans' plan was working to perfection, and with a little luck he would soon have a large force threatening the Confederate rear as the rest of the army approached, trapping and destroying the Army of Tennessee.[8]

As so often happened in the mountainous terrain of Tennessee, the weather became a major factor in the campaign. It began to rain the day the Federals began their march and continued for days. Colonel Francis T. Sherman of the 88th Illinois wrote home that the rain has "proved to be almost intolerable. The dust was allayed and became muddy, from that to mud, from mud to slosh, slosh to an almost impassable quagmire, and still it rains. I never saw anything like it." The heavy rain slowed the Union advance to a crawl and gave Bragg time to consolidate his spread-out troops before they were overwhelmed.[9]

The thorny relations between Bragg and most of his senior officers prevented them from developing a plan to launch a counterattack that everyone could agree to support, but fortunately the slowness of the Federal advance gave Bragg time to gather his forces. On June 27 he decided to pull his army back into the safety of the well fortified positions around Tullahoma. Two of Bragg's corps commanders, Lieutenant Generals Leonidas L. Polk and William J. Hardee, protested that Tullahoma was too isolated and that Federal forces were sure to try to get between the army and its supply depot in Chattanooga. Should this occur and the army was forced to retreat to the southwest, both Chattanooga and northern Georgia would be open to the enemy. Bragg eventually decided his subordinates were right and that he must protect Chattanooga at all costs. On July 1 he ordered the Army of Tennessee to fall back toward the little town that was so essential to the Confederacy.[10]

General Bragg's troops began crossing the Tennessee River on July 4 and by dark on the seventh the tired Confederates were in camp at Chattanooga. Rosecrans tried to continue the advance but the terrible weather and delays in crossing the Elk River caused him to call off the pursuit and pull the troops back to the town of Winchester for some much needed rest. General

Left: Confederate General Braxton Bragg's bad temper and inability to get along with subordinates cost him several civilian positions after the war (Library of Congress).
Right: Union General William S. Rosecrans, after the war, was active in the railroad industry and served two terms as a congressman from California (Library of Congress).

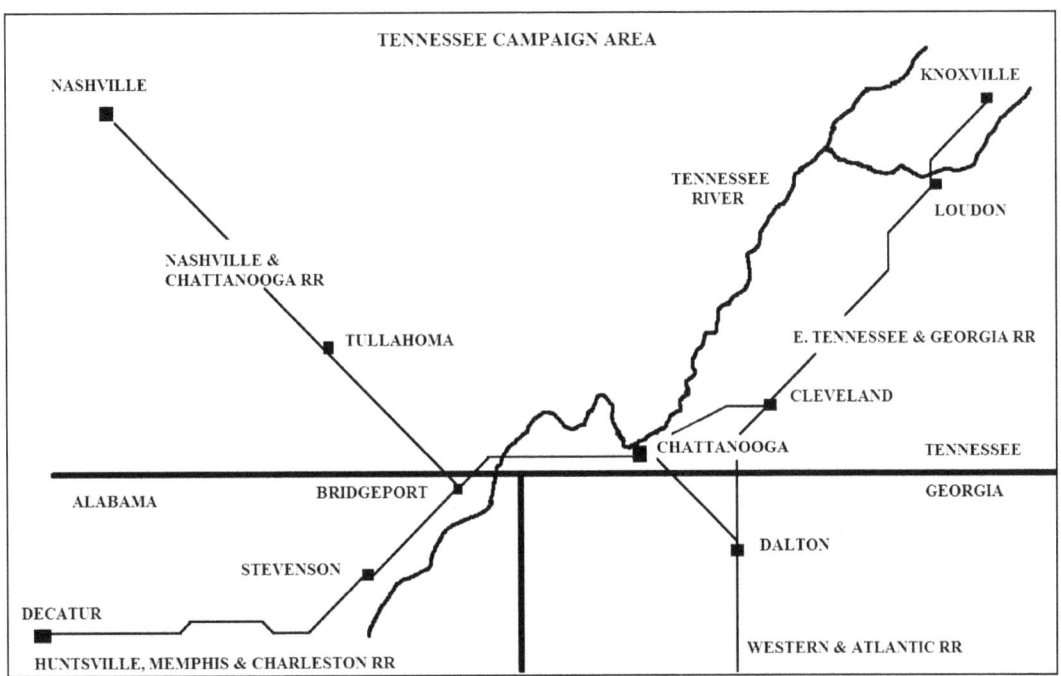

Rosecrans had reason to be pleased with his campaign so far and reported to Washington, "Thus ended a nine days' campaign, which drove the enemy from two fortified positions and gave us possession of Middle Tennessee, conducted in one of the most extraordinary rains ever known in Tennessee at that period of the year." Even Confederate Brigadier General Arthur M. Manigault gave Rosecrans credit when he later wrote that the campaign "was, I think, the most brilliant of the war." Much of Tennessee, including Chattanooga, was still under Confederate control, but Manigault clearly realized that "all the most fertile and more wealthy portion of the state was lost to us."[11]

Almost as soon as Rosecrans halted his army he began receiving messages from Washington urging him to continue moving forward. After receiving the news of Vicksburg's surrender and the victory at Gettysburg, Secretary of War Stanton tried to motivate Rosecrans to action, writing, "Lee's army overthrown; Grant victorious. You and your noble army now have the chance to give the finishing blow to the rebellion. Will you neglect the chance?" Rosecrans, however, was less than moved by Stanton's appeal and replied by noting that his army had cleared the enemy from Middle Tennessee: "I beg in behalf of this army that the War Department may not overlook so great an event because it is not written in letters of blood."[12]

The monumental victories at Vicksburg and Gettysburg had the Confederacy reeling. The authorities in Washington saw this as the perfect time to keep up the pressure and hit the enemy again. As might have been expected, however, Rosecrans strongly believed time was needed to refit his army and develop plans for the next part of the campaign. He took no action for nearly a month and a half.

Of course, just as had happened previously, Rosecrans was bombarded with messages from Washington to move forward. On August 4 Halleck wrote, "Your forces must move forward without further delay. You will daily report the movement of each corps till you cross the Tennessee." Rosecrans could not be hurried into moving until he was ready. The next part of the campaign would take the Union army over the Cumberland Plateau, a mountainous and barren region with little food for men or animals. Rosecrans felt that trying to cross this rugged terrain without a sufficient stockpile of supplies was just asking for disaster. On August 6 he answered Halleck's call for an advance. "It is necessary to have our means of crossing the river completed and our supplies provided to cross sixty miles of mountain, and sustain ourselves during the operations of crossing and fighting, before we move." Rosecrans noted that the army would be moving over narrow and difficult roads with little food and water and that "to obey your order literally would ... certainly cause ultimate delay and probable disaster." Convinced he was right to wait until all preparations were completed, Rosecrans ended his message to Halleck, "If, therefore, the movement which I propose cannot be regarded as obedience to your order, I respectfully request a modification of it, or to be relieved from the command."[13]

While Rosecrans only had to decide where and when to move forward General Bragg had about 150 miles of front to defend and had to be concerned with the possibility that the Federals might swing way around one of his flanks and get in the Confederate rear. In addition to defending Chattanooga, Bragg had to contend with a Federal advance into East Tennessee, where General Burnside was preparing to advance his Army of the Ohio against Knoxville, which would cut the important East Tennessee & Virginia Railroad. Another possibility that had to be considered was that rather than stopping at Knoxville, Burnside might continue toward Chattanooga and Bragg could be attacked by overwhelming force from two different directions. If the railroad to Knoxville were cut and a large enough Federal force got between Chattanooga and Atlanta, the Army of Tennessee would be cut off from supplies and escape, and there was only one outcome to such a scenario, surrender or destruction.[14]

On August 10 Rosecrans began his push toward Chattanooga using the same strategy that had already proved so successful, attacking with multiple forces from different directions. The goal was to get Federal forces below the Tennessee River near Bridgeport or Stevenson and cut Bragg's communication with Atlanta, exactly what the Confederate commander could not afford to let happen. One of Rosecrans' staff officers, Lieutenant Henry Cist, later wrote, "Brilliant campaigns without battles, do not accomplish the destruction of an army. A campaign like that of Tullahoma always means a battle at some other point." Chattanooga was the door that opened into the Deep South, and eventually there would have to be a fight if that door was to be forced open.[15]

The Army of the Cumberland moved forward on a broad front from Winchester northeast to McMinnville. The various corps had to spread out to avoid getting backed up by trying to go through the narrow gaps in the mountains. While this strategy was likely to confuse the enemy and conceal where the real assault might come from, it also exposed the individual Union corps to attack by a larger force, which could result in the Army of the Cumberland being destroyed piece by piece. The Confederate troops in Knoxville were recalled and stationed about thirty-five miles northeast of Chattanooga. Bragg was convinced that Rosecrans was making directly for Chattanooga and recalled a division camped at Bridgeport positioning his troops above the city to repel an assault coming from any direction north of Chattanooga. But Rosecrans had no intention of making a direct attack from that direction.[16]

Once again Rosecrans' plan was working to perfection. With the majority of the Confederates preparing for an attack on Chattanooga from the north, the Union army was able to easily get across the Tennessee River southwest of the town. In a few days four crossing sites were in operation, and by September 8 the entire Army of the Cumberland, except for a force left behind to guard the rail center at Stevenson, had crossed the river and was moving forward south of Chattanooga.[17]

Once across the river, Rosecrans quickly began moving east to cut the Western & Atlantic Railroad that brought supplies to Bragg's army from Atlanta. Knowing that he had once again outmaneuvered his enemy, Rosecrans noted, "As a prudent commander, Bragg could not afford to leave us forty miles south of his position, to get quietly down and concentrate between him and Atlanta." The dilemma facing Bragg was that he was unsure of Rosecrans' target and he did not have enough troops to properly defend Chattanooga and prevent Rosecrans from cutting his supply line at the same time. It also occurred to Bragg that the Federal moves might be just a diversion to get his army out from the safety of the town's fortifications.[18]

By September 7, Bragg received information that convinced him that the main Federal force was indeed below the city and moving east. The Confederate commander could not allow his army to be cut off from its supply base, and by evening the Army of Tennessee began to evacuate Chattanooga. It was just as well that Bragg moved when he did, because that day advance units of the Federal army arrived just a few miles from the city; one division was on the crest of Lookout Mountain, and another was less than twenty miles south. Up on Lookout Mountain the Federal advance could see the dust rising as the Confederates marched south into Georgia.[19]

On the afternoon of September 9, the town of Chattanooga was occupied by the lead division of Major General Thomas Crittenden's corps. The remainder of Crittenden's troops continued on to Rossville, about five miles south of the city. During the pursuit of the retreating enemy Rosecrans began receiving reports from prisoners and civilians that the Confederates were exhausted and demoralized. He decided that now was the moment to strike. Simply outmaneuvering the enemy was no longer enough; Rosecrans wanted to destroy the Army of Tennessee.[20]

On the same day that Chattanooga was taken Rosecrans issued new orders for his army to end the flanking movements and concentrate on the fleeing Confederate army. Rosecrans had moved units into position to delay Bragg's march south until more troops could come up or, with a little luck, one of the Federal corps could hit the retreating enemy columns in the flank or rear. Believing that he was chasing an already beaten enemy and seeing the opportunity to cut off their retreat and destroy them caused Rosecrans to abandon his usual slow and cautious approach. On the evening of September 9, Rosecrans wrote to Halleck, "Chattanooga is ours without a struggle, and East Tennessee is free. Our move on the enemy's flank and rear progresses, while the tail of his retreating column will not escape unmolested." Rosecrans' new aggressive attitude was welcome back in Washington; unfortunately, he had seriously misinterpreted the situation.[21]

In fact, instead of the Army of Tennessee running away in a panicked retreat, General Bragg was actually concentrating his own men and recently arrived reinforcements from Knoxville just twenty-five miles from Chattanooga at La Fayette, Georgia. The three advancing Federal corps were spread out far enough that they could not provide support for one another and Bragg saw a golden opportunity to attack them one at a time with overwhelming numbers.[22]

General Bragg's first target would be the corps of Major General George Thomas. Thomas' advance division commanded by Major General James Negley had gotten ahead of the rest of the corps, and Bragg put together an excellent plan to trap Negley between two Confederate forces. With the loss of this division, the rest of Thomas' corps could be destroyed in an all out assault by Bragg's full force. After Thomas' troops had been dealt with, the other two Federal corps of McCook and Crittenden, which were too far apart to support each other, could be attacked one at a time. A brilliant victory was within grasp if Bragg could get his army to move quickly enough to take advantage of the opportunity in front of them.[23]

Bragg's plan seemed about as sure as anything could be in war, but on the morning of September 10 it all began to fall apart due to the usual intransigence of some of his subordinates. Lieutenant General Daniel H. Hill reported that Major General Patrick Cleburne, the commander of the blocking force, was ill and unable to take part in the battle. Major General Thomas C. Hindman, commanding the troops who were to make the assault, stopped a mile or so short of Negley's position and just sat there. All day messages went back and forth with Bragg ordering the attack and Hindman returning messages that he needed more men. Reinforcements were sent to Hindman and once Cleburne was apprised of the situation, he turned out to be in fine health and hurried his men to their assigned position.[24]

On the morning of the 11th, Bragg rode out to the scene to take command in person. Patrick Cleburne, as tough a fighter as any in the army, had quickly brought his troops forward and was ready to attack as soon as Hindman did, and once again they waited to spring the trap. By this time, however, learning of the danger facing Negley's division, General Thomas had ordered the rest of his corps to move forward as quickly as possible. Bragg's overwhelming advantage would soon be gone, and at 3 p.m. he sent a final message to Hindman practically begging him to do something: "Time is precious. The enemy presses from the north. We must unite or both retire. The enemy is small force in line of battle in our front, and we only wait for your attack." Bragg knew that to send Cleburne's troops forward on their own in a frontal assault would only result in heavy casualties and allow Negley to simply fall back closer to the rest of Thomas' corps.[25]

By late afternoon General Negley began pulling his men back. There was some light firing between skirmishers as the Federals were withdrawing, but they soon made good their escape and the opportunity for a relatively easy Confederate victory was gone. As one might expect, Bragg was furious when he confronted Hindman, but there was nothing left to do but pull back, regroup, and look for another opportunity to strike before Rosecrans brought his scattered forces together.[26]

By September 12, Rosecrans finally deduced that Bragg was not retreating as originally thought, but was now massing his forces near La Fayette. Rosecrans began pulling his spread out army together, but it would take time for the Union army to close up, and with Bragg's forces concentrated near the center, both of Rosecrans' flanks were still dangerously exposed to attack with little chance of help from the rest of the army. Recognizing the danger he was in, Rosecrans' later wrote, "Our fate now depended, first upon prompt concentration, and next, on our choosing our own battleground, where our flanks would be protected and where we could have full use of our artillery."[27]

Another opportunity for Bragg to strike a blow against a smaller Union force came on September 12. He learned that one of Crittenden's divisions was far out in front of the rest of the corps at Lee and Gordon's Mill on the road to La Fayette. Bragg sent orders to General Polk to attack this division: "This presents you a fine opportunity of striking Crittenden in detail, and I hope you will avail yourself of it at daylight to-morrow. This division crushed, and the others are yours. I shall be delighted to hear of your success." With reinforcements ordered to support Polk, there could be little doubt of the outcome, if he followed orders.[28]

Knowing that Polk was unreliable and apt to ignore orders, Bragg sent two other messages that evening urging Polk to make the attack early the next morning. In response Polk sent messages back to headquarters complaining that he was the one who was outnumbered and asking for reinforcements. Bragg must have been frustrated beyond belief by this point, but he did order reinforcements to Polk and decided to go to the front in person. Polk's veteran troops, who were supposed to be attacking and winning an almost sure victory, were instead sitting in their works waiting for a Federal attack that was not coming. Another victory was missed because Bragg's subordinates did not trust his judgment.[29]

General Bragg was by this time physically and mentally exhausted. In addition to the frustration in dealing with subordinates, he spent many hours traveling or reading reports that flooded into headquarters, and rest was a luxury he could not afford. With the Union forces growing stronger as they concentrated, Bragg wanted to avoid a major engagement just now and decided to move his troops to the east side of Chickamauga Creek. Another reason for Bragg to avoid a fight at this time was that he would soon be receiving a large number of reinforcements. On September 9, Lieutenant General James Longstreet and 12,000 veteran soldiers from Robert E. Lee's Army of Northern Virginia began a journey that would bring them to Chickamauga Creek.[30]

The loss of Knoxville had cut the most direct route from Virginia, so these men had to travel about nine hundred miles through Virginia, North Carolina, South Carolina, and Georgia on the rundown Confederate railway system. Brigadier General E. Porter Alexander later wrote about the journey, "The roads had had but a small business before the war, and their equipment and motive power were light even for those days. The gauges were not uniform, and often the tracks of connecting roads were joined through the cities only by lines of drays, and there was no interchange of cars." Despite the many difficulties in moving the men and their equipment, the lead units of Longstreet's corps began arriving on the 18th. In addition to these fine troops, Bragg was receiving reinforcements from all over the Confederacy, including about 11,000 men from Mississippi. With the addition of these troops Bragg's army would actually have a small numerical edge over Rosecrans.[31]

Knowing that the Confederates were in position just across Chickamauga Creek, it was imperative that Rosecrans concentrate his own forces as quickly as possible. By the evening of September 17 all three Union corps were close enough to provide support for each other if needed. The army was facing east toward Chickamauga Creek with McCook on the right, Thomas in the center, and Crittenden on the left. Almost as important as concentrating the army was keeping control of the roads north to Chattanooga, so Rosecrans issued orders for the entire army to move northeast along Chickamauga Creek to cover the La Fayette road to Chattanooga. Cutting Rosecrans off from Chattanooga was exactly what Bragg was planning. On the eighteenth Bragg sent forces to several locations to get across Chickamauga Creek north of the Union army, and despite meeting some heavy resistance, by evening the Confederates had forced their way over to the west side of the creek at several points.[32]

With both armies now on the same side of Chickamauga Creek, Rosecrans took the drastic step of ordering General Thomas to leave one division behind, pull the rest of his corps out of the center of the Union line, and march behind Crittenden's corps to the far left of the army while McCook's corps moved up to fill in the space vacated by Thomas. Thomas' men made an exhausting night march, but during the morning of September 19 they filed into position on the left. Most importantly, they were north of the right flank of Bragg's troops and had control of the roads to Chattanooga.[33]

On September 18, Bragg's latest intelligence was that most of his forces were west of the creek and past the left of the Union army in position to launch a flank attack that would almost surely result in a resounding victory. Early the next morning, however, a cavalry reconnaissance reported a large force of Federal infantry in position north of Bragg's right flank. Thomas' night march had completely changed the situation, and now instead of a decisive victory the Army of Tennessee could be facing disaster.[34]

The Battle of Chickamauga began early on the morning of September 19 when reconnaissance units of both armies ran into each other on the northern end of their lines. Troops were rushed to the front and the fighting intensified and gradually spread south until both armies were engaged in mortal combat. All day the lines at different positions surged back and forth as first one side then the other attacked and counter-attacked, but the most desperate fighting took place in the northern end of the battlefield. Rosecrans had to hold his left at all costs, and it was there that Bragg made his heaviest assaults. Time after time the Confederates attacked, sometimes pushing the defenders back, but then Thomas would launch his own attack to regain the lost ground. Hour after hour they killed each other, but the La Fayette Road remained in Union hands. The fighting continued until after dark as exhausted soldiers fired at the flashes of enemy guns.[35]

The first day of battle had accomplished little other than kill and wound thousands of men. Rosecrans' lines had been pushed back in places, but he still controlled the vital La Fayette Road. During the night the Federal troops got little rest, as units were moved around to shore up the battered lines, especially the left, and the men worked feverishly to build defensive works in anticipation of what would come in the morning. That evening Rosecrans sent a message to General Halleck informing him of the situation: "We have just concluded a terrific day's fighting, and have another prospect for to-morrow. The enemy attempted to turn our left, but his design was anticipated, and a sufficient force placed there to render his attempt abortive." Rosecrans commented on the heavily wooded terrain, the lack of opportunity to use artillery, and the superior numbers of the enemy. He closed with an optimistic forecast, "The army is in excellent condition and spirits, and by the blessing of Providence, the defeat of the enemy will be total to-morrow."[36]

During the night General Bragg had moved additional troops to his right and ordered an attack on the Union left to commence at first light on the morning of the twentieth. As dawn arrived Federal troops were still moving into their new positions, and if the attack had been launched when Bragg intended, the Confederates might have found the Union troops unprepared to receive a strong assault. As it turned out, however, once again Bragg was the victim of subordinates failing to obey orders. It was not until about 9:30 a.m. that the Confederate assault against the Union left began, giving the defenders a few more crucial hours to improve their defenses.[37]

The fighting again began in the north as General Thomas' troops were hit with ferocious attacks from the front and left but held firm. As on the previous day the fighting spread south, but the Federal troops repulsed the Confederate attacks all along the line. Shortly before noon, however, the battle turned in Bragg's favor when General Longstreet sent his newly arrived veterans against the Union center and just happened to hit a gap in their lines. Rosecrans had ordered troops not actively engaged to the left to help Thomas and through a mix-up in communication the newly opened hole in the line was not filled in time. The Confederates poured through the gap and the Union lines on both sides quickly collapsed.[38]

The right side of the Union line had been shattered. Some individual units tried to make a stand, but most of the troops were soon heading north as quickly as they could. With most of the army in full retreat General Thomas continued to hold his position by moving troops around to his right, forming a horseshoe shaped line. All afternoon Thomas withstood attacks from his front and right. Rosecrans reported, "The fight on the left after 2 p. m. was that of the army. Never, in the history of this war at least, have troops fought with greater energy and determination." Thomas' magnificent defensive stand that afternoon earned him the nickname "The Rock of Chickamauga."[39]

By mid-afternoon the situation for what was left of the Army of the Cumberland had become desperate. Time after time Bragg's men assaulted the Union lines and each time they were thrown back with heavy losses. Charles Partridge of the 96th Illinois later wrote, "I cannot describe those terrific charges and countercharges, as the rebels again and again sought to drive us back." The unrelenting Confederate attacks had cost them dearly, but the defenders were being worn down and could not hang on for much longer. The fighting was reaching a critical stage around mid-afternoon when Major General Gordon Granger, hearing the sounds of the battle, left his assigned position guarding Rossville and the road to Chattanooga and arrived with two brigades of fresh troops.[40]

General Granger's reinforcements tipped the scale just enough to allow Thomas to hold his position until after dark, when he was finally able to disengage and fall back to Rossville to set up new defensive positions there and on Missionary Ridge. Once the army was safely within Chattanooga's defenses, Rosecrans notified General Burnside in East Tennessee of the defeat and requested his assistance. Assistant Secretary of War Charles Dana, who was accompanying the army, wrote to Washington, "My report today is of deplorable importance. Chickamauga is as fatal a name in our history as Bull Run." In his report to General Halleck, Rosecrans admitted, "We have met with a serious disaster; extent not yet ascertained. Enemy overwhelmed us, drove our right, pierced our center, and scattered troops there."[41]

General Bragg's army spent most of September 21 reorganizing its units and caring for the thousands of dead and wounded that littered the battlefield. General Bragg was criticized for not immediately following the beaten foe, but as he wrote, "Any immediate pursuit by our infantry and artillery would have been fruitless, as it was not deemed practicable with our weak and exhausted force to assail the enemy, now more than double our numbers, behind his entrenchments."[42]

Rosecrans wrote to President Lincoln on September 21, "After two days of the severest fighting I ever witnessed our right and center were beaten. The left held its position until sunset. Our loss is heavy and our troops worn down.... We have no certainty of holding our position here." President Lincoln understood the strategic importance of holding Chattanooga as well as anyone, and that day wrote to Halleck, "I think it very important for General Rosecrans to hold his position at or about Chattanooga, because if held from that place to Cleveland, both inclusive, it keeps all Tennessee clear of the enemy, and also breaks one of his most important railroad lines." Rosecrans was informed that assistance was on the way and he was to just stay where he was. President Lincoln also expressed his thoughts on the importance of Chattanooga when he wrote that as long as Federal forces could hold the city, "the rebellion can only eke out a short and feeble existence, as an animal sometimes may with a thorn in its vitals."[43]

General Bragg reported the victory to Richmond: "The enemy retreated on Chattanooga last night, leaving his dead and wounded in our hands. His loss is very large in men, artillery, small-arms and colors. Ours is heavy, but not yet ascertained. The victory is complete, and our cavalry is pursuing." What Bragg did not say was that the terrible battle at Chickamauga had resulted in the one thing the Confederates did not want, the Army of the Cumberland still in control of Chattanooga and now safely behind the town's fortifications.[44]

Chapter 19

A Difficult Time in Chattanooga

Although the Federal survivors had safely made their way back to Chattanooga, there was now a question of whether the city could be held by the demoralized troops. On September 22, Dana informed Secretary Stanton that "Rosecrans is considering question of retreat from here. I judge that he thinks that unless he can have assurance of ample re-enforcements within one week, the attempt to hold this place will be much more disastrous than retreat." General Bragg moved his exhausted troops up to Chattanooga over the next couple of days, taking control of most of the high ground around the city. Recovering from the shock of the battle, Rosecrans wired President Lincoln on the 23rd requesting reinforcements and assuring him that "we hold this point, and I cannot be dislodged except by very superior numbers and after a great battle."[1]

Inside the fortifications of Chattanooga, the Union soldiers faced more danger from starvation than they did from enemy assault. The army was in serious trouble and everyone could see it. One of the soldiers in the 86th Indiana put on paper what most of his comrades must have been thinking as they began to understand the difficulties they were facing: "In front was a superior force of an inveterate enemy commanded by a skillful General. In rear a large river, and beyond were rugged mountains and a stretch of country over which all supplies must be hauled a distance of sixty miles. Could the end be seen? It looked black." Fortunately for the men in Chattanooga, plans had already been drawn up and set in motion for their relief.[2]

Well before Chickamauga was fought, General Halleck had sent telegrams to Vicksburg and other commands in the west looking for troops to reinforce Rosecrans. The communication sent to Vicksburg on September 13 urged either Grant or Sherman to send any available forces to Memphis, where they would be forwarded east to join or at least cooperate with General Rosecrans' forces. Halleck also wired General Hurlbut in Memphis twice telling him to send all his available troops east to assist Rosecrans.[3]

In Knoxville, General Burnside also received appeals to send reinforcements to Rosecrans. On September 14, Halleck wired, "There are reasons why you should re-enforce General Rosecrans with all possible dispatch. It is believed that the enemy will concentrate to give him battle. You must be there to help him." And the next day Halleck sent another message saying that information had been developed "that three divisions of Lee's army have been sent to re-enforce Bragg. It is important that all the troops in your department be brought to the front with all possible dispatch, so as to help General Rosecrans."[4]

General Grant was unaware of all the requests for reinforcements for Rosecrans' army because he was in New Orleans recovering from injuries suffered when his horse fell. Grant had gone to New Orleans to discuss possible future actions with General Banks and had been bedridden for several weeks. Once he returned to Vicksburg, Grant was still incapacitated, but at least he was now aware of the seriousness of the situation and was able to begin to take action. Long distance communications during the Civil War were frequently unreliable and this was one of those times. Telegraph lines did not extend everywhere and there were frequent interruptions in service from sabotage.[5]

General Grant responded to Halleck's call for reinforcements by redirecting John E. Smith's division of McPherson's corps from Arkansas to Memphis. In addition, General Sherman was instructed to send one of his four divisions camped near Vicksburg to Memphis. General Peter Osterhaus' division began the journey east that evening. As the seriousness of the situation in Tennessee became more apparent, at Grant's headquarters the next day he ordered two more of Sherman's divisions, commanded by Brigadier Generals Giles A. Smith and John Corse, to join the troops already on the way to Memphis, with Sherman in command of the entire force.[6]

Sherman was to move his troops along the Memphis & Charleston Railroad to Athens, Alabama, much of which had been damaged and would have to be repaired as they advanced. Although this would slow down Sherman's progress, the addition of so many thousands more men to feed in the vicinity of Chattanooga made it imperative that the track be repaired so his troops "should not be dependent on the roads back to Nashville, already overtaxed by the demand of Rosecrans's army." All these troop movements from Vicksburg and Memphis turned out to be too late to help Rosecrans, who had already been defeated at Chickamauga before Grant's men began their march east.[7]

Almost immediately after the fighting ended at Chickamauga, both commanders began to receive a significant amount of criticism. Naturally, as the loser of the battle, there was dissatisfaction with Rosecrans' performance, but it was not just the battle itself that caused the storm of complaints. Chickamauga was one of the bloodiest defeats suffered by Federal forces during the entire war and this contrasted sharply with Rosecrans' well publicized campaigns that drove the Confederates out of Tullahoma and Chattanooga with a minimum of casualties. The most serious problem Rosecrans' faced, however, was that, believing the battle irretrievably lost, he abandoned the field to begin preparing for the defense of Chattanooga before the fighting had actually ended and was absent during George Thomas' magnificent defensive stand. Rosecrans' personal courage was not questioned, that had been proven on other battlefields, but the shock of the defeat appeared to leave him dazed and confused.

On the Confederate side, even though Braxton Bragg had won a great victory, he could not escape the continued criticism from both military and civilian leaders. The main complaint was that he had won only a partial victory; the majority of the enemy had been allowed to escape. It was widely believed that had Bragg vigorously pursued of the defeated Federals, he might have all but destroyed the Army of the Cumberland. Another point raised was that if Bragg had pushed troops across the Tennessee River, he could have cut the Federal supply lines and forced a quick surrender, as opposed to waiting for hunger to force Rosecrans to abandon Chattanooga. After the war, James Longstreet, who was one of Bragg's most consistent critics, wrote, "In my judgment our last opportunity was lost when we failed to follow the success at Chickamauga and capture or disperse the Union army."[8]

To be fair to Braxton Bragg, his army had lost nearly one third of its fighting force at Chickamauga. This amount of loss would devastate any army, and immediately after the battle the surviving Confederates were in no condition to pursue and assault the Federals behind the defenses of Chattanooga. Bragg's army did not have enough wagons or animals to pull them to enable the troops to move very far away from the Western & Atlantic Railroad that brought supplies up from Atlanta. Even if sufficient supplies could be obtained, most of the bridges across the Tennessee had been destroyed and the Confederates had no pontoon boats.[9]

Besides the condition of his troops, Bragg had another good reason why he did not press forward to attack the Federal troops in Chattanooga; they weren't going anywhere. At this point the exhausted men of the Army of the Cumberland were certainly not going to fight their way out of the Chattanooga area. There was already a shortage of provisions and this situation would only be getting worse over time. With control of the high ground, it would have been obvious to Bragg that the smart thing to do was to let his army recuperate and just wait until hunger accomplished what began at Chickamauga.

Considering the missed opportunities that bedeviled Bragg during the previous campaign, he decided that now was the time to get his own house in order. He relieved both Polk and Hill from their commands. Still, there was little letup in the complaining by Bragg's subordinates. In a message sent directly to Confederate Secretary of War Seddon, Longstreet concluded that Bragg's only correct decision had been to order the attack at Chickamauga: "All other things that he has done he ought not to have done. I am convinced that nothing but the hand of God can save us or help us as long as we have our present commander." The always volatile Nathan Bedford Forrest refused to serve under Bragg anymore and left the army for an independent cavalry command.[10]

The criticism of Bragg from his subordinates was still reaching Richmond, and Jefferson Davis decided it was time to take action in person. Making the long journey from Richmond on a special train, the Confederate president arrived at Bragg's headquarters on October 9. During a private meeting between Davis and Bragg, the general offered his resignation, which was not accepted. Davis wanted to hear from the army's senior generals and held a meeting with them to listen to their complaints. One by one the generals gave their assessment of their commanding officer, which were mostly negative and, fair or not, it was clear that Bragg had lost the confidence of his highest-ranking subordinates.[11]

It became clear to President Davis that if the current situation were allowed to continue, the damage done to the morale and thus the fighting effectiveness of the army would continue to deteriorate. He knew that something had to be done, but there really was no good solution. Davis would not reward what was clearly insubordination by promoting one of the officers who had been working against Bragg to command of the army, so he felt it was imperative to bring in someone from the outside. General P.G.T. Beauregard might be brought back to command the army, but Davis had already removed the difficult to get along with general from this command once before and personally disliked him, so there was little interest in making this move. Another option was to offer the command to Joseph E. Johnston, a move that could hardly be criticized by any of the senior officers. Unfortunately, Davis didn't particularly like Johnston either and blamed the loss of Vicksburg on that officer's failure to act quickly enough in Mississippi. Jefferson Davis really had no realistic option available, so he decided to leave Bragg in command and brought General Hardee back to replace Polk. Before heading back to Richmond on October 14, Davis publically pronounced his support for Braxton Bragg, expecting the senior officers to work past their differences for the good of the Confederacy.[12]

Problems between the senior officers was only one of the issues facing the Army of Tennessee. Most of the supplies came up from Atlanta on a single-track railroad that was unable to keep the army adequately supplied. Now, in addition to moving supplies, thousands of wounded had to be taken care of or transported elsewhere, and the transportation system had proven to be totally inadequate. There were also problems in distributing the supplies on hand, as Bragg had his army spread out over eight miles from Lookout Mountain to the northern end of Missionary Ridge. Moving supplies over the rugged terrain to the troops in the field presented a special challenge and shortages soon became common. But despite occasional shortages, which the Confederates were getting used to, what might be the most important problem for the Army of Tennessee was that many of the rank and file troops were beginning to suffer from low morale. The hard won victory at Chickamauga could not make up for the disasters of losing Vicksburg and the defeat at Gettysburg. These were clear signs that the Southern war effort was headed in the wrong direction. The lack of confidence in Bragg's leadership only added another cloud to the descending gloom that began to envelope the Army of Tennessee.[13]

With its limited resources already spread thin there was little the Confederacy could do to assist the Army of Tennessee, but with the vast resources available in the North there was a rapid and effective response to calls of help from Chattanooga. After the initial shock of the defeat Rosecrans seemed to calm down, and Assistant Secretary Dana was able to write to Stanton that he was now "determined to fight it out here at all hazards," but help was needed, and Dana added, "There are here ten days' full rations, sufficient for twenty days in case of need." On September 23 Dana wrote to Stanton that he believed the city "can be held by this army for from fifteen to twenty days against all efforts of the enemy, unless he should receive re-enforcements of overwhelming strength."[14]

Substantial aid for Rosecrans' army was quickly approved. Two corps from the Army of the Potomac were ordered to Washington. Following long-standing military custom, Major General George Meade, commander of the Army of the Potomac, picked two units that were at less than full strength and had not performed up to expectations, Major General Oliver Otis Howard's Eleventh Corps and Major General Henry Slocum's Twelfth Corps. Without a command since just before Gettysburg, Major General Joseph Hooker was brought back to active duty and appointed to overall command of this force. Within the Army of the Potomac there were conflicts between senior officers just like Bragg faced with the Army of Tennessee. One of the most serious was that Slocum truly disliked Hooker on both a military and personal level and threatened to resign rather than serve under him. After some serious discussions among the generals an agreement was worked out where Slocum would have very little contact with Hooker, and the troops headed to Tennessee.[15]

In an impressive display of the power that could be wielded by Federal authorities during times of crisis, national, state and local governments along with officials from several railroads were made to work together to transport Hooker's command to Chattanooga. Just two days after Dana's request for assistance was received in Washington, the first trains carrying Hooker's troops began their journey. It took only twelve days for the two army corps with their artillery and baggage to make the journey from Washington to Bridgeport. This was an amazing feat for the times and was one more illustration of the vast difference in the industrial strength between the North and the South.[16]

Although Hooker's troops were now arriving in the vicinity of Chattanooga, the safety of the city and the garrison was not assured. Much of the reason for this was due to Rosecrans' apparent inability to take any action that might alleviate the food shortage. In the past he had always been careful not to act until he felt he had a good understanding of the strategic situation and plans were completed to his satisfaction, but once he did take action it was decisive. In the aftermath of defeat, however, Rosecrans had seemingly lost confidence in his ability to formulate plans and make decisions. Dana reported to Secretary Stanton on October 17, "The general organization of this army is inefficient and its discipline defective." In another wire Dana wrote, "Our condition and prospects grow worse and worse," adding that "amid all this, the practical incapacity of the general commanding is astonishing, and it often seems difficult to believe him of sound mind. His imbecility appears to be contagious, and it is difficult for any one to get anything done."[17]

Having an ineffective commander would be a problem for any military force anywhere, but the predicament was magnified because of the army's poor position. Isolated and difficult to approach, Chattanooga is situated at the northern end of a valley, about five or six miles wide, divided by Chattanooga Creek running through the center. Missionary Ridge forms the eastern side of the valley rising from three hundred to eight hundred feet high, running mostly northeast to southwest and meeting the river east of the city. Just south of Chattanooga on the west side of the valley, Lookout Mountain towers over the landscape nearly one thousand feet high. Flowing north of the city, the Tennessee River makes a hairpin turn south then quickly turns back along the base of Lookout Mountain, leaving just enough room for the tracks of the Memphis & Charleston Railroad and a narrow road. The terrain on the northern portion of Lookout Mountain is a foreboding mix of woods, gullies and boulders that rises steeply until reaching a band of gentle sloping land containing a few small farms. Above this cultivated area is an almost vertical palisade that rises to the summit of the mountain.[18]

Control of the high ground around the city gave General Bragg excellent positions to establish his fortifications, especially along the crest of Missionary Ridge. There was another defensive line across Chattanooga Valley to Lookout Mountain. Lookout Mountain was fortified along the northern end and on some of the more gentle slopes. Other defensive positions were established in the valley west of Lookout Mountain, farther west on Raccoon Mountain, east of the city toward Lookout Mountain and down to the river covering the road along the northern embankment. Not only was the crest of Missionary Ridge heavily fortified, the Confederates added a line of rifle pits along the base and at several locations on the slope of the ridge. Down in the valley Chattanooga Creek was generally considered the dividing line between the armies, with both sides stationing pickets along each bank.[19]

When the Federal troops looked out of their fortifications in almost any direction the Confederate positions appeared unassailable. Bragg rightly believed that hunger would eventually force Rosecrans to either risk a breakout, which would almost surely be disastrous, or surrender. Since the Federal troops had arrived in Chattanooga there had been a shortage of supplies, and although there was a large Union base at Bridgeport which could easily supply the needs of the Federal troops, there was no easy way to deliver those supplies. After Chickamauga the Federal troops had streamed into Chattanooga thinking only of reaching safety. Shortly after the battle Rosecrans withdrew a brigade that had been stationed on the northern end of Lookout Mountain to consolidate his forces. General Bragg immediately recognized the importance of Lookout Mountain and ordered Longstreet to send troops to occupy this vital position. With the Confederates controlling the high ground and the best supply routes, they did not have to actually surround the city for the Federal army to believe they were under siege.[20]

Supplies for Army of the Cumberland first went by rail from the main depots in Nashville to Stevenson, Alabama, where they would then be transported to Bridgeport on the Memphis & Charleston Railroad. From there supplies could be sent to Chattanooga by the river, or the single rail line and narrow road running past Lookout Mountain. Unfortunately for the Union troops, all three of these routes were unusable because of the Confederate artillery based on the mountain. There was another road on the north side of the Tennessee from Bridgeport, but this too was covered by the Confederate guns on Lookout Mountain. The only route that was still open to transport provisions into Chattanooga was by using slow moving wagon trains traveling west of the river through the Sequatchie Valley and over Walden's Ridge north of the city. This was a winding route more

Right: Union General Joseph Hooker led a corps during Atlanta campaign but asked to be relieved when he was not given command of McPherson's army after his death (Library of Congress).

Above: Union General Oliver O. Howard—after the war he was in charge of the Freedman's Bureau and later founded Howard University (Library of Congress).

Top Right: Union General George H. Thomas in December of 1864 attacked and all but destroyed the Army of Tennessee outside Nashville (Library of Congress).

than sixty miles long over terrible mountain roads. The easiest part of the supply route was from Bridgeport north around the curve of the Tennessee to Jasper. From Jasper wagons had to travel northeast about twenty miles through the valley of the Sequatchie River. The worst part of the route was little more than a winding mountain trail southeast over Walden's Ridge. Even in good weather the troops in Chattanooga could not be adequately supplied by this route, and during the winter months that were quickly approaching, the roads became treacherous, and it was simply not possible to move a sufficient amount of supplies into Chattanooga.[21]

It did not take long for conditions inside Chattanooga to deteriorate. Rosecrans was forced to order the army to go on two-thirds rations on October 2, although many units had already reached that level. William Hartpence of the 51st Indiana later remembered that he witnessed soldiers following the few supply trains that did come into the city "holding their hats under the wagon to catch whatever might fall; following forage wagons for squares with the hope that an ear of corn, or a few grains even, might be jolted out." L. G. Bennett from the 36th Illinois noted that the short rations, tattered clothing, and wet and cold weather "were telling fearfully on the men, whose sunken cheeks and spiritless manner gave token that their powers of endurance were being greatly tried. Sometimes they were so weak that they tottered and staggered like old men." Charles Briant, of the 6th Indiana, wrote: "The supplies became so short that parts of crackers and corn, dropped in handling the packages, were eagerly seized and eaten, to stay the demands of hunger ... and no one knew how it would ultimately end."[22]

Mr. Dana wrote that on October 15, "the troops were on half rations, and officers as they went about where the men were working on the fortifications frequently heard the cry of 'Crackers!'" Dana added that during this time, "General Rosecrans seemed to be insensible to the impending danger; he dawdled with trifles in a manner which scarcely can be imagined." The situation was getting more and more desperate and the soldiers could not see anything that was being done to alleviate their suffering. "I never saw anything which seemed so lamentable and hopeless," Dana continued. "Our animals were starving, the men had starvation before them, and the enemy was bound to make desperate efforts to dislodge us." Taking little action to improve conditions, General Rosecrans seemed to use "that part of the time which was not employed in pleasant gossip to the composition of a long report to prove that the Government was to blame for his failure on the 20th."[23]

A solution to the supply problem had to be found, and quickly. The only area where Union foragers could operate relatively safely was north of the city and river which had already been picked over by troops from both sides multiple times, and there was precious little to be obtained there. Silas S. Canfield of the 21st Ohio later wrote, "Foraging meant journeys of fifty to sixty miles across a range of mountains to the north and east of Chattanooga, into a country which supposably had been previously stripped of both forage and food." The horses and mules that had to pull the supply wagons were quickly becoming too weak to haul fully loaded wagons back to Chattanooga, and many wagons had to be abandoned. "In such cases returning soldiers brought in whatever they could carry on their backs."[24]

There was no shortage of supplies in Federal depots in the region, the problem was transporting those supplies over the narrow and winding mountain roads from Bridgeport. Too many times the starving animals were simply too weak to pull fully loaded wagons over the steep hills and too many times precious supplies had to be thrown away so that at least a portion of the load could reach Chattanooga. What made the already bad situation even worse was that the frequent rain all but destroyed the so-called roads. The heavy wagons would frequently get stuck in soft mud up to their axles. One of General Granger's staff wrote, "In one instance, a wagon having sunk till its bed rested on the mud, the driver did not, as usual, beat his mules and swear; he simply sat on a rock by the wayside, looked at the wretched animals, and *cried*."[25]

The shortage of provisions was actually negatively affecting any plans that might be developed to relieve the shortage of provisions. General Hooker's force was only thirty miles away, and these men could possibly be used to take back Lookout Mountain and open the main supply routes. But the lack of food for the troops and fodder for the animals was so severe it was feared that bringing thousands more Union soldiers into the vicinity of Chattanooga would only cause the combined forces to starve before the supply line could be opened. There had been several possible plans to open various supply routes developed by Rosecrans and his staff, but despite the obvious need for something to be done, for some reason no action was ever taken.

By the middle of October the administration was just about out of patience with General Rosecrans' lack of action. Losing a major battle was bad enough, but now his army was trapped and facing starvation in Chattanooga. Due in large part to Dana's frequent reports commenting on the lack of any effort to alleviate the situation in Chattanooga, many in the administration had lost confidence in his ability to command the army. President Lincoln himself, however, did not easily give up hope that Rosecrans would be able to overcome the difficulties facing his army. Lincoln's continuing support was in recognition of Rosecrans' previous victories and the important political support the president had received due to the general's efforts. But, Rosecrans ran out of time on October 16 when Dana wrote that the situation was continuing to deteriorate and he believed that things had reached the point where "nothing can prevent the retreat of the army from this place within a fortnight, and with a vast loss of public property and possible of life, except the opening of the river." Clearly, immediate and decisive action had to be taken to save the troops in Chattanooga.[26]

The same day that Dana's message was received in Washington, a cabinet meeting was held where it was decided to make a change in the commander of the Army of the Cumberland. Lincoln decided that more than just a change in army commanders was needed; he wanted to rearrange the command structure in the West. The three main military departments in the Western Theater were the Cumberland, Ohio, and Tennessee commanded by Rosecrans, Burnside, and Grant. Lincoln decided to create the Military Division of the Mississippi with one commander over all three departments. General Grant was appointed to this command and given the authority to deal with the situation in Chattanooga as he saw fit.[27]

Secretary Stanton could see that changes had to be made in the command structure in the West before the formal reorganization took effect, because as early as October 3 a wire was sent to Grant, "It is the wish of the Secretary of War that as soon as General Grant is able he will come to Cairo and report by telegraph." Grant did not receive this message until the tenth and, even though still suffering from pain due to his injured leg, he left for Cairo immediately.[28]

Grant arrived in Cairo on October 16 with several members of his staff and immediately sent a message to General Halleck that he would wait there until he received further instructions. The next morning Grant received orders to "immediately proceed to the Galt House, Louisville, Ky., where you will meet an officer of the War Department with your orders and instructions." About two hours later as Grant's train was pulling out of Indianapolis it was halted because the "officer of the War Department" decided not to wait in Louisville.[29]

The official from Washington who was in such a hurry to meet with Grant was Secretary of War Stanton himself, who then joined Grant on his train. As they headed toward Louisville, Secretary Stanton informed Grant that he had been selected to command the new Military Division of the Mississippi, encompassing a vast area from the Alleghenies to the Mississippi, except for Louisiana. By placing just one man to command the three armies attached to the new division, the government hoped that they could be used more effectively in coordinated movements. The first thing that had to be taken care of, however, was the situation at Chattanooga. A decision had to be made whether to retain Rosecrans in command and, if not, who should take his place. Stanton had brought with him two sets of orders and Grant was given his choice as to which one to issue. One order let department commanders stay as they were, while the other relieved Rosecrans and assigned George Thomas as his replacement. Grant knew each man slightly and wasn't particularly friendly with either of them, but Rosecrans had served under Grant the previous fall in Mississippi and caused some difficulties, so Grant decided to make the change. General Thomas became the new commander of the Army of the Cumberland.[30]

Grant spent the day with Stanton discussing possible future operations. Later Grant and his wife, Julia, who had also made the trip, spent the evening in the company of some local friends. Not long after Grant had left the hotel, Secretary Stanton received a message from Dana informing him that there was reason to be concerned that Rosecrans was thinking about abandoning Chattanooga. It was later learned that this was not the case, but considering the situation in Chattanooga and Rosecrans' recent pessimistic attitude, it had to be taken seriously at the time. Grant returned to the hotel about eleven o'clock to find the secretary literally pacing the floor of his room deeply concerned about the situation in Chattanooga. Grant read Dana's telegram and "immediately wrote an order assuming command of the Military Division of the Mississippi, and telegraphed it to General Rosecrans." Grant wrote a separate wire to Rosecrans relieving him of his duties and assigning George Thomas as the new commander of the Army of the Cumberland.[31]

Grant told Thomas to "hold Chattanooga at all hazards. I will be there as soon as possible." Replying to Grant's request for an update on the supply situation, Thomas wired that he had "two hundred and four thousand four hundred and sixty-two rations in store-houses; ninety thousand to arrive to-morrow, and all the trains were loaded which had arrived at Bridgeport up to the 16th—probably three hundred wagons," adding, "I will hold the town till we starve." Grant liked the defiant tone that Thomas exhibited, but when the numbers were calculated things actually looked pretty dismal. Thomas' information revealed that there were only about five days of rations in Chattanooga with two more days worth of provisions on the way. Considering that the trip from Bridgeport to Chattanooga took at least eight days, the situation was clearly desperate.[32]

Grant later wrote in his *Memoirs*, "I appreciated the force of this dispatch later when I witnessed the condition of affairs which prompted it. It looked, indeed, as if but two courses were open: one to starve, the other to surrender or be captured."[33]

Once Grant learned the true the situation in Chattanooga, he decided to leave for Chattanooga immediately. Grant was on a train headed for Nashville on October 20, then, using the normal supply route, he proceeded south on the Nashville & Chattanooga Railroad to Stevenson, Alabama. On the evening of October 21 Grant met with General Howard, whose corps was stationed near Bridgeport about ten miles away. Howard was generally considered a good soldier who had lost an arm in Virginia, although his corps had acquired a reputation of being a little slow and not quite reliable. General Howard was meeting Grant for the first time and quickly found that he bore little resemblance to the hard fighting general depicted in the newspapers. Howard wrote that Grant "was quite the opposite of my ideal,—in size small, in color pale at that time, in manner remarkably quiet and retiring."[34]

While Grant and Howard were discussing possible operations, General Hooker, who had his headquarters in Stevenson, sent a courier to Grant's train offering to share the hospitality of his headquarters. Howard noticed that Grant did not seem upset but calmly informed the messenger, "If General Hooker wishes to see me, he will find me on this train." General Hooker duly appeared in person to pay his respects a little later that evening. To Howard this appeared to be "General Grant's method of asserting himself where he thought a general who had had large commands and considerable self-assertion might be seeking an ascendancy over him."[35]

General Rosecrans also visited Grant's train that evening as he was on his way north. He had quickly turned the army over to Thomas and quietly left Chattanooga with the majority of the troops unaware of the change in command. This meeting could not have been very pleasant for either man, but Rosecrans quickly gave his views of the situation at Chattanooga and informed Grant of several plans that had the potential to improve the flow of supplies but had not yet been implemented. Grant later wrote about this brief meeting and mentioned one of the reasons he had decided to replace Rosecrans, noting that he had "made some excellent suggestions as to what should be done. My only wonder was that he had not carried them out." When this meeting was over, Grant continued on to Bridgeport, spending the night at Howard's headquarters.[36]

Still having difficulty moving around because of his injured leg, Grant had to be lifted onto his horse when he and a small escort set out on the final stretch of the route to Chattanooga early on October 22. Grant now saw firsthand the difficulties facing the wagon trains as they moved over the treacherous roads to Chattanooga: "There had been much rain, and the roads were almost impassable from mud, knee-deep in places, and from wash-outs on the mountain sides." It took two full days fighting heavy rain and freezing mountain winds on horseback until Grant arrived at General Thomas' headquarters on the night of October 23, where the reception was only a little less unpleasant than the weather outside.[37]

Grant's relationship with Thomas could best be described as strained, in part due to Thomas being given command of Grant's army during the summer after Shiloh. Exchanging basic polite greetings, both men sat in front of the fireplace just staring at the fire and not talking while water dripping from Grant's wet uniform formed a puddle under his chair. After an uncomfortable time lapse, Colonel James Wilson mentioned that the commanding general might like something warm to eat and some dry clothes, which was quickly provided. Colonel Horace Porter, who later joined Grant's staff, remembered that Grant ate a light dinner and rather than change clothes preferred to just quietly sit in front of the fire. As officers came by to brief Grant, one of them, Brigadier General William F. Smith, whom Grant had known at West Point, offered up an impressive plan that might just break the Confederate stranglehold on the city.[38]

Chapter 20

Grant Makes Things Happen

The morning after Grant arrived at Thomas' headquarters, Dana wired Secretary Stanton to let him know that "Grant arrived last night, wet, dirty and well." This was only partially true, since Grant's injured leg was still giving him serious trouble. In fact, during the journey to Chattanooga, he "had to be carried over places where it was not safe to cross on horseback." Grant himself reported to General Halleck that in making the trip from Bridgeport, his party rode "over the worst roads it is possible to conceive of, and through a continuous drenching rain." At least the miserable journey over the mountains to Chattanooga gave Grant first-hand knowledge of how important it was to open another supply route. He wrote, "It is now clear, and so long as it continues so it is barely possible to supply this army from its present base, but when winter rains set in it will be impossible."[1]

First thing on the morning of October 24, Grant, Thomas, and William Smith, with several staff officers, took a ride to become familiar with the terrain north and west of the city. Crossing the Tennessee, they rode out to a river crossing called Brown's Ferry about three miles north of Lookout Mountain. The Confederate pickets manning their positions on the west bank of the river saw Grant's party but did not fire on this group of enemy officers, possibly as Grant guessed, because "they looked upon the garrison of Chattanooga as prisoners of war, feeding or starving themselves, and thought it would be inhuman to kill any of them except in self-defence."[2]

One of the most important factors that had to be considered when planning how to increase the flow of supplies into Chattanooga was the meandering course of the Tennessee River. Grant wanted to see for himself if there was a way to use this waterway to his advantage. Once the river passed the city it flowed almost straight south for a couple of miles until running into the northern end of Lookout Mountain and being forced back to the northwest. This turn was known as Moccasin Bend, and the land that stuck out between the two lines of water was called Moccasin Point. The Tennessee continued north for several miles, again passing the city flowing northwest around the northern end of Raccoon Mountain before heading back southwest toward Bridgeport.[3]

What made route of the river around Moccasin Bend significant is that a heavily wooded area hid a narrow road that gave direct access to the city from the western side of Moccasin Point. Starting just across the river on the northern side of the city, this road headed west for a little over a mile across the narrow strip of land formed by Moccasin Point to Brown's Ferry, the area that Grant and his party had inspected the morning after his arrival. On the other side of the river southwest from Brown's Ferry was a gap cut into Raccoon Mountain through which there was a route that led back to the river on the other side of the mountain at a place known as Kelley's Ferry. The main point of this was that Kelley's Ferry was easily accessible from the Union supply depot at Bridgeport. General Smith had formed a plan to wrest control of Raccoon Mountain away from the enemy and set up pontoon bridges across the river at Brown's Ferry, opening a shorter route from Bridgeport to Chattanooga that would ensure the speedy delivery of supplies into the city.[4]

The Federal commanders at Chattanooga had been aware of the route through Brown's Ferry when General Rosecrans had been in charge, but there was a very good reason why Union quartermasters were not already using this route. All the territory south of the river from Lookout Mountain around Moccasin Bend and north to Raccoon Mountain was controlled by the Confederates. Fortunately for the hungry troops in Chattanooga, Grant was now learning that most of the enemy forces had been concentrated on and near Lookout Mountain by General Longstreet, who was in command of the defenses in this area. On the west side of the river from near Lookout Mountain north to Raccoon Mountain, the enemy defenses were weak with small units positioned more as picket stations than a defensive line. As General Smith reported, "Evidences were against the occupation of that part of the valley by a large force of the enemy," and that a surprise attack would probably be successful.[5]

General Smith had devised a complicated plan to open this new supply route across Moccasin Point, and each phase had to be completed successfully in order for the entire plan to work. The most hazardous part of Smith's plan was to be launched in the dead of night with a brigade of infantry quietly slipping down the river and around Moccasin Bend in pontoon boats. If all went as planned and this force could safely navigate the river and remain undiscovered by Confederate pickets along the riverbank, they would land on the western shore opposite Brown's Ferry at first light. Moving quickly to surprise the Confederate pickets, they were to overwhelm the enemy troops guarding the eastern end of the gap in Raccoon Mountain. While the river force was making their way around Moccasin Point another brigade would cross over to Brown's Ferry on the eastern bank using the same road as Grant's reconnaissance party. By using the boats from the assault force to build a pontoon bridge the troops waiting at Brown's Ferry could quickly join the men who had alrady landed, and together they would advance against the Confederate forces on Raccoon Mountain to secure the road to Kelley's Ferry. In addition, Smith planned to bring several batteries of artillery up to the eastern bank to provide cover fire for the landing party from across the river. Considering how few Confederates were stationed on and around Raccoon Mountain, if the two Federal brigades successfully made it to the west side of the river, they had an excellent chance to accomplish their mission.[6]

The success of this operation not only depended on taking the road to Kelley's Ferry but holding it. Once the Federal troops began moving toward the Raccoon Mountain gap there was little doubt that Confederate commanders would understand what Grant was trying to do and send reinforcements from Lookout Mountain to block the Federal movement. The pontoon bridge at Brown's Ferry now became one of the keys to the success of the movement, because by using that bridge the Federal troops in Chattanooga would now actually be closer to the scene of the action than the Confederates on Lookout Mountain and the troops on Moccasin Point could receive reinforcements more quickly than could their enemy.

There was one final part to Smith's plan, and this might be the most important part of all if the movement was to accomplish its goal. General Bragg could not afford to just sit by and allow the Federal troops to walk over Raccoon Mountain and open a new supply route, so General Smith decided to make use of General Hooker's troops that were just sitting in their camps. To guarantee success of the movement Hooker's three divisions, the fourth was spread out guarding the railroad back to Nashville, would cross the Tennessee at Bridgeport and march along the railroad north to Wauhatchie, several miles south of Brown's Ferry. From here Hooker's force would be in position to prevent the breaking of the new supply line by a Confederate advance from Lookout Mountain.[7]

General Smith's plan was a bold and complicated maneuver consisting of several moving parts that, if successful, could bring about a solution to the Federal army's supply problem. Smith had already presented this plan, or something quite similar, to General Rosecrans, but he never authorized its implementation. Once he had been put in command, General Thomas approved the plan before Grant arrived, and Smith had already set up a shop along the river that was turning out wood planks to build pontoon boats. The project was only waiting for final approval from Grant, which was quickly given. Grant sent out orders that General Smith was to be in command of the operation and he was to be given top priority for all resources.[8]

While the preparations for the Raccoon Mountain operation were taking place, Grant received a message from General Halleck warning him that at least 20,000 men were on their way to Tennessee from the Army of Northern Virginia. It was feared in Washington that Bragg would be using these veteran troops to make an advance into East Tennessee against Knoxville, and it was up to Grant to prevent what could turn into a military and political disaster. This report was later found to be completely inaccurate; after already sending Longstreet's force to join Bragg's army, Robert E. Lee had no more troops to spare, but at the time Grant had to act on the information and make plans to deal with this new enemy force.[9]

Since the start of the war President Lincoln had been trying to get Union forces to make a serious push to enter and take control of the eastern portion of Tennessee, where many Union supporters had been suffering under Confederate rule. The problem was that any invading Federal force had to face mountainous terrain that provided little in the way of food or forage, making any attempt to move large numbers of men and animals through the region a difficult task. During the past summer, however, when Rosecrans maneuvered Bragg out of Tennessee, the Army of the Ohio led by General Burnside took advantage of the lack of Confederate resources in the area and moved down from Kentucky to take control of the city of Knoxville and the nearby countryside.

In trying to strengthen and consolidate his position, Burnside, who was not the most capable of military men, learned first-hand that he was facing two serious problems. It was quickly discovered that the lack of provisions in the area was just as serious as it was believed to be, and he had to report to Halleck that his troops "had been on half rations from the moment of their arrival in East Tennessee." The second challenge that Burnside had to overcome was that while his primary duty was to defend Knoxville and the Cumberland Gap, it was difficult to concentrate his troops for that purpose because they were spread out all over the area looking for provisions. Another consideration was that once many of the local citizens had declared their support for the Union, the government had a moral obligation to protect them from reprisals, to say nothing of the political fallout facing the government if the area were suddenly abandoned. It was decided that Burnside must stay where he was and Grant would send assistance to Burnside as soon as possible. Grant was certainly willing to help if he could, but on October 26 he was forced to admit, "Thomas' command is in bad condition to move, for want of animals of sufficient strength to move his artillery, and for want of subsistence." Still, Grant was well aware of the many reasons it was important to hold Knoxville and promised Burnside to do what he could: "If you are threatened with a force beyond what you can compete with, efforts must be made to assist you."[10]

In addition to Chattanooga and East Tennessee, one of the things that most concerned Grant was the possibility of a Confederate force moving west past Knoxville. The small town of Cleveland lay a little over twenty miles east of Chattanooga on the Western & Atlantic line that brought Bragg's supplies up from Atlanta. If the Confederate force that was reportedly heading west from Virginia were to reach Cleveland, it could be re-supplied and move north toward Nashville and cut the railroad that brought supplies to Stevenson. A break in the supply line from Nashville would mean disaster not only for the troops in Chattanooga but Hooker's forces as well. The troops in Chattanooga were too weak and Hooker's men were too far away to oppose such a Confederate advance. The only Federal troops that might be available were Sherman's men, who were still slowly making their way east along the Memphis & Charleston Railroad.[11]

General Sherman's force was just east of the Mississippi and Alabama border when Grant sent him an urgent message on October 24: "Drop everything east of Bear Creek and move with your entire force toward Stevenson until you receive further orders. The enemy are evidently moving a large force toward Cleveland, and may break through our lines and move on Nashville, in which event your troops are the only forces at command that could beat them there. With your forces here before the enemy cross the Tennessee we could turn their position so as to force them back."[12]

Informing General Halleck of Smith's plan to open the new supply route, Grant wrote on October 26, "If successful, and I think it will be, the question of supplies will be fully settled." He also informed the general-in-chief that he was concerned with the possibility of a Confederate force advancing north because "our artillery horses are not in a condition to enable us to follow, and neither is our larder," and that he had changed Sherman's orders "with a view of having his forces in a position to use if the enemy should attempt this move." If Bragg stayed put, Grant had already decided that when Sherman's troops arrived there would be "force enough to insure a line for our supplies, and enable me to move Thomas to the left, thus securing Burnside's position and give a strong hold upon that part of the line, from which I suppose a move will finally have to be made to turn Bragg." Grant added that he would "endeavor to get the troops in a state of readiness for a forward movement at the earliest possible day." Grant knew that saving the Army of the Cumberland was only one of the reasons he had been given this new command; he was a fighter and made things happen. Once Chattanooga was secure the next step was to drive Bragg out of Tennessee and open the way to Atlanta and the Deep South. But before there could be any serious discussion of advancing against the Confederate army around Chattanooga, the new supply route had to be opened. It was decided to launch the assault during the early hours of October 27.[13]

The force making the assault from the river was made up of 1,500 men from the brigade of Brigadier General William B. Hazen, who would be in command. Hazen's men would move down the river on fifty pontoon boats and two larger flat boats. Brigadier General John B. Turchin, commanding his brigade and the remainder of Hazen's troops, made up the force moving overland to Brown's Ferry that would cross the river over Hazen's pontoon boats. Preparations for the assault were very thorough, including supplying Turchin's men with extra lumber so they could quickly go to work building the pontoon bridge as soon as the boats were available. The landing party was provided with axes to cut down trees to build defensive works and fires were prepared along the river bank so the landing force might have some idea of their progress in the darkness.[14]

About one o'clock in the morning of October 27, Hazen's men were roused from their sleep and filed into their boats on the Chattanooga waterfront. Bayonets and tin cups were left behind, anything, in fact, that might make enough noise to attract the attention of Confederate pickets, only rifles and ammunition accompanied the men into the boats. It was about nine miles from the city docks around Moccasin Point and back north to Brown's Ferry, almost seven miles on open water under the noses Confederate pickets. If the Union flotilla of small boats was discovered, the Confederates had enough artillery that could reach the river to quickly turn this undertaking into a disaster.[15]

The boats carrying Hazen's landing force began their hazardous journey at about three o'clock. Troops manned the oars to power the boats until they came within sight of the first Confederate picket fire, then they steered to the right hugging the river bank as close as possible and let the current carry them soundlessly along. It had been stressed to the men how important it was to keep silent, and all was quiet until the boats were moving through the bend near Lookout Mountain when an officer in one of the lead boats was knocked overboard by a tree branch sticking out from the bank and there was a muffled shout as he disappeared into the black water. Luckily for the expedition this noise went unnoticed by the enemy pickets, and luckily for the officer he was a good swimmer and was able to stay afloat until he was picked up by another boat.[16]

During the early morning hours that Hazen's men were quietly gliding along on the water, General Turchin's column was crossing the river at Chattanooga and headed across Moccasin Point to Brown's Ferry. Accompanying the infantry was Major John Mendenhall commanding three batteries of artillery that would be used to cover the landing. Turchin's column made good time and arrived early at their designated position where all they could do was to wait in the woods until they would be needed to augment Hazen's force.[17]

When the boats first shoved off there was a little moonlight, but that was soon masked by clouds and there was the usual fog and mist on the river to hide the boats from the enemy pickets gathered around their campfires along most of the route. The plan called for the boats to arrive at the landing site just before it got light, and they could not have timed it more perfectly. Lieutenant Colonel James C. Foy of the 23rd Kentucky was in the lead boat and his assignment was to secure the landing site with the first few boats that made it to shore. As the boats passed the last of the signal fires it was still just dark enough to call it night when Hazen suddenly shouted, "Pull in Col. Foy; pull in! pull in!"[18]

As soon as he heard Hazen's shout, Colonel Foy turned his boat toward shore. Before they even came to a complete stop his men began scrambling out of the boat and straight up the river bank. The surprise was complete and the Confederate pickets were overwhelmed so quickly that they barely had time to fire off a shot or two before falling back to the slopes of the nearby hills. As the other boats landed the men branched out in all directions securing the landing area, then quickly formed their companies and began advancing toward the higher ground. As soon as the men disembarked, each boat turned around and headed back across the river to pick up Turchin's men. Hazen reported that everyone did their job so well and so quickly that "the entire crest was occupied, my skirmish lines out, and the axes working, before the reinforcements of the enemy, a little beyond the hill, came forward to drive us back."[19]

It was still just barely getting light enough to see when the fighting began to get more severe as Hazen's men continued to move further inland. The Confederates defending the hills were tough veterans from Major General Lafayette McLaw's division and although they were outnumbered, they would not give ground easily. Fighting in the early morning haze was a little confusing for both sides, but as it grew lighter the Federal numbers told and it was not long before Hazen's men were cutting down trees and building defenses to hold the positions they had already won. About 5:30 a.m. General Smith reported back to army headquarters, "We hold the crest, and the attack has just commenced."[20]

Now in control of the high ground, Hazen's troops repulsed several uncoordinated attacks, and by the time the sun was fully up, Turchin's men began arriving to bolster the thin Federal defenses. During the afternoon the pontoon bridge at Brown's Ferry was completed, Mendenhall's artillery came up to cover the infantry and the Federal positions were secure. At 3:30 p.m. General Smith sent back the message notifying headquarters that the operation was a success: "This place cannot be carried now." So far the entire operation had cost the Federals fewer than forty men and they had accomplished everything they had set out to. Just to play it safe, Brigadier General Walter C. Whitaker's brigade was moved up to Brown's Ferry in case General Smith's troops needed reinforcements, which they did not. By late afternoon the operation had gone as well as could have been hoped for, but now General Hooker had to do his part to protect the positions already won.[21]

The final phase of the plans drawn up by General Smith commenced about dawn on October 27 as General Hooker's troops began their march north. Hooker's men crossed the Tennessee River at Bridgeport with the divisions of Major General Carl Schurtz and Brigadier General Adolph von Steinwehr from Howard's corps taking the lead. Brigadier General John Geary's division from Slocum's corps followed Howard's men. They had a relatively easy and

Left: Union General John W. Geary—after the war he served two terms as governor of Pennsylvania (Library of Congress). *Right:* Union General William B. Hazen—later in his career he served on the frontier and as an observer during the Franco-Prussian War (Library of Congress).

quiet march as they moved along the railroad near the base of Raccoon Mountain, across Lookout Valley and past Wauhatchie. Encountering only a few small groups of Confederate skirmishers, Howard's advance units came to a halt a little over a mile from Brown's Ferry in the late afternoon, and during the next day the rest of Howard's troops came up in position to protect the approaches to Brown's Ferry. Coming up behind Howard's men, General Geary's small division of about 1,500 men camped about three miles behind the rear of Howard's men near Wauhatchie. General Smith's plan had been executed to perfection.[22]

The Federal movement to take Brown's Ferry and the gap in Raccoon Mountain had already succeeded before the Confederate commanders realized what was happening. It wasn't that they had been unable to prepare a stronger defense around Raccoon Mountain, but it appears that the long-standing feuding between Bragg and his subordinates, especially James Longstreet, had once again affected operations. In command of the Confederate left, Longstreet was responsible for defending the area from Chattanooga Creek west to the Tennessee River on the other side of Raccoon Mountain. Mostly concerned about the main Federal forces in Chattanooga, originally Longstreet had concentrated his forces on the northern end of Lookout Mountain and in the valley to the east facing the city. Even after Hooker's force arrived, there were no sizeable Confederate units assigned to Lookout Valley or on Raccoon Mountain until October 9, when Bragg had to finally order Longstreet to strengthen his forces in those areas. Even so, on the day of Hooker's advance there were only two regiments available to defend the area Hooker came through.[23]

Whatever friction existed between Bragg and Longstreet, they had to work together, since it was obvious that the entire situation at Chattanooga would be transformed if a new supply route was opened into the city. Something had to be done. Longstreet quickly made plans to attack Geary's isolated troops on the night of October 28 with three brigades commanded by Brigadier General Micah Jenkins and Brigadier General Evander Law's brigade. Jenkins was to "hold the point designated for General Law with a sufficient force, while a portion of his command moved up the road and captured or dispersed the rear guard." If the attack succeeded Jenkins could, "if time and circumstances favored it," move forward and attack Hooker's main body and push them across the river. Considering the relative size of both forces this was unlikely. If Jenkins found no opportunity to attack Hooker he was to fall back to the mountain by first light. Scheduled to begin at 10 p.m. the assault had to be delayed until around midnight due to the usual confusion in moving troops in darkness. Jenkins set up an ambush for any troops trying to reinforce Geary, sending one of his brigades to join Law, who was stationed among a group of hills along the road between Hooker's main force and Geary's rear guard. The actual attack on Geary's camp was to be made by Colonel John Bratton's brigade with another brigade waiting between the two Confederate forces to move in either direction to support Law or Bratton.[24]

A highly capable officer, General Geary had his troops sleep in line, fully dressed with their weapons close by ready to quickly react to any emergency. A little before 11 p.m. there had been a brief outbreak of firing along the picket line which ended as quickly as it began, and the men tried to go back to sleep. They got little rest because between midnight and one o'clock Bratton's Confederates hit the Federal camp. The fighting was fierce, but Geary's men put up a tough defense with the only light provided by the flash of hundreds of muskets. As Geary reported, "Charge after charge was made, each with redoubled effort upon our left, which they seemed determined to force, but each time the enemy's lines were hurled back under the unintermitting fire, both from infantry and artillery, that like a wall of flame opposed them."[25]

Several miles away at Hooker's camp, the sounds of the fighting at Wauhatchie woke General Howard, who shortly received a message from Hooker, "Hurry, or you cannot save Geary. He has been attacked." There was good reason for Hooker to be concerned, since he issued the orders that left Geary's command three miles away from the main force. Orders were sent to both Howard and General Schurz to immediately send reinforcements to Geary's division. Unfortunately, the hasty efforts made to mount a relief column produced some confusion and delay between the staff and field officers.[26]

General Howard formed his troops as quickly as possible and started them toward Wauhatchie, but soon encountered General Law's men waiting in the hills overlooking the road. Hard fighting took place as Howard's men repeatedly rushed up the slopes of the hills only to be thrown back. When Hooker received reports of this second battle he ordered more troops forward, not realizing that in the confusion these units were already on the march.[27]

General Geary's men held their position, but as he reported, "The contest raged with vehemence along the whole line, while our artillery threw its missiles unsparingly into the opposing ranks." On the left the 137th New York "fought the over-reaching right of the enemy by part of them fighting back to back with the other part." After nearly three hours of hard fighting the Confederates were unable to make any headway and began to pull back about 3:30 a.m. The fighting on the field was over, but the fighting between the generals was just beginning. In his report Longstreet stated that Bratton had been gaining the advantage at Geary's camp until Law fell back from the road, allowing Hooker's reinforcements to advance to Geary's aid. General Law said that around three o'clock he was informed that Bratton's attack had failed and decided it was pointless to continue fighting along the road losing more men for no good reason. There was also controversy among the Federal commanders; Hooker accused General Schurz of not obeying orders. Schurz was later cleared of any wrongdoing when it was shown that in the confusion of that morning Hooker sent orders for Schurz to perform two different tasks at the same time.[28]

Longstreet later excused his weak effort in the Wauhatchie attack, "To have put two divisions on the west side of the mountain during daylight would have exposed them to an attack from the enemy's entire force without artillery, and in a position where they could not be re-enforced." Considering the feeble physical condition of the Federal troops in Chattanooga prevented them from launching any type of serious attack, it is difficult to see what threat Longstreet's troops might have faced. Perhaps more telling was Longstreet's admission that even if successful, he felt the assault would not bring about any meaningful change in the overall situation around Chattanooga. He wrote, "My goal was merely to inflict such damage upon the enemy as might be accomplished by a surprise."[29]

The Brown's Ferry position was secure and the opening of the new supply route, known as the "cracker line" after the hardtack crackers that made up the majority of the soldiers' diet, proceeded on schedule. Grant sent a telegram to General Halleck on the evening of October 28 informing him that "General Thomas' plan for securing the river and south side road hence to Bridgeport has proven eminently successful. The question of supplies may now be regarded as settled. If the rebels give us one week more time I think all danger of losing territory now held by us will have passed away, and preparations may commence for offensive operations." As yet unknown to the Confederates, they had just been put on the defensive.[30]

The new supply line affected the Federals in more ways than just bringing more food into the city. Lt. Colonel Robert Kimberly of the 41st Ohio later wrote: "What of the relief to the men of the Union army? It was beyond description. The depression which had lasted from the days at Chickamauga was gone. The troops felt as if they had been in prison, and were now free."[31]

In his *Memoirs*, Grant wrote about the changes at Chattanooga:

> In five days from my arrival in Chattanooga the way was open to Bridgeport and, with the aid of steamers and Hooker's teams, in a week the troops were receiving full rations. It is hard for any one not an eye-witness to realize the relief this brought. The men were soon reclothed and also well fed; an abundance of ammunition was brought up, and a cheerfulness prevailed not before enjoyed in many weeks. Neither officers nor men looked upon themselves any longer as doomed. The weak and languid appearance of the troops, so visible before, disappeared at once. I do not know what the effect was on the other side, but assume it must have been correspondingly depressing.[32]

Lieutenant Joshua K. Callaway of the 28th Alabama was one of those Confederate soldiers who was could see the change in the situation at Chattanooga and for the Confederate war effort overall. In a letter to his wife dated November 1, Callaway wrote: "I am almost dead to see you and be with you. My patience is worn entirely out with the war. I am perfectly miserable; but God knows if I could see any prospect for peace, even a year hence, I could manage to bear it. But I see no prospect for it even ten years hence. The Lord help us!" Joshua Callaway would soon be killed in action on Missionary Ridge.[33]

Chapter 21

An Army Unable to Move

Now that the "cracker line" was up and running the threat of starvation and eventual surrender for the Federal troops in Chattanooga had been removed. But General Grant was there to push the enemy out of Tennessee, not just hold on to the city. Yet before he could do anything the still serious problems with transporting men and material from Nashville to Chattanooga had to be taken care of. In a later report, Grant remarked that even with using the new supply route, "The capacity of the railroad and steam-boats was not sufficient, however, to supply all the wants of the army, but actual suffering was prevented."[1]

Another part of the problem that affected Grant's ability to plan any offensive moves was that the thousands of horses and mules that pulled artillery, wagons and ambulances were so weak and worn down that the army was pretty much immobilized for the foreseeable future. John Rawlins, Grant's chief-of-staff, discussed the condition of the army's animals in a letter to General James McPherson in Vicksburg: "Owing to the difficulties of getting forward supplies and the poverty of the animals, a forward movement from here, before spring, is exceedingly problematical." Even the officer in charge of department that was responsible for providing supplies to all the armies, Quartermaster General Montgomery C. Meigs, who was on an inspection tour, thought it would be at least three months before the animals could return to their normal strength. "They should be returned to Louisville for this purpose. Hard work, exposure, short grain, and no long fodder have almost destroyed them."[2]

But apart from how long it took to rehabilitate the animals, the key to any long-term future operations was still the railroads. The railroads most heavily used were proving to be inadequate to handle the growing traffic they were now being asked to carry. Looking to increase the flow of supplies, Grant wired the superintendent of military railroads in Nashville, Colonel J. B. Anderson, on November 1 instructing him to "send thirty, and if possible more, cars through to Stevenson and Bridgeport daily, loaded with rations." Grant wanted Anderson to use the railroad to its full capacity, and if any spare cars were found, "load them with rations or forage and send them through. On no account fail to send the thirty cars daily loaded with rations." There was also a desperate need for more rolling stock and Grant had no problem requisitioning railroad equipment, telling Colonel C. L. Kilburn, the chief commissary officer in Louisville, that if it was necessary to send sufficient supplies south, "cars can also be taken from the Louisville road." Grant wrote to General McPherson in Vicksburg that he needed to immediately transfer "all the locomotives at Vicksburg with the exception of two and all the cars with the exception of ten. Let the locomotives and cars be the best you have. They are required for immediate use."[3]

Another difficulty that had to be overcome was the fact that supplies coming down from Nashville were transported on the single track of the Nashville & Chattanooga Railroad to Stevenson, where the Memphis & Charleston Railroad carried them to Bridgeport. Maintaining the army in Chattanooga with just the one rail line was difficult enough, and if Grant were to go on the offensive, which he certainly planned on doing, the demand for materials needed for an army to operate in the field would drastically increase. Grant knew that when Sherman's force arrived, there would be thousands more men and animals that would have to be supplied from Nashville. Still another factor Grant had to consider was, "All indications pointed also to the probable necessity of supplying Burnside's command in East Tennessee, twenty-five thousand more, by the same route. A single track could not do this."[4]

About seventy miles west of Stevenson was a possible solution that could dramatically increase the flow of supplies into the Chattanooga area. Another railroad line, the Nashville & Decatur, connected Nashville to Decatur, Alabama, where it intersected the Memphis & Charleston and then ran to Stevenson. But there was a reason this line was not already in use. The route from Nashville to Decatur was littered with rivers and streams, and as Grant would write, "All the bridges over these had been destroyed, and the rails taken up and twisted by the enemy. All the cars and locomotives not carried off had been destroyed as effectually as they knew how to destroy them." An immense amount of work would be required to get the Nashville & Decatur line back into operating condition.[5]

Grant assigned Brigadier General Grenville Dodge to direct the rebuilding effort of the Nashville & Decatur. He picked the right man, since as Grant noted, Dodge "besides being a most capable soldier, was an experienced railroad builder." General Dodge and his division left Sherman's force and immediately began working to put the railroad line back into working order. Materials of every kind were in short supply, including track, cars and bridge building materials, but this project was given the highest priority by Grant, who on more than one occasion intervened personally to keep the work going. Back in Nashville railroad superintendent Anderson was ordered to speed up the transfer of materials used in bridge building and to move several prefabricated bridges from Louisville to sites along the line. Many miles of new rails were needed, but there was such a delay in ordering new rails from manufacturers that Grant ordered that the rails of unused branch lines in Tennessee and Kentucky should be torn up and shipped to Dodge's work gangs. Dodge's men did an impressive job. Just over forty days after work began, trains were able to begin transporting supplies over the entire one hundred miles of track.[6]

By early November it was obvious that the Confederate force that was reported to be heading west from Virginia was not coming, removing the threat of losing Knoxville or having the Union supply line from Nashville cut. But Grant still had to deal with the fact that "Burnside was in about as desperate a condition as the Army of the Cumberland had been, only he was not yet besieged." The closest Federal supply depot to Knoxville was about one hundred miles away, and although the area around Knoxville could provide modest amounts of food and forage, as Grant noted, "It did not supply ammunition, clothing, medical supplies, or small rations, such as coffee, sugar, salt and rice." The simple fact was that no meaningful assistance could be sent to Knoxville until Sherman's troops arrived and the second railroad line was opened.[7]

Also early in November, General Bragg, who had been sitting up on Missionary Ridge waiting for the Union army in Chattanooga to starve, decided it was time to try something else, especially since the opening of the Brown's Ferry supply route ended the possibility of his simply walking into the city after the garrison surrendered. The options open to Bragg were limited and mostly unacceptable. Launching an all-out assault against the well-fortified city offered little chance of success and would almost surely produce heavy casualties. To pull his army back from the excellent positions they occupied around Chattanooga would be to admit failure, and giving up the prize for which his troops had endured the slaughter at Chickamauga would almost surely complete the ruin of the army's already low morale. It could prove just as dangerous to simply sit on the heights around Chattanooga as Grant's forces grew stronger and he eventually launched an attack where and when he wanted, which he surely would.

Surveying the area in which he could realistically hope to operate, it was clear to Bragg that an advance toward Knoxville offered the best opportunity for success. A movement to the northeast would simultaneously secure both his supply line from the south and the East Tennessee & Georgia Railroad, which ran through Knoxville into southwestern Virginia. A possible added bonus was that Major General Samuel Jones was in charge of several thousand Confederate troops guarding salt works and lead mines in southwest Virginia, troops that might be used to make a coordinated assault on Knoxville.[8]

Jefferson Davis wrote to Bragg on October 29 mentioning how beneficial if could be if the Confederacy were able to regain control of East Tennessee and restore communications with Virginia. Among other things, Davis wrote, "It has occurred to me that if the operations on your left should be delayed, or not be of prime importance that you might advantageously assign General Longstreet with his two division to the task of expelling Burnside." General Lee wanted Longstreet and his troops returned to the Army of Northern Virginia and Knoxville was at least in the right direction. Another potential advantage was that by threatening East Tennessee, pressure might be brought on Grant to reinforce Burnside with troops from Chattanooga or Sherman's force when it arrived. And there was one more possible reason why Bragg might be willing to lose several thousand veteran soldiers—he and Longstreet just could not work together and Bragg would probably be happy to see the disruptive general leave.[9]

Confederate General James Longstreet—many Southerners later turned against Longstreet when he supported his old friend Ulysses Grant for president (Library of Congress).

On November 4, Longstreet received orders to make an advance toward Knoxville to "drive Burnside out of East Tennessee first, or better, to capture or destroy him." Bragg emphasized that "every preparation is ordered to advance you as fast as possible, and the success of the plan depends on rapid movements and sudden blows." The next day Longstreet began withdrawing two divisions from their positions and began the march toward Knoxville. Learning of Longstreet's departure, Grant admitted that he could not take advantage of the weakened enemy: "The situation seemed desperate, and was more aggravating because nothing could be done until Sherman should get up."[10]

When the news of Longstreet's departure from Chattanooga, with his probable target being Knoxville, was learned back in Washington, telegrams began to flood the wires into Chattanooga. As Grant remembered it, he received several messages saying he had to "do something for Burnside's relief; calling attention to the importance of holding East Tennessee; saying the President was much concerned for the protection of the loyal people in that section, etc."[11]

Thinking that an assault on Bragg's position at Chattanooga might force Longstreet to turn his troops around, on November 7 Grant ordered General Thomas to assault on the northern end of Missionary Ridge "with all the force you can bring to bear against it, and, when that is carried, to threaten, and even attack, if possible, the enemy's line of communications between Dalton and Cleveland." If a sizable Federal force was able to move around the northern end of Missionary Ridge they would be in position to break the Confederate supply line. Not only did most of Bragg's provisions come through Dalton, but this railroad was also Longstreet's lifeline. Any threat to disrupt his supplies would probably force Longstreet to cancel or at least postpone his advance.[12]

The importance of taking some sort of action to assist Burnside was apparent when Grant told Thomas that if not enough horses were available "to move the artillery, mules must be taken from the teams or horses from ambulances; or, if necessary, officers dismounted and their horses taken.... The movement should not be made one moment later than to-morrow morning." Grant wrote to Burnside confidently predicting that the attack "must have the effect to draw the enemy back from your western flank." If, however, Longstreet failed to cooperate by withdrawing, Grant suggested that Burnside fall back through the mountain passes obstructing the roads behind him.[13]

The reality of the situation, however, was that no matter what plans Grant might make or orders sent out, there were not enough healthy animals in the entire army to move all the wagons and artillery that would be needed to carry out such an advance. Normally mules were not used to haul artillery because they were not as steady under fire as horses, and there was little point in taking officers' horses to pull artillery, as they were generally not strong enough. If the army were unable to move provisions and ammunition up to the front, breaking through the enemy lines on Missionary Ridge would accomplish little, as the army could not move far enough from Chattanooga to sever the Confederate supply route. Embarrassed by this inability to take action, Grant had to wire Halleck that "Thomas will not be able to make the attack of which I telegraphed until Sherman gets up." Grant informed Burnside that Thomas was now going to try to "drive the enemy from the west side of Lookout and move a column up the valley. This may withhold any movement against you until a larger force can be collected, and a greater effort will be made to force the enemy back."[14]

The removal of Longstreet's force presented Grant with an opportunity that he would normally have taken immediate advantage of. Considering how much Grant believed in hitting the enemy hard and often, this must have been a terribly frustrating time for him. But the simple fact was that for now the troops in Chattanooga were staying put and little could be done to change the situation. On November 21, Grant exhibited some of this exasperation in a message to General Halleck, "I have never felt such restlessness before as I have at the fixed and immovable condition of the Army of the Cumberland. General Meigs states that the loss of animals here will exceed 10,000. Those left are scarcely able to carry themselves."[15]

On November 13, Grant finally received the news he had been waiting for—the lead elements of General Sherman's troops had arrived at Bridgeport. Sherman's 17,000 men had endured wretched conditions on their journey, being constantly bombarded by cold rain as they tried to move over the narrow, muddy mountain roads. There was never enough food, so as the army approached its destination Sherman decided to bring up the supply wagons from the rear of the army and ordered that each division's wagons should follow behind that unit. While this did make the distribution of provisions more efficient, the column slowed down even more, as many of the wagons had to be pushed and pulled along over the muddy roads. Sherman's entire force would need several days to come up, so he rode ahead into Chattanooga to meet with Grant on November 14. That evening Grant, Thomas, and Sherman met for hours to discuss the situation facing them and what steps might be taken to deal with the Confederate army around Chattanooga.[16]

The next morning, while the three generals were out surveying the surrounding area in person, Sherman saw for himself the strong Confederate positions on Missionary Ridge and Lookout Mountain. Sherman later wrote that he made the comment, "'Why,' said I, 'General Grant, you are besieged'; and he said, 'It is too true.' Up to that moment I had no idea that things were so bad." It was at this time that good roads were discovered leading from Brown's Ferry north behind a series of hills that would conceal Federal troops' movement from the Confederates on Missionary Ridge. By utilizing these routes Sherman could prevent, at least for a while, Bragg's learning if his force was staying in the vicinity of Chattanooga or moving east to relieve Knoxville. Just as important was that the Federal commanders learned that the defenses on the northern end of Missionary Ridge were not as strong as had been expected. On the 16th, Sherman returned to his troops to begin preparations to confront the enemy on the northern end of the ridge.[17]

Grant's basic outline for the coming fighting was already completed with the date to begin the only major factor still undecided. After the opening of the Brown's Ferry supply route, control of Lookout Mountain became less important, so the main Federal effort was to be made against Missionary Ridge. The main thrust of the plan was for Sherman to advance behind the hills that shielded his troops from view and assault the northern end of Missionary Ridge. Over one hundred pontoon boats had been accumulated by General Smith about seven miles east of the city in North Chickamauga Creek. The movement would begin with one of Sherman's divisions floating down to the Tennessee at night. A portion of the troops were to drift a few miles past the city to the mouth of South Chickamauga Creek and build a pontoon bridge across the river. Most of troops in the initial movement were to cross the river and establish a position opposite the north end of Missionary Ridge. The main portion of Sherman's troops would then cross the river and begin the assault against the lightly defended north end of Missionary Ridge. If these troops broke through the Confederate lines, they could then continue advancing toward the railroad that brought up Bragg's supplies.[18]

The part General Hooker's troops were to play in the early stages of planning was to attack the Confederates on the northern end of Lookout Mountain, then cross Chattanooga Valley south of the Confederate lines on Missionary Ridge, where he could threaten Bragg's left and possibly get behind the Confederate lines to cut off their retreat. After Grant reflected on the difficulties in forcing his way over Lookout Mountain, it was decided for Hooker to follow Sherman's route to Chattanooga, then head south toward Rossville, because "the passage over the mountain was a difficult one to make in the face of an enemy" and he "was perfectly willing that the enemy should keep Lookout Mountain until we got through with the troops on Missionary Ridge." As the time to launch the assault was near heavy rains made the river rise dramatically and the crossing at Brown's ferry was considered too unsafe for Hooker's men to use, so he was ordered to implement the original plan and move against Lookout Mountain.[19]

All that was left to decide was what to do with the troops in Chattanooga. Grant did not really want to use Thomas' men because he feared they were still not totally recovered physically from the recent lack of food and were possibly still a little demoralized from their defeat at Chickamauga. All Grant wanted from the men in Chattanooga was to form their ranks in front of Missionary Ridge to hopefully draw attention away from the flanks where the real assaults would take place. Once the fighting began and Grant could see how Bragg responded to the first assaults, Thomas could then send men to support either of the flank attacks or feint an attack against the Confederate works in the center of Missionary Ridge.[20]

While he worked on plans to drive the enemy from Chattanooga, Grant also had to keep an eye on Burnside and Knoxville. Once Sherman's advance arrived at Bridgeport, Grant informed Burnside and asked if he could stand against Longstreet's force, "or by skirmishing and falling back can avoid serious loss to yourself, and gain time," until Sherman could move to his assistance and Grant was able to "force the enemy back from here and place a force between Longstreet and Bragg that must inevitably make the former take to the mountain passes by every available road to get back to his supplies." Grant told Burnside on November 17 that he was "doing exactly what appears to me right. I want the enemy's progress retarded at every foot all it can be, only giving up each place when it becomes evident that it cannot be longer held without endangering your force to capture." Grant also informed Burnside that plans were in motion to attack Bragg, advising him that only Sherman's advance troops were at Bridgeport and that the earliest the assault could be launched would probably be the 19th.[21]

Luckily Burnside and Knoxville were not in as much jeopardy as was feared, since once Longstreet reached Loudon he kept his troops there until November 13. The railroad line ended at that point and Grant believed "it is probable he was directed to remain there awaiting orders. He was in a position threatening Knoxville, and at the same time where he could be brought back speedily to Chattanooga." A shortage of rail transportation was the reason for the halt later given by Longstreet, but whatever the reason was that he delayed the advance, the main beneficiaries were Grant and Burnside[22]

As soon as Sherman returned to Bridgeport, he went to work and began moving his troops forward on November 17, and once again the weather played a part in the operation. Two days of heavy rain turned the already primitive roads into deep mud. Sherman's troops were slowed to a snail's pace. Adding to the delays, the pontoon bridge at Brown's Ferry was damaged due to rising water in the Tennessee River. It quickly became clear that Grant's original timetable would have to be postponed.[23]

With most of the troops still stretched out behind them, the head of Sherman's column reached Brown's Ferry on November 20, already behind schedule. Attempting to create a diversion that fooled no one, Sherman had Brigadier General Hugh Ewing turn his division south toward Lookout Mountain. Grant had received word that there was fighting near Knoxville and communication with the city had been cut, which made him even more anxious for Sherman to begin his assault, if possible the next day. Unfortunately, no matter how many orders were issued or how hard the men worked to obey those orders, the continuing rain made any immediate movement impossible. The delays forced Grant to send out orders changing the day of the assault to the 22nd. But, as Grant recorded, "The elements were against us. It rained all the 20th and 21st. The river rose so rapidly that it was difficult to keep the pontoons in place."[24]

Over the next two days Sherman's rain-soaked men crossed the river as quickly as they could, considering the conditions under which they had to work. In their original position Sherman's troops were clearly visible to Confederate observers, but once across the river, they were concealed from view in the hills. Using the hills as cover, Sherman moved his troops up to a point where he could approach the north end of Missionary Ridge. Since the combined movement of all the Union forces could not begin until Sherman was ready, Grant had to postpone the assault again. November 23 was now set as the day to begin the attacks.[25]

Back in Chattanooga there was understandable concern that the longer the attacks were delayed the more probable was the chance that Sherman's movements behind the hills would be discovered. As a diversion to draw attention and possibly troops from Missionary Ridge, on November 22 Thomas suggested that Grant change Hooker's orders again and launch an assault against the Confederate positions on Lookout Mountain. By this time, however, the troops under Hooker's orders had become a mixed group of units from different commands. Both of Howard's Eleventh Corps divisions had moved north to reinforce Sherman, and of Hooker's original four divisions, only John Geary's small division remained. In addition to Geary's troops, Hooker's force was bolstered by Brigadier General Charles Cruft's division of Gordon Granger's corps that had been sent out in case more support was needed during the Raccoon Mountain operation, and General Osterhaus' division that had been unable to return to Sherman's force when the pontoon bridge at Brown's Ferry became unusable. Although these units and their commanders had never worked together, Grant felt that even if an attack on Lookout Mountain failed, it would provide a diversion that might assist the main assault on Missionary Ridge. Hooker was told to prepare to assault the seemingly unassailable positions on the mountain.[26]

General Grant had received a message from Bragg back on November 20 saying, "As there may still be some non-combatants in Chattanooga, I deem it proper to notify you that prudence would dictate their early withdrawal." Grant immediately believed that "this was a device intended to deceive; but I did not know what the intended deception was." The plainspoken Charles Dana simply wrote, "Of course, we all knew this was a bluff." This message took on a new meaning when a few days later a Confederate deserter informed Federal officers that Bragg was considering pulling his army back. That day reports came in that two more Confederate divisions commanded by Generals Cleburne and Buckner had pulled out of the lines on Missionary Ridge and were heading east to reinforce Longstreet. Being unable to account for at least part of Sherman's force, Bragg apparently believed that Grant had or soon would detach some of his forces to support Burnside. Added to his confidence in the strength of his position, this belief convinced Bragg that it would be safe to further reduce his forces around Chattanooga.[27]

This new information convinced Grant that it was now time to move: "Hearing nothing from Burnside, and hearing much of the distress in Washington on his account, I could no longer defer operations for his relief. I determined, therefore, to do on the 23d, with the Army of the Cumberland, what had been intended to be done on the 24th." To learn if Bragg really was reducing his forces, Grant instructed Thomas to make a serious demonstration in front of Missionary Ridge on November 23. Orders were also sent to Hooker that if Osterhaus could not rejoin Sherman's force by the next morning, he would be under Hooker's command and the attack on Lookout Mountain was to commence that morning. Confident that Sherman would by then be in position to launch his assault in the north, Grant would have both ends of the Confederate line under attack and Thomas in the center to reinforce either side or launch a separate assault with his own troops.[28]

About a mile out in front of the Federal lines was a thinly manned advance defensive line established by the Confederates on a group of low hills near the center of the valley. Sticking up about one hundred feet above the surface of the valley, the highest of these hills was a desolate looking place known as Orchard Knob. Grant decided to make this bump in the terrain the target of the first Federal assault, not only because he needed to remove any enemy positions from his front, but he also wanted to keep the enemy's attention focused on the center instead of the flanks, where the real attacks were to be made.[29]

General Thomas was well known for his careful planning and attention to detail, which some believed caused him to be a little slow to act; but when he did take action it was with overwhelming strength. Thomas massed about twenty thousand men out in front of the Federal lines where they were clearly visible to the Confederates on Orchard Knob and up on the ridge itself. General Granger's two divisions were formed in the center with Major General Philip H. Sheridan on the right and Brigadier General Thomas J. Wood on the left. In addition, Howard's corps was stationed to Wood's left, extending the line to Citico Creek and making it available for support if needed. The long rows of men in blue formed up in straight lines with flags waving and bayonets glistening in the sun, a magnificent vision of what war was like before the killing began. Looking down on the Federal formations from Missionary Ridge, most of the Confederates thought they were forming for some sort of review.[30]

A little before two o'clock the signal to advance was given and Wood and Sheridan led their men forward. It was not until the lines of blue clad soldiers were coming straight at them that the Confederate pickets and those manning the rifle-pits on Orchard Knob and the lower hills realized they were about to be attacked. Along the hills Confederate muskets fired a volley or two, and from up on Missionary Ridge artillery fire began to fall among the Federal lines. Here and there the dead and wounded fell out of ranks dotting the field with blue spots, but there was no hesitation as the Federals moved forward. General Wood's men headed directly for Orchard Knob as Brigadier General August Willich's brigade stormed up the hill, driving the defenders before them while Hazen's brigade overran another lower hill to the right. At the same time General Sheridan's men easily captured the rifle pits further to the right. In less than an hour the entire Confederate line was taken and the surviving Confederates had dashed back to the line of rifle pits below the ridge.[31]

One of the men observing the assault was Quartermaster General Montgomery Meigs, who wrote to Secretary Stanton that it appeared the Confederates were not expecting any attack until it had begun. "Prisoners assert that they thought the whole movement was a review and general drill, and then it was too late to send to their camps for reinforcements, and they were overwhelmed by force of numbers. It was a surprise in open daylight."[32]

A little later that day the new Federal line was extended on the left of Wood's position by Howard's troops and artillery was brought up to improve the defenses. Each side suffered about two hundred casualties, but this minor engagement was more important than it might seem. Grant confirmed that Bragg was still firmly lodged on the ridge and now the distance to the first line of rifle pits at the base of the ridge had been almost cut in half, which was a major advantage for assaulting troops. Another result from the assault on Orchard Knob was that the massive Federal buildup in the center caused Bragg enough concern that he weakened the defenses on Lookout Mountain by transferring General William Walker's division from the far left to strengthen his center.[33]

There could no longer be any doubt in Bragg's mind that Grant was positioning his forces for a major offensive. Although Bragg was still confident in the strength of his positions, he immediately tried to recall the troops that had just recently left for Knoxville. Most of Buckner's men were by now too far away, but General Cleburne was able to return with his division and one of Buckner's brigades. The build-up of Federal forces in the center also forced Bragg to increase the defenses on the crest of the ridge. Initially the height and difficult terrain on the slopes convinced the senior Confederate officers that no one would be foolish enough to launch an assault up the face of the ridge. The only real defensive lines that had been set up were the rifle pits near the base of the ridge. Now that the center appeared to be more seriously threatened than had been expected, Bragg initiated a rushed program of building fortifications on the crest and in various places on the face of the ridge, hoping that it was not too late.[34]

Chapter 22

The Battle Begins

Joseph Hooker must have been feeling pretty good on the morning of November 24 when he looked out and saw that most of Lookout Mountain was covered by fog and thick low-lying clouds. His command was originally going to play only a minor role in the coming battle by providing a diversion for the main attack made by General Sherman on the north end of Missionary Ridge, after which Hooker was to try to get in the rear of the Confederate army and do what he could to disrupt their retreat. The overall situation around Chattanooga had changed dramatically in the last few days. Now Hooker had the opportunity to repair his military reputation that had been so damaged at Chancellorsville. Because of the inclement weather Hooker's part in the coming battle had already been changed twice, and now his role in the assault on Lookout Mountain had become an integral part of the overall operation.[1]

With the opening of the Brown's Ferry supply route, Lookout Mountain had lost most of its military importance. Missionary Ridge and the Confederate supply line east of the ridge were Grant's main targets in the upcoming assaults, and the enemy troops stationed on the mountain had little effect on that outcome. Now that General Osterhaus' division was still unable to get back across the river, he was ordered by Grant to join Hooker's command. Hooker now commanded three full divisions and this was too large a force to allow the men to just sit in camp, so on the evening of the 23rd Hooker received orders to attack and drive the enemy off Lookout Mountain the next morning.[2]

No doubt General Hooker was pleased to be entrusted with a meaningful assignment, but he also must have been realized how difficult it would be to take control of that immense rock from the veteran soldiers who manned the enemy defenses. The troops making the assault would have to move up steep and heavily wooded terrain which rose up the western slope to a sheer rock palisade about fifty feet from the crest. About two-thirds of the way up the mountain the slope was broken up by a narrow strip of relatively level land, almost like a shoulder, where a few plucky farmers made their homes working small fields. On the north end of the mountain and for a few miles on either side, this rock palisade prevented access to the flat summit, which was narrow at the northern end and widened to about two miles to the south.[3]

The Confederate defenses were set up in two distinct areas with one group of troops defending the shoulder area and below and another force stationed on the crest. Two brigades of Major General Benjamin Cheatham's division defended the lower portion of the mountain, with the western side defended by Brigadier General Edward C. Walthall's Mississippi Brigade mostly facing west, downhill toward the creek. Walthall's flank was protected by a relatively weak line set up on their left stretching up the slope. There was also a thinly manned picket line extending from Lookout Creek around the north end of the mountain to Chattanooga Creek. High up on the plateau, three brigades of Carter Stevenson's division were stationed to support artillery that had been placed there to shell Federal positions around Chattanooga.[4]

The most extensive Confederate defenses were on the flat shoulder of the mountain. A series of rifle pits and trenches strengthened with logs stretched across the northern end of the mountain and formed a continuous line along both the east and west sides. General Hooker reported on the enemy defenses, "A continuous line of earth-works had been thrown up, while redoubts, redans, and pits appeared lower down the slope, to repel an assault from the direction of the river." Along either side on the slopes "were rifle-pits, epaulements for batteries, walls of stone, and abatis to resist attack from either the Chattanooga or Lookout Valleys."[5]

Taking advantage of the early morning fog, General Geary began his advance past Wauhatchie around daybreak with his division and General Whitaker's brigade of Cruft's division. About 8:30 a.m. Geary's force forded Lookout Creek while at the same time the remainder of Cruft's division moved forward to capture two damaged bridges near the railroad which they and Osterhaus' division would use to cross the creek. One of the bridges was quickly taken by Colonel William Grose's brigade, but the firing brought Confederate reinforcements down from the lower slopes into positions along the railroad, which, as Hooker reported, "enabled them, without exposure, to sweep, with a fire of musketry, the field over which our troops would be compelled to march for a distance of 300 or 400 yards."[6]

Unable to see much of what was going on, Hooker had to wait for news of Geary's troops before continuing the assault, and it was about 10:30 a.m. before he decided to make a move. Leaving two regiments behind to continue repairs on the captured bridge, Cruft was instructed to send the rest of Grose's brigade to construct another bridge about half a mile up the creek and then join Geary's troops. In addition, several batteries of artillery were sent forward to cover the infantry along the creek and fire on the enemy positions on the slopes.[7]

Continuing his advance while Cruft and Osterhaus were engaged along the creek, Geary was able to take advantage of the cover provided by the clouds and mists farther up the valley until his men were past the enemy defensive lines. With Whitaker's brigade in the lead, they now began an arduous climb up the side of the mountain and drove back the Confederate pickets as they went. Once his men reached the level ground of the shoulder in the slope, Whitaker halted his advance and formed his troops with their right near the sheer rock formation, and in combination with the rest of Geary's troops formed a line that covered the slope from the shoulder down the mountain side facing north.[8]

General Geary now led his men forward across the western face of Lookout Mountain. The broken terrain made moving at anything more than a slow walk difficult. One of Whitaker's men, Isaac C. Doan, of the 40th Ohio, later wrote that when his unit reached the base of the palisade, they "swept the slope to the northeast, descending into ravines that furrow the slope, climbing the opposite bank with infinite labor." The going was slow but Geary's men continued to move forward. Doan remembered, "We make up for lack of speed, with yells, while the opposite mountain sends back the echoing battle cry, until the rebels afterward captured said they thought there was a million of us."[9]

The left flank of Walthall's line was defended by only one regiment and they were totally outmanned by Geary's advancing troops. While the fighting on the slope was slowly moving north, down near the base of the mountain Osterhaus and Cruft had been making progress against the defenders along the creek. Once the second bridge was finally completed, Osterhaus' troops moved forward and engaged the defenders in their front at about eleven thirty. Grose later wrote that his men moved forward "as fast as the men and officers could climb (for all were on foot), sweeping everything before them, over rebel camps and rebel rifle-pits." Hit from the front and flank, the Confederate front facing downhill was pushed back into a series of works which Geary describes as "covering the whole plateau in front of the left of my right and my center, formidable in natural defense and seemingly impregnable with rocks, stone, and earth breastworks, surrounded by tangled slashings."[10]

Rather than falling back to the stronger positions on the northern end of the mountain, Walthall did all he could to hold his positions on the west side, but even putting in his reserve force did little to slow down the Union soldiers advancing along the slope. In his report General Geary stated that Colonel David Ireland's brigade accompanied by the 29th and 111th Pennsylvania regiments "hurled themselves upon their flank with furious effort. Our fire was delivered in continuous volleys." Geary also noted the determination of his men as they moved forward: "The ardor of our men surprised and stultified the enemy, and we punished him severely in his irresolution." The men in blue continued to force their way forward through the broken terrain as they received continuous fire from Confederates hidden in the many ravines and depressions on the mountain side and from the crest above. Walthall's Mississippians did their best to hold the positions, but the weight of the Federal assault took its toll, and by noon they were forced to finally give way back to the northern end of the mountain.[11]

The Confederates had erected their strongest defensive works on and around the farm of Robert Craven located on the shoulder of the northern end of the mountain. This was where the battle would be won or lost. The defensive line was fortified with rifle-pits and low walls made from piles of rocks and supported by several artillery pieces that could sweep the ground of what had once been a quiet little farm. If the Union advance could not be stopped here, there was little to prevent them from moving around the end of Lookout Mountain into Chattanooga Valley on the far left of Missionary Ridge. Another advantage for the defenders was that the slope of the mountain was even steeper in this area and the ground was covered with large boulders and small ravines, making it even more difficult to move forward under the enemy fire.[12]

Walthall's remaining troops manned the defenses around the farm and were joined by Brigadier General John Moore's brigade on the right defending a line from the farm down the slope. The beleaguered Confederates put up a good fight, but once again they were overwhelmed by the Union attack. Walthall's left flank, closest to the palisade, was hit hard, while at the same time the center around the Craven house was attacked relentlessly. The Union soldiers found the going tough and in many places were forced to jump over logs and climb over and around boulders, but they did not stop. The Confederates were unable to use their artillery with effect in the close quarters, so most of the gunners joined their comrades fighting on the lines. General Moore did his best to hold his position on the slope, but as the defenders above his line began to falter he could not take the chance of being flanked and cut off, so Moore had to pull his men out with some falling back around the mountain to the east or escaping into the valley below.[13]

Throughout the morning the sounds of battle on Lookout Mountain could be heard by the Union troops down in Chattanooga, but the mountain itself combined with the fog and low clouds prevented them from actually viewing any of the fighting. As the Confederates fell back toward the Craven farm and the intensity of the fighting increased, so did the noise from the mountainside as the battle lines moved closer. As the boom of artillery and the crack of musket fire echoed between the mountains, down in the valley the Union troops could only wonder what was going on behind the fog and smoke.[14]

One of the Federal soldiers wondering what was happening up on Lookout Mountain was Major James A. Connolly of the 123rd Illinois, who wrote his wife that as they waited anxiously for news about the fighting, "All eyes are turned toward the Mountain, and the stillness of death reigns among us in the valley, as we listen to the sounds of battle on the other side of the Mountain while all was quiet as a Puritan Sabbath on our side of it. How hope and despair alternated in our breasts." Suddenly, as if it were a planned event, the clouds and smoke and fog drifted away, and for a few short minutes Lookout Mountain was bathed in sunlight, revealing an amazing sight to the soldiers around Chattanooga.[15]

Around the northern end of Lookout Mountain came the Confederates in full retreat. Following close behind them were swarms of men in blue with flags whipping in the cool mountain air and rifle barrels glistening in the sun. Thomas' men went wild, throwing their caps in the air and cheering as loudly as they could. Major Connolly wrote, "Oh! Such a cheer as then went up in the valley! Manly cheeks were wet with tears of joy." General Hooker reported that during most of the morning his troops in the valley only caught an occasional glimpse of their comrades on the mountain, but when the air cleared for that brief time and "our true condition was revealed to them, their painful anxiety yielded to transports of joy which only soldiers can feel in the earliest moments of dawning victory." The celebrating did not last long, as the clouds and fog soon returned to mask the mountain, but the Federal soldiers in the valley saw enough to know they had witnessed victory.[16]

During the early afternoon the main area of fighting had moved around the northern end of the mountain to the eastern slopes, where the Confederates ended their retreat and formed another defensive line. Up to this point in the fighting the angle of the slope on the western side had prevented General Stevenson's men up on the summit from assisting their comrades below. Once the fighting moved around to the east, however, Stevenson hurried reinforcements to bolster Walthall's defenses. General Geary reported that "about 500 yards beyond Craven's house, and in front of the mountain road, the enemy, already reported, appeared in heavy force." The defenders were able to get a brief rest behind the new set of works that extended up the slope to the palisade, effectively preventing the flanking tactics that the Union troops had used to force the defenders out of their previous positions.[17]

Around one o'clock the weather began to get even worse as the rain increased and the fog became even thicker than earlier. Hooker's men had pushed the enemy completely off the western and northern slopes and the Federals now had control of a good part of the eastern side of the mountain overlooking the Confederate works in the valley. Every reasonable objective had been accomplished, and Hooker decided it was time for the tired troops to rest. Not willing to concede defeat just yet, however, the Confederates were more than willing to continue the contest. In his report Geary wrote that around "1 o'clock the enemy made an assault in force upon my left," which was beaten back. And still later, about three o'clock, "the enemy were observed massing a force under the cliff of the extreme right held by Cobham." A relatively weak assault was made shortly after, but this was easily repulsed and the fighting ended for the day except for some occasional firing through the night. Geary proudly noted that even though his men were exhausted from the fighting and suffered from the cold wind that swept over the mountainside, "many expressed their impatience for the coming of day that the attack might be renewed."[18]

General Hooker had won an impressive victory because the Confederates could not come up with an answer to the spirited Federal assault despite the great advantage they held in defending such difficult terrain. General Bragg put most of the blame for the loss on Stevenson, but this was hardly fair, since he had only taken over the command of the Lookout Mountain forces the night before the battle and had no time to get acquainted with the terrain or the defensive positions and was unable to make any adjustments he might have liked to. The outnumbered Confederates had fought well but were simply overwhelmed by the much larger Federal force. Since the opening of the new supply route Lookout Mountain had lost much of its value, and Bragg had decided before the fighting began there was no good reason to weaken other areas in order to make a major effort to hold the mountain. From the Federal point of view, however, control of the northern end of the mountain gave Hooker an almost open road to the rear of the Missionary Ridge position, which most certainly would be taken advantage of by General Grant.[19]

During the night before Hooker's men began moving up Lookout Mountain, the main part of Grant's plan was put into motion on the northern end of the Federal lines. Shortly after midnight Brigadier General Giles A. Smith began loading his brigade into pontoon boats on North Chickamauga Creek. Floating quietly into the darkness, they headed down the creek into the Tennessee and continued until about 2:30 a.m. when they approached the mouth of South Chickamauga Creek, where two regiments landed on the south bank quickly and quietly, capturing the few enemy pickets in the immediate vicinity. Once again the Federal scheme went as well as anyone could want. The remainder of Smith's brigade continued downriver past the creek and quickly established a beachhead. As soon as they disembarked the boats were returned to retrieve more of Sherman's men from the opposite shore, and by sunrise nearly eight thousand men were consolidating their positions on the Confederate side of the Tennessee. As happened at Lookout Mountain, the dark skies and misty rain made it difficult for Confederate lookouts on the ridge to see what was going on along the river.[20]

As the sun was coming up General William Smith and his engineer details began building a pontoon bridge out of the boats that ferried the advance troops across the river. The work done by these men impressed General Sherman so much that he later wrote, "I have never beheld any work done so quietly, so well, and I doubt if the history of war can show a bridge of that extent (viz. 1,350 feet) laid down so noiselessly and well in so short a time." Another pontoon bridge was quickly laid over South Chickamauga Creek to connect Sherman's two forces.[21]

While the engineers were feverishly working on the pontoon bridges, the troops on the far shore secured their positions and the steamboat *Dunbar* ferried Sherman's third division across the river. The Union commanders were pleasantly surprised that the Confederates did not launch an attack against the small beachhead before reinforcements arrived. The only enemy fire Sherman's men faced was light musket fire from pickets and just occasional artillery fire from Missionary Ridge. General Howard brought a brigade of his corps up from Chattanooga about noon. Soon the pontoon bridge was completed and Brigadier General Jefferson C. Davis's division also crossed over to the east side if the river. Around noon Sherman had a dozen brigades and several batteries of artillery on the eastern side of the Tennessee and was ready to launch his assault.[22]

About a mile and a half from Sherman's position were the low hills that formed the northern end of Missionary Ridge. With no major obstacles between Sherman's men and the hills, it appeared that the Union forces had only to brush aside whatever light resistance they might encounter, seize the northern end of the ridge, and then advance along the crest driving in Bragg's right flank. Not wanting to give the enemy time to concentrate, Sherman gave the order to move forward about one o'clock, sending forward three divisions under the overall command of Major General Frank P. Blair. Morgan L. Smith led his division along South Chickamauga Creek, with John E. Smith's division in the center and Hugh Ewing's division to his right. Davis' division was assigned to guard the all-important bridge and provide a reserve force, if necessary. Sherman's troops moved steadily forward against light resistance as Captain S.H.M. Byers of the 5th Iowa reported, "All the afternoon we maneuvered and fought for position, chasing the enemy off one high hillspur only to find him better intrenched behind another."[23]

Around 3:30 p.m. Sherman's men had advanced far enough to take two hills that were believed to be the north end of Missionary Ridge. Just about a mile away was Tunnel Hill where the railroad ran through the ridge and connected to the line that brought Bragg's supplies up from Atlanta. This site was one of the major objectives of Sherman's movement, but he decided it was too late in the day to attempt to capture this vital position. There was a weak Confederate assault late in the afternoon which was easily beaten off. Sherman's men halted for the night, throwing up earthworks to secure their position.[24]

Believing that his troops were firmly planted on Missionary Ridge, Sherman sent word to Grant that he would continue the advance the next morning with Tunnel Hill as the objective. Grant replied by telling Sherman to "attack the enemy at the point most advantageous from your position at early dawn to-morrow morning (25th instant)." Grant also informed Sherman that he had ordered Thomas "to commence the attack early to-morrow morning. He will carry the enemy's rifle-pits in his immediate front, or move to the left to your support, as circumstances may determine best."[25]

From all appearances Grant's plan seemed to be coming together rather nicely and a great Union victory was just over the horizon. In the morning Sherman would begin assaulting Bragg's right flank, Thomas was prepared to hit, or at least demonstrate against, the center, and Hooker would be marching around the left flank of the Confederate line heading toward their rear. As happens all too often in war, however, the best laid plans do not always work out. This time it was mostly because Sherman's men were not camping on the northern end of Missionary Ridge but rather on a separate hill with a steep little valley between it and the actual ridge. Sherman's present location was not just a bad place from which to renew the attack in the morning, it was exceptionally bad. Understanding what Sherman was trying to accomplish, General Bragg sent Patrick Cleburne over to command the defense at Tunnel Hill and the northern portion of the ridge. Cleburne's troops had been on the way to Knoxville but Bragg recalled them just in time to arrive on the scene late that afternoon. During the night they made ready for the coming fight by preparing a series of excellent defensive positions which were made even stronger by reinforcements from Lookout Mountain that arrived early that morning.[26]

All along the slopes and crest, Missionary Ridge is covered with ravines, small depressions in the ground, and little knolls, terrain that was made for defense. The northern end of the ridge was narrow enough so that a determined number of defenders could hold off a much larger force. In addition to the abundantly available natural defensive positions, the very capable Cleburne added heavy log barricades to defend both slopes and the crest, adding well placed artillery to cover his front and both sides.[27]

Left: Confederate General John C. Breckinridge—won the Battle of New Market in May 1864 and was appointed Confederate secretary of war in February 1865 (Virginia Military Institute Archives).
 Right: Confederate General William Hardee wrote the manual for drill and infantry tactics used by both sides during the Civil War and after (Library of Congress).

In a meeting at Confederate headquarters, the senior commanders on Missionary Ridge, General Hardee and Major General John C. Breckinridge, joined Bragg to plan their moves to counter the coming Federal assault. The generals decided that even without Lookout Mountain, they had such confidence in the positions on the ridge that there was little doubt that any assault would be thrown back with heavy casualties. For the coming day Hardee was given command of the northern end of the ridge. More reinforcements were moved over to that sector so that Hardee would have about half the available forces to defend a third of the ground. The remainder of the army was tasked with defending the rest of the ridge under the command of General Breckinridge.[28]

When the fighting began Grant did his best to keep General Halleck informed of the progress made so far. After the capture of Orchard Knob the previous day, Grant wired that Thomas' men had taken the "first line of rifle-pits running over the knoll, 1,200 yards in front of Fort Wood. Our loss small. The troops moved under fire with all the precision of veterans on parade." Once the fighting died down that evening, Grant sent another message informing Halleck that the battle was proceeding favorably: "Sherman carried the end of Missionary Ridge, and his right is now at the tunnel, and left at Chickamauga Creek. Troops from Lookout Valley carried the point of the mountain, and now hold the eastern slope and point high up. I cannot yet tell the amount of casualties, but our loss is not heavy." Of course Grant was unaware that Sherman was not where he reported he was.[29]

On the morning of November 25 Grant received congratulatory messages from Halleck and President Lincoln with both men also making sure that Burnside was not forgotten. Halleck wrote, "I congratulate you on the success thus far of your plans. I fear that General Burnside is hard pressed, and that any further delay may prove fatal. I know that you will do all in your power to relieve him." From the president came the short message, "Well done. Many thanks to all. Remember Burnside."[30]

Since Grant's plan seemed to be working to perfection, his orders for November 25 called to just continue what had been begun. Sherman's task was to take Tunnel Hill and continue advancing across the ridge. Beginning his advance at first light, Hooker was to clear Lookout Mountain of any remaining defenders, then cross Chattanooga Creek coming up on the Confederate left. If that end of the ridge was occupied Hooker was to attack, but if undefended Grant wanted Hooker to advance on Rossville to cut off Bragg's retreat. Thomas was to keep his troops stationary until events determined if he should stage a diversionary attack in the center or join the attack on the Confederate right. If all went as planned, the battle for Chattanooga would end today.[31]

Chapter 23

A Change of Plans

Around dawn on November 25 several brave souls from the 8th Kentucky Infantry were able to make their way to the very tip of the palisade on the northern end of Lookout Mountain and unfurl a large American flag that could be seen across the valley and quickly resulted in an emotional outburst of cheering from the Federal troops below. Isaac Doan of the 40th Ohio remembered that as he joined in the cheering, "the whole mountain side resounded with huzzahs of joy and triumph.... It is no derogation to the manhood of soldiers whose valor had been fully proved, to say, that the tears of joy coursed down over many a war-worn face." From the mountain itself General Geary's men joined the celebration: "The enthusiasm," he reported, "was such as can only emanate from hearts of patriots, overflowing with gratitude for a great and signal victory."[1]

It was also on that morning General Grant learned Sherman was in fact in a relatively poor position to continue the attack. General Bragg did not wait to see what his opponents might do when morning came, but had spent much of the night repositioning his troops in preparation for the attack that was surely coming. Two divisions were brought over from Lookout Mountain to reinforce the right along the ridge. It took most of the night to make this realignment, and at dawn they were still moving along the summit of the ridge, clearly visible from Thomas' lines. Also during the night General Cleburne had reorganized his defenses to even better positions a little to their rear, and by first light preparations had been completed to challenge Sherman's assaults from any direction.[2]

Just as the sun was coming up Sherman's men moved forward with General Corse's brigade leading the advance down into the valley between their position and the first high ground of the ridge. There was no telling where Confederates might be positioned in the rough terrain and Corse's skirmishers were on their guard as they carefully moved forward. The defenders made their presence known soon enough, hitting Corse's men with musket and artillery fire as they descended into the valley, fire that only increased as they tried to move up the opposite slope. The Confederates occupied well fortified positions on both the slope and the crest of the next hill, with other works on higher ground farther back. The firing came down on the advancing Federals from several directions and continued for much of the morning. Not one to hesitate when the going got tough, Corse called for reinforcements, but as Sherman saw, "The space was narrow and it was not well to crowd the men, as the enemy's artillery and musketry fire swept the approach to his position, giving him great advantage."[3]

As Corse's men slowly moved forward the fighting got more violent. It was hours before they forced their way up the hillside to where they could actually assault Missionary Ridge proper. Once the Federals reached the crest, they found it so narrow that only Corse's brigade could operate effectively. Sherman had sent supporting troops to both sides of the ridge with Morgan L. Smith's division on the east and three brigades led by Colonel John M. Loomis on the west side, but these troops could do little to affect the outcome on the crest. Sherman reported that as Corse continued advancing, "a close, severe contest ensued, lasting more than an hour, gaining and losing ground, but never the position first obtained, from which the enemy in vain attempted to drive him." The Union troops hurled themselves at the Confederates and in some places there was desperate hand-to-hand fighting as the men grappled over every piece of dirt, but Cleburne's main lines held firm.[4]

Reporting on one of several charges his men made that morning, Colonel Charles C. Walcutt of the 46th Ohio wrote, "The advance was sounded, and the several lines rushed over the brow of the hill under a most terrific fire. Being in easy canister and musket range, it seemed almost impossible for any troops to withstand it, but so eager were the men to take the new position that they charged through it, all with a fearlessness and determination that was astonishing." Captain S.H.M. Byers of the 5th Iowa later wrote that the sounds echoed through the hills as "the battle raged for over an hour for the possession of a single hill-crest." The more numerous Federals could not gain an advantage against the Confederates who were well dug in on the higher ground. "So close were they, and so protected behind rifle-pits, logs, and bowlders, that they could throw stones on the assaulting column and do almost as much harm with them as with bullets."[5]

The Confederate defenders who were fighting off the unrelenting attacks saw Patrick Cleburne everywhere that morning encouraging his men at one location to hold firm under multiple assaults and then quickly moving on to prepare a counterattack at a different position. The most desperate fighting took place on the Federal right, with the lines moving back and forth for some time with Confederate artillery above the tunnel preventing the Union troops from holding their advance positions for very long. After hours of heavy fighting both sides seemed to decide the best thing to do was to take cover where they could find it and hold their positions for the time being. On the left, however, Corse's men moved forward under cover provided by a wooded area and abandoned Confederate works. During an assault against one of his advance batteries, Cleburne reported, "The artillerymen stood bravely to their guns under a terrible cross-fire, and replied with canister at short range, but still the enemy advanced." In an attempt to force the Federals back, a counterattack was launched with part of Colonel Roger Mills' regiment and Colonel Hiram Granbury's 7th Texas. As the Confederates charged, however, they came under heavy fire from Morgan L. Smith's Federal troops to the north and were driven back.[6]

During the assault on the Confederate battery, all the officers and so many men were casualties that Granbury had to send some of his infantry troops to help man the guns. Fighting just as stubbornly as their enemy, Corse's men hung on to most of their positions despite several ferocious counterattacks. During one of the attacks General Corse was wounded and Colonel Walcutt took over the command. Around noon the assaults were halted and for the next few hours both sides held their positions on the crest, but the firing continued unabated.[7]

After hours of hard fighting Sherman's assault had accomplished very little, so he decided to go up to the front to see what was going on in person. Sherman quickly realized the narrowness of the crest limited the number of troops that could be brought to bear on the enemy positions, which basically eliminated the Federal advantage in numbers. The rough terrain made advancing difficult while at the same time provided excellent cover for the defenders. Seeing no point in continued attacks that only increased casualties, Sherman decided to shift the focus of the attack to either the western slope facing Chattanooga or the opposite side of the ridge on the northeast. Unfamiliar with the terrain on either side, Sherman decided to launch his assault on the western slope simply because it was more accessible for bringing up supplies and reinforcements to that side of the ridge. With only a portion of his manpower committed to the crest, Sherman could easily support another assault from a different direction. So the decision was made.[8]

Early in the afternoon Colonel Loomis' brigade began making its way up the slope, with two brigades of John E. Smith's troops for support. Loomis' men were soon facing heavy fire from enemy positions on both the slope and crest and were forced to take shelter behind trees and boulders a short distance from the crest. Loomis, who was in a dangerously exposed position, reported he was "threatened on my entire front and left flank by the enemy coming down the hill-sides and the road." The assault on the western slope bogged down just as it did on the crest, with both sides able to hold their positions but nothing more. Cleburne reported that when the attacking troops concentrated their fire on one of his batteries, "Tier after tier of the enemy, to the foot of the hill and in the valley beyond, supplied this fire and concentrated the whole on a space of not more than 40 yards, till it seemed like one continuous sheet of hissing, flying lead." The heavy fire prevented the men on both sides from changing positions to more effectively return fire but caused few casualties, since most of the bullets went over the enemy's heads due to the angle of the slope.[9]

Neither side could gain an advantage over the other, but Cleburne did receive much needed reinforcements from General Alfred Cumming's brigade and Brigadier General George Maney's brigade that came over from Lookout Mountain and were immediately put into positions to support the front lines. After nearly two hours of hard fighting Lieutenant Colonel E. Warfield told Cleburne, "Our men were wasting ammunition and becoming disheartened at the persistency of the enemy, and proposed a charge down upon them with the bayonet." Cleburne was quick to agree, and now he had the men to act more aggressively.[10]

Near mid-afternoon Cleburne launched a surprise attack on Smith's two reserve brigades on the western slope. Sherman reported that the enemy "suddenly appeared on the right and rear of this command. The suddenness of the attack disconcerted the men, and, exposed as they were in the open field, they fell back in some disorder to the lower edge of the field and reformed." As the Confederates were pushing Smith's men down the slope, suddenly they "were caught in flank by the well-directed fire of one brigade on the

Confederate General Patrick Cleburne was killed leading his men in an assault at Franklin, Tennessee, in November 1864 (Library of Congress).

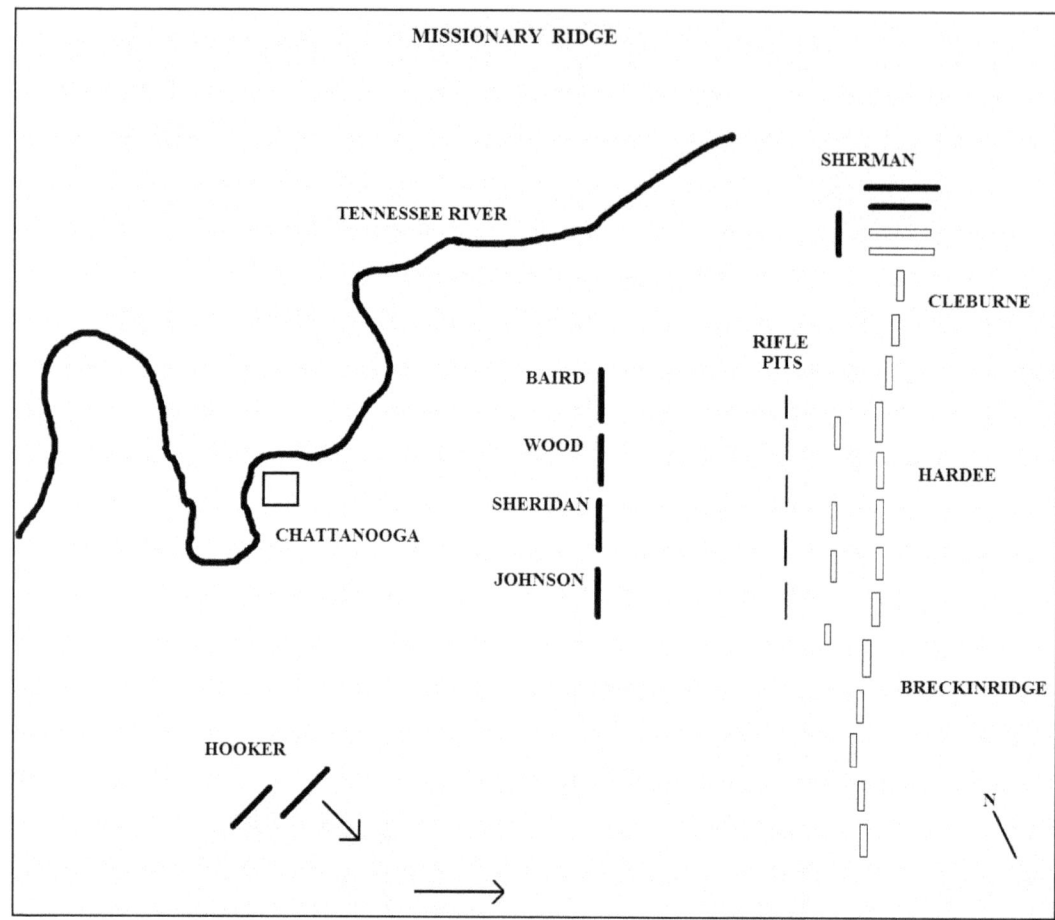

wooded crest" and were forced to quickly take cover. From their vantage point above the slope Walcutt's men had witnessed the Confederate attack, and as he reported, "In an instant every man was at his post and poured into the enemy volley after volley, that sent him running to his works. That this firing punished the enemy good is evidenced by the haste in which those coming upon us went back." By about three o'clock most of the troops on the slope and crest were just trying to hang on where they were. It was obvious that Sherman was not going to be rolling up the Confederate right flank as had been expected.[11]

The fighting along the crest and slopes of Missionary Ridge could be heard, and depending on the location, in some cases seen, from Orchard Knob. Once it became clear that Sherman was not going to advance across the crest of the ridge as expected, Grant had to again modify his plans. He instructed Thomas to send reinforcements to aid the assault on the ridge. Sherman had already been reinforced by two divisions of General Howard's corps and now Brigadier General Absalom Baird's division headed toward Sherman's vicinity only to learn that he had plenty of men; the advance was being held up by the terrain and Cleburne's defenses. With the assault on the Confederate right stalled, Grant sent word to General Hooker to begin his attack on the southern end of Missionary Ridge. Grant reasoned that if attacks on both ends of their line did not cause Bragg's troops to break, then he might weaken the center to strengthen the flanks, which could be taken advantage of by Thomas.[12]

Like Sherman, General Hooker was having his own problems that morning although for vastly different reasons. With most of the Confederate troops withdrawn from Lookout Mountain to bolster the defenses on Missionary Ridge, it looked like Hooker would have a relatively easy march to the Confederate left. With Osterhaus' division in the lead, Hooker's started out early in the morning meeting little resistance until reaching the bridge over Chattanooga Creek around noon. The bridge had been destroyed and the recent rain raised the water level in creek so high that it was unfordable. Hooker's advance came to a halt until the bridge was rebuilt. A footbridge was rigged by the 27th Missouri but it was too narrow and unstable to allow more than a few men to cross at the same time. As Grant later wrote, "Thus was lost the immediate advantage I expected from his forces. His reaching Bragg's flank and extending across it was to be the signal for Thomas' assault of the ridge." It took several hours to repair the bridge and Hooker's main force was not able to move forward again until after three o'clock.[13]

Once over the creek, General Osterhaus quickly moved forward with Brigadier General Charles R. Woods' brigade advancing on the right and Colonel James Williamson's brigade on the left. The Confederate defenders were forced out of Rossville Gap losing their artillery and a large amount of supplies. When Hooker brought up the rest of his infantry and the artillery, he began moving north along Missionary Ridge with Osterhaus "parallel with the ridge on the east, Cruft on the ridge, and Geary in the valley, to the west of it, within easy supporting distance."[14]

The Confederate defenders found some degree of shelter in old field works as they attempted to fight off Hooker's advancing troops, but as he reported, "Such was the impetuosity of our advance that his front line was routed before an opportunity was afforded him to prepare for a determined resistance." There was no place to go for the defenders who tried to escape down either side of the ridge. Those who headed down the eastern slope ran into Osterhaus' troops while those that fled to the west fell into Geary's hands. The majority of Confederates continued to resist Hooker's advance by falling back to a second defensive line but were soon forced to flee for their lives as the Federals continued to press their assault. General Hooker reported, "Whenever the accidents of the ground enabled the rebels to make an advantageous stand, Geary and Osterhaus, always in the right place, would pour a withering fire into their flanks, and again the race was renewed." Light resistance continued until evening, "when those of the enemy who had not been killed or captured gave way, and in attempting to escape along the ridge, ran into the arms of Johnson's division, of the Fourteenth Corps, and were captured."[15]

Back in front of the city, General Grant later noted that all morning he could see "column after column of Bragg's forces moving against Sherman. Every Confederate gun that could be brought to bear upon the Union forces was concentrated upon him." There was a growing concern among Union commanders that with these reinforcements the Confederates might be used in a counterattack on Sherman's troops. The fact was, however, that while Sherman's assault had not gotten anywhere, his men had built up their own solid defensive positions and were almost as well protected against attack as were the Confederates. With Sherman stalled in the north and Hooker too far away to affect the outcome of the battle, Grant's overall plan was not working out, and it was becoming apparent that "Sherman's condition was getting so critical that the assault for his relief could not be delayed any longer."[16]

After spending most of the day on Orchard Knob waiting to hear that Sherman had broken through the Confederate lines, Grant finally decided by around three o'clock it was time to try something else. Usually attacking both flanks of the enemy's defenses would have resulted in one of the flanks cracking, but since that had obviously not worked, Grant decided to try the direct approach. Grant's ability to remain calm and hide his emotions during times of crisis was already well established, but behind his usually sober expression he was always considering what other actions might produce the desired result if things did not go his way at first. The answer was in the center of the battlefield where George Thomas had over 20,000 men waiting for orders, facing enemy positions that had been noticeably weakened by transferring troops to face Sherman's assault.

The Army of the Cumberland had been formed in front of Missionary Ridge primarily to force Bragg to keep most of his men in the center instead of sending reinforcements to Cleburne on the northern end of the ridge. In addition, once the enemy's flanks had been driven in, Thomas' troops could join in the pursuit of the defeated Confederates. Making an all-out assault on the center of Missionary Ridge was never part of Grant's original plan simply because that looked like a disaster waiting to happen. Just to get to the Confederate defenses appeared to be a difficult task. In front of Orchard Knob there was almost a mile of relatively level open ground broken by a few small wooded areas which offered little cover from artillery fire that would fall on any massed bodies of troops all the way to the base of the ridge. There was a line of rifle pits at the base of the ridge with the ground well out in front littered with felled trees to slow down assaulting troops, making them easy targets for musket fire from the rifle pits. This portion of Missionary Ridge is about five hundred or six hundred feet high, and there was another line of trenches about half-way up the steep slope, which although not yet completed, provided another serious obstacle. Finally, any assaulting troops that were able to get past the first two defensive lines and make the difficult climb up the slope would find the crest lined with infantry and artillery. The man-made works combined with the steep and broken terrain made the Confederate position so strong that all their senior commanders believed the Federals would never be foolish enough to actually try to storm the center of the ridge.[17]

General Thomas' troops were lined up in front of Orchard Knob with Baird's division on the left, Wood and Sheridan in the center, and Brigadier General Richard W. Johnson on the far right. It was getting late in the day when Grant decided it was time to use the last option. Thomas was instructed to advance with his entire force "and carry the rifle-pits at the foot of Missionary Ridge, and when carried to reform his lines on the rifle-pits with a view to carrying the top of the ridge."[18]

What looked to be the desperate act of a general trying anything to win a battle was not quite as risky as it appeared. Confederate reinforcements had been moving north most of the morning and Grant was taking a calculated risk that Bragg had weakened his center enough to give Thomas an opportunity to break through. There was also the possibility that an attack on Bragg's center might induce him to recall some of those troops sent against Sherman, possibly providing him with an opportunity to break through the enemy's right. By attacking in the center, Grant was manufacturing two chances to drive the enemy from their position, and he was willing to take the risk that one of them would succeed. At this point Grant probably didn't care much where the enemy lines were broken, all that really mattered to him was defeating the enemy.

Chapter 24

A Legend Is Created

The decision had been made and the orders had been issued; now General Grant could only wait for the assault to begin. After a while Grant saw no discernable movement toward launching the assault, and as he was not known for his patience, he went in person to find out from Thomas why the assault was delayed. Grant found Thomas casually talking with General Wood. Grant asked Wood "why he did not charge as ordered an hour before. He replied very promptly that this was the first he had heard of it, but that he had been ready all day to move at a moment's notice." Grant then promptly directed Wood to join his division and begin the assault at once.[1]

It was nearing 4 p.m. when finally the signal was given for Thomas to begin the assault. Cheers echoed throughout the valley as over 20,000 men in four divisions formed up in a thick line of blue over a mile wide out in front of Orchard Knob. Similar to the formation that took Orchard Knob two days earlier, Thomas' men appeared to be getting ready for a review with regiments and companies lined up in neat rows rank after rank. Few Civil War battles offered the opportunity for both sides to have such a clear view of as much of the battlefield as did Chattanooga. It was very possible that many of the Confederates looking down on the Federal formations could not believe that they would be so foolish as to try a head-on attack against what they believed was an impregnable position. It is also just possible that at least some of the Confederates looking down on this juggernaut coming their way were beginning to wonder just how impregnable their position really was.[2]

After Grant took command and the opening of the new supply line and the flood of reinforcements that arrived, it became obvious to Bragg that he was going to be on the defensive, so he naturally concentrated the majority of effort on strengthening the flanks, where it was expected the assaults would fall. None of the Confederate commanders, including Breckinridge, who was in charge of the center of the Confederate line, devoted much thought toward having to defend against an attack up the steep and rugged slope. But with the loss of Orchard Knob the center of the Confederate line was now also threatened, forcing them to quickly improve the defenses in that sector.[3]

One of the most glaring problems with the Confederate defenses was that with the artillery on the very top of the ridge, the guns could not be depressed far enough to cover the entire slope. Another cause for concern was there had been little coordination in the layout of the trenches and fortifications. In some areas troops had been removed from the rifle pits at the base to strengthen the defenses on the crest. There was also a second line of works about halfway up the ridge but there were many gaps in this line which prevented the formation of a solid defensive front. During a fight these troops in the second line would have to fire over the heads of their comrades below, always a dangerous proposition. Even worse was that if the men stationed at the base had to retreat back up the slope, they would be right in the line of fire of their comrades above. Apparently Bragg had counted on the difficulty of the terrain to deter any serious attack. In any event, it was now too late to correct any deficiencies in the defenses—thousands of Federal soldiers were heading toward Missionary Ridge and they looked like they meant business.[4]

Once Thomas' men left the woods near Orchard Knob there was from 500 to 700 yards of open ground in front of the first line of rifle pits. General Bragg had nearly fifty pieces of artillery along the crest and they immediately opened fire with a deafening roar, sending shot and shell down on the advancing troops like hail. Lieutenant Colonel Robert Kimberly from the 41st Ohio later wrote that the men were at first stunned by the explosion of artillery fire, "but in a moment it was plain that no harm was being done. The much-talked-of moral effect of big guns was missing; there was no wavering in the lines. Rather, a feeling of new confidence came upon the men as they moved on, always too fast for the Confederates' depressing of their pieces." Major James Connolly remembered that as the enemy shells began falling, "the very heavens above us seemed to be rent asunder; shells go screaming over our heads, bursting above and behind us, but they hurt nobody and the men don't notice them." William Bircher of the 2nd Minnesota later wrote that as his regiment came out into the open, "the top of the ridge was one sheet of flame and smoke from the enemy's batteries, and the grape tore up the ground around us; but the troops being deployed as they were, there were very few casualties." Alfred G. Hunter, a Hoosier in the 82nd Indiana, had the same experience when his regiment moved forward: "The enemy soon opened a most terrific artillery fire from the ridge, yet it did but little injury as we advanced so rapidly that they could not get proper range upon us, the missiles falling behind us tearing up the earth."[5]

With men falling all around it must have felt like it took hours for Thomas' men to cross the open ground and make their way through the downed trees before they were near the enemy rifle pits where the already heavy fire seemed to actually increase in intensity. As the wave of men in blue was almost upon them some defenders broke and ran, but many stayed and kept firing. Henry Aten of the 85th Illinois remembered that as they reached the rifle pits, "There is a moment of death and terror, and the men leap over the parapet and into the trench, capturing the defenders to a man, who, as they stream to the rear, are pursued by the iron hail beating down from the hill top on both friend and foe." Grant was watching the progress of the assault from Orchard Knob, and in the sectors that the Confederates were able to fall back up the ridge, he thought they looked like "bees from a hive." One of the Confederates watching the fighting from the crest of the ridge was W. J. Worsham of the 19th Tennessee, who saw that the men escaping from the rifle pits had to climb up the slope "through a shower of bullets that plowed the ground and skinned the trees all around them." The Federal troops spread out through the works and the Confederates who stayed and fought were quickly overwhelmed.[6]

On first occupying the Confederate works, Thomas' men caught their breaths and gave thanks for surviving. As it turned out, however, they celebrated a little too soon, since fewer than half the attacking force could fit into the captured trenches. Once the former occupants had made it to safety their comrades up on the ridge sent a barrage of bullets and shells down on Thomas' men. The rifle pits were built to provide protection against fire coming from the front, but as Judson Bishop of the 2nd Minnesota noted, "It was only knee high and no protection at all against the musketry and canister that rained down upon us from the crest of the ridge." Lieutenant Colonel Kimberly later wrote that from up above, the enemy "opened a severe fire, and the artillery, by firing obliquely down the face of the steep slope, was able to be effective. Both arms together made the firing hot." And General Sheridan reported that his front lines "reached the first line of pits simultaneously, passed over them, and lay down on the face of the mountain. The enemy had now changed from shot and shell to grape and canister and musketry. The fire was terrific."[7]

L. G. Bennett of the 36th Illinois later wrote that they could not stay where they were for very long, and "to retreat was out of the question, after such a success, and over such a plain, and yet there were no orders to advance." Grant would later say that his orders to General Thomas had been to "carry the rifle-pits at the foot of Missionary Ridge, and when carried to reform his lines on the rifle-pits with a view to carrying the top of the ridge." These orders were more than a little vague, and most of the men were not sure whether they were supposed to continue up the slope or just sit there and keep taking casualties.[8]

There was just as much confusion over what to do next among the officers on the field. General Wood was confident the orders had been carried out, as he reported, "The goal for which we had started was won. Our orders carried us no farther. We had been instructed to carry the line of intrenchments at the base of the ridge and there halt." But other officers in Wood's division were not so sure about what to do next. General Willich later said that he only learned of the order to stop at the base of the ridge after the battle. But it was obvious to everyone "that to stay in this position would be certain destruction and final defeat; every soldier felt the necessity of saving the day and the campaign by conquering, and every one saw instinctively that the only place of safety was in the enemy's works on the crest of the ridge." General Hazen stated, "On commencing the advance, the thought of storming Mission Ridge had not entered the mind of any one, but now the necessity was apparent to every soldier of the command." What had to be done next was also obvious to General Wood: "The intrenchments were no protection against the enemy's artillery on the ridge. To remain would be destruction—to return would be both expensive in life and disgraceful. Officers and men all seemed impressed with this truth."[9]

Over on the left of the Federal line, General Baird stated that he was informed by one of Thomas' aides "that I would be following his wishes were I to push on to the summit." Sheridan was also unsure of his orders and had sent one of his staff back to General Granger for verification. Sheridan's men were already in the rifle pits when he learned that "the original order was to carry the first line of pits, but that, if in my judgment, the ridge could be taken, to do so." General Johnson, who commanded on the far right, understood his orders were to stay in contact with Sheridan's right flank and "to conform to his movements."[10]

While the officers pondered what to do, it was quite obvious to the Federal soldiers in the rifle pits at the base of Missionary Ridge that they could not stay where they were. Retreating back to Orchard Knob was never considered, so that left only one place to go and they did. William Calkins of the 104th Illinois remembered that "their musketry was telling rapidly on our ranks in the rifle pits below. Stung to madness, knowing that it would be death to stay there; scorning retreat, and inspired by one common impulse, there was suddenly an involuntary movement begun along the entire front, up the ridge." The story of Missionary Ridge is that on their own, Thomas' troops simply decided to charge to the top of the ridge. While this is certainly the stuff that legends are made of, the reality of what occurred was probably a little different.[11]

Most likely the movement up the ridge began with a few soldiers and lower ranking officers who could see that they would be much safer among the rocks and gullies on the slope than sitting in the open rifle pits. At first a few men then larger groups and finally regiments began to climb the rugged slope. In some cases if a unit advanced their neighboring troops would follow, as they had been ordered to stay aligned with the advancing unit. General Hazen wrote that he gave "the men about five minutes to breathe, and receiving no orders, I gave the word forward, which was eagerly obeyed. Not much regard to lines could be observed, but the strong men, commanders and color bearers, took the lead in each case." Some of Willich's men had already started up and, in a matter of minutes thousands of men in blue were making their way up the steep slopes of Missionary Ridge. Lieutenant Colonel Kimberly wrote, "Once the ascent was begun, however, the men came together, for the gullied and broken face of the Ridge afforded shelter not to be found on the level ground below. All the Confederate fire was also less effective, though it was not lessened." Mr. Dana later reported to Secretary Stanton that he believed both Sheridan and Wood ordered their men to move up the slope, "because the men were not to be held back, dangerous as the attempt appeared to military prudence. Besides, the generals had caught the inspiration of the men, and were ready themselves to undertake impossibilities."[12]

At headquarters on Orchard Knob the sudden advance up the ridge caught Grant, Thomas, and other high ranking officers by surprise. General Granger's chief-of-staff, Major J. S. Fullerton, later wrote about the confusion among the generals: "Grant quickly turned to Thomas, who stood by his side, and I heard him angrily say: 'Thomas, who ordered those men up the ridge?' Thomas replied, in his usual slow, quiet manner: 'I don't know; I did not.'" Grant then turned to General Granger asking, "'Did you order them up, Granger?' 'No,' said Granger; 'they started up without orders. When those fellows get started, all hell can't stop them.'" Dana reported that in his view the thousands of men slowly making their way up the side of the ridge appeared "as awful as a visible interposition of God."[13]

As Thomas' men felt their way up the steep slope quickly moving from cover to cover, it was impossible to stay in anything that resembled a normal formation. Captain Tilmon D. Kyger of the 73rd Illinois wrote in his diary that as he and his men climbed the ridge, they moved "from tree to tree, from stump to stump, and from log to log." Most of the men moved forward in small groups of a few dozen or a few hundred using trails cut across the face of the slope, and taking advantage of the protection offered by the many large rock formations and small ravines covering the face of the ridge, they followed their regimental flags up the slope.[14]

The Confederates had always relied on the difficulty of advancing over the steep and rugged slope of the ridge as their main form of defense on Missionary Ridge, but now it appeared that what was thought of as an advantage for the defense was being used against them. In addition to the fact that the angle and roughness of the slope provided many places where the attackers could find shelter from Confederate fire, the bullets were flying in both directions. In many instances the defenders were silhouetted against the sky as they stood up above their parapets to see what they were shooting at, which made them excellent targets.

Without knowing the number of Confederates that made it out of the rifle pits, Thomas' men probably had about a two to one edge over the defenders, not much of an advantage during Civil War assaults. The fire coming down the slope was causing heavy casualties among the attackers, but they continued to advance. General Willich noted that "many men fell down exhausted in climbing up under the enemy's fire, some fainted, but irresistible was the general advance." Ephraim Wilson of the 10th Illinois thought the roar from the artillery and musket fire sounded like "the very heavens above and earth beneath were at eternal war with each other." One of the things that John Hartzell of the 105th Ohio still remembered years later were the many trees that had been cut down "so forming as abatis over which we made slow progress. We just crowded over and under and through, and made headway slowly but surely."[15]

In spite of all the reasons they should not be doing what they were doing, the Federal troops continued moving up the slope, passing over the makeshift defenses around the center. In a letter to his wife, Major James Connolly described how he and his men advanced "mostly on hands and knees, amid a terrible storm of shot, shell and bullets," and after pushing the defenders out of the second line of trenches, "on our gallant boys went, officers and men mingled together, all rank forgotten, following their old flag away to the mountain top." The Confederates on the crest were getting more anxious by the minute as they watched the seemingly unstoppable Federal troops come closer and closer. W. J. Worsham later remembered that "the ridge where we were was quite steep but the enemy came on, crawling up the steep ascent like bugs, and were so thick they were almost in each other's way."[16]

One of the problems facing the defenders was that the top of the ridge was not wide enough for them to create a secondary defensive line if they were forced back from the edge of the crest. The assault had to be stopped before Thomas' men were able to breach the line at the edge of the crest, or the position would be lost. As the most forward of the Union troops approached the summit, Confederate artillery pieces could not be depressed enough to be of much use, so some of the artillerymen desperately tried to assist in the defense by lighting the fuses of their shells and rolling them down the slope to explode among the attackers.[17]

John Hartzell later wrote that as he came near to the top, in front was an artillery position built up with logs and dirt. "On it were two field guns which were being worked industriously, but could not be depressed enough to do us much harm. We all began to cluster up against this log pen like a swarm of bees on a limb." After pausing for a few moments to catch their breath, up and over into the enemy lines they went. Chaos erupted on the crest of Missionary Ridge as men fought desperately, firing their muskets at point-blank range and then not having the time to reload, using them as clubs. John Hartzell described what happened as he and his comrades made their move. "all at once, without orders, we burst up over the logs onto the gun platform. It was hand to hand fighting, and the 'devil take the hindmost.' The gunners stood to their guns like heroes, and the musket butts were pitted against sweat sticks and rammers."[18]

The Confederate lines were breached in several places almost simultaneously. Tough little Phil Sheridan went over the works with his men. Colonel John Martin of the 8th Kansas later wrote that his regiment pierced the enemy line at virtually the same time as "one or two regiments of Hazen's brigade on our right, and the 25th Illinois of our own brigade." Leading the 24th Wisconsin onto the summit of the ridge was eighteen-year-old Lieutenant Arthur MacArthur, waving the flag and shouting, "On Wisconsin!"[19]

All along the crest the results were the same, and although small groups of Confederates tried to stand and fight, most of the defenders were overcome with panic and fear even as their officers tried to regain control, but it was too late. Doing what he could to rally the men, General Bragg rode back and forth among his troops working hard to get them to continue fighting, but there was nothing he could do now, the battle was lost. The fighting spirit of the Confederate soldiers had slowly deteriorated as they had watched day by day their once defeated and starving foe relentlessly grow stronger until the Federal superiority in men and equipment proved to be more than the hungry and disheartened Confederates could resist.[20]

Before long the fighting began to die down. Thousands of beaten enemy soldiers fled down the eastern side of Missionary Ridge while the victorious Federal soldiers began to realize what they had just accomplished and the celebrating began. Major Connolly saw "dead and wounded rebels under our feet by hundreds, cannon by scores scattered up and down the ridge with yelling soldiers astraddle them, rebel flags lying around in profusion, and soldiers and officers completely and frantically drunk with excitement." Nixon B. Stewart of the 52nd Ohio remembered that "cheer after cheer, rang like bells, through the valley of the Chickamauga. Men flung themselves, exhausted, on the ground. They laughed, they wept, they shook hands and embraced each other.... It was as wild as a carnival." John Hartzell probable echoed the thoughts of many of his comrades in writing, "Such a scene of wild exultation. We had accomplished that which, for more than two months, we had looked upon as an impossibility. To attack and carry the fortified ridge had in nowise entered into our calculations; but here we were."[21]

All over the eastern slope of the ridge Confederate troops were trying to get away as fast as they could, throwing away anything that might slow them down, including items they would surely need later, like weapons and blankets. Those who stayed on the high ground of the ridge and headed south ran into Hooker's troops moving north and were gathered up by the hundreds. For the Confederate survivors who headed north along the crest, the day ended on a much better note. When the Federal troops began their assault General Hardee had sent orders to Cleburne, who was still firmly holding the northern end of the ridge, to send reinforcements to the center as soon as possible. Cleburne did send men to reinforce the center but the fighting was over before they arrived. Knowing how important it was to keep control of the northern part of the ridge, Cleburne was able to put together an effective defensive line across the ridge facing south, providing safety for the men retreating from the center and even more importantly preventing any Federal units from coming up behind his own command.[22]

Union General Philip H. Sheridan—in summer of 1864 he defeated Confederate forces in the Shenandoah Valley using a scorched earth policy (U.S. Army Military History Institute).

Even though in reality the Federal assault against the center of Missionary Ridge was probably not the impulsive charge made by troops without orders, it was still a very special event. In a message to Secretary Stanton, Charles Dana wrote, "The storming of the ridge by our troops was one of the greatest miracles in military history." In a personal observation he added that "no man who climbs the ascent by any of the roads that wind along its front can believe that 18,000 men were moved up its broken and crumbling face unless it was his fortune to witness the deed."[23]

During the night the remainder of the Confederate troops were pulled off the northern end of the ridge and headed for safety with Cleburne commanding the rear guard to cover the retreat. Most of the Federal troops were too exhausted to do anything but drop where they were to rest for the night, but the always aggressive Sheridan wanted to damage Bragg's army as much as possible while they were still running; he sent two brigades down the eastern side of the ridge in pursuit of the retreating Confederates. About a mile from the ridge they ran into a strong enemy position supported by artillery, and after a brief fight Sheridan's men drove the defenders away adding to the number of prisoners already captured and taking several pieces of artillery as a bonus. After this short fight Sheridan continued east toward Chickamauga Station.[24]

Sheridan knew that if he could take the railroad station, Cleburne's rear guard could be cut off from the rest of the Confederate army. Sheridan also knew that to be successful against Cleburne's force he would need more men than he had at hand, so he rode back to Missionary Ridge to get help. Both Grant and Thomas had already returned to Chattanooga and the highest ranking officer in the area was General Granger, who had gone to bed. Sheridan did his best to convince Granger how important it was to take advantage of this opportunity to cut off a substantial number of enemy troops, but Granger refused to give Sheridan any additional men. Returning to his troops, Sheridan continued pressing forward, and by midnight they pushed the Confederate skirmishers to within about half a mile of Chickamauga Station, where Sheridan halted and once again requested reinforcements. This request was also ignored, so Sheridan finally gave up for the night and had his men camp where they were. Early the next morning Cleburne was able to get his men far enough away to be out of immediate danger and continued to guard the rear of the retreating Confederates as they headed to safety in Georgia.[25]

Chapter 25

The Aftermath of Victory

Considering that the fighting at Chattanooga took place over several days and the severity of the combat, especially the rush up Missionary Ridge, the casualties were not as high as were suffered in many other Civil War battles. As was usually the case, it is difficult to obtain accurate casualty numbers, especially from the Confederate side. General Grant states in his official report that for the entire series of battles at Chattanooga the Federals sustained 757 killed, 4,529 wounded, and 330 missing, for a total of 5,616. General Bragg gave no reliable casualty figures in his report, but later figures from other sources reported 361 killed, 2,160 wounded, 4,146 missing, for a total of 6,667. The high number of Federal killed and wounded was indicative of the fact that they were the aggressors during most of the fighting. While Grant was in command at Chattanooga he reported that 6,142 Confederates became prisoners of war, two thousand more than it is believed were captured in battle. This is also an indication that many Confederates just gave up and allowed themselves to be captured away from the main fighting or simply deserted to escape the poor conditions and worsening morale that existed in the Army of Tennessee.[1]

There is little doubt that General Grant's taking over command at Chattanooga in person turned probable defeat into a glorious victory. Since the first day Grant arrived in Chattanooga his naturally aggressive nature had served him well. From opening the "cracker line" to the final assault on Missionary Ridge, every step he took had been a calculated risk that had paid off handsomely. Gaining control of Chattanooga and the surrounding area gave the Union control of most of the central portion of Tennessee.

Coincidentally, November 26 had been designated by President Lincoln back in October as America's first official national Thanksgiving Day. As news of the victory at Chattanooga sped across the country by telegraph, there really was a reason to be thankful. While another victory brought about by Ulysses Grant was being celebrated throughout the North, the man himself was still hard at work trying to press the enemy wherever possible. Grant was mostly known for his quiet manner and work ethic but he was also well aware of the important part politics played in this war, and he certainly knew how important the fate of the loyal citizens of East Tennessee was to President Lincoln. Confident of victory at Chattanooga even before the decision was final, Grant had instructed General Granger to move his corps toward Knoxville as soon as Bragg was defeated. Those orders were still in effect on the evening of November 25, but by then circumstances made Grant rethink this move, and he decided that Burnside could wait a day or two. Grant was always looking to do as much damage as possible to the enemy and decided he could not ignore the opportunity of catching the fleeing Confederate army and turning their retreat into a demoralizing rout. "On reflection," Grant wrote to Sherman, "I think we will push Bragg with all our strength to-morrow, and try if we cannot cut off a good portion of his rear troops and trains. His men have manifested a strong disposition to desert for some time past, and we will now give them a chance."[2]

The pursuit of Bragg's defeated troops was begun by General Hooker, who was in the best position to lead the chase. Following close behind the retreating Confederates, Hooker's men found many signs of a beaten and demoralized enemy. J. R. Kinnear of the 86th Illinois later wrote that his regiment "found all manner of things, burning and broken.... As the command advanced, every kind of plunder lined the road, the private soldier having even thrown away his provisions and clothing, being in the utmost confusion and excitement." As the pursuit continued the weather turned bad. Heavy rain that slowed the infantry and made it almost impossible for the men to move wagons over the muddy roads and close on the rear of the enemy. In addition, the men had little opportunity for rest the last two days, and most were near exhaustion from the fighting and weeks of living on short rations. Further inhibiting the pursuit, the Confederate rear guard, command by General Cleburne, was able to significantly delay the Federal troops by staging ambushes, obstructing roads and burning bridges. Hooker's troops were continually picking up stragglers and a few artillery pieces here and there, but the only way to inflict serious damage on the retreating Confederates was to catch up to their rear and force them into a real fight.[3]

Hooker's men did catch up with the Confederate rear guard on the morning of November 27 where the Western & Atlantic Railroad cut its way through a narrow gap in the mountains known as Ringgold Gap. As was so often the case, General Cleburne chose an excellent place to stop and face the pursuing Federals. Hooker's force had no artillery and his officers were unfamiliar with the terrain, but nevertheless Hooker sent his men forward hoping to hit the Confederates before they could complete their defenses. But Hooker was too late. Time after time Cleburne's men, well positioned with plenty of cover, received the Federal assaults, and time after time, they were sent reeling back with heavy casualties. After a day of heavy fighting Cleburne's men still held firm and the Confederate supply trains and artillery had made good their escape.[4]

General Grant had joined Hooker's force and could now clearly see for himself that it was pointless to continue pursuing Bragg's army. There was also the problem of sending aid to General Burnside, and Grant decided that it was time to call off the pursuit and turn his attention toward Knoxville. Information had been received stating that Burnside was low on provisions and only had enough to last through early December. There could be no more delay in sending assistance to Knoxville. "Had it not been for the imperative necessity of relieving Burnside," Grant reported, "I would have pursued the broken and demoralized retreating enemy as long as supplies could have been found in the country."[5]

General Granger had not yet begun his advance toward Knoxville because during Hooker's pursuit of Bragg's retreating army Grant had sent instructions for Granger's troops to remain near Chattanooga until he received further orders. There had been rumors that Bragg might attempt to double-back north and join with Longstreet's troops still in the vicinity of Knoxville and attack Burnside's positions. When Grant witnessed in person how quickly Bragg was trying to get as far south as possible, he became convinced that there was nothing to fear from Bragg's army in the immediate future. He noted, "The enemy had been throwing away guns, caissons and small-arms, abandoning provisions, and, altogether, seemed to be moving like a disorganized mob, with the exception of Cleburne's division." Grant sent orders back to Thomas to immediately start Granger's force toward Knoxville. Now that the relief force was on the way to Knoxville there was no reason for Grant to hurry back to Chattanooga, so he decided to remain in the field with Hooker. As frequently happened, things did not go as planned.[6]

When Grant returned to Chattanooga on November 29 and found that Granger's corps was still in camp, he quickly decided that if Granger was not anxious to make the march to Knoxville, the relief force would have a new commander. General Sherman was the man that Grant trusted above all others so he informed his friend that while Granger's troops would still be sent to Knoxville, "I have lost all faith in his energy or capacity to manage an expedition of the importance of this one. I am inclined to think, therefore, I shall have to send you." Wanting Sherman to move as quickly as possible, Grant told him to just take some of his own men and whatever troops he needed from Granger's corps: "In plain words, you will assume command of all the forces now moving up the Tennessee, including the garrison at Kingston, and from that force organize what you deem proper to relieve Burnside." If in Sherman's opinion he accumulated more troops than were needed to relieve Burnside, any surplus should be returned to Chattanooga. Displaying his total confidence in Sherman's ability to get the job done, Grant added, "I leave this matter to you, knowing that you will do better acting upon your discretion than you could trammeled with instructions."[7]

The situation in Knoxville turned out to be not as grave as Burnside had originally reported. Given sufficient notice of Longstreet's advance as the Confederates approached the city, Burnside was able to pull most of his troops within the relatively secure fortifications around Knoxville. Since Longstreet did not have sufficient manpower to conduct a proper siege of the city, Burnside's army was able to maintain access to the countryside south of the Holston River and could avoid any real danger of starvation. Shortly after a failed attempt to storm the Federal works on November 29, Longstreet learned of the defeat at Chattanooga and, realizing that Federal reinforcements would soon be on their way, decided there was now no chance of taking Knoxville. He marched his troops over fifty miles to the northeast and settled down to camp for the winter. Sherman's relief force had closed to about fifteen miles of Knoxville by December 5 when he learned that the Confederates had left the area and were no longer a threat. Leaving Granger's corps to reinforce Burnside's Army of the Ohio, Sherman brought his own troops back to Chattanooga, ending the active campaigning in Eastern Tennessee for the year.[8]

On December 8, Grant received a wire from President Lincoln: "Understanding that your lodgment at Knoxville and at Chattanooga is now secure, I wish to tender you, and all under your command, my more than thanks, my profoundest gratitude for the skill, courage, and perseverance with which you and they, over so great difficulties, have effected that important object. God bless you all."[9]

After General Bragg had his army safely camped around Dalton, Georgia, he turned his thoughts to how the once promising situation at Chattanooga could have gone so horribly wrong. In his official report Bragg simply could not account for the loss of Missionary Ridge: "Every effort which could be made by myself and staff and by many other mounted officers availed but little. A panic which I had never before witnessed seemed to have seized upon officers and men, and each seemed to be struggling for his personal safety, regardless of his duty or his character." Like virtually all the senior officers, Bragg believed that the position on the ridge was invulnerable and that the Federals would never launch an assault up the face. "No satisfactory excuse can possibly be given for the shameful conduct of our troops on the left in allowing their line to be penetrated. The position was one which ought to have been held by a line of skirmishers against any assaulting column." Just climbing the ridge required an extraordinary effort by the Federal troops, and Bragg rightly pointed out that "those who reached the ridge did so in a condition of exhaustion from the great physical exertion in climbing, which rendered them powerless, and the slightest effort would have destroyed them." He insisted that "had all parts of the line been maintained with equal gallantry and persistence no enemy could ever have dislodged us." There was only one way he believed to account for the failure of his veteran troops to hold such a strong position. For two days the Confederates on Missionary Ridge had to just sit and watch "the enemy, marshaling his immense forces in plain view, and exhibiting to their sight such a superiority in numbers as may have intimidated weak-minded and untried soldiers." However, Bragg also rightly pointed out that since "our veterans had so often encountered similar hosts," he had total confidence in the strength of the position and believed that his men would stand firm when the time came.[10]

When Bragg sent in his official report on December 1, he also sent a separate personal letter to Jefferson Davis. In it he said, "The disaster admits of no palliation, and is justly disparaging to me as a commander," but added, "I trust, however, you may find under full investigation that the fault is not entirely mine." Bragg also reminded Davis of how many difficulties he had to contend with due to the insubordination and lack of cooperation from many of the senior officers under his command, mentioning Generals Breckinridge and Cheatham by name. "I fear we both erred in the conclusion for me to retain command here after the clamor raised against me. The warfare has been carried on successfully, and the fruits are bitter. You must make other changes here, or our success is hopeless." Whether or not Bragg had been a capable army commander, he truly believed in the Confederate cause and told Davis, "I can bear to be sacrificed myself, but not to see my country and my friends ruined by the vices of a few profligate men who happen to have an undue popularity." Stating that "I shall ever be ready to do all in my power for our common cause, but feel that some little rest will ender me more efficient than I am now," Bragg offered his resignation to President Davis, who accepted it and placed General Hardee in command of the Army of Tennessee. Despite replacing him as a commander in the field, Davis continued to believe that Bragg had much to offer the Confederacy and made him his personal military advisor.[11]

The only sizeable body of Confederate troops in Tennessee that still concerned Grant was Longstreet's force now peacefully camping in the far-eastern part of the state. Grant wrote to Halleck on December 17 that he was going to look into the situation and see if there was anything that could be done to remove Longstreet from Tennessee. He planned to "accumulate supplies in East Tennessee to enable me to fight a battle there with a large army if the spring movements of the enemy should make it necessary." The main reason Grant wanted any enemy troops removed from East Tennessee was "so as to be able to select my own campaign in the spring instead of having the enemy dictate it for me." As far as any possible concern about enemy movements in the rest of Tennessee, Grant noted that "reports of deserters and citizens show the army of Bragg to be too much demoralized and reduced by desertion to do anything this winter."[12]

General Grant soon learned that any plans he might have had to force Longstreet back into Virginia could not be acted upon. General Burnside became ill and had to relinquish command of his army. Eventually the commander of the garrison at St. Louis, Major General John M. Schofield, a young and active officer, was put in command at Knoxville. But it was quickly learned that there was a shortage of animals to pull wagons and artillery and almost everything else an army needed to conduct a campaign, which prevented any meaningful movement through the winter months. General Longstreet just stayed where he was for the next few months and eventually returned to the Army of Northern Virginia on his own.[13]

The summer of 1863 is generally considered the turning point in the Civil War. The Federal victory at Gettysburg and Grant's capture of Vicksburg were twin disasters for the Confederacy, and the loss of Chattanooga would prove to be just as real a catastrophe. The Mississippi was open to the Gulf of Mexico and the states of Kentucky and Tennessee were now firmly under Federal control. With control of the Tennessee River and the mountain passes around Chattanooga, the Federal armies had a direct route into the heart of the Deep South. Over the next several months Chattanooga would be built up into one of the Union's largest supply centers in preparation for the campaigns of 1864, with one of the main objectives being Atlanta. This major rail and industrial center was just a little over 100 miles south from Chattanooga, along the tracks of the Western & Atlantic Railroad, and it was a place that the Confederacy could not survive without.

In March of 1864 Ulysses S. Grant was formally promoted to be the only lieutenant general in the army. He took over as general-in-chief from Henry Halleck, who became Grant's chief-of-staff. William T. Sherman, who was Grant's most trusted subordinate and friend, was given command of the Union armies in the West. With these men in charge of the Union armies, the war was going to be waged differently from now on, and although the sacrifices would be great, there was little doubt of the final outcome.

Chapter Notes

Chapter 1

1. Samuel Carter III, *The Final Fortress: The Campaign for Vicksburg 1862–1863* (New York: St. Martin's Press, 1980), 1–2.
2. Brooks D. Simpson and Jean V. Berlin, eds., *Sherman's Civil War: Selected Correspondence of William T. Sherman, 1860–1865* (Chapel Hill: University of North Carolina Press, 1999), 149.
3. Alfred T. Mahan, *The Gulf and Inland Waters* (New York: Charles Scribner's Sons, 1883), 10–11.
4. Carter, 4; Henry Walke, "Operations of the Western Flotilla," *The Century*, January 1885, 424.
5. Walke, 424–25; Howard P. Nash, Jr., *A Naval History of the Civil War* (New York: A. S. Barnes, 1972), 100.
6. Spencer C. Tucker, *Unconditional Surrender: The Capture of Forts Henry and Donelson* (Abilene, TX: McWhiney Foundation Press, 2001), 18–19; Stephen D. Engle, *Struggle for the Heartland: The Campaigns from Fort Henry to Corinth* (Lincoln: University of Nebraska Press, 2001), 30; James M. McPherson, *Battle Cry of Freedom: The Civil War Era* (New York: Oxford University Press, 1988), 578.
7. Henry Coppee, *Life and Services of Gen. U.S. Grant* (Chicago: Western News Company, 1868), 18–28; Adam Badeau, "General Grant," *The Century*, May 1885, 155–56.
8. United States War Department, *The War of the Rebellion: A Compilation of the Official Records of the Union and Confederate Armies* (Washington, D.C.: Government Printing Office, 1880–1901), Vol. 7, 625; John G. Nicolay and John Hay, "Abraham Lincoln: A History, the Mississippi and Shiloh," *The Century*, September 1888, 659.
9. Mahan, 29; Nicolay, 659–60.
10. Walke, 439–43; Mahan, 30–34.
11. Nicolay, 661–62; Walke, 443–44.
12. Walke, 444–45; Mahan, 40–45.
13. Walke, 445–46; Mahan, 46–48.
14. Nash, 122; Mahan, 58–59.
15. Nash, 126–27; United States Naval War Records Office, *Official Records of the Union and Confederate Navies in the War of the Rebellion* (Washington, D.C.: Government Printing Office, 1894–1922), Vol. 18, 7–8.
16. John S. C. Abbott, "Heroic Deeds of Heroic Men: Opening the Mississippi," *Harper's New Monthly Magazine*, August 1866, 298; Nash, 127–28.
17. Nash, 129–30; *Official Records Navy*, Vol. 18, 160.
18. *Official Records Navy*, Vol. 18, 156–57; Mahan, 73–85.
19. Nash, 137–39; *Official Records Navy*, Vol. 18, 158–59.
20. Abbott, "Opening the Mississippi," 300; Mahan, 90.

Chapter 2

1. Nicolay, 675; *Official Records Navy*, Vol. 18, 491–92.
2. *Official Records Navy*, Vol. 18, 492.
3. *Official Records Navy*, Vol. 18, 493.
4. James Russell Soley, "Naval Operations in the Vicksburg Campaign," *Battles and Leaders of the Civil War*, Vol. 3, Robert Underwood Johnson and Clarence Clough Buell, eds. (New York: Thomas Yoselof, 1956), 553–54; Duane Schultz, *The Most Glorious Fourth: Vicksburg and Gettysburg, July 4, 1863* (New York: W. W. Norton, 2002), 78; Abbott, "Opening the Mississippi," 300.
5. Peter F. Walker, *Vicksburg: A People at War, 1860–1865* (Chapel Hill: University of North Carolina Press, 1960), 97; Nash, 142–43.
6. Nash, 143; David D. Porter, *Incidents and Anecdotes of the Civil War* (New York: D. Appleton, 1886), 97.
7. Robert J. Schneller, Jr., *Farragut: America's First Admiral* (Washington, D.C.: Brassey's, 2002), 56; Mahan, 90–91; Nash, 143–44.
8. Mahan, 94–95; Schneller, 56; Nash, 143.
9. *Official Records Navy*, Vol. 18, 609; Mahan, 94–95; Schneller, 57.
10. Schneller, 57; Mahan, 95–96; Gideon Welles, "Admiral Farragut and New Orleans," *The Galaxy*, December 1871, 829.
11. Abbott, "Opening the Mississippi," 302–03; Coppee, 135–36; Nash, 144.
12. Nicolay, 675; Nash, 144.
13. Nash, 149; Nicolay, 675; Welles, "Admiral Farragut," 829.
14. Mahan, 91, 104; Schneller, 60.
15. Schneller, 60; Welles, "Admiral Farragut," 829.
16. Steven E. Woodworth, *Jefferson Davis and His Generals: The Failure of Confederate Command in the West* (Lawrence: University Press of Kansas, 1990), 112; Abbott, "Opening the Mississippi," 303.
17. Nash, 144–45; Mahan, 98–99.
18. Mahan, 99; Nash, 146; Soley, 555.
19. Nash, 146; Mahan, 99–101; Schneller, 61.
20. Schneller, 61; Nash, 146–47; Mahan, 101–02.
21. Soley, 557–58; Mahan, 102; Nash, 148.

22. Nash, 148–49; Mahan, 103–04; Abbott, "Opening the Mississippi," 306.
23. Mahan, 104–05; Soley, 558.
24. Nash, 149–50; Schneller, 64.
25. Nash, 150; Schneller, 64.
26. Nash, 151; Mahan, 106.
27. Nash, 151–53; Mahan, 107, 110–13; Schneller, 70.
28. S. H. Lockett, "The Defense of Vicksburg," *Battles and Leaders of the Civil War*, Vol. 3, Robert Underwood Johnson and Clarence Clough Buell, eds. (New York: Thomas Yoselof, 1956), 484.

Chapter 3

1. David D. Porter, *Incidents*, 95–96.
2. Michael B. Ballard, *Civil War Mississippi: A Guide* (Jackson: University Press of Mississippi, 2000), 36; Schultz, 75.
3. William L. Shea and Terrence J. Winschel, *Vicksburg Is the Key: The Struggle for the Mississippi River* (Lincoln: University of Nebraska Press, 2003), 17; John C. Pemberton, *Pemberton: Defender of Vicksburg* (Chapel Hill: University of North Carolina Press, 1942), 59.
4. Schultz, 80–81; Pemberton, *Pemberton*, 8–9.
5. Schultz, 81; Pemberton, *Pemberton*, 58–59.
6. Richard L. Kiper, *Major General John Alexander McClernand, Politician in Uniform* (Kent, OH: Kent State University Press, 1999), 135–36.
7. Kiper, *McClernand*, 136; Rowena Reed, *Combined Operations in the Civil War* (Annapolis, MD: Naval Institute Press, 1978), 229.
8. Terrence J. Winschel, *Vicksburg: Fall of the Confederate Gibraltar* (Abilene, TX: McWhiney Foundation Press, 1999), 33–35; Lloyd Lewis, *Sherman: Fighting Prophet* (New York: Harcourt, Brace, 1932), 255.
9. Kiper, *McClernand*, 138; Victor Hicken, *Illinois in the Civil War* (Urbana: University of Illinois Press, 1991), 91.
10. Kiper, *McClernand*, 137–38; Rowena Reed, 229; Lewis, 255.
11. *Official Records*, Vol. 17, Pt. 2, 282.
12. Kiper, *McClernand*, 140–41; Roy P. Basler, *The Collected Works of Abraham Lincoln*, Vol. 5 (New Brunswick, NJ: Rutgers University Press, 1953), 469.
13. *Official Records*, Vol. 17, Pt. 2, 332–33.
14. *Official Records*, Vol. 17, Pt. 2, 296; Ulysses S. Grant, *Personal Memoirs of U.S. Grant*, Vol. 1 (New York: Charles L. Webster, 1885), 424.
15. Kiper, *McClernand*, 143; *Official Records*, Vol. 17, Pt. 1, 469.
16. Grant, *Memoirs*, Vol. 1, 422–23; Coppee, 137; William T. Sherman, *Memoirs of Gen. W. T. Sherman, Written by Himself*, Vol. 1 (New York: Charles L. Webster, 1891), 307–08.
17. A. F. Brown, "Van Dorn's Operations in Northern Mississippi—Recollections of a Cavalryman," *Southern Historical Society Papers*, October 1878, 151–52.
18. A. F. Brown, 152; *Official Records*, Vol. 17, Pt. 1, 470, Pt. 2, 365.
19. Grant, *Memoirs*, Vol. 1, 427–28; Charles A. Dana and James H. Wilson, *The Life of Ulysses S. Grant: General of the Armies of the United States* (Springfield, MA: Gurden Bill, 1868), 95–96.
20. Sherman, 309–11; *Official Records*, Vol. 17, Pt. 1, 601.
21. Grant, *Memoirs*, Vol. 1, 430–31; Sherman, 310.
22. *Official Records*, Vol. 17, Pt. 1, 474.
23. Grant, *Memoirs*, Vol. 1, 426–27, 430–31; *Official Records*, Vol. 52, Pt. 1, 314.
24. *Official Records*, Vol. 17, Pt. 1, 474.
25. *Official Records*, Vol. 17, Pt. 2, 392; Simpson, *Sherman's Civil War*, 344.
26. Sherman, 313–14.
27. *Official Records*, Vol. 17, Pt. 2, 372.
28. *Official Records*, Vol. 17, Pt. 2, 401.
29. *Official Records*, Vol. 17, Pt. 2, 415, 420.
30. *Official Records*, Vol. 17, Pt. 2, 432–33, 425.
31. *Official Records*, Vol. 17, Pt. 2, 462.
32. Bruce Catton, *Grant Moves South* (Boston: Little, Brown, 1960), 340.
33. Martha L. Crabb, *All Afire to Fight: The Untold Tale of the Civil War's Ninth Texas Cavalry* (New York: Avon Books, 2000), 141; McPherson, 578.
34. A. F. Brown, 154–58; *Official Records*, Vol. 17, Pt. 1, 512–13, 477–78.
35. Crabb, 136–37; A. F. Brown, 158–59; *Official Records*, Vol. 17, Pt. 1, 478.
36. *Official Records*, Vol. 17, Pt. 2, 463.
37. *Official Records*, Vol. 17, Pt. 1, 478; Grant, *Memoirs*, Vol. 1, 435.

Chapter 4

1. Sherman, 317.
2. Sherman, 317–18; J. T. Woods, *Services of the Ninety-sixth Ohio Volunteers* (Toledo, OH: Blade, 1874), 20–21.
3. Sherman, 317–18.
4. Woods, 21; Winchester Hall, *The Story of the 26th Louisiana Infantry* (n. p., 1890), 38; Rowena Reed, 237.
5. Sherman, 318–19.
6. Sherman, 319.
7. George W. Morgan, "The Assault on Chickasaw Bluffs," *Battles and Leaders of the Civil War*, Robert Underwood Johnson and Clarence Clough Buell, eds. (New York: Thomas Yoselof, 1956), 463; *Official Records*, Vol. 17, Pt. 1, 655.
8. Morgan, 465–66.
9. Morgan, 466–67.
10. Sherman, 319; Hall, 46; Morgan, 468.
11. Otto F. Bond, *Under the Flag of the Nation: Diaries and Letters of Owen Johnston Hopkins, A Yankee Volunteer in the Civil War* (Columbus: Ohio State University Press, 1998), 46; *Official Records*, Vol. 17, Pt. 1, 649–50.
12. *Official Records*, Vol. 17, Pt. 1, 656.
13. Woods, 21; *Official Records*, Vol. 17, Pt. 1, 634; Sherman, 320.
14. Sherman, 320; Morgan, 468–69.
15. Sherman, 320–21.
16. Sherman, 321–22; Catton, *Grant Moves South*, 343–44.

17. Sherman, 324; Mahan, 120.
18. David D. Porter, *Incidents*, 131; Sherman, 324–25.

Chapter 5

1. Mahan, 120; Nash, 157.
2. Mahan, 120–21; Sherman, 325–26.
3. Sherman, 326–27; Mahan, 121; Stewart Bennett and Barbara Tillery, eds., *The Struggle for the Life of the Republic: A Civil War Narrative by Brevet Major Charles Dana Miller, 76th Ohio Volunteer Infantry* (Kent, OH: Kent State University Press, 2004), 77–78.
4. *Official Records*, Vol. 17, Pt. 1, 723–24.
5. Mahan, 122; *Official Records*, Vol. 17, Pt. 1, 724; Sherman, 331.
6. Mahan, 122; Nash, 157–58.
7. Grant, *Memoirs*, Vol. 1, 438; *Official Records*, Vol. 17, Pt. 2, 542.
8. *Official Records*, Vol. 17, Pt. 2, 546–47; Grant, *Memoirs*, Vol. 1, 439.
9. *Official Records*, Vol. 17, Pt. 2, 553.
10. *Official Records*, Vol. 17, Pt. 2, 553–54.
11. *Official Records*, Vol. 17, Pt. 2, 559.
12. *Official Records*, Vol. 17, Pt. 2, 555, 557.
13. *Official Records*, Vol. 17, Pt. 2, 570; Grant, *Memoirs*, Vol. 1, 439–40.
14. *Official Records*, Vol. 17, Pt. 2, 571; Grant, *Memoirs*, Vol. 1, 440.
15. Sherman, 333; Grant, *Memoirs*, Vol. 1, 441.
16. T. Harry Williams, *Lincoln and His Generals* (New York: Alfred A. Knopf, 1952), 223.
17. Grant, *Memoirs*, Vol. 1, 441; *Official Records*, Vol. 24, Pt. 1, 11.
18. *Official Records*, Vol. 24, Pt. 1, 12, Vol. 17, Pt. 2, 282.
19. *Official Records*, Vol. 24, Pt. 3, 19.
20. *Official Records*, Vol. 24, Pt. 1, 13.
21. *Official Records*, Vol. 24, Pt. 1, 13–14.
22. *Official Records*, Vol. 24, Pt. 1, 11.

Chapter 6

1. *Official Records Navy*, Vol. 24, 189, 180.
2. J.F.C. Fuller, *The Generalship of Ulysses S. Grant* (New York: Da Capo Press, 1991), 132–33; Catton, *Grant Moves South*, 370.
3. Edward G. Longacre, *General Ulysses S. Grant: The Soldier and the Man* (Cambridge, MA: Da Capo Press, 2006), 169–70; Badeau, "General Grant," 153.
4. *Official Records*, Vol. 24, Pt. 1, 14.
5. *Official Records*, Vol. 24, Pt. 1, 14.
6. *Official Records Navy*, Vol. 24, 181.
7. Grant, *Memoirs*, Vol. 1, 446; Coppee, 153–54.
8. Coppee, 153–54; Grant, *Memoirs*, Vol. 1, 446–47; Committee of the Regiment, *The Story of the Fifty-fifth Regiment Illinois Volunteer Infantry in the Civil War, 1861–1865* (Clinton, MA: W. J. Coulter, 1887), 211.
9. Catton, *Grant Moves South*, 377–78; *Official Records*, Vol. 24, Pt. 1, 44.
10. Committee of the Regiment, 211; Stewart Bennett, 86–87.
11. Simpson, *Sherman's Civil War*, 372; Terrence J. Winschel, ed., *The Civil War Diary of a Common Soldier: William Wiley of the 77th Illinois Infantry* (Baton Rouge: Louisiana State University Press, 2001), 37.
12. Lynda Lasswell Crist, ed., *The Papers of Jefferson Davis*, Vol. 9 (Baton Rouge: Louisiana State University Press, 1997), 59–60.
13. *Official Records*, Vol. 24, Pt. 1, 44; Coppee, 154.
14. *Official Records*, Vol. 24, Pt. 3, 17–18, 33.
15. *Official Records*, Vol. 24, Pt. 1, 44–45; Coppee, 155.
16. McPherson, 587; Catton, *Grant Moves South*, 381; Coppee, 155.
17. *Official Records*, Vol. 24, Pt. 3, 36; Catton, *Grant Moves South*, 379; Coppee, 155–56.
18. Mahan, 142; Soley, 561.
19. Nash, 159–60; Mahan, 142–43; Soley, 561–62.
20. Mahan, 142–43; Soley, 561.
21. Aaron Dunbar, *History of the Ninety-third Regiment Illinois Volunteer Infantry* (Chicago: Blakely Printing, 1898), 21; Alonzo L. Brown, *History of the Fourth Regiment of Minnesota Infantry Volunteers During the Great Rebellion, 1861–1865* (St. Paul, MN: Pioneer Press, 1892), 168–69.
22. Mahan, 143; Nash, 160; Soley, 562–63.
23. Nash, 160; Soley, 563; Mahan, 144.
24. Nash, 160–61; Mahan, 145.
25. Mahan, 146; Soley, 563.
26. Nash, 161; Mahan, 146; Soley, 563.
27. Sherman, 334.
28. Coppee, 157; Mahan, 147; Soley, 563; Nash, 161.
29. *Official Records Navy*, Vol. 24, 474; Soley, 563.
30. *Official Records Navy*, Vol. 24, 474; Chester G. Hearn, *Admiral David Dixon Porter: The Civil War Years* (Annapolis, MD: Naval Institute Press, 1996), 186–87.
31. *Official Records Navy*, Vol. 24, 475; Mahan, 148; Nash, 162.
32. *Official Records Navy*, Vol. 24, 475; Hearn, 187.
33. Hearn, 188; Mahan, 148–49.
34. Mahan, 149; *Official Records Navy*, Vol. 24, 476.
35. Soley, 563–64; *Official Records Navy*, Vol. 24, 476; Nash, 162.
36. *Official Records Navy*, Vol. 24, 477; Mahan, 150–51.
37. *Official Records Navy*, Vol. 24, 477–79; Sherman, 339.
38. Dana, *Life of Grant*, 108–09.
39. Joseph Orville Jackson, ed., *"Some of the Boys..." The Civil War Letters of Isaac Jackson 1862–1865* (Carbondale: Southern Illinois University Press, 1960), 78; Lucius F. Hubbard, *Civil War Papers of Lucius F. Hubbard* (St. Paul: Minnesota Historical Society, 1908), 561.
40. J. Grecian, *History of the Eighty-third Regiment, Indiana Volunteer Infantry* (Cincinnati, OH: John F. Uhlhorn, 1865), 22.

Chapter 7

1. John Eaton, *Grant, Lincoln and the Freedmen* (New York: Negro Universities Press, 1969), 26–27.

2. *Official Records*, Vol. 24, Pt. 3, 46–47, 105.
3. *Official Records*, Vol. 24, Pt. 3, 156–57.
4. *Official Records*, Vol. 24, Pt. 3, 157.
5. *Official Records*, Vol. 24, Pt. 3, 187.
6. Catton, *Grant Moves South*, 403.
7. John K. Duke, *History of the Fifty-third Regiment Ohio Volunteer Infantry During the War of the Rebellion 1861 to 1865* (Portsmouth, OH: Blade, 1900), 103.
8. *Official Records*, Vol. 24, Pt. 3, 220; James Grant Wilson, *General Grant's Letters to a Friend, 1861–1810* (New York: T. Y. Crowell, 1897), 7.
9. Schultz, 71; Catton, *Grant Moves South*, 388.
10. Schultz, 71; Charles A. Dana, *Recollections of the Civil War* (New York: D. Appleton, 1902), 20–21.
11. Dana, *Recollections*, 30.
12. Dana, *Recollections*, 61.
13. James H. Wilson, "Reminiscences of General Grant," *The Century*, October 1885, 947.
14. Mary A. Livermore, *My Story of the War: A Woman's Narrative of Four Years Personal Experience* (Hartford, CT: A. D. Worthington, 1896), 310–11.
15. Eaton, 90.
16. Sherman, 342; *Official Records Navy*, Vol. 24, 479.
17. Grant, *Memoirs*, Vol. 1, 543.
18. *Official Records*, Vol. 24, Pt. 3, 126; Catton, *Grant Moves South*, 408.
19. *Official Records*, Vol. 24, Pt. 1, 46, Pt. 3, 151–52; Catton, *Grant Moves South*, 409–10; Dana, *Life of Grant*, 110–11.
20. *Official Records*, Vol. 24, Pt. 1, 46–47; Bond, 50; John S. C. Abbott, "Heroic Deeds of Heroic Men: Siege of Vicksburg," *Harper's New Monthly Magazine*, January 1865, 157–58.
21. *Official Records*, Vol. 24, Pt. 1, 47; Abbott, "Vicksburg," 158; Catton, *Grant Moves South*, 410.
22. *Official Records*, Vol. 24, Pt. 3, 151–52.
23. *Official Records*, Vol. 24, Pt. 3, 152; Hearn, 208.
24. *Official Records*, Vol. 24, Pt. 3, 168.
25. *Official Records*, Vol. 24, Pt. 1, 25–26.
26. Mahan, 154–55; Nash, 176; *Official Records Navy*, Vol. 24, 554–55.
27. Dana, *Recollections*, 32–33; Catton, *Grant Moves South*, 413.
28. Richard L. Kiper, ed., *Dear Catharine, Dear Taylor: The Civil War Letters of a Union Soldier and His Wife* (Lawrence: University Press of Kansas, 2002), 99.
29. *Official Records*, Vol. 24, Pt. 3, 188.
30. Joseph E. Johnston, "Jefferson Davis and the Mississippi Campaign," *The North American Review*, December 1886, 591; Lockett, 486.

Chapter 8

1. Hearn, 209; *Official Records Navy*, Vol. 24, 553–54.
2. Hearn, 210; *Official Records*, Vol. 24, Pt. 3, 735, 740.
3. Mahan, 155; Hearn, 211.
4. Catton, *Grant Moves South*, 414–15; Hearn, 211–12.
5. Mahan, 156; Hearn, 212; David D. Porter, *Incidents*, 175–76; *Official Records Navy*, Vol. 24, 682.

6. J. T. Hogane, "Reminiscences of the Siege of Vicksburg," *Southern Historical Society Papers*, April–May 1883, 224.
7. Hearn, 212–13; Grant, *Memoirs*, Vol. 1, 463–64; David D. Porter, *Incidents*, 176.
8. David D. Porter, *Incidents*, 176; Hogane, 224.
9. Nash, 176–77; Mahan, 156–57; *Official Records Navy*, Vol. 24, 552.
10. Sherman, 345–46.
11. Hearn, 216; *Official Records Navy*, Vol. 24, 554; David D. Porter, *The Naval History of the Civil War* (New York: Sherman, 1886), 311.
12. *Official Records Navy*, Vol. 24, 717.
13. Catton, *Grant Moves South*, 416.
14. Hearn, 217; *Official Records*, Vol. 24, Pt. 3, 212, 216, Vol. 24, Pt. 1, 77–79.
15. *Official Records*, Vol. 24, Pt. 3, 188, 212–13.
16. Catton, *Grant Moves South*, 417–18; *Official Records*, Vol. 24, Pt. 3, 211, 201.
17. *Official Records*, Vol. 24, Pt. 3, 207.
18. *Official Records*, Vol. 24, Pt. 3, 211.
19. *Official Records*, Vol. 24, Pt. 3, 222.
20. *Official Records*, Vol. 24, Pt. 3, 231.
21. Albert O. Marshall, *Army Life: From a Soldier's Journal* (Joliet, IL: Albert O. Marshall, 1884), 195, 199; S. C. Jones, *Reminiscences of the Twenty-second Iowa Volunteer Infantry* (Iowa City, IA: S. C. Jones, 1907), 27.
22. Alonzo Brown, 184; Kenneth Carley, *Minnesota in the Civil War* (Minneapolis, MN: Ross and Haines, 1961), 79.
23. *Official Records*, Vol. 24, Pt. 1, 47.
24. S.H.M. Byers, *With Fire and Sword* (New York: Neale, 1911), 66.
25. *Official Records*, Vol. 24, Pt. 1, 48; Nash, 177; Winschel, *Vicksburg*, 52–53.
26. Catton, *Grant Moves South*, 422; *Official Records*, Vol. 24, Pt. 3, 50, 95; Hicken, 154–55.
27. Hicken, 154–55; Catton, *Grant Moves South*, 422; *Official Records*, Vol. 24, Pt. 1, 34.
28. *Official Records*, Vol. 24, Pt. 3, 240.
29. *Official Records*, Vol. 24, Pt. 3, 242–43.
30. *Official Records*, Vol. 24, Pt. 3, 243–44.
31. *Official Records*, Vol. 24, Pt. 1, 32; Dana, *Life of Grant*, 115–16.
32. Grant, *Memoirs*, Vol. 1, 480–81.

Chapter 9

1. Warren E. Grabau, *Ninety-eight Days: A Geographer's View of the Vicksburg Campaign* (Knoxville: University of Tennessee Press, 2000), 168–69; *Official Records*, Vol. 24, Pt. 1, 48.
2. Grant, *Memoirs*, Vol. 1, 488; Jeffrey L. Patrick, ed., *Three Years with Wallace's Zouaves: The Civil War Memoirs of Thomas Wise Durham* (Macon, GA: Mercer University Press, 2003), 151.
3. Isaac H. Elliott, *History of the Thirty-third Regiment Illinois Veteran Volunteer Infantry in the Civil War* (Gibson City, IL: Regimental Association, 1902), 38.
4. Grant, *Memoirs*, Vol. 1, 482; Ballard, *Civil War*, 55–56.
5. Grant, *Memoirs*, Vol. 1, 483.

6. Elliott, 38; Grant, *Memoirs*, Vol. 1, 483.
7. Patrick, 116–17; Ballard, *Civil War*, 57–59.
8. Grant, *Memoirs*, Vol. 1, 483–84; *Official Records*, Vol. 24, Pt. 1, 49.
9. Ballard, *Civil War*, 58; *Official Records*, Vol. 24, Pt. 1, 660.
10. *Official Records*, Vol. 24, Pt. 3, 260, 807.
11. Grant, *Memoirs*, Vol. 1, 489–90; *Official Records*, Vol. 24, Pt. 3, 269.
12. *Official Records*, Vol. 24, Pt. 3, 821; Mahan, 163.
13. *Official Records*, Vol. 24, Pt. 1, 33.
14. Grant, *Memoirs*, Vol. 1, 491.
15. Grant, *Memoirs*, Vol. 1, 491–92.
16. Geoffrey Perret, *Ulysses S. Grant, Soldier and President* (New York: Random House, 1997), 256; John Fiske, *The Mississippi Valley in the Civil War* (Boston: Houghton, Mifflin, 1900), 231–32; *Official Records*, Vol. 24, Pt. 3, 268–69.
17. Ballard, *Civil War*, 59; *Official Records*, Vol. 24, Pt. 3, 248, 268, Vol. 24, Pt. 1, 84.
18. Grant, *Memoirs*, Vol. 1, 481; *Official Records*, Vol. 24, Pt. 1, 50.
19. Grant, *Memoirs*, Vol. 1, 492.
20. *Official Records*, Vol. 24, Pt. 3, 285; Grant, *Memoirs*, Vol. 1, 492–93.
21. Patrick, 127; Byers, *Fire and Sword*, 67; Ira Blanchard, *I Marched with Sherman: Civil War Memoirs of the 20th Illinois Volunteer Infantry* (San Francisco: J. D. Huff, 1992), 87.
22. Wilber F. Crummer, *With Grant at Fort Donelson, Shiloh and Vicksburg* (Oak Park, IL: E. C. Crummer, 1915), 100; John A. Bering and Thomas Montgomery, *History of the Forty-eighth Ohio Vet. Vol. Inf.* (Hillsboro, OH: Highland News Office, 1880), 80–81.
23. Grant, *Memoirs*, Vol. 1, 496–97; Dana, *Life of Grant*, 120.
24. *Official Records*, Vol. 24, Pt. 3, 842, 808, 815.
25. *Official Records*, Vol. 24, Pt. 3, 810, 828, 845.
26. *Official Records*, Vol. 24, Pt. 3, 846, 859.
27. *Official Records*, Vol. 24, Pt. 3, 288, Pt. 1, 36.
28. *Official Records*, Vol. 24, Pt. 1, 704, 737.
29. *Official Records*, Vol. 24, Pt. 1, 708; Osborn H. Oldroyd, *A Soldier's Story of the Siege of Vicksburg* (Springfield, IL: H. W. Rokker, 1885), 16.
30. Blanchard, 88.
31. *Official Records*, Vol. 24, Pt. 1, 738, 740, 744; Oldroyd, 17.
32. *Official Records*, Vol. 24, Pt. 1, 740–41, 748.
33. *Official Records*, Vol. 24, Pt. 1, 738; William F. Fox, *Regimental Losses in the American Civil War, 1861–1865* (Albany, NY: Albany Publishing Company, 1889), 98.

Chapter 10

1. Grabau, 241; Edwin C. Bearss and Warren Grabau, *The Battle of Jackson, the Siege of Jackson, Three Other Post-Vicksburg Actions* (Baltimore: Gateway, 1981), 3–4; Grant, *Memoirs*, Vol. 1, 499.
2. Grabau, 240–41; Bearss, 4; Grant, *Memoirs*, Vol. 1, 499.
3. Grant, *Memoirs*, Vol. 1, 499–500.
4. *Official Records*, Vol. 24, Pt. 1, 36; Grabau, 241; Grant, *Memoirs*, Vol. 1, 500.
5. *Official Records*, Vol. 24, Pt. 1, 215.
6. Joseph E. Johnston, *Narrative of Military Operations, Directed, During the Late War Between the States* (New York: D. Appleton, 1874), 175–76; *Official Records*, Vol. 24, Pt. 1, 239, 215.
7. *Official Records*, Vol. 24, Pt. 3, 876; Johnston, "Jefferson Davis," 594.
8. Grant, *Memoirs*, Vol. 1, 501; Bearss, 5–6.
9. Bearss, 6–7; Grant, *Memoirs*, Vol. 1, 501.
10. Grant, *Memoirs*, Vol. 1, 501.
11. Grant, *Memoirs*, Vol. 1, 503; *Official Records*, Vol. 24, Pt. 1, 50–51.
12. *Official Records*, Vol. 24, Pt. 1, 50; Bond, 59.
13. Johnston, *Narrative*, 176–77; Bearss, 9.
14. Bearss, 12–13; *Official Records*, Vol. 24, Pt. 1, 785–86.
15. Grant, *Memoirs*, Vol. 1, 503–04; Bearss, 14–15; *Official Records*, Vol. 24, Pt. 1, 638, 753, 775.
16. Bearss, 18; *Official Records*, Vol. 24, Pt. 1, 638, 782.
17. Grant, *Memoirs*, Vol. 1, 505; Bearss, 18; *Official Records*, Vol. 24, Pt. 1, 753, 767–68.
18. *Official Records*, Vol. 24, Pt. 1, 753, Pt. 2, 284–85.
19. *Official Records*, Vol. 24, Pt. 1, 753–54, 759, 762.
20. Grant, *Memoirs*, Vol. 1, 505–06; *Official Records*, Vol. 24, Pt. 1, 754, 759, 766, 768, 770.
21. *Official Records*, Vol. 24, Pt. 1, 638, 729, 775, 777, 782–83, 786; Bearss, 24.
22. *Official Records*, Vol. 24, Pt. 1, 639, 751, 786; Bearss, 25–26.
23. Sherman, 349; *Official Records*, Vol. 24, Pt. 3, 310, 312; Grant, *Memoirs*, Vol. 1, 506–08.
24. *Official Records*, Vol. 24, Pt. 1, 36, 754, Pt. 2, 251; Bearss, 27–29.
25. Grant, *Memoirs*, Vol. 1, 507.
26. Bearss, 30; *Official Records*, Vol. 24, Pt. 1, 754, Pt. 3, 315.
27. *Official Records*, Vol. 24, Pt. 1, 84.
28. Lockett, 487; Ballard, *Civil War*, 63.
29. *Official Records*, Vol. 24, Pt. 2, 125–26.
30. Grant, *Memoirs*, Vol. 1, 512–13; *Official Records*, Vol. 24, Pt. 1, 52.

Chapter 11

1. Grant, *Memoirs*, Vol. 1, 513–14; Coppee, 172–73; Dunbar, 27–29; *Official Records*, Vol. 24, Pt. 2, 42.
2. Coppee, 173.
3. Dunbar, 27; Grant, *Memoirs*, Vol. 1, 512; Dana, *Life of Grant*, 122.
4. Catton, *Grant Moves South*, 443; *Official Records*, Vol. 24, Pt. 2, 42.
5. *Official Records*, Vol. 24, Pt. 2, 94–95; Dunbar, 28–29.
6. *Official Records*, Vol. 24, Pt. 2, 55, 49.
7. Patrick, 130; *Official Records*, Vol. 24, Pt. 2, 42.
8. *Official Records*, Vol. 24, Pt. 2, 100.
9. *Official Records*, Vol. 24, Pt. 2, 100; E. Z. Hays, ed., *History of the Thirty-second Regiment Ohio Veteran*

Volunteer Infantry (Columbus, OH: Cott and Evans, 1896), 45, 43.
  10. *Official Records*, Vol. 24, Pt. 1, 264, Pt. 2, 110–11.
  11. *Official Records*, Vol. 24, Pt. 2, 111, 49, 102.
  12. *Official Records*, Vol. 24, Pt. 2, 42, 44, Pt. 1, 52; Dana, *Life of Grant*, 123.
  13. *Official Records*, Vol. 24, Pt. 2, 50; Dunbar, 30.
  14. Mark Grimsley and Todd D. Miller, eds., *The Union Must Stand: The Civil War Diary of John Quincy Adams Campbell, Fifth Iowa Volunteer Infantry* (Knoxville: University of Tennessee Press, 2000), 97; Byers, *Fire and Sword*, 76–77.
  15. Dunbar, 30; *Official Records*, Vol. 24, Pt. 2, 44.
  16. Dana, *Life of Grant*, 123; *Official Records*, Vol. 24, Pt. 2, 44; G. B. McDonald, *A History of the 30th Illinois Veteran Volunteer Regiment of Infantry* (Sparta, IL: Sparta News, 1916), 44.
  17. Grant, *Memoirs*, Vol. 1, 517; *Official Records*, Vol. 24, Pt. 1, 53.
  18. Dana, *Life of Grant*, 124; Elliott, 40; Grant, *Memoirs*, Vol. 1, 519–20.
  19. *Official Records*, Vol. 24, Pt. 1, 53, 264–65, Pt. 2, 76–77.
  20. *Official Records*, Vol. 24, Pt. 1, 265.
  21. *Official Records*, Vol. 24, Pt. 1, 265.
  22. *Official Records*, Vol. 24, Pt. 2, 77–78; Catton, *Grant Moves South*, 444; Grant, *Memoirs*, Vol. 1, 518; Coppee, 174.
  23. Catton, *Grant Moves South*, 445; *Official Records*, Vol. 24, Pt. 2, 10, 44, 82, 99, 112, Pt. 1, 53; Grant, *Memoirs*, Vol. 1, 518.

Chapter 12

  1. Fuller, 153; Grant, *Memoirs*, Vol. 1, 522.
  2. Grant, *Memoirs*, Vol. 1, 523–24; Marshall, 216; *Official Records*, Vol. 24, Pt. 1, 54, Pt. 2, 113, 135; Elliott, 41.
  3. Grant, *Memoirs*, Vol. 1, 524; Catton, *Grant Moves South*, 445–46.
  4. Catton, *Grant Moves South*, 446; *Official Records*, Vol. 24, Pt. 1, 54, 152.
  5. Catton, *Grant Moves South*, 446; *Official Records*, Vol. 24, Pt. 2, 137; Elliott, 41.
  6. Marshall, 226.
  7. Elliott, 41; W. S. Morris and others, *History of the 31st Regiment Illinois Volunteers* (Carbondale: Southern Illinois University Press, 1998), 66.
  8. Grant, *Memoirs*, Vol. 1, 526; *Official Records*, Vol. 24, Pt. 2, 138; Hicken, 160–61.
  9. Grant, *Memoirs*, Vol. 1, 524, 526.
  10. Grant, *Memoirs*, Vol. 1, 526–27; Sherman, 352; *Official Records*, Vol. 24, Pt. 3, 321–22.
  11. Coppee, 175; Charles Swift Northen III, ed., *All Right Let Them Come: The Civil War Diary of an East Tennessee Confederate* (Knoxville: University of Tennessee Press, 2003), 94.
  12. Dora Miller Richards, "A Woman's Diary of the Siege of Vicksburg," *The Century*, September 1885, 771.
  13. Mary Ann Loughborough, *My Cave Life in Vicksburg* (Wilmington, NC: Broadfoot, 1989), 34.
  14. *Official Records*, Vol. 24, Pt. 1, 54; Adam Badeau, *Military History of Ulysses S. Grant: From April 1861 to April 1865*, Vol. 1 (New York: D. Appleton, 1885), 281.
  15. *Official Records*, Vol. 24, Pt. 3, 888.
  16. *Official Records*, Vol. 24, Pt. 3, 890.
  17. *Official Records*, Vol. 24, Pt. 2, 366.
  18. Morris, 67.
  19. Grant, *Memoirs*, Vol. 1, 535–36; *Official Records*, Vol. 24, Pt. 2, 169.
  20. Catton, *Grant Moves South*, 450, 452; *Official Records*, Vol. 24, Pt. 2, 169–70.
  21. Lockett, 488.
  22. Benjamin P. Thomas, ed., *Three Years with Grant as Recalled by War Correspondent Sylvanus Cadwallader* (New York: Alfred A. Knopf, 1955), 87–88; Grabau, 355; Bond, 63.

Chapter 13

  1. Charles B. Johnson, *Muskets and Medicine or Army Life in the Sixties* (Philadelphia: F. A. Davis, 1917), 97.
  2. *Official Records*, Vol. 24, Pt. 3, 892.
  3. Dana, *Life of Grant*, 128.
  4. Grant, *Memoirs*, Vol. 1, 529.
  5. Bering, 86; J. J. Kellogg, *War Experiences and the Story of the Vicksburg Campaign* (Washington, IA: Evening Journal, 1913), 27.
  6. Winschel, *Civil War Diary*, 49; Kellogg, 28.
  7. *Official Records*, Vol. 24, Pt. 2, 231; Winschel, *Civil War Diary*, 49.
  8. Kellogg, 31.
  9. Sherman, 353; *Official Records*, Vol. 24, Pt. 1, 54.
  10. Hicken, 168–69; Grant, *Memoirs*, Vol. 1, 530–31; *Official Records*, Vol. 24, Pt. 1, 55.
  11. R. L. Howard, *History of the 124th Regiment Illinois Infantry Volunteers* (Springfield, IL: H. W. Rokker, 1880), 104–05.
  12. Bryner, 84; Elliott, 44.
  13. Crummer, 111.
  14. Sherman, 354; Bryner, 85.
  15. Grimsley, 101; R. L. Howard, 108.
  16. Winschel, *Civil War Diary*, 50; Marshall, 234–35.
  17. *Official Records*, Vol. 24, Pt. 2, 140, 244.
  18. Sherman, 354–55; *Official Records*, Vol. 24, Pt. 1, 55.
  19. Grant, *Memoirs*, Vol. 1, 531; Sherman, 355.
  20. *Official Records*, Vol. 24, Pt. 1, 56.
  21. Dunbar, 36–37.
  22. R. L. Howard, 108; Jackson, 97; Elliott, 44–45.
  23. *Official Records*, Vol. 24, Pt. 2, 344.
  24. Sherman, 355; Simpson, *Sherman's Civil War*, 472; Bond, 65; *Official Records*, Vol. 24, Pt. 2, 165.
  25. Thomas, 92.
  26. *Official Records*, Vol. 24, Pt. 1, 37.
  27. *Official Records*, Vol. 24, Pt. 2, 170; W. H. Bentley, *History of the 77th Illinois Volunteer Infantry, Sept. 2, 1862–July 10, 1865* (Peoria, IL: Edward Hine, 1883), 158.
  28. Grant, *Memoirs*, Vol. 1, 532; *Official Records*, Vol. 24, Pt. 1, 37.

Chapter 14

1. *Official Records*, Vol. 24, Pt. 1, 37.
2. *Official Records*, Vol. 24, Pt. 1, 37–38.
3. Dana, *Life of Grant*, 128; Grant, *Memoirs*, Vol. 1, 532.
4. Badeau, *Military History*, Vol. 1, 335; *Official Records*, Vol. 24, Pt. 2, 170–71.
5. *Official Records*, Vol. 24, Pt. 2, 177.
6. Winschel, *Civil War Diary*, 55–56; Lucius W. Barber, *Army Memoirs of Lucius W. Barber* (Chicago: J.M.W. Jones Stationery and Printing, 1894), 111.
7. Blanchard, 97; Bond, 67; Woods, 30.
8. *Official Records*, Vol. 24, Pt. 1, 90.
9. Woods, 32; Alonzo Brown, 230.
10. Coppee, 180; Catton, *Grant Moves South*, 460; Grant, *Memoirs*, Vol. 1, 544–45.
11. Winschel, *Vicksburg*, 113; Grant, *Memoirs*, Vol. 1, 543; Coppee, 180.
12. Catton, *Grant Moves South*, 457; Hall 82.
13. Stephen E. Ambrose, ed., *A Wisconsin Boy in Dixie: The Selected Letters of James K. Newton* (Madison: University of Wisconsin Press, 1961), 70; Catton, *Grant Moves South*, 460.
14. *Official Records*, Vol. 24, Pt. 2, 247.
15. *Official Records*, Vol. 24, Pt. 3, 449.
16. Kellogg, 55; R. L. Howard, 112.
17. Crummer, 143; Jackson, 104; Thomas M. Stevenson, *History of the 78th Regiment O.V.V.I.* (Zanesville, OH: Hugh Dunne, 1865), 132.
18. Kellogg, 51.
19. Crummer, 128–29.
20. Jesse Grant Cramer, ed., *Letters of Ulysses S. Grant to His Father and His Youngest Sister, 1857–78* (New York: G. P. Putnam's Sons, 1912), 98–99.
21. James H. Wilson, *Under the Old Flag*, Vol. 1 (New York: D. Appleton, 1912), 182.
22. James H. Wilson, *Under the Old Flag*, Vol. 1, 182–83.
23. Catton, *Grant Moves South*, 466.
24. *Official Records*, Vol. 24, Pt. 1, 162.
25. *Official Records*, Vol. 24, Pt. 1, 162–63.
26. *Official Records*, Vol. 24, Pt. 1, 164–65.
27. *Official Records*, Vol. 24, Pt. 1, 164–65.
28. James H. Wilson, *Under the Old Flag*, Vol. 1, 184–85.
29. *Official Records*, Vol. 24, Pt. 1, 222.
30. Grant, *Memoirs*, Vol. 1, 549, 551; *Official Records*, Vol. 24, Pt. 2, 222.
31. Stewart Bennett, 103; Byron R. Abernethy, ed., *Private Elisha Stockwell, Jr. Sees the Civil War* (Norman: University of Oklahoma Press, 1958), 63.
32. Andrew Hickenlooper, "The Vicksburg Mine," *Battles and Leaders of the Civil War*, Vol. 3, Robert Underwood Johnson and Clarence Clough Buell, eds. (New York: Thomas Yoselof, 1956), 540; Crummer, 119.
33. Kiper, *Dear Catharine*, 114–15; Donald C. Elder III, ed., *A Damned Iowa Greyhound: The Civil War Letters of William Henry Harrison Clayton* (Iowa City: University of Iowa Press, 1998), 74; Steven E. Woodworth, ed., *The Musick of the Mocking Birds, the Roar of the Cannon: The Civil War Diary and Letters of William Winters* (Lincoln: University of Nebraska Press, 1998), 55–56.
34. Hickenlooper, 540–41; Morris, 73.
35. Morris, 73; Hickenlooper, 541.
36. Crummer, 138–39; Morris, 73–74.
37. Catton, *Grant Moves South*, 469.

Chapter 15

1. Crist, 189; *Official Records*, Vol. 24, Pt. 3, 929–30.
2. Woodworth, *Jefferson Davis*, 210–11; Crist, 239.
3. Richards, 771; Loughborough, 8; Gordon A. Cotton, ed., *From the Pen of a She-Rebel: The Civil War Diary of Emilie Riley McKinley* (Columbia: University of South Carolina Press, 2001), 9.
4. Loughborough, 52.
5. Schultz, 124–25.
6. Loughborough, 84–85.
7. W. H. Tunnard, *The History of the Third Regiment Louisiana Infantry* (Baton Rouge, LA: Printed for the author, 1866), 247.
8. Hall, 89.
9. Northen, 95; Tunnard, 252.
10. *Official Records*, Vol. 24, Pt. 3, 964.
11. *Official Records*, Vol. 24, Pt. 1, 227.
12. *Official Records*, Vol. 24, Pt. 1, 227.
13. *Official Records*, Vol. 24, Pt. 1, 228.
14. *Official Records*, Vol. 24, Pt. 3, 974.
15. *Official Records*, Vol. 24, Pt. 3, 979.
16. *Official Records*, Vol. 24, Pt. 3, 980.
17. *Official Records*, Vol. 24, Pt. 3, 982–83.

Chapter 16

1. Grant, *Memoirs*, Vol. 1, 553; *Official Records*, Vol. 24, Pt. 2, 365.
2. *Official Records*, Vol. 24, Pt. 2, 347.
3. *Official Records*, Vol. 24, Pt. 2, 347, 349.
4. *Official Records*, Vol. 24, Pt. 2, 374, 368.
5. R. W. Memminger, "The Surrender of Vicksburg—A Defence of General Pemberton," *Southern Historical Society Papers*, Vol. 12, July–September 1884, 359; Lockett, 492.
6. Lockett, 492.
7. Schultz, 264–65; Lockett, 492.
8. Lockett, 492.
9. *Official Records*, Vol. 24, Pt. 1, 59.
10. Grant, *Memoirs*, Vol. 1, 556–57.
11. *Official Records*, Vol. 24, Pt. 1, 60; Grant, *Memoirs*, Vol. 1, 557–58.
12. Grant, *Memoirs*, Vol. 1, 558–59; Ulysses S. Grant, "General Grant on the Terms at Vicksburg," *The Century*, August 1887, 617; Catton, *Grant Moves South*, 471–72.
13. John C. Pemberton, "The Terms of Surrender," *Battles and Leaders of the Civil War*, Vol. 3, Robert Underwood Johnson and Clarence Clough Buell, eds. (New York: Thomas Yoselof, 1956), 544.
14. Grant, *Memoirs*, Vol. 1, 559; Pemberton, "Terms of Surrender," 544; Grant, "Terms at Vicksburg," 617.

15. Grant, *Memoirs*, Vol. 1, 560–61; Catton, *Grant Moves South*, 473.
16. Grant, "Terms at Vicksburg," 617; Pemberton, "Terms of Surrender," 545.
17. *Official Records*, Vol. 24, Pt. 1, 60, Pt. 3, 460.
18. *Official Records*, Vol. 24, Pt. 1, 61.
19. *Official Records*, Vol. 24, Pt. 1, 61.
20. *Official Records*, Vol. 24, Pt. 1, 61.
21. *Official Records*, Vol. 24, Pt. 3, 460–61.
22. R. L. Howard, 120–21.
23. Elder, 78.
24. Alonzo Brown, 238; R. L. Howard, 121; Kiper, *Dear Catharine*, 124.
25. Schultz, 345–46, 360.
26. Carley, 74.
27. Schultz, 362; Crummer, 159.
28. Catton, *Grant Moves South*, 483.
29. Edmund Newsome, *Experience in the War of the Great Rebellion* (Carbondale, IL: Edmund Newsome, 1880), 76–77.
30. James H. Wilson, *Under the Old Flag*, Vol. 1, 223.
31. Catton, *Grant Moves South*, 478; Schultz, 363–64.
32. Jackson, 112; Woodworth, *Musick*, 63.
33. Ambrose, *Wisconsin Boy*, 80–81.
34. Richards, 774; Frank A. Montgomery, *Reminiscences of a Mississippian in Peace and War* (Cincinnati, OH: Robert Clarke, 1901), 127.
35. *Official Records*, Vol. 24, Pt. 3, 473, 470.
36. *Official Records*, Vol. 24, Pt. 3, 473.
37. *Official Records*, Vol. 24, Pt. 3, 472.

Chapter 17

1. *Official Records*, Vol. 24, Pt. 3, 483.
2. *Official Records*, Vol. 24, Pt. 3, 498.
3. *Official Records*, Vol. 24, Pt. 3, 540, 547.
4. Basler, Vol. 6, 326.
5. Grant, *Memoirs*, Vol. 1, 576; Sherman, 359.
6. Official Records, Vol. 24, Pt. 3, 528; Sherman, 360.
7. *Official Records*, Vol. 24, Pt. 3, 528, 533–34.
8. Sherman, 360; Grant, *Memoirs*, Vol. 1, 577.
9. Grant, *Memoirs*, Vol. 1, 569.
10. Grant, *Memoirs*, Vol. 1, 569.
11. *Official Records*, Vol. 24, Pt. 3, 1000, 1010.
12. *Official Records*, Vol. 24, Pt. 3, 529.
13. *Official Records*, Vol. 24, Pt. 3, 546; Thomas, 125.
14. *Official Records*, Vol. 24, Pt. 3, 539, 538.
15. *Official Records*, Vol. 24, Pt. 3, 538.
16. *Official Records*, Vol. 24, Pt. 2, 528, Pt. 3, 507–08; Dana, *Recollections*, 102.
17. Grant, *Memoirs*, Vol. 1, 578–80.
18. *Official Records*, Vol. 24, Pt. 3, 499–500.
19. *Official Records*, Vol. 24, Pt. 3, 497–98.
20. *Official Records*, Vol. 24, Pt. 3, 530, 528.
21. *Official Records*, Vol. 24, Pt. 3, 569, Vol. 26, Pt. 1, 666.
22. *Official Records*, Vol. 24, Pt. 3, 578.
23. *Official Records*, Vol. 24, Pt. 3, 584.
24. *Official Records*, Vol. 24, Pt. 3, 584, 547.
25. *Official Records*, Vol. 24, Pt. 3, 570–71.
26. Sherman, 363.
27. Sherman, 364.
28. Sherman, 368; *Official Records*, Vol. 30, Pt. 3, 698.
29. *Official Records*, Vol. 30, Pt. 3, 698–99.
30. Bruce Catton, *Grant Takes Command* (Boston: Little, Brown, 1969), 3–5.
31. *Official Records*, Vol. 52, Pt. 1, 416.
32. Dana, *Recollections*, 72; Gideon Welles, *Diary of Gideon Welles*, Vol. 1 (Boston: Houghton Mifflin, 1911), 386.
33. Catton, *Grant Takes Command*, 4–5.
34. Welles, *Diary*, Vol. 1, 387.
35. *Official Records*, Vol. 30, Pt. 3, 592.

Chapter 18

1. William S. Rosecrans, "The Campaign for Chattanooga," *The Century*, May 1887, 130.
2. *Official Records*, Vol. 20, Pt. 1, 698–99; Rosecrans, 129; Peter Cozzens, *This Terrible Sound: The Battle of Chickamauga* (Urbana: University of Illinois Press, 1992), 3.
3. *Official Records*, Vol. 23, Pt. 2, 119, 171; Cozzens, 16.
4. *Official Records*, Vol. 23, Pt. 2, 369, 383; Cozzens, 16.
5. *Official Records*, Vol. 23, Pt. 1, 10.
6. Cozzens, 21–22; Steven E. Woodworth, *Six Armies in Tennessee: The Chickamauga and Chattanooga Campaigns* (Lincoln: University of Nebraska Press, 1998), 12–13; Julie A. Doyle, et al., eds., *This Wilderness of War: The Civil War Letters of George W. Squire, Hoosier Volunteer* (Knoxville: University of Tennessee Press, 1998), 71.
7. *Official Records*, Vol. 23, Pt. 1, 9–10.
8. Woodworth, *Six Armies*, 19–21; *Official Records*, Vol. 23, Pt. 1, 405, 465–66; Cozzens, 17–18.
9. C. Knight Aldrich, *Quest for a Star: The Civil War Letters and Diaries of Colonel Francis T. Sherman of the 88th Illinois* (Knoxville: University of Tennessee Press, 1999), 50.
10. Gilbert C. Kniffin, "Manoeuvring Bragg Out of Tennessee," *Battles and Leaders of the Civil War*, Vol. 3, Robert Underwood Johnson and Clarence Clough Buel, eds. (New York: Thomas Yoseloff, 1956), 637; *Official Records*, Vol. 23, Pt. 1, 618, 621–23, Pt. 2, 884; Woodworth, *Six Armies*, 32–35, 40.
11. Rosecrans, 130; *Official Records*, Vol. 23, Pt. 1, 408; R. Lockwood Tower, ed., *A Carolinian Goes to War: The Civil War Narrative of Arthur Middleton Manigault, Brigadier General, C.S.A.* (Columbia: University of South Carolina Press, 1983), 76–77.
12. *Official Records*, Vol. 23, Pt. 2, 518; Cozzens, 23.
13. Rosecrans, 131.
14. Thomas Lawrence Connelly, *Autumn of Glory: The Army of Tennessee, 1862–1865* (Baton Rouge: Louisiana State University Press, 1871), 149.
15. James R. Sullivan, *Chickamauga and Chattanooga Battlefields* (Washington, D.C.: National Park Service, 1961), 8; Rosecrans, 131; Henry M. Cist, *The Army of the Cumberland* (New York: Charles Scribner's Sons, 1882), 170.
16. Sullivan, 8–9; *Official Records*, Vol. 30, Pt. 1, 51.

17. Cozzens, 44–45; Sullivan, 9; *Official Records*, Vol. 30, Pt. 1, 51–52.
18. *Official Records*, Vol. 30, Pt. 1, 50; Rosecrans, 132.
19. Rosecrans, 132; *Official Records*, Vol. 30, Pt. 2, 27; Connelly, 173; Steven E. Woodworth, *Decision in the Heartland: The Civil War in the West* (Westport, CT: Praeger, 2008), 75.
20. Rosecrans, 132; *Official Records*, Vol. 30, Pt. 1, 53; Cozzens, 63; Catton, *Never Call Retreat* (Garden City, NJ: Doubleday, 1965), 242.
21. *Official Records*, Vol. 30, Pt. 1, 53, Pt. 3, 479; Catton, *Never Call Retreat*, 242.
22. Sullivan, 10, 12; Rosecrans, 132.
23. Connelly, 175; Catton, *Never Call Retreat*, 243.
24. Sullivan, 13; *Official Records*, Vol. 30, Pt. 2, 28–29, 301–02.
25. *Official Records*, Vol. 30, Pt. 2, 29, Pt. 4, 634.
26. *Official Records*, Vol. 30, Pt. 1, 54, Pt. 2, 30; Woodworth, *Decision*, 76.
27. *Official Records*, Vol. 30, Pt. 1, 53–54, Pt. 3, 564–65; Woodworth, *Decision*, 76; Rosecrans, 132.
28. *Official Records*, Vol. 30, Pt. 1, 603–04, Pt. 2, 30; Connelly, 186–87.
29. *Official Records*, Vol. 30, Pt. 2, 30–31, 44.
30. Cozzens, 86–87; Sullivan, 12–13.
31. Sullivan, 12; Catton, *Never Call Retreat*, 241; Connelly, 191–92. E. Porter Alexander, "Longstreet at Knoxville," *Battles and Leaders of the Civil War*, Vol. 3, Robert Underwood Johnson and Clarence Clough Buel, eds. (New York: Thomas Yoseloff, 1956), 746.
32. Cozzens, 87–88; *Official Records*, Vol. 30, Pt. 1, 54–55, 447, Pt. 2, 32, 239; Woodworth, *Decision*, 77–78.
33. *Official Records*, Vol. 30, Pt. 1, 55–56, 248–49; Woodworth, *Decision*, 78.
34. Cozzens, 128; Connelly; 199–200; Woodworth, *Decision*, 78.
35. *Official Records*, Vol. 30, Pt. 1, 249–50, 400, 539, Pt. 2, 32, 154; D. H. Hill, "Chickamauga—The Great Battle of the West," *The Century*, April 1887, 949; Connelly, 203–07.
36. Sullivan, 19; *Official Records*, Vol. 30, Pt. 1, 251, 136.
37. *Official Records*, Vol. 30, Pt. 2, 33, 58; Hill, 952.
38. Hill, 952; Gates P. Thruston, "The Crisis at Chickamauga," *Battles and Leaders of the Civil War*, Vol. 3, Robert Underwood Johnson and Clarence Clough Buel, eds. (New York: Thomas Yoseloff, 1956), 663–64; Sullivan, 21; *Official Records*, Vol. 30, Pt. 1, 59, 580.
39. *Official Records*, Vol. 30, Pt. 1, 59–60, 580–81; Rosecrans, 134; Thruston, 664.
40. *Official Records*, Vol. 30, Pt. 1, 60, 854–55; Hill, 961; J. S. Fullerton, "The Reserve Corps at Chickamauga," *The Century*, April 1887, 962–63; Sullivan, 22.
41. *Official Records*, Vol. 30, Pt. 1, 253–54, 142–43, 192.
42. Hill, 962; *Official Records*, Vol. 30, Pt. 2, 35.
43. *Official Records*, Vol. 30, Pt. 1, 148–50.
44. *Official Records*, Vol. 30, Pt. 2, 22.

Chapter 19

1. *Official Records*, Vol. 30, Pt. 1, 197, 168.
2. James A. Barnes, et al., *The Eighty-sixth Regiment, Indiana Volunteer Infantry* (Crawfordsville, IN: Journal Company, 1895), 214.
3. *Official Records*, Vol. 30, Pt. 3, 592, 594, 620.
4. *Official Records*, Vol. 30, Pt. 3, 638, 655.
5. Grant, *Memoirs*, Vol. 1, 581–82; Catton, *Grant Takes Command*, 29–30.
6. Grant, *Memoirs*, Vol. 1, 582–83; Sherman, 375.
7. Sherman, 378.
8. James Longstreet, *From Manassas to Appomattox* (Old Saybrook, CT: Konecky and Konecky, n.d.), 466.
9. *Official Records*, Vol. 30, Pt. 2, 36–37.
10. Bruce Catton, *Never Call Retreat*, 252; *Official Records*, Vol. 30, Pt. 4, 706.
11. Catton, *Never Call Retreat*, 253; Longstreet, *From Manassas*, 465–66.
12. Catton, *Never Call Retreat*, 253–54; Connelly, 245–47.
13. Woodworth, *Decision*, 84–85.
14. *Official Records*, Vol. 30, Pt. 1, 197.
15. Catton, *Never Call Retreat*, 255; *Official Records*, Vol. 29, Pt. 1, 156.
16. Catton, *Never Call Retreat*, 255–56; Sullivan, 27.
17. *Official Records*, Vol. 30, Pt. 1, 220–21.
18. Grant, *Memoirs*, Vol. 2, 32–33.
19. Grant, *Memoirs*, Vol. 2, 33–34.
20. James M. McCaffrey, *This Band of Heroes: Granbury's Texas Brigade, C.S.A.* (College Station: Texas A&M University Press, 1996), 84; Catton, *Never Call Retreat*, 256; W.F.G. Shanks, "Chattanooga, and How We Held It," *Harper's New Monthly Magazine*, January 1868, 145.
21. McCaffrey, 84; Catton, *Never Call Retreat*, 256–57.
22. Charles C. Briant, *History of the Sixth Regiment Indiana Volunteer Infantry of Both the Three Months' and Three Years' Services* (Indianapolis: William Burford, 1891), 253–54; L. G. Bennett and William M. Haigh, *History of the Thirty-sixth Regiment Illinois Volunteers, During the War of the Rebellion* (Aurora, IL: Knickerbocker and Hodder, 1876), 509; William R. Hartpence, *History of the Fifty-first Indiana Veteran Volunteer Infantry* (Cincinnati, OH: Robert Clarke, 1894), 189.
23. Dana, *Recollections*, 127–28.
24. Silas S. Canfield, *History of the 21st Regiment Ohio Volunteer Infantry, in the War of the Rebellion* (Toledo, OH: Vrooman, Anderson and Bateman, 1893), 159.
25. J. S. Fullerton, "The Army of the Cumberland at Chattanooga," *The Century*, May 1887, 137.
26. Catton, *Never Call Retreat*, 257; *Official Records*, Vol. 30, Pt. 1, 218.
27. Grant, *Memoirs*, Vol. 2, 18–19; *Official Records*, Vol. 30, Pt. 4, 404.
28. Grant, *Memoirs*, Vol. 1, 583–84.
29. *Official Records*, Vol. 30, Pt. 4, 404; Grant, *Memoirs*, Vol. 2, 17–18.
30. Grant, *Memoirs*, Vol. 2, 18–19.
31. Grant, *Memoirs*, Vol. 2, 26; *Official Records*, Vol. 30, Pt. 4, 455.
32. *Official Records*, Vol. 30, Pt. 4, 479; Catton, *Grant Takes Command*, 35.
33. Grant, *Memoirs*, Vol. 2, 26–27.

34. Catton, *Grant Takes Command*, 35–36; Oliver O. Howard, "Chattanooga," *The Atlantic Monthly*, August 1876, 206; Oliver O. Howard, *Autobiography of Oliver Otis Howard*, Vol. 1 (New York: Baker and Taylor, 1908), 460.
35. Oliver O. Howard, "Chattanooga," 206.
36. Catton, *Grant Takes Command*, 36–37; Grant, *Memoirs*, Vol. 2, 28.
37. Grant, *Memoirs*, Vol. 2, 28; Catton, *Grant Takes Command*, 38.
38. Catton, *Grant Takes Command*, 40–41; Horace Porter, *Campaigning with Grant* (New York: Mallard Press, 1991), 4–5.

Chapter 20

1. *Official Records*, Vol. 31, Pt. 1, 70, 739; Grant, *Memoirs*, Vol. 2, 28.
2. Grant, *Memoirs*, Vol. 2, 31.
3. Grant, *Memoirs*, Vol. 2, 32–33; Catton, *Grant Takes Command*, 44.
4. *Official Records*, Vol. 31, Pt. 1, 77; Catton, *Grant Takes Command*, 45–46.
5. *Official Records*, Vol. 31, Pt. 1, 77; Catton, *Grant Takes Command*, 45.
6. *Official Records*, Vol. 31, Pt. 1, 77–78; Matt Spruill, *Storming the Heights: A Guide to the Battle of Chattanooga* (Knoxville: University of Tennessee Press, 2003), 26–27.
7. *Official Records*, Vol. 31, Pt. 1, 48–49; Sullivan, 32.
8. Grant, *Memoirs*, Vol. 2, 28–29.
9. *Official Records*, Vol. 31, Pt. 1, 712.
10. *Official Records*, Vol. 30, Pt. 3, 904–05, Vol. 31, Pt. 1, 745.
11. *Official Records*, Vol. 31, Pt. 1, 713; Catton, *Grant Takes Command*, 48.
12. *Official Records*, Vol. 31, Pt. 1, 713.
13. *Official Records*, Vol. 31, Pt. 1, 739–40.
14. *Official Records*, Vol. 31, Pt. 1, 77–78; Catton, *Grant Takes Command*, 50–51.
15. Catton, *Grant Takes Command*, 51; Fullerton, "Army Cumberland," 139.
16. William B. Hazen, *A Narrative of Military Service* (Boston: Ticknor, 1885), 157; Robert L. Kimberly and Ephraim S. Holloway, *The Forty-first Ohio Veteran Volunteer Infantry in the War of the Rebellion, 1861–1865* (Cleveland, OH: W. R. Smellie, 1897), 60–61.
17. Fullerton, "Army Cumberland," 139; *Official Records*, Vol. 31, Pt. 1, 77.
18. Catton, *Grant Takes Command*, 52; Kimberly, 60–61.
19. Hazen, 157; Kimberly, 61–62.
20. Kimberly, 62; *Official Records*, Vol. 31, Pt. 1, 49, 78.
21. Kimberly, 62; Fullerton, "Army Cumberland," 139; *Official Records*, Vol. 31, Pt. 1, 54, 78.
22. Fullerton, "Army Cumberland," 139–40; John Bowers, *Chickamauga and Chattanooga: The Battles That Doomed the Confederacy* (New York: HarperCollins, 1994), 192–93; *Official Records*, Vol. 31, Pt. 1, 54–57.
23. Connelly, 256–57; Bowers, 192–93.
24. *Official Records*, Vol. 31, Pt. 1, 217–18; Longstreet, *Manassas*, 475–76; Connelly, 260.
25. *Official Records*, Vol. 31, Pt. 1, 113–14; Fullerton, "Army Cumberland," 140.
26. Oliver O. Howard, "Chattanooga," 208; Oliver O. Howard, *Autobiography*, 467.
27. Woodworth, *Six Armies*, 166–67; Oliver O. Howard, "Chattanooga," 208–09.
28. *Official Records*, Vol. 31, Pt. 1, 115; James Longstreet, "Report of General Longstreet," *Southern Historical Society Papers*, Vol. 8, July 1880, 268.
29. *Official Records*, Vol. 31, Pt. 1, 218.
30. *Official Records*, Vol. 31, Pt. 1, 56.
31. Kimberly, 63.
32. Grant, *Memoirs*, Vol. 2, 38–39.
33. Judith Lee Hallock, ed., *The Civil War Letters of Joshua K. Callaway* (Athens: University of Georgia Press, 1997), 157, 166.

Chapter 21

1. *Official Records*, Vol. 31, Pt. 2, 29.
2. *Official Records*, Vol. 31, Pt. 1, 729, Pt. 3, 23.
3. *Official Records*, Vol. 31, Pt. 3, 10, 26.
4. Grant, *Memoirs*, Vol. 2, 46–47.
5. Grant, *Memoirs*, Vol. 2, 46; Catton, *Grant Takes Command*, 57.
6. Grant, *Memoirs*, Vol. 2, 47–48; Catton, *Grant Takes Command*, 57–58.
7. Grant, *Memoirs*, Vol. 2, 44.
8. Woodworth, *Decision*, 87; Catton, *Grant Takes Command*, 58–59; *Official Records*, Vol., 52, Pt. 2, 555.
9. Bowers, 196; *Official Records*, Vol. 52, Pt. 2, 554.
10. *Official Records*, Vol. 31, Pt. 3, 634; Longstreet, *Manassas*, 482; Grant, *Memoirs*, Vol. 2, 49.
11. Grant, *Memoirs*, Vol. 2, 49.
12. *Official Records*, Vol. 31, Pt. 3, 73.
13. *Official Records*, Vol. 31, Pt. 3, 73, 76.
14. Grant, *Memoirs*, Vol. 2, 50; *Official Records*, Vol. 31, Pt. 3, 84, 88.
15. *Official Records*, Vol. 31, Pt. 3, 216.
16. Sherman, 388–89; Catton, *Grant Takes Command*, 69; Oliver O. Howard, "Chattanooga," 210–11.
17. Sherman, 389; Thomas B. Van Horne, *History of the Army of the Cumberland its Organization, Campaigns, and Battles*, Vol. 1 (Cincinnati, OH: Robert Clarke, 1875), 410.
18. Grant, *Memoirs*, Vol. 2, 54–56.
19. Grant, *Memoirs*, Vol. 2, 57–58.
20. Francis F. McKinney, *Education in Violence: The Life of George H. Thomas and the History of the Army of the Cumberland* (Detroit, MI: Wayne State University Press, 1961), 281–82.
21. *Official Records*, Vol. 31, Pt. 3, 145–46, 177; Grant, *Memoirs*, Vol. 2, 50–51.
22. Grant, *Memoirs*, Vol. 2, 52; Longstreet, *Manassas*, 483.
23. Catton, *Grant Takes Command*, 69.
24. Sherman, 391; Grant, *Memoirs*, Vol. 2, 59.
25. Oliver O. Howard, "Chattanooga," 211; Catton, *Grant Takes Command*, 69.

26. Grant, *Memoirs*, Vol. 2, 64–66; Catton, *Grant Takes Command*, 69–70; Van Horne, 412.
27. Grant, *Memoirs*, Vol. 2, 61; Dana, *Recollections*, 142; Van Horne, 413.
28. Grant, *Memoirs*, Vol. 2, 62–63; *Official Records*, Vol. 31, Pt. 2, 32.
29. Fullerton, "Army Cumberland," 141.
30. Fullerton, "Army Cumberland," 141; Grant, *Memoirs*, Vol. 2, 63.
31. Van Horne, 414–15; McKinney, 288.
32. Montgomery C. Meigs, *The Three Days' Battle of Chattanooga, 23d, 24th, 25th November 1863: An Unofficial Dispatch from General Meigs* (Washington, D.C.: McGill and Witherow, 1864), 3–4.
33. Spruill, 99; Fullerton, "Army Cumberland," 142.
34. Fullerton, "Army Cumberland," 142; Grant, *Memoirs*, Vol. 2, 64.

Chapter 22

1. Catton, *Grant Takes Command*, 73.
2. *Official Records*, Vol. 31, Pt. 2, 32.
3. Van Horne, 418; *Official Records*, Vol. 31, Pt. 2, 315; Steven E. Woodworth, *This Grand Spectacle: The Battle of Chattanooga* (Abilene, TX: McWhiney Foundation Press, 1999), 57.
4. Woodworth, *Grand Spectacle*, 57, 60; *Official Records*, Vol. 31, Pt. 2, 315.
5. *Official Records*, Vol. 31, Pt. 2, 315.
6. *Official Records*, Vol. 31, Pt. 2, 315–16, 391.
7. *Official Records*, Vol. 31, Pt. 2, 143–44.
8. Oliver O. Howard, "Chattanooga," 213; Grant, *Memoirs*, Vol. 2, 71–72.
9. Isaac C. Doan, *Reminiscences of the Chattanooga Campaign: A Paper Read at the Reunion of Company B, Fortieth Ohio Volunteer Infantry, at Xenia, O., August 22, 1894* (Richmond, IN: J. M. Coe's Printery, 1894), 13.
10. Fullerton, "Army Cumberland," 142–43; *Official Records*, Vol. 31, Pt. 2, 144, 392; William Grose, *The Story of the Marches, Battles and Incidents of the 36th Regiment Indiana Volunteer Infantry* (New Castle, IN: Courier Company Press, 1891), 195.
11. Woodworth, *Grand Spectacle*, 61–62; *Official Records*, Vol. 31, Pt. 2, 392–93.
12. *Official Records*, Vol. 31, Pt. 2, 393–94; Woodworth, *Grand Spectacle*, 62.
13. *Official Records*, Vol. 31, Pt. 2, 394–95; Woodworth, *Grand Spectacle*, 62, 64.
14. Fullerton, "Army Cumberland," 143; Oliver O. Howard, "Chattanooga," 214.
15. Paul M. Angle, ed., *Three Years in the Army of the Cumberland: The Letters and Diary of Major James A. Connolly* (Bloomington: Indiana University Press, 1959), 153; Catton, *Grant Takes Command*, 74.
16. Angle, 154; *Official Records*, Vol. 31, Pt. 2, 317.
17. *Official Records*, Vol. 31, Pt. 2, 396; Woodworth, *Grand Spectacle*, 64.
18. *Official Records*, Vol. 31, Pt. 2, 317, 397–99; Fullerton, "Army Cumberland," 143.
19. *Official Records*, Vol. 31, Pt. 2, 664.
20. Fullerton, "Army Cumberland," 143–44; *Official Records*, Vol. 31, Pt. 2, 572.
21. Grant, *Memoirs*, Vol. 2, 67–68; *Official Records*, Vol. 31, Pt. 2, 572–73.
22. *Official Records*, Vol. 31, Pt. 2, 573–74; Van Horne, 422.
23. Grant, *Memoirs*, Vol. 2, 68; *Official Records*, Vol. 31, Pt. 2, 573; S.H.M. Byers, "Sherman's Attack at the Tunnel," *Battles and Leaders of the Civil War*, Vol. 3, Robert Underwood Johnson and Clarence Clough Buel, eds. (New York: Thomas Yoseloff, 1956), 712.
24. *Official Records*, Vol. 31, Pt. 2, 573; Van Horne, 422–23.
25. *Official Records*, Vol. 31, Pt. 2, 43.
26. Van Horne, 423–24; Fullerton, "Army Cumberland," 144; *Official Records*, Vol. 31, Pt. 2, 573, 746.
27. Van Horne, 423; *Official Records*, Vol. 31, Pt. 2, 574.
28. *Official Records*, Vol. 31, Pt. 2, 664–65; Connelly, 273.
29. *Official Records*, Vol. 31, Pt. 2, 24.
30. *Official Records*, Vol. 31, Pt. 2, 25.
31. Grant, *Memoirs*, Vol. 2, 75; *Official Records*, Vol. 31, Pt. 2, 43–44.

Chapter 23

1. Fullerton, "Army Cumberland," 143; Doan, 15; *Official Records*, Vol. 31, Pt. 2, 399.
2. Fullerton, "Army Cumberland," 144; *Official Records*, Vol. 31, Pt. 2, 746.
3. Catton, *Grant Takes Command*, 77; *Official Records*, Vol. 31, Pt. 2, 574.
4. Grant, *Memoirs*, Vol. 2, 76; *Official Records*, Vol. 31, Pt. 2, 574–75; Byers, "Sherman's Attack," 713.
5. *Official Records*, Vol. 31, Pt. 2, 636; Byers, "Sherman's Attack," 713.
6. *Official Records*, Vol. 31, Pt. 2, 575, 749–50; Fullerton, "Army Cumberland," 144.
7. *Official Records*, Vol. 31, Pt. 2, 575, 750; Woodworth, *Grand Spectacle*, 71.
8. Woodworth, *Grand Spectacle*, 71–72; *Official Records*, Vol. 31, Pt. 2, 575.
9. *Official Records*, Vol. 31, Pt. 2, 634, 750, 574–75; Grant, *Memoirs*, Vol. 2, 77.
10. *Official Records*, Vol. 31, Pt. 2, 751; Woodworth, *Six Armies*, 192.
11. *Official Records*, Vol. 31, Pt. 2, 575, 636–37.
12. Fullerton, "Army Cumberland," 145–46; Grant, *Memoirs*, Vol. 2, 77; Catton, *Grant Takes Command*, 78.
13. *Official Records*, Vol. 31, Pt. 2, 318; Grant, *Memoirs*, Vol. 2, 78.
14. *Official Records*, Vol. 31, Pt. 2, 318.
15. *Official Records*, Vol. 31, Pt. 2, 319.
16. Grant, *Memoirs*, Vol. 2, 77–78.
17. Fullerton, "Army Cumberland," 146; Van Horne, 429; Catton, *Grant Takes Command*, 78.
18. Bowers, 221; *Official Records*, Vol. 31, Pt. 2, 34.

Chapter 24

1. Grant, *Memoirs*, Vol. 2, 79; *Official Records*, Vol. 31, Pt. 2, 68.

2. Fullerton, "Army Cumberland," 146; Van Horne, 429.
3. Bowers, 225–26; Connelly, 273.
4. Bowers, 225–26; John D. Fowler, *Mountaineers in Gray: The Nineteenth Tennessee Volunteer Infantry regiment, C.S.A.* (Knoxville: University of Tennessee Press, 2004), 121.
5. Van Horne, 430; Angle, 157; Kimberly, 69; Alfred G. Hunter, *History of the Eighty-second Indiana Volunteer Infantry, Its Organization, Campaigns and Battles* (Indianapolis: William B. Buford, 1893), 106; William Bircher, *A Drummer-Boy's Diary: Comprising Four Years of Service with the Second Regiment Minnesota Veteran Volunteers* (St. Paul, MN: St. Paul Book and Stationery, 1889), 85–86.
6. Henry J. Aten, *History of the Eighty-fifth Regiment Illinois Volunteer Infantry* (Hiawatha, KS: Regimental Association, 1901), 135; *Official Records*, Vol. 31, Pt. 2, 34; W. J. Worsham, *The Old Nineteenth Tennessee Regiment, C.S.A.* (Knoxville, TN: Press of Paragon Printing, 1902), 100.
7. Kimberly, 69; Judson W. Bishop, *The Story of a Regiment: Being a Narrative of the Service of the Second Regiment, Minnesota Veteran Volunteer Infantry, in the Civil War of 1861–1865* (St. Paul, MN: Regimental Association, 1890), 126; *Official Records*, Vol. 31, Pt. 2, 190.
8. L. G. Bennett, *Thirty-sixth*, 526; *Official Records*, Vol. 31, Pt. 2, 34.
9. *Official Records*, Vol. 31, Pt. 2, 258, 264, 281.
10. *Official Records*, Vol. 31, Pt. 2, 508, 190–91, 459.
11. William Wirt Calkins, *The History of the One Hundred and Fourth Regiment of Illinois Volunteer Infantry* (Chicago: Donohue and Henneberry, 1895), 178–79.
12. *Official Records*, Vol. 31, Pt. 2, 282, 69; Kimberly, 70.
13. *Official Records*, Vol. 31, Pt. 2, 69; Fullerton, "Army Cumberland," 147.
14. Catton, *Grant Takes Command*, 83; W. H. Newlin and others, *A History of the Seventy-third Regiment of Illinois Infantry Volunteers* (Regimental Reunion Association, 1890), 266.
15. Bowers, 226; *Official Records*, Vol. 31, Pt. 2, 264; Charles I. Switzer, ed., *Ohio Volunteer: The Childhood and Civil War Memoirs of Captain John Calvin Hartzell, OVI* (Athens: Ohio University Press, 2005), 150; Ephraim A. Wilson, *Memoirs of the War* (Cleveland, OH: W. M. Bayne, 1893), 262.
16. Angle, 150; Worsham, 100.
17. Fullerton, "Army Cumberland," 148–49.
18. Switzer, 150.
19. Woodworth, *Decision*, 92; Fullerton, "Army Cumberland," 149.
20. Bowers, 231–32; Van Horne, 432.
21. Nixon B. Stewart, *Dan McCook's Regiment, 52nd O.V.I.* (Alliance, OH: Nixon B. Stewart, 1900), 75–76; Angle, 158; Switzer, 150.
22. Bowers, 232; *Official Records*, Vol. 31, Pt. 2, 752; Catton, *Grant Takes Command*, 84.
23. *Official Records*, Vol. 31, Pt. 2, 69.
24. *Official Records*, Vol. 31, Pt. 2, 35, 191; Fullerton, "Army Cumberland," 149.
25. Catton, *Grant Takes Command*, 89–90; *Official Records*, Vol. 31, Pt. 2, 192; Philip H. Sheridan, *Personal Memoirs of P. H. Sheridan*, Vol. 1 (New York: Charles L. Webster, 1888), 314–16.

Chapter 25

1. *Official Records*, Vol. 31, Pt. 2, 36; Fox, 551.
2. Grant, *Memoirs*, Vol. 2, 84; Sherman, 393.
3. *Official Records*, Vol. 31, Pt. 2, 319–20; Connelly, 276; J. R. Kinnear, *History of the Eighty-sixth Regiment Illinois Volunteer Infantry* (Chicago: Tribune Company's Book and Job Printing Office, 1866), 33.
4. Grant, *Memoirs*, Vol. 2, 91; *Official Records*, Vol. 31, Pt. 2, 320–22; Connelly, 276.
5. *Official Records*, Vol. 31, Pt. 2, 35; Catton, *Grant Takes Command*, 87.
6. Grant, *Memoirs*, Vol. 2, 90–91.
7. Grant, *Memoirs*, Vol. 2, 92; Sherman, 394–95.
8. Orlando M. Poe, "The Defense of Knoxville," *Battles and Leaders of the Civil War*, Vol. 3, Robert Underwood Johnson and Clarence Clough Buel, eds. (New York: Thomas Yoseloff, 1956), 743–45; Sherman, 395–96.
9. Grant, *Memoirs*, Vol. 2, 98.
10. *Official Records*, Vol. 31, Pt. 2, 665–66.
11. *Official Records*, Vol. 52, Pt. 2, 745–46; Connelly, 277–78.
12. Official Records, Vol. 31, Pt. 3, 429–30.
13. Catton, *Grant Takes Command*, 99–100.

Bibliography

Books

Abernethy, Byron R., ed. *Private Elisha Stockwell, Jr. Sees the Civil War*. Norman: University of Oklahoma Press, 1958.

Aldrich, C. Knight, ed. *Quest for a Star: The Civil War Letters and Diaries of Colonel Francis T. Sherman of the 88th Illinois*. Knoxville: University of Tennessee Press, 1999.

Ambrose, Stephen E. *Halleck: Lincoln's Chief of Staff*. Baton Rouge: Louisiana State University Press, 1962.

Ambrose, Stephen E., ed. *A Wisconsin Boy in Dixie: The Selected Letters of James K. Newton*. Madison: University of Wisconsin Press, 1961.

Angle, Paul M., ed. *Three Years in the Army of the Cumberland: The Letters and Diary of Major James A. Connolly*. Bloomington: Indiana University Press, 1959.

Aten, Henry J. *History of the Eighty-fifth Regiment, Illinois Volunteer Infantry*. Hiawatha, KS: Regimental Association, 1901.

Badeau, Adam. *Military History of Ulysses S. Grant: From April 1861 to April 1865*, 3 vols. New York: D. Appleton, 1885.

Ballard, Michael B. *The Campaign for Vicksburg*. Eastern National Park and Monument Association, 1996.

Ballard, Michael B. *Civil War Mississippi: A Guide*. Jackson: University Press of Mississippi, 2000.

Barber, Lucius W. *Army Memoirs of Lucius W. Barber*. Chicago: J.M.W. Jones Stationery and Printing, 1894.

Barnes, James A., James R. Carnahan and Thomas H. B. McCain. *The Eighty-sixth Regiment, Indiana Volunteer Infantry*. Crawfordsville, IN: Journal Company, 1895.

Basler, Roy P., ed. *The Collected Works of Abraham Lincoln*, 8 vols. New Brunswick, NJ: Rutgers University Press, 1953.

Beach, John N. *History of the Fortieth Ohio Volunteer Infantry*. London, OH: Shepherd and Craig, 1884.

Bearss, Edwin C., and Warren Grabau. *The Battle of Jackson, The Siege of Jackson, Three Other Post-Vicksburg Actions*. Baltimore, MD: Gateway Press, 1981.

Belknap, William W. *History of the Fifteenth Regiment, Iowa Veteran Volunteer Infantry*. Keokuk, IA: R.B. Ogden and Son, 1887.

Bennett, L. G., and William M. Haigh. *History of the Thirty-sixth Regiment Illinois Volunteers, During the War of the Rebellion*. Aurora, IL: Knickerbocker and Hodder, 1876.

Bennett, Stewart, and Barbara Tillery, eds. *The Struggle for the Life of the Republic: A Civil War Narrative by Brevet Major Charles Dana Miller, 76th Ohio Volunteer Infantry*. Kent, OH: Kent State University Press, 2004.

Bentley, W. H. *History of the 77th Illinois Volunteer Infantry, Sept. 2, 1862–July 10, 1865*. Peoria, IL: Edward Hine, 1883.

Bering, John A., and Thomas Montgomery. *History of the Forty-eighth Ohio Vet. Vol. Inf.* Hillsboro, OH: Highland News Office, 1880.

Bircher, William. *A Drummer-Boy's Diary: Comprising Four Years of Service with the Second Regiment Minnesota Veteran Volunteers*. St. Paul, MN: St. Paul Book and Stationery Company, 1889.

Bishop, Judson W. *The Story of a Regiment: Being a Narrative of the Service of the Second Regiment, Minnesota Veteran Volunteer Infantry, in the Civil War of 1861–1865*. St. Paul, MN: Regimental Association, 1890.

Blanchard, Ira. *I Marched with Sherman: Civil War Memoirs of the 20th Illinois Volunteer Infantry*. San Francisco: J. D. Huff, 1992.

Bond, Otto F., ed. *Under the Flag of the Nation: Diaries and Letters of Owen Johnston Hopkins, a Yankee Volunteer in the Civil War*. Columbus: Ohio State University Press, 1998.

Bowers, John. *Chickamauga and Chattanooga: The Battles That Doomed the Confederacy*. New York: HarperCollins, 1994.

Boyd, James P. *The Life of General William T. Sherman*. Philadelphia: Publishers Union, 1891.

Briant, Charles C. *History of the Sixth Regiment Indiana Volunteer Infantry of Both the Three Months' and Three Years' Services*. Indianapolis: William E. Burford, 1891.

Brown, Alonzo L. *History of the Fourth Regiment of Minnesota Infantry Volunteers During the Great Rebellion 1861–1865*. St. Paul, MN: Pioneer Press, 1892.

Bryner, Cloyd. *Bugle Echoes: The Story of Illinois 47th*. Springfield, IL: Phillips Bros., 1905.

Byers, S.H.M. *With Fire and Sword*. New York: Neale, 1911.

Calkins, William Wirt. *The History of the One Hundred and Fourth Regiment of Illinois Volunteer Infantry*. Chicago: Donohue and Henneberry, 1895.

Canfield, S. S. *History of the 21st Regiment Ohio Volunteer Infantry, in the War of the Rebellion*. Toledo, OH: Vrooman, Anderson and Bateman, 1893.

Carley, Kenneth. *Minnesota in the Civil War*. Minneapolis, MN: Ross and Haines, 1961.

Carpenter, John A. *Ulysses S. Grant*. New York: Twayne, 1970.

Carter, Samuel III. *The Final Fortress: The Campaign for Vicksburg 1862–1863*. New York: St. Martin's, 1980.

Catton, Bruce. *Grant Moves South*. Boston: Little, Brown, 1960.

Catton, Bruce. *Grant Takes Command*. Boston: Little, Brown, 1969.

Catton, Bruce. *Never Call Retreat*. Garden City, NJ: Doubleday, 1965.

Christ, Mark K., ed. *Getting Used to Being Shot At: The Spence Family Civil War Letters*. Fayetteville: University of Arkansas Press, 2002.

Church, William Conant. *Ulysses S. Grant and the Period of National Preservation and Reconstruction*. New York: G. P. Putnam's Sons, 1897.

Cist, Henry M. *The Army of the Cumberland*. New York: Charles Scribner's Sons, 1882.

Coburn, Mark. *Terrible Innocence: General Sherman at War*. New York: Hippocrene Books, 1993.

Committee of the Regiment. *The Story of the Fifty-fifth Regiment Illinois Volunteer Infantry in the Civil War 1861–1865*. Clinton, MA: W. J. Coulter, 1887.

Conger, A. L. *The Rise of U.S. Grant*. Freeport, NY: Books for Libraries Press, 1970.

Connelly, Thomas Lawrence. *Autumn of Glory: The Army of Tennessee, 1862–1865*. Baton Rouge: Louisiana State University Press, 1971.

Coppee, Henry. *Life and Services of Gen. U.S. Grant*. Chicago: Western News Company, 1868.

Cotton, Gordon A., ed. *From the Pen of a She-Rebel: The Civil War Diary of Emilie Riley McKinley*. Columbia: University of South Carolina Press, 2001.

Cotton, Gordon A., and Jeff T. Giambrone. *Vicksburg and the War*. Gretna, LA: Pelican, 2004.

Cozzens, Peter. *This Terrible Sound: The Battle of Chickamauga*. Urbana: University of Illinois Press, 1992.

Crabb, Martha L. *All Afire to Fight: The Untold Tale of the Civil War's Ninth Texas Cavalry*. New York: Avon Books, 2000.

Cramer, Jesse Grant, ed. *Letter of Ulysses S. Grant to His Father and His Youngest Sister 1857–78*. New York: G. P. Putnam's Sons, 1912.

Crist, Lynda Lasswell, ed. *The Papers of Jefferson Davis*. Baton Rouge: Louisiana State University Press, 1997.

Crummer, Wilbur F. *With Grant at Fort Donelson, Shiloh and Vicksburg*. Oak Park, IL: E. C. Crummer, 1915.

Dana, Charles A. *Recollections of the Civil War*. New York: D. Appleton, 1902.

Dana, Charles A., and James H. Wilson. *The Life of Ulysses S. Grant, General of the Armies of the United States*. Springfield, MA: Gurden Bill, 1868.

Davis, William C., ed. *Diary of a Confederate Soldier: John S. Jackman of the Orphan Brigade*. Columbia: University of South Carolina Press, 1990.

Day, Lewis W. *Story of the One Hundred and First Ohio Infantry*. Cleveland, OH: W. M. Bayne, 1894.

Deaderick, Barron. *Shiloh, Memphis and Vicksburg*. Memphis: West Tennessee Historical Society, 1960.

Deming, Henry C. *The Life of Ulysses S. Grant, General United States Army*. Hartford, CT: S. S. Scranton, 1868.

Dodge, William S. *History of the Old Second Division, Army of the Cumberland, Commanders: M'Cook, Sill, and Johnson*. Chicago: Church and Goodman, 1864.

Dodge, William S. *A Waif of the War or, the History of the Seventy-fifth Illinois Infantry*. Chicago: Church and Goodman, 1866.

Downey, Fairfax. *Storming of the Gateway: Chattanooga, 1863*. New York: David McKay, 1960.

Doyle, Julie A., John David Smith, and Richard M. McMurry, eds. *This Wilderness of War: The Civil War Letters of George W. Squier, Hoosier Volunteer*. Knoxville: University of Tennessee Press, 1998.

Duke, John K. *History of the Fifty-third Regiment Ohio Volunteer Infantry During the War of the Rebellion 1861 to 1865*. Portsmouth, OH: Blade Printing, 1900.

Dunbar, Aaron. *History of the Ninety-third Regiment Illinois Volunteer Infantry*. Chicago: Blakely Printing, 1898.

Dyer, Frederick H. *A Compendium of the War of the Rebellion*. Des Moines, IA: Dyer, 1908.

Eaton, John. *Grant, Lincoln and the Freedmen*. New York: Negro Universities Press, 1969.

Elder, Donald C. III, ed. *A Damned Iowa Greyhound: The Civil War Letters of William Henry Harrison Clayton*. Iowa City: University of Iowa Press, 1998.

Elliott, Isaac H. *History of the Thirty-third Regiment Illinois Veteran Volunteer Infantry in the Civil War*. Gibson City, IL: Regimental Association, 1902.

Engle, Stephen D. *Struggle for the Heartland: The Campaigns from Fort Henry to Corinth*. Lincoln: University of Nebraska Press, 2001.

Farragut, Loyall. *The Life of David Glasgow Farragut, First Admiral of the United States Navy*. New York: D. Appleton, 1882.

Ferrel, Robert H., ed. *Holding the Line: The Third

Tennessee Infantry 1861–1864. Kent, OH: Kent State University Press, 1994.

Fiske, John. *The Mississippi Valley in the Civil War*. Boston: Houghton, Mifflin, 1900.

Foote, Shelby. *The Beleaguered City: The Vicksburg Campaign, December 1862–July 1863*. New York: Modern Library, 1995.

Fowler, John D. *Mountaineers in Gray: The Nineteenth Tennessee Volunteer Infantry Regiment, C.S.A*. Knoxville: University of Tennessee Press, 2004.

Fox, William F. *Regimental Losses in the American Civil War, 1861–1865*. Albany, NY: Albany Publishing Company, 1889.

Frost, M. O. *Regimental History of the Tenth Missouri Volunteer Infantry*. Topeka, KS: M. O. Frost, 1892.

Fuller, J.F.C. *The Generalship of Ulysses S. Grant*. New York: Da Capo Press, 1991.

Garland, Hamlin. *Ulysses S. Grant: His Life and Character*. New York: Macmillan, 1920.

Gosnell, H. Allen. *Guns on the Western Waters: The Story of River Gunboats in the Civil War*. Baton Rouge: Louisiana State University Press, 1949.

Gottschalk, Phil. *In Deadly Earnest: The History of the First Missouri Brigade, CSA*. Columbia: Missouri River Press, 1991.

Grabau, Warren E. *Ninety-eight Days: A Geographer's View of the Vicksburg Campaign*. Knoxville: University of Tennessee Press, 2000

Grant, Ulysses S. *Personal Memoirs of U.S. Grant*. New York: Charles L. Webster, 1885.

Grecian, J. *History of the Eighty-third Regiment, Indiana Volunteer Infantry*. Cincinnati, OH: John F. Uhlhorn, 1865.

Grimsley, Mark, and Todd D. Miller, eds. *The Union Must Stand: The Civil War Diary of John Quincy Adams Campbell, Fifth Iowa Volunteer Infantry*. Knoxville: University of Tennessee Press, 2000.

Grose, William. *The Story of the Marches, Battles and Incidents of the 36th Regiment Indiana Volunteer Infantry*. New Castle, IN: Courier Company Press, 1891.

Hale, Douglas. *The Third Texas Cavalry in the Civil War*. Norman: University of Oklahoma Press, 1993.

Hall, Winchester. *The Story of the 26th Louisiana Infantry*. N.P., 1890.

Hallock, Judith Lee, ed. *The Civil War Letters of Joshua K. Callaway*. Athens: University of Georgia Press, 1997.

Hartpence, William R. *History of the Fifty-first Indiana Veteran Volunteer Infantry*. Cincinnati, OH: Robert Clarke, 1894.

Hays, E. Z., ed. *History of the Thirty-second Regiment Ohio Veteran Volunteer Infantry*. Columbus, OH: Cott and Evans, 1896.

Hazen, William B. *A Narrative of Military Service*. Boston: Ticknor, 1885.

Hearn, Chester G. *Admiral David Dixon Porter: The Civil War Years*. Annapolis, MD: Naval Institute Press, 1996.

Hicken, Victor. *Illinois in the Civil War*. Urbana: University of Illinois Press, 1991.

Hoppin, James Mason. *Life of Andrew Hull Foote, Rear-Admiral United States Navy*. New York: Harper and Brothers, 1874.

Horn, Stanley F. *Tennessee's War, 1861–1865: Described by Participants*. Nashville: Tennessee Civil War Centennial Commission, 1965.

Howard, Oliver Otis. *Autobiography of Oliver Otis Howard, Major General United States Army*. New York: Baker and Taylor, 1907.

Howard, R. L. *History of the 124th Regiment Illinois Infantry Volunteers*. Springfield, IL: H. W. Rokker, 1880.

Howell, H. Grady, Jr. *Going to Meet the Yankees: A History of the "Bloody Sixth" Mississippi Infantry, C.S.A*. Jackson, MS: Chickasaw Bayou Press, 1981.

Howland, Edward. *Grant as a Soldier and Statesman*. Hartford, CT: J. B. Burr, 1868.

Hubbard, Lucius F. *Civil War Papers of Lucius F. Hubbard*. St. Paul: Minnesota Historical Society, 1908.

Hunter, Alfred G. *History of the Eighty-second Indiana Volunteer Infantry, Its Organization, Campaigns and Battles*. Indianapolis: William B. Buford, 1893.

Jackson, Joseph Orville, ed. *"Some of the Boys..." The Civil War Letters of Isacc Jackson 1862–1865*. Carbondale: Southern Illinois University Press, 1960.

Johnson, Charles B. *Muskets and Medicine or Army Life in the Sixties*. Philadelphia: F. A. Davis, 1917.

Johnson, R. W. *A Soldier's Reminiscences in Peace and War*. Philadelphia: J. B. Lippincott, 1886.

Johnston, Joseph E. *Narrative of Military Operations, Directed, During the Late War Between the States*. New York: D. Appleton, 1874.

Jones, S. C. *Reminiscences of the Twenty-Second Iowa Volunteer Infantry*. Iowa City, IA: S. C. Jones, 1907.

Kellogg, J. J. *War Experiences and the Story of the Vicksburg Campaign*. Washington, IA: Evening Journal, 1913.

Kimberly, Robert L., and Ephraim S. Holloway. *The Forty-first Ohio Veteran Volunteer Infantry in the War of the Rebellion, 1861–1865*. Cleveland, OH: W. R. Smellie, 1897.

Kinnear, John R. *History of the Eighty-sixth Regiment Illinois Volunteer Infantry*. Chicago: Tribune Company's Book and Job Printing Office, 1866.

Kiper, Richard L. *Major General John Alexander McClernand, Politician in Uniform*. Kent, OH: Kent State University Press, 1999.

Kiper, Richard L., ed. *Dear Catharine, Dear Taylor: The Civil War Letters of a Union Soldier and His Wife*. Lawrence: University Press of Kansas, 2002.

Larke, Julian K. *General Grant and His Campaigns*. New York: J. C. Derby and N. C. Miller, 1864.

Lewis, Lloyd. *Sherman: Fighting Prophet.* New York: Harcourt, Brace, 1932.

Livermore, Mary A. *My Story of the War: A Woman's Narrative of Four Years Personal Experience.* Hartford, CT: A. D. Worthington, 1896.

Longacre, Edward G. *General Ulysses S. Grant: The Soldier and the Man.* Cambridge, MA: Da Capo Press, 2006.

Longstreet, James. *From Manassas to Appomattox.* Old Saybrook, CT: Konecky and Konecky, n. d.

Loughborough, Mary Ann. *My Cave Life in Vicksburg.* Wilmington, NC: Broadfoot, 1989. Reprint.

Mahan, Alfred T. *The Gulf and Inland Waters.* New York: Charles Scribner's Sons, 1883.

Marshall, Albert O. *Army Life: From a Soldier's Journal.* Joliet, IL: Albert O. Marshall, 1884.

McCaffrey, James M. *This Band of Heroes: Granbury's Texas Brigade, C.S.A.* College Station: Texas A&M University Press, 1996.

McDonald, G. B. *A History of the 30th Illinois Veteran Volunteer Regiment of Infantry.* Sparta, IL: Sparta News, 1916.

McDonough, James Lee. *Chattanooga: A Death Grip on the Confederacy.* Knoxville: University of Tennessee Press, 1984.

McKinney, Francis F. *Education in Violence: The Life of George H. Thomas and the History of the Army of the Cumberland.* Detroit, MI: Wayne State University Press, 1961.

McPherson, James M. *Battle Cry of Freedom: The Civil War Era.* New York: Oxford University Press, 1988.

Montgomery, Frank A. *Reminiscences of a Mississippian in Peace and War.* Cincinnati, OH: Robert Clarke, 1901.

Morris, W. S., L. D. Hartwell, and J.B. Kuykendall. *History of the 31st Regiment Illinois Volunteers.* Carbondale: Southern Illinois University Press, 1998.

Nash, Howard P. Jr. *A Naval History of the Civil War.* New York: A. S. Barnes, 1972.

Newlin, W. H., D. F. Lawler, and J. W. Sherrick. *A History of the Seventy-third Regiment of Illinois Infantry Volunteers.* Springfield, IL: Regimental Reunion Association, 1890.

Newsome, Edmund. *Experience in the War of the Great Rebellion.* Carbondale, IL: Edmund Newsome, 1880.

Northen, Charles Swift III, ed. *All Right Let Them Come: The Civil War Diary of an East Tennessee Confederate.* Knoxville: University of Tennessee Press, 2003.

O'Connor, Richard. *Sheridan the Inevitable.* New York: Konecky and Konecky, 1993.

Oldroyd, Osborn H. *A Soldier's Story of the Siege of Vicksburg.* Springfield, IL: H. W. Rokker, 1885.

Partridge, Charles A. *History of the Ninety-sixth Regiment Illinois Volunteer Infantry.* Chicago: Brown, Pettibone, 1887.

Patrick, Jeffrey L., ed. *Three Years with Wallace's Zouaves: The Civil War Memoirs of Thomas Wise Durham.* Macon, GA: Mercer University Press, 2003.

Pemberton, John C. *Pemberton: Defender of Vicksburg.* Chapel Hill: University of North Carolina Press, 1942.

Perret, Geoffrey. *Ulysses S. Grant: Soldier and President.* New York: Random House, 1997.

Perry, Henry Fales. *History of the Thirty-eighth Regiment Indiana Volunteer Infantry.* Palo Alto, CA: F. A. Stuart, 1906.

Porter, David D. *Incidents and Anecdotes of the Civil War.* New York: D. Appleton, 1886.

Porter, David D. *The Naval History of the Civil War.* New York: Sherman Publishing Company, 1886.

Porter, Horace. *Campaigning with Grant.* New York: Mallard Press, 1991.

Pratt, Fletcher. *Civil War on Western Waters.* New York: Henry Holt, 1956.

Reed, David W. *Campaigns and Battles of the Twelfth Regiment Iowa Veteran Volunteer Infantry.* Evanston, IL: N. P., 1903.

Reed, Rowena. *Combined Operations in the Civil War.* Annapolis, MD: Naval Institute Press, 1978.

Reed, Samuel Rockwell. *The Vicksburg Campaign, and the Battles About Chattanooga Under the Command of General U.S. Grant.* Cincinnati, OH: Robert Clarke, 1882.

Rerick, John H. *The Forty-fourth Indiana Volunteer Infantry: History of Its Services in the War of the Rebellion.* LaGrange, IN: John H. Rerick, 1880.

Richardson, Albert D. *A Personal History of Ulysses S. Grant.* Hartford, CT: American Publishing Company, 1868.

Schneller, Robert J., Jr. *Farragut, America's First Admiral.* Washington, D.C.: Brassey's, 2002.

Schultz, Duane. *The Most Glorious Fourth: Vicksburg and Gettysburg, July 4, 1863.* New York: W. W. Norton, 2002.

Shea, William L., and Terrence J. Winschell. *Vicksburg Is the Key: The Struggle for the Mississippi River.* Lincoln: University of Nebraska Press, 2003.

Sheridan, Philip H. *Personal Memoirs of P. H. Sheridan.* New York: Charles L. Webster, 1888.

Sherman, William T. *Memoirs of Gen. W. T. Sherman, Written by Himself.* New York: Charles L. Webster, 1891.

Simpson, Brooks D. *Ulysses S. Grant: Triumph Over Adversity, 1822–1865.* Boston: Houghton Mifflin, 2000.

Simpson, Brooks D., and Jean V. Berlin, eds. *Sherman's Civil War: Selected Correspondence of William T. Sherman, 1860–1865.* Chapel Hill: University of North Carolina Press, 1999.

Spruill, Matt. *Storming the Heights: A Guide to the Battle of Chattanooga.* Knoxville: University of Tennessee Press, 2003.

Stevenson, Thomas M. *History of the 78th Regiment O.V.V.I.* Zanesville, OH: Hugh Dunne, 1865.

Stewart, Nixon B. *Dan McCook's Regiment, 52nd O.V.I.* Alliance, OH: Nixon B. Stewart, 1900.

Stillwell, Leander. *The Story of a Common Soldier of Army Life in the Civil War, 1861–1865.* Kansas City, KS: Franklin Hudson, 1920.

Sullivan, James R. *Chickamauga and Chattanooga Battlefields.* Washington, D.C.: National Park Service, 1961.

Sutherland, Daniel E., ed. *Reminiscences of a Private: William E. Bevens of the First Arkansas Infantry, C.S.A.* Fayetteville: University of Arkansas Press, 1992.

Switzer, Charles I., ed. *Ohio Volunteer: The Childhood and Civil War Memoirs of Captain John Calvin Hartzell, OVI.* Athens: Ohio University Press, 2005.

Thomas, Benjamin P., ed. *Three Years with Grant as Recalled by War Correspondent Sylvanus Cadwallader.* New York: Alfred A. Knopf, 1955.

Tower, R. Lockwood, ed. *A Carolinian Goes to War: The Civil War Narrative of Arthur Middleton Manigault, Brigadier General, C.S.A.* Columbia: University of South Carolina Press, 1983.

Tucker, Spencer C. *Unconditional Surrender: The Capture of Forts Henry and Donelson.* Abilene, TX: McWhiney Foundation Press, 2001.

Tunnard, W. H. *The History of the Third Regiment Louisiana Infantry.* Baton Rouge, LA: Printed for the Author, 1866.

United States Naval War Records Office. *Official Records of the Union and Confederate Navies in the War of the Rebellion.* Washington, D.C.: Government Printing Office, 1894–1922.

United States War Department. *The War of the Rebellion: A Compilation of the Official Records of the Union and Confederate Armies.* Washington, D.C.: Government Printing Office, 1880–1901.

Van Horne, Thomas B. *History of the Army of the Cumberland Its Organization, Campaigns, and Battles.* Vol. 1. Cincinnati, OH: Robert Clarke, 1875.

Walker, Peter F. *Vicksburg: A People at War 1860–1865.* Chapel Hill: University of North Carolina Press, 1960.

Welles, Gideon. *Diary of Gideon Welles*, 3 vols. Boston: Houghton Mifflin, 1911.

Wheeler, Richard. *The Siege of Vicksburg.* New York: Thomas Y. Crowell, 1978.

Williams, Kenneth P. *Grant Rises in the West, from Iuka to Vicksburg.* Lincoln: University of Nebraska Press, 1997.

Williams, Kenneth P. *Lincoln Finds a General.* Vol. 4. New York: Macmillan, 1956.

Williams, T. Harry. *Lincoln and His Generals.* New York: Alfred A. Knopf, 1952.

Wilson, Ephraim A. *Memoirs of the War.* Cleveland, OH: W. M. Bayne, 1893.

Wilson, James Grant. *General Grant's Letters to a Friend, 1861–1880.* New York: T. Y. Crowell, 1897.

Wilson, James H. *Under the Old Flag.* New York: D. Appleton, 1912.

Winschel, Terrence J. *Vicksburg: Fall of the Confederate Gibraltar.* Abilene, TX: McWhiney Foundation Press, 1999.

Winschel, Terrence J., ed. *The Civil War Diary of a Common Soldier: William Wiley of the 77th Illinois Infantry.* Baton Rouge: Louisiana State University Press, 2001.

Woods, J. T. *Services of the Ninety-sixth Ohio Volunteers.* Toledo, OH: Blade, 1874.

Woodworth, Steven E. *Decision in the Heartland: The Civil War in the West.* Westport, CT: Praeger, 2008.

Woodworth, Steven E. *Jefferson Davis and His Generals: The Failure of Confederate Command in the West.* Lawrence: University Press of Kansas, 1990.

Woodworth, Steven E. *Six Armies in Tennessee: The Chickamauga and Chattanooga Campaigns.* Lincoln: University of Nebraska Press, 1998.

Woodworth, Steven E. *This Grand Spectacle: The Battle of Chattanooga.* Abilene, TX: McWhiney Foundation Press, 1999.

Woodworth, Steven E. ed. *The Musick of the Mocking Birds, the Roar of the Cannon: The Civil War Diary and Letters of William Winters.* Lincoln: University of Nebraska Press, 1998.

Worsham, W. J. *The Old Nineteenth Tennessee Regiment, C.S.A.* Knoxville, TN: Press of Paragon Printing, 1902.

Magazines, Diaries, Letters

Abbott, John S. C. "Heroic Deeds of Heroic Men: Opening the Mississippi," *Harper's New Monthly Magazine*, August 1866.

Abbott, John S. C. "Heroic Deeds of Heroic Men: Siege of Vicksburg." *Harper's New Monthly Magazine*, January 1865.

Alexander, E. Porter. "Longstreet at Knoxville." *Battles and Leaders of the Civil War.* 4 Vols. Robert Underwood Johnson and Clarence Clough Buel, eds. New York: Thomas Yoseloff, 1956.

Badeau, Adam. "General Grant." *The Century*, May 1885.

Brown, A. F. "Van Dorn's Operations in Northern Mississippi—Recollections of a Cavalryman." *Southern Historical Society Papers*, October 1878.

Byers, S.H.M. "Sherman's Attack at the Tunnel." *Battles and Leaders of the Civil War.* 4 Vols. Robert Underwood Johnson and Clarence Clough Buel, eds. New York: Thomas Yoseloff, 1956.

Doan, Isaac C. *Reminiscences of the Chattanooga Campaign: A Paper Read at the Reunion of Company B, Fortieth Ohio Volunteer Infantry, at Xenia, O., August 22, 1894.* Richmond, IN: J. M. Coe's Printery, 1894.

Force, Manning F. *Personal Recollections of the Vicksburg Campaign: A Paper Read Before the Ohio Commandery of the Military Order of the Loyal Legion of the United States*. Cincinnati, OH: Henry C. Sherick, 1885

Fullerton, J. S. "The Reserve Corps at Chickamauga." *The Century*, April 1887.

Fullerton, J. S. "The Army of the Cumberland at Chattanooga." *The Century*, May 1887.

Grant, Ulysses S. "General Grant on the Terms at Vicksburg." *The Century*, August 1887.

Hickenlooper, Andrew. "The Vicksburg Mine." *Battles and Leaders of the Civil War*, 4 vols. Robert Underwood Johnson and Clarence Clough Buell, eds. New York: Thomas Yoselof, 1956.

Hill, D. H. "Chickamauga: The Great Battle of the West." *The Century*, April 1887.

Hogane, J. T. "Reminiscences of the Siege of Vicksburg." *Southern Historical Society Papers*, April-May 1883.

Howard, Oliver O. "Chattanooga." *The Atlantic Monthly*, August 1876.

Johnston, Joseph E. "Jefferson Davis and the Mississippi Campaign." *The North American Review*, December 1886.

Kniffin, Gilbert C. "Manoeuvring Bragg Out of Tennessee." *Battles and Leaders of the Civil War*. 4 vols. Robert Underwood Johnson and Clarence Clough Buel, eds. New York: Thomas Yoseloff, 1956.

Lawrence, Eugene. "Grant on the Battle-field." *Harper's New Monthly Magazine*, July 1869.

Lockett, S. H. "The Defense of Vicksburg." *Battles and Leaders of the Civil War*, 4 vols. Robert Underwood Johnson and Clarence Clough Buell, eds. New York: Thomas Yoselof, 1956.

Longstreet, James. "Report of General Longstreet." *Southern Historical Society Papers*, July 1880.

Meigs, Montgomery C. *The Three Days' Battle of Chattanooga, 23d, 24th, 25th November, 1863: An Unofficial Dispatch from General Meigs*. Washington, D.C.: McGill and Witherow, 1864.

Memminger, R. W. "The Surrender of Vicksburg—A Defence of General Pemberton." *Southern Historical Society Papers*, July-September 1884.

Morgan, George W. "The Assault on Chickasaw Bluffs." *Battles and Leaders of the Civil War*, 4 vols. Robert Underwood Johnson and Clarence Clough Buell, eds. New York: Thomas Yoselof, 1956.

Nicolay, John G., and John Hay. "Abraham Lincoln: A History, the Mississippi and Shiloh." *The Century*, September 1888.

Pemberton, John C. "The Terms of Surrender." *Battles and Leaders of the Civil War*, 4 vols. Robert Underwood Johnson and Clarence Clough Buell, eds. New York: Thomas Yoselof, 1956.

Perry, Leslie J. "The Rise of General Grant." *The Century*, November 1896.

Poe, Orlando M. "The Defense of Knoxville." *Battles and Leaders of the Civil War*. 4 vols. Robert Underwood Johnson and Clarence Clough Buel, eds. New York: Thomas Yoseloff, 1956.

Rice, Allen Thorndike, ed. "Unpublished War Letters by Generals Grant and Halleck." *The North American Review*, March 1886.

Richards, Dora Miller. "A Woman's Diary of the Siege of Vicksburg." *The Century*, September 1885.

Rosecrans, William S. "The Campaign for Chattanooga." *The Century*, May 1887.

Shanks, W.F.G. "Chattanooga, and How We Held It." *Harper's New Monthly Magazine*, January 1868.

Shanks, W.F.G. "Lookout Mountain and How We Won It." *Harper's New Monthly Magazine*, June 1868.

Soley, James Russell. "Naval Operations in the Vicksburg Campaign." *Battles and Leaders of the Civil War*, 4 vols. Robert Underwood Johnson and Clarence Clough Buell, eds. New York: Thomas Yoselof, 1956.

Thruston, Gates P. "The Crisis at Chickamauga." *Battles and Leaders of the Civil War*. 4 vols. Robert Underwood Johnson and Clarence Clough Buel, eds. New York: Thomas Yoseloff, 1956.

Walke, Henry. "Operations of the Western Flotilla." *The Century*, January 1885.

Welles, Gideon. "Admiral Farragut and New Orleans." *The Galaxy*, December 1871.

Wilson, James H. "Reminiscences of General Grant." *The Century*, October 1885.

Index

Adams, Brig. Gen. John: at Jackson 76, 77
Alabama River 130
Alexandria, Louisiana 16
Anaconda Plan 3
Anderson, Col. J.B. (railroad superintendent) 164, 165
CSS *Arkansas* (Confederate gunboat) 12–15
Arkansas River 30–32
Army of Mississippi 17
Army of Northern Virginia 141, 166, 198
Army of Tennessee 95; Chattanooga 147, 148, 194, 197; Tullahoma 134, 136, 138, 139
Army of the Cumberland 133, 135, 138, 158, 165, 168; change commander 153; Chattanooga 144, 147, 150, 152; Missionary Ridge 186
Army of the Gulf 51
Army of the Mississippi 30
Army of the Ohio 138, 157
Army of the Potomac 37, 69, 148
Aten, Henry 188
Athens, Alabama 146
Atlanta, Georgia 1, 135, 138; supply center 139, 147, 158, 178, 198
Autry, Col. J.L. 9

Bailey, Col. W.K.: Big Black 88
Baird, Brig. Gen. Absalom 184, 186; Missionary Ridge 189
Baker's Creek 81
Baldwin, Brig. Gen. William: Port Gibson 64
Banks, Maj. Gen. Nathaniel 63, 66, 70, 71, 89, 129, 130, 145; Army of the Gulf 51; New Orleans 32, 33; Port Hudson 53, 54, 115, 125
Barber, Lucius: Vicksburg 101
Barton, Brig. Gen. Seth M.: Champion's Hill 82, 83; Vicksburg 117
Baton Rouge, Louisiana 8, 14, 15; Grierson's raid 60
Bayou Baxter 40
Bayou Macon 40
Bayou Pierre 65
Bayou Sara 54
Bayou Vidal 51, 52
Beauregard, Gen. G.P.T. 147
Belmont, Battle of 18

Bennett, L.G. 151; Missionary Ridge 189
Bentley, W.H.: Vicksburg 99
USS *Benton* 4, 6, 53; Porter's flagship 55–57
Bering, John A. 70, 94
Big Black River 21, 40, 52, 79, 86, 90, 93, 102, 127; battle 87–89; Grant follows 65, 68, 70, 73; Sherman defends 103, 107, 114, 126
Bingham, Col. J.D. (chief quartermaster) 67
Bishop, Judson: Missionary Ridge 188
Black Bayou 43, 44
USS *Black Hawk* (Porter flagship) 31, 124
Blair, Brig. Gen. Francis P. 68, 75, 80, 103; Champion's Hill 81, 83; Chattanooga 178; Chickasaw Bayou 26–29; Vicksburg 93
Blanchard, Ira 69, 71; Vicksburg 102
Blue Wing 30, 33
Bolton, Mississippi 68, 78, 127
Boomer, Col. George 98; Champion's Hill 84
Bowen, Brig. Gen. John 64, 65, 74, 87; Champion's Hill 81–86; surrender 119, 120; Vicksburg 92
Bragg, Gen. Braxton 37, 54, 140, 141, 167–71; Chattanooga 136, 138–41, 145; Chickamauga 142–44; complaints 146, 147; defeat 193–96; Knoxville 157, 166; Longstreet 161; Missionary Ridge 172, 178, 179, 181, 185–88, 191; positions 149; reinforce 141; resign 197
Bratton, Col. John: Wauhatchie 161, 162
Breckinridge, Maj. Gen. John C. 179, 187
Briant, Charles: Chattanooga 151
Bridgeport, Alabama 138, 148–51, 153, 155; new supply route 156, 160, 162–64; Sherman 168, 169
Bridgeport, Mississippi 89
USS *Brooklyn* 10, 11
Brown, Col. A.F. 24
Brown, Alonzo 41, 59; Vicksburg 123
Brown, Cdr. Isaac 13

Brown's Ferry 155, 156; Sherman 168–70; supply route 158–62, 165
Bruinsburg, Mississippi (landing place) 61, 63–65
Bryner, Cloyd 96
Buckner, Maj. Gen. Simon Bolivar 119; Chattanooga 170, 172
Burbridge, Brig. Gen. Stephen G. 25; Chickasaw Bayou 31, 32
Bureau of Navigation 15
Burnside, Maj. Gen. Ambrose 37, 135, 145, 152; Army of the Ohio 138, 157; Knoxville 143, 158, 166–67, 169, 170, 180, 194–97
Butler, Maj. Gen. Benjamin 7, 8
Byers, Capt. S.H.M. 60, 69; Champion's Hill 84; Missionary Ridge 178, 182

Cadwallader, Sylvanus 99
USS *Cairo* 4, 7
Cairo, Illinois: Union base 3, 4, 7, 23, 120, 152
Calkins, William: Missionary Ridge 189
Callaway, Lt. Joshua K. 163
Campbell, John Quincy Adams: Champion's Hill 84; Vicksburg 96
Canfield, Silas S. 151
Canton, Mississippi 76, 77, 122
USS *Carondelet* 4, 6, 13, 43; Grand Gulf 60; Memphis 7; Vicksburg 53, 55, 56
Carr, Brig. Gen. Eugene 63, 64, 75, 87, 88; Champion's Hill 81, 85, 86; Vicksburg 93
Champion's Hill, Battle of 80, 81, 83, 86, 87, 89, 93
Charleston, South Carolina 17
Chase, Sec. of Treasury Salmon P. 3, 17, 128, 129
Chattanooga Creek 149, 161, 173; Hooker 180, 185
Chattanooga, Tennessee 161, 177, 187, 193, 194, 196; Bragg 134, 136, 138, 144, 166, 170, 196; casualties 194; Chickamauga 141–43; Confederate defenses 173–75; Grant takes command 154, 155, 158, 163, 167, 194; Hooker 168, 180, 185; importance 1, 143, 198; location 135,

149, 150; occupy city 139, 143; planning moves 169, 170, 173; railroads 135; reinforcements 148; Rosecrans 134, 138, 139; Sherman 168, 182; supply line 155, 156, 159, 164, 165; Thomas 153; under siege 145–47, 151, 152
Cheatham, Maj. Gen. Benjamin 173, 197
Chickamauga, Battle of 142–44, 146–49, 163, 166, 169
Chickamauga Creek 141, 179, 192
Chickamauga Station 193
Chickasaw Bayou 25–27, 30, 32, 37, 41, 90
USS *Chillicothe* 41, 42
Churchill, Brig. Gen. Thomas J. 32
USS *Cincinnati* 4, 6; Vicksburg 31, 32, 43
Cincinnati, Ohio 16
Cist, Lt. Henry 138
Clayton, William 110, 122
Cleburne, Maj. Gen. Patrick 140, 195; Chattanooga 170, 172, 178, 181, 182; Missionary Ridge 183, 184, 192, 193
Cleveland, Tennessee 143, 158, 167
Clinton, Mississippi 73–82
Cockrell, Col. Francis: Champion's Hill 83
Coldwater River 38, 41
College Hill, Mississippi 20
USS *Colorado* 7
Colquitt, Col. P.H. 76, 77
Columbus, Kentucky 4, 5, 9, 19
Comstock, Capt. Cyrus B.: Vicksburg defenses 91, 92, 99, 101
USS *Conestoga* 4
Connolly, Maj. James A. 176; Missionary Ridge 188, 191, 192
Corinth, Mississippi 6, 12, 133
Corse, Brig. Gen. John 146; Missionary Ridge 181, 182
Cracker Line 162, 164, 194
Craven, Robert 175, 176
Craven, Capt. Thomas 8
Crittenden, Maj. Gen. Thomas 139–41
Crocker, Brig. Gen. Marcellus 74, 76, 93; Champion's Hill 81, 83–85; Jackson 77
Cruft, Brig. Gen. Charles 170, 185; Lookout Mountain 174
Crummer, Wilber 69; Vicksburg 96, 104, 105, 109, 110, 123
Cumberland Gap 157
Cumberland Plateau 138
Cumberland River 4, 5
Cumming, Brig. Gen. Alfred 82, 183

Dalton, Georgia 135, 167, 196
Dana, Asst. Sec. of War Charles A. 49, 50, 55, 67, 79, 143, 145; Chattanooga 148, 149, 151–53, 155, 170, 190; Missionary Ridge 192; Vicksburg 102, 129, 132
Davis, Commodore Charles H. 6, 13–15

Davis, Confederate Pres. Jefferson 12, 16, 17; Bragg 134, 147, 166, 197; brother 111; Johnston 39, 111; Pemberton 65, 70, 93, 128
Davis, Brig. Gen. Jefferson C. 177–78
Davis, Joseph 111
Decatur, Alabama 165
DeCourcy, Col. John: Chickasaw Bayou 27–29, 32
Deer Creek 43, 44
Deimling, Maj.Francis C. 77
USS *De Kalb* 4, 31, 32, 41, 42
DeSoto Point 16, 56
Diamond Island 57
Dillon's, Mississippi 74
District of Cairo 19
Doan, Isaac: Lookout Mountain 174, 181
Dodge, Brig. Gen. Grenville 165
Drumgould's Bluff 17
Duke, John K. 48
Dunbar 177
Dunbar, Aaron 41; Champion's Hill 84; Vicksburg 98
Durham, Thomas 63, 64, 69; Champion's Hill 82
Duvall's Bluff 32

Eads, James B. 4
Earnest, John Guilford 90, 113
East Tennessee 12, 158; Burnside 139, 143, 157, 167; Confederates threaten 165–66, 194, 197
East Tennessee & Georgia Railroad 166
East Tennessee & Virginia Railroad 138
Eaton, Chap. John 47, 50
Edwards Station, Mississippi 68, 73–75, 79
8th Kansas Infantry: Missionary Ridge 191
8th Kentucky Infantry 181
88th Illinois Infantry 136
85th Illinois Infantry: Missionary Ridge 188
81st Illinois Infantry 124
86th Illinois Infantry 195
86th Indiana Infantry 145
83rd Indiana Infantry 46
83rd Ohio Infantry: Vicksburg 98, 124
11th Indiana Infantry 64; Champion's Hill 82
11th Wisconsin Infantry: Vicksburg 97
Elk River 136
Ellet, Lt. Col. Charles R. 6, 14
Elliott, Isacc H. 63, 85, 87; Big Black 88; Vicksburg 96, 98
USS *Essex* 14, 15
Ewing, Brig. Gen. Hugh 169; Chattanooga 178

Farquharson, Col. Robert: Jackson 76, 77
Farragut, Flag Officer David Glasgow 38, 51, 55, 130; New Orleans 7, 8; Vicksburg 10–15
Featherston, Brig. Gen. Winfield 44
Ferguson, Col. Samuel 44
Fifteenth Corps 39, 46, 58, 75, 76, 94, 127
15th Illinois Infantry 101
5th Iowa Infantry 69, 96, 178; Champion's Hill 84; Missionary Ridge 182
5th Minnesota Infantry 76
58th Ohio Infantry 29
55th Illinois Infantry 39
54th Indiana Infantry: Chickasaw Bayou 28
52nd Ohio Infantry: Missionary Ridge 192
53rd Ohio Infantry 48
Foote, Flag Officer Andrew Hull 4–6; Fort Donelson 5
Forest Queen 55, 56
Forney, Brig. Gen. J.H.: Vicksburg 91, 117, 118
Forrest, Brig. Gen. Nathan Bedford 23, 24, 147
Fort Donelson 5, 18, 38, 119
Fort Henry 5, 18
Fort Hill 110
Fort Hindman (Post of Arkansas) 30, 31
Fort Jackson 7, 8
Fort Pemberton 42–44
Fort Pillow 6, 9
USS *Fort Rose* 41
Fort St. Philip 7
40th Ohio Infantry: Lookout Mountain 174, 181
48th Ohio Infantry 69, 94
45th Illinois Infantry 69, 71, 123; Vicksburg 96
41st Ohio Infantry 163; Missionary Ridge 188
42nd Ohio Infantry: Chickasaw Bayou 28, 29; Vicksburg 98
47th Illinois Infantry: Vicksburg 96
46th Ohio Infantry: Missionary Ridge 182
Foster, Lt. Cdr. John G. 42
Fourteen Mile Creek 70, 71, 74, 75, 81
14th Wisconsin Infantry: Vicksburg 109
4th Minnesota Infantry: Vicksburg 123
Foy, James C. 159
Fredericksburg, Virginia 37
Friar's Point 22
Fullerton, Maj. J.S. 190
USS *Fulton* 41

Galt House 152
Galveston, Texas 130
Gardner, Maj. Gen. Franklin 70
Geary, Brig. Gen. John 160, 170, 185; Lookout Mountain 174–76, 181; Wauhatchie 161, 162

General Orders No. 13 35
General Orders No. 50 131
USS *General Sterling Price* 53, 56
Gettysburg, Pennsylvania 131, 137, 148, 198
Granbury, Col. Hiram 71; Missionary Ridge 182
Grand Gulf, Mississippi 63, 64, 73, 75, 79, 87, 126; attack 60, 61; Grant's first target 51, 52, 54, 58, 59; supply base 65–67, 69
Grand Junction, Tennessee 19
Granger, Maj. Gen. Gordon 143, 170, 193; Knoxville 194–96; Missionary Ridge 189, 190; Orchard Knob 171
Grant, Julia 4, 153
Grant, Maj. Gen. Ulysses S. 1, 4, 18, 22, 30, 45, 49, 50, 60, 72, 87, 109, 112, 115, 125, 131, 164, 173, 184, 194, 197; approaching Vicksburg 89–93; Banks 51, 66, 129; build up forces 165, 166; Burnside 157, 165, 167, 169, 194, 195; Champion's Hill 80, 83, 85, 86, 89; to Chattanooga 153–55; Chattanooga casualties 194; Chattanooga offensive plans 164, 167–70, 177, 178, 180; command Military Division of the Mississippi 152, 153; cotton trade 128, 129; east of Mississippi River 63, 64, 66–70; failed assaults 93–95, 97, 99; first Vicksburg campaign 19–21, 24; former slaves 47, 48; future operations 129, 130, 133; Grant qualities 5, 38, 49–50; Grierson raid 60, 61; Halleck 19, 21, 32, 33, 47, 52, 65, 66, 71, 73, 99, 126, 145, 158, 179, 180; history 4, 5; Hooker 184, 185; Jackson 73–75, 78; lieutenant general 198; Lincoln 132, 133, 180, 196; McClernand 21, 32, 33, 35, 40, 54, 58, 65, 97, 107; McClernand removed 107, 108; Missionary Ridge 185–90; Mississippi campaign command 18, 19, 21, 23, 34, 36, 79; new supply line 155–57, 162, 163; occupy Vicksburg 128, 131; Orchard Knob 171, 172; Porter 40, 52, 58; pursue Bragg 193, 195; routes around Vicksburg 37–41, 43; Sherman 20, 33, 34, 43, 59, 61, 104, 107, 122, 127, 158, 178, 194, 106, 168; siege of Vicksburg 99, 100–3, 117; Thomas 186; troops marching down river 51, 53, 55–58, 60; Vicksburg surrender 119–22, 124
Grecian, J. 46
Greeley, Horace 49
Green, Brig. Gen. Martin 64; Champion's Hill 83
Greenwood, Mississippi 42
Greer, Lt. Cdr. James A. 55, 56
Gregg, Brig. Gen. John 71, 72; Jackson 74–78

Grenada, Mississippi 20, 22, 50, 122
Grierson, Col. Benjamin H.: Mississippi raid 60, 61
Grose, Col. William: Lookout Mountain 174

Hall, Winchester 27, 28; Vicksburg 103, 113
Halleck, Maj. Gen. Henry W. 6, 11, 12, 15, 34, 35, 69, 89, 105, 126, 145, 146; Grant 19, 21, 32, 33, 36, 47, 52, 61, 65, 71, 73, 78, 99, 100, 126, 128–31, 133, 152, 155, 157, 158, 162, 167, 179, 180, 197; history 4; McClernand 18, 19, 23, 35; Rosecrans 134, 135, 137–39, 142, 143; Sherman 131, 133
Hard Times, Louisiana 57, 59, 61, 65
Hardee, Lt. Gen. William J. 136, 147, 197; Chattanooga 179, 192
USS *Hartford* 7, 10, 11; New Orleans 8
Hartpence, William: Chattanooga 151
Hartzell, John: Missionary Ridge 191, 192
Haynes' Bluff: above Vicksburg 12, 15, 26, 30, 38, 61, 89, 90, 100, 103
Hays, E.Z.: Champion's Hill 83
Hazen, Brig. Gen. William B.: Chattanooga 156, 158–60; Missionary Ridge 189–91; Orchard Knob 171
Hebert, Brig. Gen. Louis 117
Helena, Arkansas 35
Henry Clay 55–57
Herron, Maj. Gen. Francis J. 103
Hill, Lt. Gen. Daniel H. 140, 147
Hill's Plantation 44, 45
Hindman, Maj. Gen. Thomas C. 140
Hogane, Maj. J.T. 56
Holly Springs, Mississippi 19, 20, 32; attack 24, 25
Holmes, Col. Samuel A.: Champion's Hill 84; Jackson 76
Holston River 196
Hooker, Maj. Gen. Joseph 148, 152, 154, 156–58, 160, 161, 178, 180; Lookout Mountain 173, 174, 176, 177; Missionary Ridge 184, 185, 192; Ringgold 195; Wauhatchie 162, 163, 168–71
Hopkins, Capt. Owen J. 52, 75; Chickasaw Bayou 28, 29; Vicksburg 92, 98, 102
Hovey, Brig. Gen. Charles E. 64, 75, 79, 80, 93; Champion's Hill 81–86
Howard, Maj. Gen. Oliver Otis 148, 160, 161, 170, 171, 177, 184; meet Grant 153, 154; Wauhatchie 162
Howard, R.L.: Vicksburg 95, 96, 98, 104, 122, 123
Hunter, Alfred G.: Missionary Ridge 188

Hurlbut, Maj. Gen. Stephen A. 23, 102, 145

Ireland, Col. David: Lookout Mountain 175
USS *Iroquois* 10
Island No. 10 4, 5, 9; captured 6

Jackson, Isacc 45; Vicksburg 104
Jackson, Mississippi 17, 65, 70, 73, 84, 85, 114, 128, 131; assault 76–78; destruction 127; first campaign 19, 20; Grant advances 52, 54, 65, 68, 69, 72–75, 90; Johnston 63, 74, 115, 127; railroads 19, 57, 67; Sherman 122, 126, 129
Jasper, Tennessee 151
Jenkins, Brig. Gen. Micah: Wauhatchie 161
Johnson, Dr. Charles B. 93
Johnson, Brig. Gen. Richard W.: Missionary Ridge 185, 186, 189
Johnson's Plantation 25
Johnston, Gen. Joseph E.: 40, 67, 73, 86, 109, 121, 122, 125, 129, 133, 134, 147; commander in West 39; Davis 39, 111; Jackson 63, 68, 75, 78, 127; Pemberton 70, 74, 79, 90, 91, 111, 114, 115; Seddon 74, 114, 115; threaten Union lines 87, 91, 93, 95, 100, 102, 105; Vicksburg 9, 103, 108, 113, 118, 126
Jones, S.C. 59
Jones, Maj. Gen. Samuel 166

USS *Katahdin* 10, 11
Kelley's Ferry 155–56
Kellogg, J.J.: Vicksburg 94, 104
Kelton, Col. J.C. 38
USS *Kennebec* 10, 11
Kilburn, Col. C.L. 164
Kimball, Brig. Gen. Nathan 102
Kimberly, Lt. Col. Robert 163; Missionary Ridge 188, 190
Knoxville, Tennessee 135, 138, 141, 165, 169; Burnside 145, 157; Longstreet 166, 167; relieve 194–96
Kyger, Capt. Tilmon D. 190

USS *Lafayette* 53, 55, 56, 60
LaFayette, Georgia 139, 140
LaFayette Road 141, 142
Lake Pontchartrain 130
Lake Providence 38, 40
Lake St. Joseph 51
Law, Brig. Gen. Evander: Wauhatchie 161, 162
Lawler, Brig. Gen. Michael K.: Big Black 88, 89, 97
Lee, Brig. Gen. Albert 94
Lee, Capt. Charles N. 97
Lee, Gen. Robert E. 17, 37, 69, 111, 131, 137, 141, 145, 157, 166
Lee, Cdr. S. Phillips: Vicksburg 9, 10

Lee, Brig. Gen. Stephen D. 26, 118; Champion's Hill 82, 83, 85
Lee & Gordon's Mill 140
Leggett, Brig. Gen. Mortimer 89
USS *Lexington* 4, 31
Lincoln, Pres. Abraham 3, 7, 37, 49, 157; Grant 50, 126, 130, 132, 180, 196; McClernand 18, 22, 23, 34, 35; Rosecrans 134, 143, 145, 152; Thanksgiving 194; Vicksburg 16, 17
Lindsay, Mayor L. 9
USS *Lioness* 41
Livermore, Mary 50
Lockett, Col. S.H.: surrender 118, 124; Vicksburg 15, 91
Logan, Maj. Gen. John A. 65; Champion's Hill 81-85; Jackson 76, 77; Raymond, 71, 72; Vicksburg 110, 119, 123
Longstreet, Lt. Gen. James 141, 157, 161, 170, 197, 198; Chickamauga 142, 146, 147; Knoxville 166, 167, 169, 195, 196; Lookout Mountain 149, 156; Wauhatchie 161, 162
Lookout Creek 173, 174
Lookout Mountain 139, 152, 157, 159, 176, 178, 181, 183; assault 173-75, 177; defenses 148, 161, 168; Grant's plan 168-72, 177, 180; Hooker 185; importance 149, 150, 155, 156
Lookout Valley 161, 174, 179
Loomis, Col. John M.: Missionary Ridge 181, 183
Loring, Maj. Gen. William W. 42, Champion's Hill 81-83, 85, 86, 88
Loudon, Tennessee 169
Loughborough, Mary: Vicksburg 90, 112, 113
USS *Louisville* 4, 7, 31, 43, 53, 55, 56, 60
Louisville, Kentucky 152, 153, 164, 165

MacArthur, Lt. Arthur 191
Magnolia Church 64
Maney, Brig. Gen. George: Missionary Ridge 183
Manigault, Brig. Gen. Arthur M. 137
USS *Marmora* 41
Marshall, Albert O. 59, 88; Vicksburg 96
Martin, Col. John 191
Matthies, Col. C.L. 76
Maximillian, Archduke 130
McClernand, Maj. Gen. John A. 21, 30, 34, 36, 58, 68, 70, 74, 75, 85, 87, 105, 107, 126, 132; congratulation order 107, 108; failed assaults 97-99; Grant 23, 33-35, 40, 58, 65, 78, 79, 97; history 17, 18; Lincoln 18, 23, 34; Mississippi plan 17-19, 22; move below Vicksburg 51-53, 59, 61; Port Gibson 63, 64; Port of Arkansas 30-32; Rawlins explanation 132, 133;
relieved 108; Vicksburg 90, 93, 96-98; Wilson 107
McCook, Maj. Gen. Alexander 135, 140, 141
McDonald, G.B.: Champion's Hill 84
McGavock, Col. Randal: Raymond 71, 72
McGinnis, Brig. Gen. George F.: Champion's Hill 82-84
McKinley, Emilie Riley 112
McLaw, Maj. Gen. Lafayette: Wauhatchie 159
McMillen, Col. William L. 77
McMinnville, Tennessee 138
McNutt Lake 27
McPherson, Maj. Gen. James B. 23, 33, 34, 47, 58, 68, 79, 90, 102, 126, 131, 164; Big Black 87, 89; Champion's Hill 81, 83; Jackson 74-78; Lake Providence 40; McClernand 99, 107, 108; Port Gibson 65; Raymond 70, 71, 73; Vicksburg 93, 96-98, 119
Meade, Maj. Gen. George G. 148
Meigs, QM Gen. Montgomery C. 164, 168, 171
Memphis, Tennessee 4, 6, 100, 129; build army 19-23; cotton 131; fleet action 7, 10, 18; Grant falls back 32, 34, 38, 50, 54; transfer troops 145, 146
Memphis & Charleston Railroad 135, 146, 149, 150, 164, 165
Mendenhall, Maj. John 159, 160
Military Division of the Mississippi 152, 153
Miller, Charles 31, 39
Milliken's Bend 25, 32, 33, 38, 51, 57; supply line 59, 67
Mills, Col. Roger 182
Missionary Ridge 143, 148, 175, 177, 193, 196, 197; assault in center 186, 188-92; defenses 168, 178, 179, 186, 187; Grant's plans 167-69, 171; Hooker 184, 185; Sherman 170, 173, 177, 178, 181, 184
USS *Mississippi* 7
Mississippi Central Railroad 19, 21, 122
Mississippi River 1, 8, 11, 14, 23, 24, 30, 31, 50, 51, 70, 87, 90, 91, 103, 128; *Arkansas* 12, 13, 15; bypass Vicksburg 38, 40-43, 45; forts 4, 5; Grant 20, 21, 34, 36, 54, 58, 62; importance 3, 4, 16; McClernand 17-19, 21, 23, 32, 33, 35, 107; moving below Vicksburg 56-59, 67; naval forces 6, 7, 13, 15; Sherman 22, 25; Vicksburg 8-10, 17, 37, 105
Mississippi Springs, Mississippi 73-76
Mississippi Squadron 15, 125
Mobile, Alabama 8, 130
Mobile Bay 130
Moccasin Bend 155, 156
Moccasin Point 155, 156, 159
Monroe Doctrine 130
Montgomery, Col. Frank 124
Montgomery, Col. Louis 119, 120
Moon Lake 40, 41
Moore, Brig. Gen. John 175
Morgan, Brig. Gen. George W. 21; Chickasaw Bayou 25-30; Port of Arkansas 31, 32
Morris, W.S. 110
USS *Mound City* 4, 6, 43, 53, 55, 56, 60
Mower, Brig. Gen. Joseph A.: Jackson 76, 78
Murfreesboro, Tennessee 37, 134, 135
Murphy, Lt. J.M. 44
Murphy, Col. R.C. 24

Napoleon III (emperor) 130
Nashville & Chattanooga Railroad 135, 153
Nashville & Decatur Railroad 165
Natchez, Mississippi 8, 129
Negley, Maj. Gen. James 139, 140
New Carthage, Louisiana 38, 51-53, 57
New Madrid, Missouri 4-6
New Orleans, Louisiana 4, 35, 38, 57, 67; Banks 32; Farragut 7-10, 12, 14, 16, 18; Grant 130, 145; importance 3, 51, 66
New Orleans, Jackson & Great Northern Railroad 67, 77
New York Tribune 49
Newsome, Edmund: Vicksburg 124
Newton, James K.: Vicksburg 103, 124
95th Ohio Infantry: Jackson 77
99th Illinois Infantry: Big Black 88
97th Illinois Infantry: Vicksburg 97
96th Illinois Infantry: Chickamauga 143
96th Ohio Infantry 25; Vicksburg 102
93rd Illinois Infantry 41; Vicksburg 98
Ninth Army Corps 103; Jackson 127
North Chickamauga Creek 168, 177

Ohio River 3
Old River 25
Oldroyd, Osborn H. 71
111th Pennsylvania Infantry: Lookout Mountain 175
105th Ohio Infantry: Missionary Ridge 191
104th Illinois Infantry: Missionary Ridge 189
113th Illinois Infantry: Vicksburg 94, 104
137th New York Infantry: Wauhatchie 162
124th Illinois Infantry: Vicksburg 95, 96, 104, 122

Index

123rd Illinois Infantry: Chattanooga 176
USS *Oneida* 10
Orchard Knob 171, 172, 179, 184–86; assault 187–90
Ord, Maj. Gen. E.O.C. 108, 119
Osterhaus, Brig. Gen. Peter J. 75, 87, 88, 146; Champion's Hill 79–81, 85, 86; join Hooker 170, 171, 173; Lookout Mountain 174; Missionary Ridge 185; Port Gibson 64, 65; Vicksburg 93
Oxford, Mississippi 20

Parke, Maj. Gen. John G. 103
Partridge, Charles 143
Pearl River 78, 127
Peirce, Taylor 54; Vicksburg 109, 123
Pemberton, Lt. Gen. John C. 20, 45, 51, 66, 68, 73, 78, 79, 117, 125, 128; Champion's Hill 81, 83, 85; concentrate troops 64, 65; Davis 70, 93, 128; Grant's first campaign 20, 21, 22, 25; history 17; Johnston 70, 74, 79, 90, 111, 113–15; Kirby Smith 70; retreat to Vicksburg 86–88; soldier's letter 116; surrender 117–22, 124; Vicksburg 54, 55, 57, 60, 91, 92, 100, 103, 109
USS *Pinola* 10
USS *Pittsburg* 4, 6, 43, 60; Vicksburg 53, 55, 56
Polk, Lt. Gen. Leonidas L. 136, 140, 141; relieved 147
Pope, Brig. Gen. John 5, Island No. 10 6
Port Gibson, Louisiana 12, 63, 70, 71, 74, 119, 126; battle 64, 65
Port Hudson, Louisiana 4, 8, 15, 17, 39, 40, 53, 57, 65, 71, 89, 95, 115, 125; Banks 51, 54, 63, 66; captured 129; orders to hold 70
Porter, Rear Adm. David D. 12, 20, 22, 30, 58, 103, 124, 125; Fort Hindman 30, 31; Grand Gulf 58–60, 65; Mississippi Squadron 15; New Orleans 7, 10; new plan 50; passing Vicksburg 52–57; prisoners 120; Vicksburg 37, 38, 41; Yazoo River 43, 44, 45
Porter, Col. Horace 154
Porter, Cdr. William D. 14
Post of Arkansas (Fort Hindman) 30, 32, 33
Prime, Capt. Frederick E. 91; Vicksburg 92, 99, 101
Putnam, Col. Holden: Vicksburg 98

Queen of the West 13, 14
Quinby, Brig. Gen. Isaac F. 42; Vicksburg 93, 97

Raccoon Mountain 149, 155–57, 161, 170
USS *Rattler* 41
Rawlins, Col. John 103, 108, 164; to Washington 132, 133

Raymond, Mississippi 68, 70, 74, 75, 81, 85; battle 71–73
Raymond Road 75, 77, 81, 86
Red River 15, 16, 38, 40, 57; Banks 66
Reynolds, Col. A.W. 117
Richards, Dora Miller: Vicksburg 90, 111, 124
USS *Richmond* 10
Richmond, Virginia 111, 135, 144, 147
Ringgold Gap 195
Rock of Chickamauga: George Thomas 143
Rocky Springs, Mississippi 68
Rodgers, Cdr. John 4
Rolling Fork 43, 44
USS *Romeo* 41
Rosecrans, Maj. Gen. William S. 37, 129, 133, 140, 146, 148, 149, 152; Chattanooga 138, 139, 151; Chickamauga 141–43, 145; Halleck 134, 135, 137, 138, 143; replaced 153, 154; Tullahoma 134–37
Ross, Brig. Gen. Leonard 41
Rossville, Georgia 139, 143, 169, 180
Rossville Gap 185
Roundaway Bayou 38

St. George, Arkansas 32
Sanborn, Col. John B. 59, 77
Sanitary Commission 50
Savannah, Georgia 130
Schofield, Maj. Gen. John M. 129, 197
Schurtz, Maj. Gen. Carl 160
USS *Sciota* 10
Scott, Winfield 3
2nd Illinois Cavalry 24
2nd Iowa Cavalry 60
2nd Minnesota Infantry: Missionary Ridge 188
Seddon, James
Sequatchie Valley 150, 151
Seventeenth Corps 23, 58, 94
7th Illinois Cavalry 60
78th Ohio Infantry 104
77th Illinois Infantry 39; Vicksburg 94, 99
76th Ohio Infantry 31; Vicksburg 39
73rd Illinois Infantry: Missionary Ridge 190
Sheridan, Maj. Gen. Philip H.: Missionary Ridge 186, 189–91; Orchard Knob 171; pursuit 193
Sherman, Col. Francis T. 136
Sherman, U.S. Sen. John 22
Sherman, Maj. Gen. William T. 3, 20, 21, 33, 37, 53, 67–70, 83, 86, 89, 110, 117, 126, 131, 146, 158, 166, 167, 198; brother 22, 39; Chattanooga 168–71; Chickasaw Bayou 22, 23, 25–27, 29, 30; Grant 20, 33, 34, 43, 51, 59, 61, 66, 80, 125, 127, 128, 194; Halleck 131–33; Jackson 73–78, 125, 127; Knoxville 196; Missionary Ridge 177–85; Port of Arkansas 30, 31; Vicksburg 39, 44, 45, 50, 57, 58, 61, 90, 91, 93–99, 102, 103, 107, 108, 122
Shiloh, Battle of 6, 12, 18, 38, 48, 154
Shreveport, Louisiana 16, 25, 70
USS *Signal* 41
Silver Wave 55
Sixteenth Corps 23
16th Ohio Infantry: Chickasaw Bayou 28
6th Illinois Cavalry 60
6th Indiana Infantry 151
6th Missouri Infantry: Chickasaw Bayou 29
67th Indiana Infantry: Vicksburg 109, 124
Slack, Col. James R.: Champion's Hill 82
Slocum, Maj. Gen. Henry 148, 160
Smith, Brig. Gen. A.J. 21, 25, 64, 75, 79, 80, 119, 120; Champion's Hill 81; Chickasaw Bayou 26, 29, 31, 32; Vicksburg 93
Smith, Lt. Gen. Edward Kirby 70, 115, 129
Smith, Brig. Gen. Giles A. 45, 146, 177
Smith, Brig. Gen. John E. 65, 146; Chattanooga 178, 183
Smith, Brig. Gen. Martin L. 9; Vicksburg 92
Smith, Brig. Gen. Morgan L. 22, 25; Chattanooga 178, 181, 182; Chickasaw Bayou 26;
Smith, Brig. Gen. Sooy 103
Smith, Lt. Cdr. Watson 41, 42
Smith, Brig. Gen. William F. 154; build bridge 177; Chattanooga 155–57, 160, 161, 168
Smith's Plantation 51, 52, 59
Snyder's Bluff 43
Snyder's Mill 111
South Chickamauga Creek 168, 177, 178
Southern Railroad of Mississippi 16, 19, 67, 70
Special Field Orders No. 2 47
Squier, George W. 135
Stanton, Sec. of War Edwin M. 11, 18, 36, 137, 171; Dana 49, 67, 102, 129, 145, 148, 149, 155, 190, 192; Grant 79, 152, 153; McClernand 19, 22, 23, 34, 35
Steele, Brig. Gen. Frederick 19, 22, 31, 48, 58, 127; Chickasaw Bayou 25, 26, 30; Jackson 77, 78; Vicksburg 93
Steele's Bayou 43
Steinwehr, Brig. Gen. Adolph von 160
Stevenson, Maj. Gen. Carter L. 44, 55, 86, 92; Champion's Hill 81, 82; Lookout Mountain 173, 176, 177; Vicksburg 98, 117

Stevenson, Brig. Gen. John D. 85; Champion's Hill 82, 84; Jackson 77
Stevenson, Thomas M. 104
Stevenson, Alabama 135; supply depot 138, 139, 150, 153, 158, 164, 165
Stewart, Nixon B.: Missionary Ridge 192
Stockwell, Elisha: Vicksburg 109
Stone's River, Battle of 37
Stuart, Brig. Gen. David 26, 30, 31
Sullivan, Brig. Gen. J.C. 67
USS *Sumter* 14
Sunflower River 43

Tallahatchie River 20, 21, 24, 42
Tennessee River 5, 24; Chattanooga 136, 138, 146, 149, 155, 160, 161, 169, 198
Tensas Bayou 40
Tensas River 40
10th Illinois Infantry: Missionary Ridge 190
10th Missouri Infantry 77
10th Tennessee Infantry 71
Thayer, Brig. Gen. John M.: Chickasaw Bayou 28
Thirteenth Corps 23, 35, 51, 58, 63, 94, 107, 108, 127
13th Illinois Infantry: Chickasaw Bayou 29
30th Illinois Infantry Champion's Hill 84
30th Tennessee Infantry 71
31st Illinois Infantry: Vicksburg 110
31st Missouri Infantry: Chickasaw Bayou 29
32nd Ohio Infantry: hampion's Hill 83
36th Illinois Infantry 151
33rd Illinois Infantry 59, 63; Champion's Hill 85, 87, 88; Vicksburg 96
Thomas, Maj.Gen. George 139, 140; Army of the Cumberland 153–55; assault plans 171, 178, 180; Chattanooga 157, 158, 162, 167, 170; Chickamauga 141–43, 146; Knoxville 195; Missionary Ridge 184, 186–90, 193
Thomas, Maj. Gen. Lorenzo 48
Thompson, Col. Alfred P. 76
Thompson's Lake 28
Thurston, John H. 123
Tilghman, Brig. Gen. Lloyd: Champion's Hill 85, 86
Tinclad 15, 31, 40, 41
Tracy, Brig. Gen. Edward 64

Trans-Mississippi 3, 16, 17, 70, 115, 129, 131
Tullahoma, Tennessee 74, 134, 136, 138, 146
Tunnard, Willie: Vicksburg 113
Tunnel Hill 178, 180
Turchin, Brig. Gen. John B. 158–60
Turner, Lt. Col. James J. 71
USS *Tuscumbia* 53, 55, 60
Tuscumbia, Mississippi 133
Tuttle, Brig. Gen. James M. 19, 74; Jackson 76–78; Vicksburg 93
Twentieth Army Corps 135
20th Illinois Infantry 69; Raymond 71; Vicksburg 102
20th Ohio Infantry: Raymond 71
25th Illinois Infantry 191
21st Illinois Infantry 5
21st Iowa Infantry: Vicksburg 97
21st Ohio Infantry 151
24th Iowa Infantry: Champion's Hill 82
24th South Carolina Infantry: Jackson 77
24th Wisconsin Infantry: Missionary Ridge 191
29th Missouri Infantry 29
29th Pennsylvania Infantry: Lookout Mountain 175
22nd Iowa Infantry 59; Vicksburg 97, 109, 123
22nd Kentucky Infantry: Chickasaw Bayou 28, 29
27th Missouri Infantry 185
27th Ohio Infantry 47
23rd Indiana Infantry 71
23rd Kentucky Infantry: Chattanooga 159
USS *Tyler* 4, 13

Van Dorn, Maj. Gen. Earl 12–15, 20; Holly Springs 24
Vicksburg, Mississippi 1, 4; assault 94, 96–99; east of city 63, 65; first campaign 19–21; Grant takes command 33, 36; importance 16, 17; Jackson 74, 75; passing city 55–57; plans 50, 51; surrender 119–22
Virginia & Tennessee Railroad 135

Walcutt, Col. Charles C.: Missionary Ridge 182, 184
Walden's Ridge 150, 151
Walke, Cdr. Henry 4, 13
Walker, Brig. Gen. William H.T.: Jackson 76, 77; Chattanooga 172
Walnut Hills 25, 26, 90
Walthall, Brig. Gen. Edward C.: Lookout Mountain 173–76

Warfield, Lt. Col. E. 183
Warrenton, Mississippi 15, 39, 51, 52, 67, 100
Washburne, U.S. Congressman Elihu B. 48
Washita River 40
Wauhatchie, Tennessee 157, 161, 174; battle 162
Waul, Col. Thomas 92
Welles, Sec. of the Navy Gideon 7, 11, 12, 37, 38, 132, 133
West Tennessee 21, 24
Western & Atlantic Railroad 135, 139, 147, 158, 195, 198
Western Flotilla 7, 8, 10–12, 14, 15
Western Gulf Squadron 7
Whitaker, Brig. Gen. Walter C. 160; Lookout Mountain 174
White River 31, 33
Wiley, William 39; Vicksburg 94, 96, 101, 102
Williams, Brig. Gen. Thomas 10, 11, 14, 38
Williamson, Col. James 185
Willich, Brig. Gen. August 171; Missionary Ridge 189, 190
Willow Bayou 38
Willow Springs, Mississippi 65, 68
Wilson, Ephraim: Missionary Ridge
Wilson, Lt. Col. James H. 38, 41, 49, 124, 154; McClernand 107, 108
Winchester, Tennessee 136, 138
Winters, William: Vicksburg 109, 124
USS *Wissahickon* 10
Wood, Brig. Gen. Thomas J.: Chattanooga 171; Missionary Ridge 186, 187, 189, 190
Woods, Brig. Gen. Charles R.: Chattanooga 185
Woods, J.T. 102; Chickasaw Bayou 25, 29
Worsham, W.J.: Missionary Ridge 188, 191

Yalobusha River 20, 42
Yates, Richard 17
Yazoo City 13
Yazoo Delta 40
Yazoo Pass 38, 40, 41, 43
Yazoo River 11, 17, 19, 30, 38, 45, 61, 87, 90; *Arkansas* 12, 13; Grant reaches 91, 102, 103, 115; route around Vicksburg 40–43; Sherman 21, 25, 26
Yazoo Valley 41
Young's Point: canal 34, 38–40

www.ingramcontent.com/pod-product-compliance
Ingram Content Group UK Ltd.
Pitfield, Milton Keynes, MK11 3LW, UK
UKHW050529150426
5217IPUK00026B/1867